SPANISH GRAMMAR in REVIEW

KENNETH CHASTAIN

National Textbook Company
a division of *NTC Publishing Group* • Lincolnwood, Illinois USA

Published by National Textbook Company, a division of NTC Publishing Group.
© 1994 by NTC Publishing Group, 4255 West Touhy Avenue,
Lincolnwood (Chicago), Illinois 60646-1975 U.S.A.

3 4 5 6 7 8 9 0 VP 9 8 7 6 5 4 3 2 1

Contents

PART VII · Simple Sentence Transformations

PART VIII · Complex Sentence Transformations

Preface

One of the major challenges in learning a second language is establishing a solid linguistic base from which to launch communicative practice activities. As Chomsky has pointed out, competence underlines performance in language usage. Of course, these two language components are not mutually exclusive. Each is interrelated with the other, and each influences the other. However, without a basic understanding of how the language system functions, students cannot be expected to generate the structural forms necessary for self expression. With practice, this knowledge can grow into solid linguistic competence and functional communicative skills.

Spanish Grammar in Review: Patterns for Communication has been designed to help students establish a solid linguistic base and has two principal purposes. The first is to assist those students who have forgotten aspects of the Spanish they learned previously and need to regain a working comprehension of the Spanish language system. The second is to involve students in some sort of communicative self expression.

Organization The text is organized into eight major parts: I. Nouns and Noun Phrases; II. Regular Verb Forms in the Indicative; III. Irregular Verb Forms in the Indicative; IV. Uses of Selected Verbs; V. Verb Phrases; VI. Non-Finite Verbs; VII. Simple Sentence Transformations; and VIII. Complex Sentence Transformations. The objective of this organization is to focus students' attention first on related elements in the basic components of the Spanish sentence and second on the processes by which basic sentences may be transformed into other types of sentences.

Format The eight parts are divided into several sections; each section generally treats the following aspects of language: (1) Linguistic forms of the grammar being studied; (2) Contrast of these forms with other forms; (3) Use of the forms in context; (4) Contrast of the uses with those of other related grammatical structures; (5) Communication pattern exercises; and (6) *Actividades de comunicación*. During this sequence attention is focused on one concept at a time. First, an objective is stated; then a short explanation with examples is presented and followed by exercises. All the concepts needed to comprehend and to use a particular grammar point are studied and practiced separately; however, progress is always moving toward self expression and toward total use of Spanish.

Explanations Explanations at the beginning of each section summarize the material to follow. The explanations within the sections are limited to the concept(s) delineated in the objectives. Thus, they deal with only a small, comprehensible portion of the grammar being treated in the section. Explanations, accompanied by pertinent examples, are brief and to the point. Unity of focus on small segments of the total concept being studied makes it possible to condense grammatical explanations. The explanations are designed to help students understand the grammar point and to understand how it fits into the total language system. The explanations emphasize a systematic approach based on examples rather than on abstract grammatical discussions.

Exercises   The exercises in *Spanish Grammar in Review* serve to verify understanding and to practice various patterns. They provide practice in comparing and discriminating among related forms and patterns. Whenever necessary, a background context is supplied that enables the students to choose the structures that correctly express the desired meaning. Furthermore, in each case the exercises have been selected, not on the basis of some prejudged philosophy, but on the type of practice needed by the students in order to learn to use the grammar under consideration. An effort has been made to select exercise types that are appropriate to comprehension and learning of the grammar point being studied and that simulate the mental processes needed to use that same structure to express one's own thoughts.

Task Analyses   Explanations have been prepared and exercises have been selected only after careful analysis of what the students should already know and what they need to learn in order to master the linguistic concepts under consideration. In many cases this analysis has led to more complete explanations presented in smaller units and to exercises chosen to practice each step in concept comprehension and progress toward communicative practice.

Stress   The stress is on the underlying system that makes language not only learnable but extendable, and on the patterns that enable students to understand and/or create needed language forms as the appropriate situation occurs.

The approach taken in this book is based on ideas from Bull, *Spanish for Teachers;* Stockwell, Bowen, and Martin, *The Grammatical Structures of English and Spanish;* Wolfe, Hadlick and Inman, *A Structural Course in Spanish;* transformational-generative grammar theories, various Spanish grammars, and the author's own teaching experience.

The approach taken is based on the belief that the language system can be simplified and organized into more meaningful relationships for the students thereby improving the efficiency of their efforts in learning the language and enhancing their ability to retain and to use what they have learned.

Using the Book   It is recommended that the responsibility for learning much of the material in this text be placed on the students themselves. If the instructor desires, he or she can provide the answers so that the students can do most of the work in the first part of each section without assistance. Toward the end of the section in the Communication Pattern Exercises and the *Actividades de comunicación*, the instructor may need to become involved as he or she seeks to give the students an opportunity to incorporate the material into communicative exchanges. Many of the *Actividades de comunicación* are designed to stimulate oral interaction in small groups or oral or written presentation to the class, instructor, or classmates. Students can do the Communication Pattern Exercises in pairs, and the *Actividades de comunicación* in groups.

Flexibility   It is recommended that the instructor not attempt to cover all the material. Assignments should be selective, the selection being based on identified needs and weaknesses of the students in the class. Only those portions containing unfamiliar material or material incompletely understood should be reviewed. Ideally, students who already know material needed by a large portion of the class will be guided into other more productive, challenging, and stimulating activities.

Some students may need to review forms, while others may already know the forms but need practice in using the structure in communicative situations. Some classes may need work on the subjunctive or on irregular verbs, but not the indicative of regular verbs. In each case, the instructor should choose the most beneficial exercises and activities dealing with the least understood and most important points of Spanish grammar. It is not necessary that the class go through the book in the order of presentation.

Acknowledgments

No book is ever the product of the author alone, and this one is no exception. I readily and gratefully acknowledge the following contributions.

The seeds that later grew into these present materials were planted by Charles A. S. Heinle and Charles H. Heinle several years ago.

As the contents evolved toward their present format and content, David Wolfe (Temple University) read and commented on the first manuscript. Later, Professor Marcel Andrade (University of North Carolina at Asheville), Joseph Chrzanowski (California State University–Los Angeles), Janet Dirlam (Stephen F. Austin State University), Marie Rentz (University of Maryland), Charles Stansfield (University of Colorado), Barbara Wing (University of New Hampshire), and Ronald Young (San Diego State University) evaluated and critiqued the materials. All their comments and suggestions were considered carefully and incorporated into the text whenever and wherever possible.

Native speakers checked the appropriateness and the correctness of the Spanish on three separate occasions. Mrs. Violeta Daydí-Tolson, Ms. Elba Baryna, and finally Professor José Buergo (University of Illinois–Chicago) deleted, corrected, altered, and added to the original Spanish content.

I would also like to express my deep personal indebtedness to Charlie Heinle for having accepted the manuscript for publication and for having obtained the various reviews to stimulate and guide needed revisions. To Carlyle Carter, supervisor of the project; to Kevin Thornton, director of the publication process; to Jane Wall Meinike, editor of the manuscript; and to Kara N. Lindstrom, who provided valuable editorial assistance throughout all phases of production; I would like to say thanks for a job done well, efficiently, promptly, and courteously.

At the publication of this second edition of *Spanish Grammar in Review*, I am especially grateful to Professor Marcel Andrade for urging and initiating a second edition; to Professor Andrade and Ms. Edra Staffieri (North Central High School, Indianapolis, IN) for reviewing the first edition; to the editors of NTC Publishing Group for publishing this second edition; and to Timothy J. Rogus, Tim Collins, Jill Ginsburg, and Michael O'Neill for the time, energy, interest, and expertise they put into the production of this edition.

And last but not least, I wish to recognize the contributions of my wife, Jan, and my boys, Brian and Michael. It is their love and support that make my life worthwhile and my work possible.

Much of the credit for the published version of this text must go to the above-named individuals, and I am pleased to express publicly my sincere appreciation for their many valuable suggestions and contributions. I trust that at this point the book has more redeeming qualities than deficiencies, for which I alone assume full responsibility, and I hope that its contents will be of value to both students and teachers of Spanish.

Preface to the Second Edition

Hearing of Spanish teachers who continued to use *Spanish Grammar in Review* years after the text had gone out of print was always gratifying. However, even after receiving positive feedback and listening to laments about having to make do with the few deteriorating copies available, my thinking had not gone beyond the to-be-expected sense of satisfaction until Marcel Andrade contacted me to recommend that the materials to made available again and to suggest that I contact the NTC Publishing Group about publishing a second edition.

This edition is the result of his initiative, his efforts, his confidence, and his persistence. Therefore, I certainly would be remiss if I did not extend to him a special word of appreciation for his confidence in the book and for the stimulus he provided to bring it to life again.

I also wish to thank Tim Rogus and the other officials at NTC for their affirmative reaction to the materials and their willingness to publish a second edition.

As always, I recognize the indispensable support, patience, encouragement, and love of my helpmate, Jan, without whom none of my work would be possible not worthwhile. She deserves as much, if not more, credit for this book than do I. Before I learned to compose on a typewriter and before we had word processors and scanners to do much of our work for us, she typed the original manuscript for this book at least three times on a manual typewriter.

In conclusion, I would like to extend a work of thanks to teachers who choose to use *Spanish Grammar in Review*. Best wishes to you and to your students. I trust that you both will find the contents beneficial in understanding Spanish grammar and in learning to use the basic forms and patterns to communicate.

Nouns and Noun Phrases

Introduction

A sentence consists of two basic components: a noun or noun phrase and a verb or verb phrase. Part I of this review text deals with the noun or noun substitute and its modifiers.

One of the Spanish words for "noun" is *nombre*. The word *nombre* also means "name." Thus we can easily understand that a noun is a naming word. A noun may name either a concrete entity such as John or student, Chicago or city, Statue of Liberty or statue; it may also name an abstract entity such as honesty or love.

The ending of most nouns indicates whether the word refers to one or more than one (*casa, casas;* house, houses) and in some cases the ending indicates whether the word refers to a male or a female (*inglés, inglesa;* English [male], English [female]). In those cases in which the ending does not indicate number, the article, or another word, does so (*el viernes, los viernes;* Friday, Fridays). In those cases in which the ending does not indicate whether the word refers to a male or female, the meaning of the word itself does so (*mujer;* woman) or the article or other modifying word does so (*la joven, el joven;* the young woman, the young man).

A noun phrase is made up of a noun plus one or more words that tell something about the noun. The basic patterns are as follows:

1. Article + noun
   a. Definite   el hombre   *the man*
   b. Indefinite   un hombre   *a man*
2. Demonstrative + noun   esta mujer   *this woman*
3. Possessive + noun   mi libro   *my book*
4. Limiting adjective + noun   dos libros   *two books*
5. Descriptive adjective + noun   blanca nieve   *white snow*
6. Noun + differentiating adjective   casa blanca   *white house*
7. Noun + limiting adjective   libro dos   *book two*
8. Noun + possessive   libro mío   *book of mine* or
                                              my *book*

9. Noun + phrase	libro de Ana *Ana's book*
10. Noun + clause	libro que me *book that interests*
	interesa *me*

Of course, these patterns may also be used in various combinations.

Two important considerations must be kept in mind while studying and learning to use the noun and the various components of the noun phrase. First, word order is important. The words in the noun phrase must be placed in a certain order. Second, at times agreement is necessary. The words used in the noun phrase must fit the noun with which they are used.

1 Number and Gender of Nouns

GOAL 1

To form the plural of a noun.

A noun that ends in a vowel forms the plural by adding -s.

planta	plantas	gato	gatos	*plant*	*plants*	*cat*	*cats*
noche	noches	tribu	tribus	*night*	*nights*	*tribe*	*tribes*

A noun that ends in a consonant or in -*i* forms the plural by adding -*es*.

papel	papeles	*paper*	*papers*
habilidad	habilidades	*ability*	*abilities*
rubí	rubíes	*ruby*	*rubies*

Nouns that end in unaccented -*is* or -*es* have only one form.

el martes	los martes	*Tuesday*	*Tuesdays*
la tesis	las tesis	*thesis*	*theses*

A noun that ends in -*z* changes the *z* to *c* before adding the plural suffix.

luz	luces	*light*	*lights*
lápiz	lápices	*pencil*	*pencils*

When a singular noun is made plural, the stress must be retained on the same syllable. In the case of a noun ending in -*n*, it is necessary either to add or to remove an accent mark. A noun with the last syllable stressed loses the accent mark in the plural; a noun with an unaccented last syllable gains an accent mark.

balcón	balcones	*balcony*	*balconies*
joven	jóvenes	*youth*	*youths*

EXERCISE

Give the plural of each word.

1. abogado _____
2. interior _____
3. nación _____
4. jueves _____
5. colegio _____
6. periódico _____
7. autor _____
8. pez _____
9. reloj _____
10. chófer _____

11. felicidad _____
12. guante _____
13. animal _____
14. joven _____
15. escuela _____
16. actriz _____
17. pantalón _____
18. placer _____
19. calle _____
20. mamá _____

GOAL 2

To recognize whether a noun refers to a male or female.

In some cases, very different words are used to indicate males and females.

| hombre | man | mujer | woman |
| toro | bull | vaca | cow |

Gender is indicated in a large number of cases by the endings -o and -a. The -o ending designates a male, and the -a ending designates a female.

| esposo | husband | esposa | wife |
| perro | male dog | perra | female dog |

Many Spanish nouns that refer to a male and end in a consonant form the feminine by adding -a.

| escritor | male writer | escritora | female writer |
| inglés | English man | inglesa | English woman |

Some Spanish nouns have the same form for both males and females. In these cases gender is indicated by one of the modifiers.

| el turista | the male tourist | la turista | the female tourist |
| el estudiante | the male student | la estudiante | the female student |

If a noun is used to refer to a male and a female, the masculine plural form of the noun is used.

chico y chica—chicos   chicos y chicas—chicos

EXERCISE

Indicate whether each of the following nouns refers to a male, a female, or to either or both by indicating *M, F,* or *M-F.*

_____ 1. actrices

_____ 2. profesor

_____ 3. terroristas

_____ 4. gata

_____ 5. abuelo

_____ 6. representante

_____ 7. joven

_____ 8. alemanes

_____ 9. reina

_____ 10. ingeniero

_____ 11. señora

_____ 12. caballo

_____ 13. orador

_____ 14. francés

_____ 15. gato

_____ 16. estudiantes

_____ 17. soldado

_____ 18. tíos

_____ 19. maestra

_____ 20. rey

Communication Pattern Exercise

Change the gender and number of each noun to the opposite. If the noun is plural, make it singular or vice versa. If the noun is masculine, make it feminine and vice versa.

1. socialista _____

2. padre _____

3. hijos _____

4. portuguesa _____

5. bailador _____

6. cocineros _____

7. parientes _____

8. vacas _____

9. hombre _____

10. dentistas _____

11. senadora _____

12. abogado _____

13. mexicanos _____

14. perra _____

15. joven _____

Actividades de comunicación

Se dice que vivimos en una sociedad materialista y que a veces somos víctimas de nuestros deseos. A ver si tú eres materialista. Piensa en diez cosas que quieres muchísimo. Puede ser algo material o concreto como una motocicleta o algo abstracto como la paz en el mundo. Enfrente de cada deseo escribe la letra *C* si es concreto y *A* si es abstracto. Cuenta la lista de *C* para averiguar lo materialista que eres tú. ¿Es materialista la clase o no?

| *Refrán* | La necesidad es la madre de la ciencia.
Explica el sentido. Da ejemplos de la vida. |

2 Definite and Indefinite Articles

GOAL 1

To use the appropriate form of the definite article to agree with the noun.

In English there is only one definite article, "the." In Spanish the definite article has two forms and three endings, *el* and *l* + *-a, -as, -os*. Which form to use depends upon the gender or ending of the noun with which it is used.

Forms and Agreements of Definite Articles

		Singular		Plural
With nouns referring to males or nouns ending in -o, -e, -l, -n, -r, -s	el	señor libro café corral pan amor mes	los	señores libros cafés corrales panes amores meses
With nouns referring to females or nouns ending in -a, -d, -ción, -sis, -ie, -umbre	la	mujer casa libertad nación tesis serie costumbre	las	mujeres casas libertades naciones tesis series costumbres

Common exceptions to the above rules include *la mano, la sal, la calle, la noche, el mapa, el día,* and many more words ending in *-ma: el problema, el programa, el tema,* etc.

EXERCISE

Supply the definite article for each noun.

1. _los_ castillos
2. _la_ lámpara
3. _el_ edificio
4. _las_ pinturas
5. _los_ programas
6. _los_ manos
7. _la_ día
8. _las_ profesoras
9. _la_ novelista
10. _el_ bailador
11. _las_ habilidades
12. _las_ poemas
13. _la_ papá
14. _los_ lunes
15. _el_ tesis
16. _los_ escritores
17. _el_ reunión
18. _el_ examen
19. _los_ jóvenes
20. _la_ botella

GOAL 2

> To use the Spanish definite article in patterns similar in both Spanish and English.

In both Spanish and English the definite article is used to point out a specific noun or nouns.

Dame **el** libro que está en **la** mesa.   *Give me **the** book on **the** table.*

In using the definite article there are two slight irregularities that you should remember. First, *a + el* contract to *al* and *de + el* contract to *del*. The other forms are regular.

Voy **al** mercado y **a la** tienda.   *I go **to the** market and **to the** store.*
Voy **a los** mercados y **a las** tiendas.   *I go **to the** markets and **to the** stores.*

Second, with a feminine word that begins with a stressed *a* or *ha* the article *la* changes to *el*.

Sufren **del hambre.**   *They suffer from **hunger.***
Me gusta **el agua** fría.   *I like **cold water.***

The other forms are regular.

Sufren de las hambres **del espíritu.**   *They suffer from spiritual **hunger.***
Me gustan **las aguas** frías.   *I like **cold water.***

There are a few common exceptions to this rule.

La novena letra del alfabeto es   *The ninth letter of the (Spanish)*
   la hache.   *alphabet is **h.***
La Haya es una ciudad de Holanda.   ***The Hague** is a city in Holland.*

EXERCISE

Complete each sentence with the appropriate definite article or contraction.

1. Tengo _____ fotografía que me diste.

2. Estos son _____ discos que querías.

3. _____ reloj está descompuesto. No funciona.

4. _____ paisaje en las montañas es magnifico.

5. Buscamos _____ oportunidad de darle las gracias.

6. _____ mujer que tiene el pelo rubio es mi hermana.

7. Tenemos _____ lección diez para mañana.

8. _____ abogada representó a _____ criminal.

9. _____ guantes en _____ silla son de _____ hombre que acaba de salir.

10. Hablaba con _____ turista guapa a quien conocimos anoche.

11. _____ águila es _____ símbolo de _____ gobierno de _____ Estados Unidos.

12. Todos _____ candidatos políticos nuevos son miembros del congreso.

GOAL 3

To omit the definite article in patterns similar in both Spanish and English.

In general, neither Spanish nor English uses articles before singular proper nouns. Both languages use the definite article with family names.

Juan es mi amigo.   *Juan is my friend.*
Los García viven aquí.   *The Garcías live here.*

EXERCISE

Complete each sentence with the appropriate definite article, if needed. In some sentences no article will be necessary.

1. _____ Pedro siempre llega tarde.

2. Llamaré a _____ María.

3. Buscábamos _____ camisas de colores.

4. _____ palacios de España son muy viejos.

5. _____ Fernández son de Puerto Rico.

6. La familia de _____ Anita habla español en casa.

7. _____ parque es un buen sitio para pasar _____ día al aire libre.

GOAL 4

To use the definite article in Spanish in contexts different from English.

The definite article is used much more in Spanish than in English. The following examples show common uses of the definite article in Spanish in situations in which the definite article is not used in English.

A. The definite article is used in Spanish to refer to parts of the body and to articles of clothing when they are used as objects of verbs.

José, cierra **los** ojos.   *José, close **your** eyes.*
Marta tiene **los** ojos azules.   *Marta has blue eyes.*
Pepe, ponte **el** sombrero.   *Pepe, put on **your** hat.*
Los niños se ponen **el abrigo.**[1]   *The children put on **their** coats.*

EXERCISE

Complete each sentence with the appropriate form of the definite article.

1. Jorge tiene _____ nariz grande.

2. Miguel, lávate _____ orejas cuando te bañes.

3. Señor, abra usted _____ boca, por favor.

4. Señor, quítese _____ sombrero dentro de la iglesia.

5. Señora, póngase _____ zapatos.

6. María tiene _____ pelo rubio.

---

1. In Spanish the singular is used if each person has only one of the article mentioned.

B. The definite article is used in Spanish to refer to days of the week, dates, and seasons of the year.

Voy **el jueves.**	*I am going **on Thursday.***
Juan regresa **los viernes.**	*Juan returns **on Fridays.***
El domingo es el primer día de la semana.	***Sunday** is the first day of the week.*

However, after *ser* the Spanish structure is just like English.

Hoy es **miércoles.**	*Today is **Wednesday.***

EXERCISE

Complete each sentence with the appropriate form of the definite article, if needed. In some sentences no article will be necessary.

1. Llega _____ martes.

2. Vamos _____ quince de este mes.

3. _____ sábado es mi día favorito.

4. Vienen _____ domingo por la noche.

5. Salen _____ sábados por la tarde.

6. Hoy es _____ jueves.

7. Volverán _____ tres de junio en un avión de reacción.

8. _____ primavera es mi estación favorita.

C. The definite article in Spanish is also used to express an abstract idea or to refer to a general class.

El amor es muy importante en la vida.	***Love** is very important in life.*
El dinero es necesario.	***Money** is necessary.*

However, the article is not used when the idea is "some" or part of a class.

Tiene **dinero** en el banco.	*He has (some) **money** in the bank.*

EXERCISE

Complete each sentence with the appropriate form of the definite article if necessary.

1. _____ leyes nos ayudan a tener una vida mejor.

2. Es necesario ganarse _____ pan para vivir.

3. _____ inteligencia es una característica deseable.

4. Se preparan las comidas con _____ aceite de oliva.

5. _____ recreo es necesario para descansar del trabajo y de la vida rutinaria.

6. Tiene _____ amigos en esa ciudad.

D. *La* or *las* is used with cardinal numbers to tell time.

Viene a **la una.**	*She is coming at **one o'clock.***
Los otros llegan a **las dos.**	*The others arrive at **two o'clock.***

EXERCISE

Complete each sentence with either *la* or *las.*

1. La clase comienza a _____ la _____ una y quince.
2. Termina de trabajar a _____ las _____ dos.
3. Los alumnos llegan a _____ las _____ ocho menos cinco.
4. Son exactamente _____ las _____ seis y media.
5. Te llamo a _____ la _____ una menos veinte.
6. Es _____ la _____ una y diez de la tarde.

E. *El* is used with the name of a language.

El español es fácil.   ***Spanish** is easy.*

However, the article is not used after the verbs *hablar, estudiar, aprender, entender, leer,* and *saber,* or after the prepositions *en* and *de.*

Hablo español y francés.   *I speak Spanish and French.*
Es un libro de español.   *It is a Spanish book.*
Sabe escribir en francés.   *He (she) knows how to write in French.*

EXERCISE

Complete each sentence with *el* or a contraction of *el,* if needed.

1. Hablamos _____ español en la clase de _____ español.
2. Miguel habla bien _____ inglés.
3. ¿Estudian ustedes _____ alemán?
4. Sí, y escribimos composiciones en _____ alemán?
5. La lengua nacional del Brasil es _____ portugués.
6. _____ francés es una lengua romántica.

F. The definite article is used with certain titles like *señor, profesor,* etc. when talking about a person.

El señor García es muy amable.   ***Mr. Garcia** is very kind.*

However, the article is normally not used with *don* or *doña,* nor when talking directly to the person.

Don Pepe es muy amable.   ***Don Pepe** is very kind.*
Buenos días, **señor Garcia.**   *Good morning, **Mr. Garcia.***

EXERCISE

Complete each sentence with a definite article, if needed.

1. Buenas tardes, _____ señora Gómez. ¿Qué tal?
2. _____ profesor Fernández nunca pierde la paciencia.
3. Raúl sale con _____ señorita Alborg.
4. ¿Quiere usted ir con nosotros, _____ señorita Rodríguez?
5. _____ señora Sánchez es la presidente del club.
6. _____ don Carlos es respetado por todos.

G. The definite article is used before modified expressions of time.

El fue **la semana pasada.**   *He went **last week.***

EXERCISE

Complete each sentence with the appropriate form of the definite article.

1. El paquete llegó _____ primer día de mis vacaciones.

2. Saldremos _____ mes que viene en ferrocarril.

3. _____ semana próxima habrá una fiesta.

4. _____ día siguiente llovió en la costa.

5. ¡Esta es _____ última vez!

6. Es _____ próximo martes.

GOAL 5

To use the appropriate form of the indefinite article to agree with the noun.

The ending of the indefinite article (*un* and *un* + *-a, -as, -os*) must agree with the gender or ending of the noun it modifies.

Forms and Agreement of Indefinite Articles

	Singular	Plural
With nouns referring to males or nouns ending in *-o, -e, -l, -n, -r, -s*	**un** chico *a boy*	**unos** chicos *some boys*
	un animal *an animal*	**unos** anim**al**es *some animals*
With nouns referring to females or nouns ending in *-a, -d, -ción, -sis, -ie, -umbre*	**una** chica *a girl*	**unas** chicas *some girls*
	una fiesta *a party*	**unas** fiestas *some parties*

EXERCISE

Supply the appropriate indefinite article for each noun.

1. _____ castillos

2. _____ lámpara

3. _____ edificio

4. _____ pinturas

5. _____ programas

6. _____ manos

7. _____ día

8. _____ profesoras

9. _____ novelista

10. _____ bailador

11. _____ habilidades

12. _____ poemas

13. _____ padre

14. _____ francés

15. _____ tesis

16. _____ escritores

17. _____ reunión

18. _____ examen

19. _____ jóvenes

20. _____ botella

GOAL 6

To use the Spanish indefinite article in patterns similar in both
Spanish and English.

In general, the indefinite article in both Spanish and English is used in the same
way.

Veo **un** coche.	*I see **a** car.*
Lleva **una** falda azul.	*She is wearing **a** blue skirt.*

EXERCISE

Complete each of the following sentences with the appropriate indefinite article.

1. _____ abeja trabaja mucho en el verano.

2. _____ abogado estudia las leyes.

3. _____ ciudad es más grande que _____ pueblo.

4. Hay _____ cuantos edificios altos en esa ciudad.

5. Esperan _____ jóvenes en el pasillo.

6. Llegaron _____ directores de la oficina central.

7. Tiene _____ enfermedades que el médico no conoce.

8. Tomo _____ refresco cuando tengo calor.

9. Cantaban _____ canción española.

GOAL 7

To omit the Spanish indefinite article in patterns different from English.

The indefinite article is often omitted in Spanish in situations in which it is used
in English.

A. When the complement following the verb *ser* indicates a profession, a nationality, or a religious group, the indefinite article is omitted.

El señor Granadillo es profesor.	*Mr. Granadillo is **a** teacher.*
Juana es abogada.	*Juana is **a** lawyer.*

However, if the complement is modified, an indefinite article is generally used.

Es **un buen** profesor.	*He is **a good** teacher.*

EXERCISE

Write each sentence in Spanish.

1. Juan is a Mexican.

   Juan es mexicano.

2. María is a Catholic.

3. Mr. Sánchez is a well-known psychologist.

_____

4. Raúl is a student.

_____

5. He is an intelligent student.

Es un b esn

6. His father is a doctor.

Se pore es medio

B. After a negative verb or after the preposition _sin_, the indefinite article is also omitted.

No tengo libro.	**I don't** have a book.
Está prohibido manejar **sin licencia.**	Driving **without a license** is prohibited.

EXERCISE

Complete each sentence with the appropriate word.

1. He left without a coat. Salió sin _____.

2. We do not have a record player. No tenemos _____.

3. I am not wearing a hat. No llevo _____.

4. He is reading without a light. Está leyendo sin _____.

5. She did not bring a gift. No trajo _____.

6. We never travel without an umbrella.

   Nunca viajamos sin _____.

C. The indefinite article is omitted in certain expressions and after words such as the following:

cierta casa	_a certain house_
otro hombre	**another** _man_
tal clase	_such_ **a** _class_
¡Qué mujer!	_What_ **a** _woman!_
mil caballos	_a thousand horses_
cien flores	_a hundred flowers_
año y medio	_a year and_ **a** _half_

EXERCISE

Complete each sentence in Spanish.

1. We have traveled a thousand miles. Hemos viajado

   _____.

2. There is another thing to buy. Hay _____ que comprar.

3. Such a test scares me. _____ me asusta.

4. What a game! ¡Qué _____!

5. We lived there a year and a half. Vivimos allí _____.

6. He bought a thousand books. Compró _____.

Communication Pattern Exercises

I. Complete each sentence with an appropriate definite article, if needed.

1. _____ Estados Unidos están en el hemisferio occidental.

2. Dicen que _____ libertad vale mucho.

3. Isabel viene a Washington _____ próximo año.

4. _____ señora de Gómez se preocupa mucho.

5. Buenas tardes, _____ señor Martínez.

6. Hoy es _____ sábado y mi hermano viene a _____ dos.

7. ¿Habla usted _____ alemán?

8. Sí, _____ alemán es interesante.

9. _____ don Manuel González vive allí.

10. _____ leche es nutritiva.

11. _____ águila es un pájaro magnífico.

12. _____ miércoles y _____ martes yo trabajo desde _____ ocho hasta _____ una.

II. Complete each sentence with an appropriate indefinite article, if needed.

1. La Argentina es _____ país grande.

2. Su padre es _____ representante.

3. Tiene _____ casa bien arreglada.

4. _____ estudiante no sabe que hacer. Los demás sí.

5. Josefina ha escrito _____ cartas a unos marineros.

6. La señora Gómez es _____ buena deportista.

7. ¿Hay _____ corrida de toros todos los domingos?

8. Ella es _____ vecina nuestra.

9. Ellos son _____ fieles protestantes.

10. ¡Qué _____ carrera!

11. No lo creo. Tal _____ cosa nunca ocurrió.

12. ¡Pobrecita! Ya tiene _____ otra cita con él.

13. Los jóvenes son _____ ecuatorianos.

14. Estoy muy ocupado. Tengo _____ mil cosas que hacer.

III. Express the idea of each sentence in Spanish.

1. Mrs. Fernández is coming next week.

_____

2. Mr. García is a Catholic.

_____

3. Teresa has blond hair.

_____

4. What a family!

_____

5. There are some papers on the table.

_____

6. On Saturdays we go to the movies.

_____

7. Miss Fernández is a good lawyer.

_____

8. Canada is to the north of the United States.

_____

9. The train arrives at one o'clock.

_____

10. He has a hundred books in his room.

_____

11. Mrs. Robledo is a Cuban.

_____

12. Toledo is a Spanish city.

_____

13. Spanish is a very important language.

_____

14. Do you speak Spanish in class?

_____

Actividades de comunicación

I. Hablando con un(a) amigo(a) o un grupo pequeño, usa las siguientes preguntas como base de una conversación.

1. ¿Hablas tú español? ¿Es fácil o difícil el español? ¿Escribes en español? ¿Estudias otras lenguas? ¿Habla tu familia otras lenguas?

2. ¿Eres astronauta? ¿Son ustedes espías internacionales? ¿Son ustedes detectives? ¿Es médico tu padre? ¿Qué es tu padre? ¿Qué es tu madre?

3. ¿Qué hora es? ¿A qué hora es la clase de español? ¿Qué es hoy? ¿A qué hora llegas a la escuela? ¿En qué días no asistes a las clases? ¿Cuál es tu día favorito?

4. ¿Hay unos cuantos estudiantes buenos en esta clase? ¿Hay una plaza en la ciudad donde vives? ¿Qué hay de interés en tu ciudad?

5. ¿Llevas puesto el abrigo en la casa? ¿Es necesario el agua para vivir? ¿Es muy importante la religión en la sociedad? ¿Qué es más importante en tu vida?

6. ¿Tienes cien discos? ¿Tiene tu familia una casa como la del señor Rockefeller? ¿Tienen ustedes algo en exceso? ¿Tienen ustedes algo que no tiene el señor Rockefeller?

7. ¿Vas mucho al cine? ¿A qué hora vuelves del cine? ¿Con quién vas al cine? ¿Cuándo van ustedes?

II. Completa las oraciones haciendo comparación.

1. Para mí el amor es como un(a) _____.

2. Para mi mamá la casa es como _____.

3. Para mis amigos la amistad es como _____.

4. Para nosotros el español es como _____.

5. Para el profesor _____.

6. Para el drogadicto _____.

III. Pon las cosas nombradas desde A hasta J en el orden de importancia que tengan en tu vida.

A. el dinero
B. el tiempo libre
C. la amistad
D. la salud
E. la educación

F. el trabajo
G. el recreo
H. la religión
I. el amor
J. los deportes

1. _____

2. _____

3. _____

4. _____

5. _____

6. _____

7. _____

8. _____

9. _____

10. _____

Compara tu lista con la de un(a) compañero(a) de clase, y discute con la clase la importancia de cada uno.

IV. Discute lo siguiente con otros miembros de la clase.

"Sólo hay cuatro cosas necesarias en la vida—el amor, la risa, la música y la religión—y todas son libres."

¿Estás de acuerdo o no? Si no, ¿qué otras cosas hay? Si no, ¿qué importancia tiene el dinero?

Refrán

De la discusión nace la luz.
La ociosidad es madre de todos los vicios.
Explica el sentido. Da ejemplos de la vida.

---

3 Demonstratives

GOAL 1

To use the appropriate form of the demonstrative to agree with the noun it points out.

In Spanish one must say *el hermano, la hermana, los hermanos,* and *las hermanas* to make the article and noun endings agree with each other. The endings on demonstratives (*est + -e, -a, -os, -as*) also change to agree with the gender or the ending of the noun indicated.

Forms and Agreements of Demonstratives

	Singular	**Plural**
With nouns referring to males or nouns ending in -o, -e, -l, -n, -r, -s	est**e** señor *this gentleman* est**e** parque *this park*	est**os** señor**es** *these gentlemen* est**os** parques *these parks*
With nouns referring to females or nouns ending in -a, -d, -ción, -sis, -ie, -umbre	est**a** señora *this lady* est**a** ciudad *this city*	est**as** señoras *these ladies* est**as** ciuda**des** *these cities*

Ese ("that") and *aquel* ("that") also have four endings.

ese	esos
esa	esas

aquel	aquellos
aquella	aquellas

EXERCISE   Write new sentences using the cues, changing the endings of the demonstrative to agree with the new noun.

1. Quiere comprar ese traje. (libros/blusa/manzana/disco)

   Quiere comprar esos libros.

   Quiere comprar esas blusa

   Quiere comprar esa

2. ¿Ves aquella montaña? (helicóptero/vacas/edificios/contaminación)

3. ¿Por qué me das estos papeles? (dinero/bombillas/antena/boletos)

GOAL 2

To distinguish between the use of *este*, *ese*, and *aquel*.

In English we say "this table" and "that table," "these books" and "those books," "this year" and "that year," and "these times" and "those times." That is, English speakers divide time and space into two categories. In Spanish there are three categories.

Distinction Among Demonstratives

	Singular	Plural
Near the speaker	**este** libro *this* book	**estos** libros *these* books
Near the person spoken to or "just over there"	**esa** pluma *that* pen	**esas** plumas *those* pens
In the distance from both the speaker and the person spoken to	**aquel** pico *that* peak	**aquellos** picos *those* peaks

EXERCISE   Complete each sentence with the correct form of the appropriate demonstrative.

1. María mira el vestido en una tienda y dice, "¡Qué bonito es _____ vestido!"

2. Pepe coge una pelota y dice, "_____ pelota es mía."

3. Papá observa una casa grande en una colina a lo lejos y dice, "¡Qué preciosa es _____ casa!"

4. Josefina habla con Pepita y le dice, "_____ zapatos que llevas son muy bonitos. Me gustan muchísimo."

5. La familia hace una excursión por la bahía de Nueva York. El guía indica un edificio alto y les dice, "_____ edificio alto es el edificio Empire State."

6. Mamá le pide a papá, "Dáme _____ revista. No es interesante _____ cuento que leo ahora."

7. La señora entró en el almacén y le dijo al dependiente, "_____ vasos están rotos. Quisiera otros."

8. La pareja entra a una panadería; ella señala unos dulces y dice, "¡Cuánto me gustan _____ pasteles!"

GOAL 3

To distinguish between the use of *este* and *éste*, *ese* and *ése*, and *aquel* and *aquél*.

Unaccented demonstratives function as adjectives, and accented demonstratives function as pronouns.

Forms of *este, ese,* and *aquel* are used directly before nouns.

No me gusta **esta limonada.**	*I do not like **this lemonade.***
¿Qué te parecen **esas fotos?**	*What do you think of **those pictures?***

When no noun follows the demonstrative, an accent mark is added: *éste, ése, aquél.*

¿Las tarjetas? No, no me gustan **éstas.**	*The cards? No, I don't like **these.***
¿Prefieres este final o **ése?**	*Do you prefer this ending or **that one?***

Forms of *éste* and *aquél* are also used to mean "the latter" and "the former," respectively.

Visitamos a García y a Gómez. **Este** (Gómez) es mi cuñado y **aquél** (García) es mi tío.	*We are visiting García and Gómez. **The latter** is my brother-in-law, and **the former** is my uncle.*

EXERCISE   Complete each sentence with the appropriate form of either the unaccented or the accented demonstrative, as the context indicates.

1. El guía les dice a los turistas, "_____ casa (aquí) es del señor Michael Jordan y _____ (en la distancia) son de unos actores y actrices muy conocidos."

2. La niña le dice a su mamá, "De todas _____ muñecas que tengo aquí me gusta más _____."

3. El chico compara su bicicleta con la de su amigo, "_____ bicicleta que tienes tú está bien, pero _____ que tengo yo es mejor."

4. Los hermanos dividen los sellos en dos grupos. Uno le dice al otro, "_____ son míos. _____ son tuyos."

5. La profesora le dice a Juana, "No, _____ (aquí) bolsa es mía. _____ es suya."

6. El joven entra en la sala de recreo con un perrito y les dice a sus padres, "Encontré _____ perrito en _____ edificio desocupado al norte de la escuela."

7. Alberto tiene que juzgar el mejor vino en un concurso de gourmets. Prueba uno y dice, "Ah, _____ me gusta!" Luego prueba otro y exclama, "_____ es superior! Me gusta _____ más que _____."

8. Miguel pregunta a su amigo, "¿Son _____ pantalones que tengo yo más nuevos que _____ que tienes tú?"

GOAL 4

To distinguish between the use of *este*, *éste*, and *esto*; *ese*, *ése*, and *eso*; and *aquel*, *aquél*, and *aquello*.

There are three neuter demonstratives in Spanish: *esto*, *eso*, and *aquello*. (*Lo* and *ello* are the only other neuters in Spanish.) The neuter is used to refer to something for which the speaker does not know the name or to refer to a generality.

¿Qué es **esto**?   *What is **this**?*

No me gusta **eso**.   *I don't like **that** (whatever is happening).*

EXERCISE Complete each sentence with the appropriate accented, unaccented, or neuter form of the demonstrative, as the context indicates.

1. Dos niños están compartiendo sus juguetes. Joselito habla. "_____ es mío. _____ es tuyo. _____ son míos."

2. Josefina se sienta en la clase de educación física y se queja, "No me gusta _____ clase. No me gusta _____ de hacer ejercicios todos los días."

3. La familia está paseándose por el parque, y mamá dice, "¡Qué bonitos son _____ árboles al otro lado de la valle!" Luego pregunta Raúl, "Sí, son hermosos, pero ¿qué es _____ en el centro del bosque?"

4. Juan pinta un cuadro. Jorge encuentra que está mal hecho. Le dice, "_____ no vale nada. Tienes que hacerlo de nuevo."

5. Dos señoritas hablan de sus faldas. "Me gusta _____ falda que llevas. _____ que llevo yo no tiene ningún color vivo."

6. Amigos, _____ es lo que vamos a hacer. Carlos va a traer _____ cajas aquí. Pablo, lleva _____ y Tomás, lleva _____ que están en el otro edificio.

Communication Pattern Exercise

Answer the questions. Then work with a partner. Take turns asking and answering the questions.

1. ¿Es éste un libro de español?

   _____

2. ¿Es difícil este libro?

   _____

3. ¿Es más difícil éste que el del año pasado?

   _____

4. Y ese lápiz que tienes, ¿es de México?

   _____

5. ¿Son nuevos esos zapatos que llevas?

   _____

6. Y esa pluma que tienes, ¿es del Japón?

_____

7. (El turista mira una casa grande y elegante a la distancia.) ¿Vive gente
   rica en aquella casa?

_____

8. ¿Y en aquélla?

_____

9. (El turista mira Pikes Peak en Colorado.) ¿Siempre hay nieve en aquel
   pico?

_____

10. ¿Y en aquél?

_____

Actividades de comunicación

I. Usa formas de *este* para preparar una conversación que describa una excursión
imaginaria de la escuela o universidad. Indica los puntos y sitios interesantes a
un estudiante de un país de habla española que visita esta escuela.

II. Usa formas de *ese* para describir lo que lleva un(a) compañero(a) de clase.

III. Usa formas de *aquel* para describir tu pueblo o ciudad. Imagínate que eres
el guía en un autobús de turistas españoles.

Refrán

Tonto que calla, por sabio pasa.
La práctica hace al maestro.
Explica el sentido. Da ejemplos de la vida.

4 Possession

GOAL 1

To use the pattern *de* + noun to express possession.

In Spanish, to show that a noun possesses something, the pattern *de* + noun
is always used. This pattern is like that used in English when the possessor is
an inanimate object.

El techo **de** la casa es verde.	*The roof **of** the house is green.*
El coche **de** Juan es rojo.	*Juan**'s** car is red.*
La bicicleta **del** profesor es azul.	*The teacher**'s** bicycle is blue.*

Note that the English forms *'s* and *s'* are never used in Spanish.

EXERCISE   Combine each pair of sentences into one using a *de* phrase to indicate possession.

1. La profesora tiene un gato. Es blanco.

   El gato de la profesora es blanco

2. Quiero una revista. José tiene una revista.

   Quiero la revista de José.

3. María tiene una blusa. Es bonita.

4. Los González tienen un barco. Es nuevo.

5. El banquero tiene una caja fuerte. Es grande.

6. La señora lleva un sombrero. Es cómico.

7. Quiero unos discos. El joven tiene unos discos.

8. Quiero un refresco. La señora toma un refresco.

9. Queremos unas plantas. Los Gómez tienen unas plantas.

10. Quiere la nota. Sue hermano tiene la nota.

GOAL 2

To use the pattern possessive + noun.

The following possessives go before the noun:

Forms of Before-Noun Possessives

	Singular	Plural
Person speaking	mi, -s *my*	nuestro, -a, -os, -as *our*
Person spoken to (familiar)	tu, -s *your*	vuestro, -a, -os, -as *your*
Person spoken to (formal)	su, -s *your*	su, -s *your*
Person spoken about	su, -s, *his, her, its*	su, -s *their*

A. The stem of the possessive indicates the possessor. The ending attached to the possessive agrees with the thing possessed, not the possessor. The possessive must be either singular or plural to agree with the thing possessed.

Mi casa es grande.
Mis libros son nuevos.

My house is big.
My books are new.

All Spanish possessives have at least two forms: singular and plural. Some have two additional endings: masculine *(-o)* and feminine *(-a)*. English possessives in the pattern possessive + noun have only one form.

Tu conferencia fue interesante.
Tu cuaderno es grande.
Nuestra clase es corta.
Nuestro trampolín es ancho.
Nuestros bolsos son caros.

Your lecture was interesting.
Your notebook is big.
Our class is short.
Our diving board is wide.
Our purses are expensive.

EXERCISE

Complete each sentence using the appropriate form of the possessive indicated.

1. *(Nuestro)* _____Nuestra_____ farmacia está en la esquina.

2. ¿Es *(su)* _____ medicina?

3. Este es *(mi)* _____ cinturón.

4. *(Su)* _____ silla no es muy cómoda.

5. *(Su)* _____ maletas están en el coche.

6. *(Nuestro)* _____ botes son útiles.

7. ¿Es rojo *(tu)* _____ impermeable?

8. ¿De qué color son *(vuestro)* _____ cuartos?

9. *(Mi)* _____ paraguas está cerca de la puerta.

10. ¿Dónde están *(vuestro)* _____ hamburguesas?

11. Pongan ustedes *(su)* _____ bicicleta aquí.

12. *(Mi)* _____ programas favoritos son los de los deportes.

13. ¿Son nuevos *(tu)* _____ anteojos?

B. The stem of the possessive changes to indicate the possessor. Using the possessive *su* correctly seems to be especially difficult for speakers of English. Remember that the base word *su* indicates the possessor ("your," "his," "her," "its," "their"). The singular form *su* indicates that the thing possessed is singular. The suffix *-s* indicates that the thing possessed is plural.

Señor, ¿es **su** asiento?
Muchachos, ¿es **su** casa?
Señor, ¿son **sus** papeles?
Muchachos, ¿son **sus** papeles?
Las actrices escondían **su** tristeza.
El turista declaró **sus** recuerdos.

*Sir, is this **your** seat?*
*Boys, is this **your** house?*
*Sir, are these **your** papers?*
*Boys, are these **your** papers?*
*The actresses were hiding **their** sadness.*
*The tourist declared **his** souvenirs.*

EXERCISE

Complete the answer to each question using the appropriate possessive.

1. ¿Tienen ustedes una tabla de surf?

   Sí, _____*nuestra*_____ tabla de surf es blanca.

2. Pepita, ¿tengo yo un paraguas aquí?

   No, _____ paraguas está perdido.

3. ¿Tiene María unos dibujos originales?

   Sí, _____ dibujos son originales.

4. ¿Tienen los chicos una familia simpática?

   Sí, _____ familia es simpática.

5. Señores, ¿tenemos un equipo agresivo?

   Sí, _____ equipo es agresivo.

6. José, ¿tenemos jugadores entusiasmados?

   Sí, _____ jugadores están entusiasmados.

7. ¿Tenéis unos profesores exigentes?

   Sí, _____ profesores son exigentes.

8. ¿Tiene usted una silla cómoda?

   Sí, _____ silla es cómoda.

9. ¿Tienes plumas con tinta negra?

   Sí, _____ plumas tienen tinta negra.

10. ¿Tienen Diana y Catalina un tocadiscos caro?

    Sí, _____ tocadiscos es caro.

11. ¿Tiene el chico unos cuantos juguetes rotos?

    Sí, _____ juguetes están rotos.

12. ¿Tienen los Hernández unas alfombras orientales?

    Sí, _____ alfombras son orientales.

13. ¿Tiene Josefina un anillo de oro?

    Sí, _____ anillo es de oro.

14. ¿Tienen Raúl y Carlos un caballo dócil?

    Sí, _____ caballo es dócil.

15. ¿Tienen ustedes barbas largas?

    Sí, _____ barbas son largas.

GOAL 3

To use the pattern noun or *ser* + possessive.

The following possessives are used after *ser* or after a noun. All have four endings.

Forms of After-Noun Possessives

	Singular	**Plural**
Person speaking	mío, -a, -os, -as *mine*	nuestro, -a, -os, -as *ours*
Person spoken to (familiar)	tuyo, -a, -os, -as *yours*	vuestro, -a, -os, -as *yours*
Person spoken to (formal)	suyo, -a, -os, -as *yours*	suyo, -a, -os, -as *yours*
Person spoken about	suyo, -a, -os, -as *his, hers, its*	suyo, -a, -os, -as *theirs*

A. The ending attached to the possessive agrees with the thing possessed, not the possessor.

libro suyo   *your, his, her, its, their book*
libros suyos   *your, his, her, its, their books*
cama suya   *your, his, her, its, their bed*
camas suyas   *your, his, her, its, their beds*

EXERCISE

Complete each sentence with the appropriate form of the possessive indicated.

1. La chaqueta es *(suyo)* _____.

2. Unos primos *(nuestro)* _____ tocan en la banda.

3. El cuaderno es *(mío)* _____.

4. ¿Es *(tuyo)* _____ esta frazada?

5. Las plantas *(vuestro)* _____ son hermosísimas.

6. Madre *(mío)* _____, te amo mucho.

7. ¿Son *(suyo)* _____ estas bebidas?

8. El reloj *(suyo)* _____ funciona bajo agua.

9. La colección de sellos es *(suyo)* _____.

10. Unos amigos *(nuestro)* _____ vienen esta noche.

B. Remember that the ending of the possessive word agrees with the thing possessed, while the base word agrees with the possessor.

¿Es ésta la casa de Felipe?	*Is this Felipe's house?*
No, no es **suya.**	*No, it's not **his.***
¿Es de Ana?	*Is it Ana's?*
No, no es **suya.**	*No, it's not **hers.***
¿Es **mía?**	*Is it **mine?***
No, no es **tuya.**	*No, it's not **yours.***
¿Es **nuestra?**	*Is it **ours?***
No, no es **suya.**	*No, it's not **yours.***
¿Es de los García?	*Is it the García's?*
Sí, es **suya.**	*Yes, it is **theirs.***

EXERCISE

Answer each question using the appropriate possessive.

1. ¿Es ésta mi tarea? _____ *Sí, es tuya.* _____

2. ¿Son éstas las raquetas de ustedes? _____

3. ¿Es ésta vuestra toalla? _____

4. ¿Son éstos tus pijamas? _____

5. ¿Es éste el jabón de María? _____

6. ¿Son éstas las notas de José? _____

7. ¿Es ésta la comida de Irene y Marta? _____

8. ¿Son éstos los helados de los chicos? _____

9. Jorge, ¿son tus esquíes? _____

C. Depending upon its use in the sentence, the Spanish after-noun possessive may have different meanings in English. For example, *mío* may mean "my" (spoken emphatically), "mine," "of mine," or "my."

- Emphatic "my": definite article + noun + possessive

Las sandalias **mías** son hermosísimas.	***My** sandals are especially beautiful.*

- "Mine": *ser* + possessive

Las corbatas son **mías.**	*The ties are **mine.***

- "Of mine": indefinite article + noun + possessive

Es un amigo **mío.**	*He is a friend of **mine.***

- "My" in direct address: noun + possessive.

Amigos **míos,** escuchadme.	*(My) friends, listen to me.*

EXERCISE

Give the English equivalent of each sentence.

1. Un primo nuestro toca en la banda.

   _____

2. El collar es mio.

   _____

3. Señor, ¿es suya esta pluma?

   _____

4. La pulsera tuya es más brillante.

   _____

5. Señores, el equipo suyo no juega bien.

   _____

6. Hijos míos, cállense, por favor.

   _____

7. ¿Unas amigas vuestras son de Colombia?

   _____

8. Querida mía, te adoro mucho.

   _____

GOAL 4

To use the pattern article + possessive in all other sentence positions.

The forms of the possessives used in other contexts are as follows:

Forms of Possessive Pronouns

	Singular	**Plural**
Person speaking	el mío, la mía los míos, las mías *mine*	el nuestro, etc. *ours*
Person spoken to (familiar)	el tuyo, etc. *yours*	el vuestro, etc. *yours*
Person spoken to (formal)	el suyo, etc. *yours*	el suyo, etc. *yours*
Person spoken about	el suyo, etc. *his, hers, its*	el suyo, etc. *theirs*

A. The ending attached to the possessive and the article with which it is used agree with the thing possessed, not the possessor.

Este broche es mío. Veo **el** tuy**o** en la mesa.	*This brooch is mine. I see yours on the table.*
Estas monedas son mí**as. Las** tuy**as** están en la mesa.	*These coins are mine. Yours are on the table.*

EXERCISE

Write sentences using the correct form of the article and possessive to agree with the article possessed.

1. (a. refrescos/nuestro), (b. coche/mío), (c. padres/tuyo), (d. tareas/suyo), (e. regalos de Navidad/suyo), (f. madre/suyo), (g. familia/suyo)

a. *Los nuestros no están aquí.* _____

b. _____

c. _____

d. _____

e. _____

f. _____

g. _____

2. (a. perfume/tuyo), (b. comidas/suyo), (c. silla/mío), (d. partidos/nuestro), (e. apartamento/suyo), (f. hermanos/suyo), (g. amiga/suyo)

a. *Me gusta el tuyo.* _____

b. _____

c. _____

d. _____

e. _____

f. _____

g. _____

B. In order to use the possessives correctly, you must remember that the ending agrees with the thing possessed while the base word agrees with the possessor.

Mis libros están en la mesa.	**My** books are on the table.
Y los de María, ¿dónde están?	And María's, where are they?
Los **suyos** están en el sofá.	**Hers** are on the sofa.
¿Y los de Ana y Josefina?	And Ana and Josefina's?
Los **suyos** están arriba.	**Theirs** are upstairs.
¿Y los de Miguel?	And Miguel's?
Los **suyos** están en el sótano.	**His** are in the basement.

EXERCISE

Complete the answer to each question using the appropriate possessive.

1. ¿Es peligroso el perro de usted? Sí, _el mío_ es peligrosísimo.

2. ¿Son éstas las cerámicas de ustedes? No, _____ están en otra mesa.

3. ¿Dónde está nuestro coche? _____ está en la calle veinte.

4. ¿Compra tu ropa? Sí, compra _____.

5. ¿Es éste el secador de María? No, _____ está en el dormitorio.

6. ¿Son éstas las llaves de José? No, _____ están en casa.

7. ¿Dónde está la peluquera de Juana y Ana? _____ está en otro edificio.

8. ¿Viste los paquetes de los estudiantes? Sí, _____ son pequeños.

GOAL 5

To distinguish among the uses of the three types of possessives.

There are three types of possessives in Spanish: *mi, tu,* etc.; *mío, tuyo,* etc.; *el mío, el tuyo,* etc. We have only two in English: "my," "mine," etc.

- Possessive + noun

  Tu casa es grande.   *Your house is big.*

- Noun or *ser* + possessive

  Un amigo **suyo** llamó.   *A friend of his called.*

- Other possessives

  a. Possessive + verb

  El nuestro es mejor.   *Ours is better.*

  b. Verb + possessive.

  Veo **el nuestro.**   *I see ours.*

  c. Preposition + possessive

  El suyo está cerca **del nuestro.**   *Theirs is near ours.*

Note that a possessive used with a verb or a preposition is preceded by a corresponding definite article, which is not used in English.

EXERCISES

I. Complete each sentence with the appropriate possessive, according to the context. Patterns contrasted: possessive + noun versus noun + possessive.

1. _____ madre me da regalos para _____ cumpleaños.

2. La señora siempre llama a unas amigas _____ cuando está descontenta.

3. Querida _____, te adoro ahora y para siempre.

4. A Roberto le gusta la universidad. Dice que _____ clases son interesantes.

5. Pero su hermano dice que las clases _____ son muy aburridas.

6. Unos compañeros _____ vinieron a visitarnos anoche.

7. El huésped no pagó el hotel porque _____ dinero se le perdió, pero un amigo _____ le prestó el dinero.

II. Complete each sentence with the appropriate possessive. Patterns contrasted: possessive + noun versus noun + possessive versus possessives used with verbs and prepositions.

1. Amigo _____, tengo hambre. ¿Por qué no vamos a comer?

2. ¿Podemos ir en _____ coche? No puedo manejar _____.

3. Ellos creen que las propinas _____ (de ellos) son generosas.

4. Josefina ha cambiado completamente. Antes _____ cuarto siempre estaba desarreglado, pero ahora _____ es el mejor arreglado.

5. Señor, ¿son éstas _____ compras? No, _____ ya están en el taxi.

6. Chicos, ¿son _____ estos modelos? No, _____ modelos están en el sótano.

7. Marta, Raúl, éstas son _____.

8. Unos parientes _____ vinieron a visitarme anoche. Jorge, ¿vinieron _____ también?

GOAL 6

To substitute clarifying phrases for third-person possessives.

The possessives *su, suyo,* and *el suyo* may refer to many different people: for example, *usted, él, ella, el chico, la chica, Juan, María, ustedes, ellos, ellas, los chicos, las chicas,* or *Juan y María.* Generally, the context in which the possessive is used makes the meaning clear. However, if the meaning is not clear, an explanatory phrase may be substituted to make the meaning absolutely clear.

Juan y María tienen un coche cada uno. **El de él** es azul. **El de ella** es verde.	*Juan and María each have a car.* ***His*** *is blue.* ***Hers*** *is green.*
¿Es éste el coche **de él?**	*Is this **his** car?*
No, es **de ella.**	*No, it's **hers.***
¿Dónde está el coche **de el?**	*Where is **his** car.*
El de él está en el garaje.	***His** is in the garage.*

EXERCISES

I. Complete each sentence using the appropriate explanatory phrase instead of *su* to indicate the possessor.

1. (hablando del chico/sombrero)

    _____*El de él*_____ está en el suelo.

2. (hablando de la señorita Gómez/conocimientos de política)

    _____ son extraordinarios.

3. (hablando de los obreros/habilidades)

    _____ son la base de la sociedad industrializada.

4. (hablando de Rodrigo/guantes)

    _____ son de lana.

5. (hablando al señor/abrigo)

    _____ está aquí.

6. (hablando de las chicas/actitud)

    _____ es muy positiva.

II. Complete each sentence using the appropriate explanatory phrase instead of *suyo* to indicate the possessor.

1. (hablando del chico)

    Sí, el sombrero es _____*de él*_____.

2. (hablando de las chicas)

    Sí, los alimentos naturales son _____.

3. (hablando de los pasajeros)

No, las habitaciones _____ no están cerca.

4. (hablando del señor Vera)

Sí, los cuadros surrealistas son _____.

5. (hablándole a una señora)

Señora, este espejo es _____.

6. (hablándoles a las señoras)

Señoras, los asientos de la primera fila son _____.

III. Complete each sentence using the pattern definite article + explanatory phrase instead of *el suyo*.

1. (hablando de los pantalónes de Rosa)

Si, _____*los de ella*_____ son atractivos.

2. (hablando de las tiendas de la señora González)

No me gustan _____.

3. (hablando del trabajo de los empleados)

_____ es muy eficiente.

4. (hablando de la biblioteca de Gómex)

_____ tiene muchos libros antiguos.

5. (hablando de los planes del joven)

¡Ojalá que se cumplan _____!

6. (hablando de la ropa de las hermanas)

Me gustaría tener _____.

Communication Pattern Exercises

I. Answer the questions. Then work with a partner. Take turns asking and answering the questions.

1. ¿Es éste tu cuaderno?

Sí, es mío. **or** *No, no es mío.*

2. Señora, ¿son éstas mis tareas?

_____

3. José, ¿es ésta mi camisa?

_____

4. Marina, ¿son éstos mis discos?

_____

5. Señores, ¿son éstos sus asientos?

_____

6. ¿Son éstas vuestras maletas?

_____

7. Mamá, ¿es éste nuestro horario?

_____

8. ¿Es éste el coche de los González?

_____

9. ¿Es ésta su cartera?

_____

II. Answer the questions. Then work with a partner. Take turns asking and answering the questions.

1. ¿Son unas camisas de él?

   _Sí, son unas camisas suyas._____

2. ¿Es una amiga tuya?

   _____

3. ¿Son unas cintas de usted?

   _____

4. ¿Es una casa de ellos?

   _____

5. ¿Es un coche de ustedes?

   _____

6. ¿Es un mensaje de ella?

   _____

7. ¿Es una hija de los García?

   _____

8. ¿Son unos estudiantes del señor?

_____

9. ¿Son unas joyas de la profesora?

_____

III. Answer the questions. Then work with a partner. Take turns asking and answering the questions.

1. ¿Es tu chaqueta de lana?

   No, la mía no es de lana.

2. Señorita, ¿están sus cartas en el buzón?

   _____

3. Rosa, ¿quieres mis discos?

   _____

4. Profesor, ¿se reúne mi club en esta aula?

   _____

5. ¿Son jóvenes vuestros padres?

   _____

6. Señoras, ¿son de algodón sus pañuelos?

   _____

7. ¿Está en el campo vuestra casa?

   _____

8. Señorita, ¿le gusta nuestra compañía?

   _____

9. Es admirable la actitud de los jóvenes, ¿no?

   _____

10. ¿Prefiere el vuelo de Rosa y María?

   _____

IV. Read each statement and answer the questions. Then work with a partner. Take turns asking and answering the questions.

1. Nuestra casa es grande, pero mi cuarto no lo es.

   ¿Cómo es nuestra casa?

   _____

¿Cómo es mi cuarto?

_____

¿Es grande el cuarto de tu amigo?

_____

¿Son grandes las casas de tus amigos?

_____

¿Son grandes las casas de los profesores?

_____

¿Es grande vuestra casa?

_____

¿Es grande tu cuarto?

_____

2. El presidente de esta universidad es un amigo mío.

¿Es un amigo mío el presidente?

_____

¿Es un amigo suyo?

_____

¿Es un amigo de su padre?

_____

¿Es un amigo de su madre?

_____

¿Es un amigo de los estudiantes?

_____

3. Hablando de los profesores, los míos son interesantes y justos pero muy exigentes.

¿Cómo son los míos?

_____

¿Cómo son los tuyos?

_____

¿Cómo son los de tu mejor amigo?

_____

¿Cómo son los de tus hermanos?

_____

Actividades de comunicación

I. Escribe un párrafo en el que describes lo que tienes: ropa, estéreo, discos, coches, etc. Compáralo con el de tu mejor amigo(a) y los de otros estudiantes.

Compara tu descripción con la de un(a) compañero(a) de clase y discute las posesiones similares y distintas.

II. Prepara dos listas de cosas que te hacen sentirte orgulloso de tu familia y de tu escuela o universidad.

1. Mi familia . . .
2. Nuestra escuela . . .

Refrán

Ver la paja en el ojo del vecino y no la viga en el nuestro.
Cada oveja con su pareja.
Explica el sentido. Da ejemplos de la vida.

5 Adjectives

GOAL 1

To use the appropriate form of the adjective to agree with the noun or nouns it modifies.

Although there are a few Spanish adjectives that have only one form (for example, *cada*), most adjectives in Spanish must change endings to agree with the gender or the ending of the noun modified.

Adjectives that end in *-o* or *-or* (other than comparatives) and adjectives of nationality have four forms.

Four-Ending Adjectives

	Singular	**Plural**
With nouns referring to males or nouns ending in *-o, -e, -l, -n, -r, -s*	señor alto partido conservador castillo español	señores altos partidos conservadores castillos españoles
With nouns referring to females or nouns ending in *-a, -d, -ión, -sis, -ie, -umbre*	señora alta religión conservadora cuidad espanola	señoras altas religiones conservadoras ciudades españolas

Other adjectives have only singular and plural forms.

Two-Ending Adjectives

	Singular	**Plural**
With all nouns	señor diligente señor sentimental señora diligente senora sentimental	señores diligentes señores sentimentales señoras diligentes señoras sentimentales

EXERCISES

I. Form sentences using the noun, either *es* or *son,* and the appropriate form of the adjective.

1. los dibujos/realista _____ *Los dibujos son realistas.* _____

2. mi novio/tímido _____

3. las ideas/radical _____

4. la iglesia/moderno _____

5. los jóvenes/español _____

6. las olas/enorme _____

7. Juan/perezoso _____

8. su hermana/muy trabajador _____

9. los pájaros/animado _____

10. la joven/mexicano _____

11. las enfermeras/paciente _____

12. la catedral y el palacio/viejo _____

13. Juan y María/muy popular _____

14. Timoteo/muy elegante _____

II. Form new sentences using the cues.

1. El chico es guapo.

   _____ son _____.

   Las _____.

   _____ chica _____.

2. Ese señor es delgado.

   _____ mujer _____.

   _____ interesante.

   _____ reuniones _____.

La _____.

_____ coches _____.

_____ importado.

3. Este parque es muy bonito en el verano.

_____ calle _____ en el verano.

Estas _____.

_____ lago _____.

_____ árboles _____ en el invierno.

GOAL 2

To use the appropriate forms of adjectives that have shortened forms.

A. Some adjectives that end in -o drop the -o in certain sentence positions. For example, in Spanish the adjective *uno* has five forms. One says *un libro, una pluma, unos libros,* and *unas plumas.* The -o of *uno* is dropped when it appears in front of the noun. There are other adjectives that follow the same pattern.

uno (un), primero (primer), *and* tercero (tercer); bueno (buen) *and* malo (mal); alguno (algún) *and* ninguno (ningún)

Es el **primer** edificio.	*It is the **first** building.*
Es la **primera** clase.	*It is the **first** class.*
Son las **primeras** clases.	*They are the **first** classes.*
Son los **primeros** edificios.	*They are the **first** buildings.*

All these adjectives, except *uno,* can occasionally follow the noun. When they do, the -o is retained. When the -o form precedes a noun, the -o is dropped.

EXERCISE

Complete the sentences with the correct forms of the adjectives in parentheses.

1. Es la *(primero)* _____ página, pero no es el *(primero)* _____ ejercicio. Los *(primero)* _____ ejercicios son número dos y número tres.

2. Sí, es el *(tercero)* _____ ejercicio el que me fatiga más. Es la *(tercero)* _____ vez que lo he practicado.

3. ¿Llevas *(uno)* _____ impermeable hoy? Sí, llevo *(uno)* _____.

   ¿Llevas también *(uno)* _____ bufanda? No, no llevo *(uno)* _____.

4. José y María son *(bueno)* _____ tenistas. El es *(bueno)*
_____ tenista y ella es *(bueno)* _____
tenista. Su hermanito también es un tenista *(bueno)*
_____ .

B. Certain other adjectives have shortened forms.

- *Grande* becomes *gran* before a singular noun.

Es un **gran** señor.	*He is a **great** man.*
Es una **gran** señora.	*She is a **great** lady.*
Son **grandes** señores.	*They are **great** people.*
Es un señor **grande.**	*He is a **big** man.*

- *Ciento* becomes *cien* before a noun or a number larger than itself.

Le faltan **cien** dólares.	*She needs **one hundred** dollars.*
Tiene **cien mil** habitantes.	*It has **a hundred thousand** inhabitants.*
Hay **ciento veinte** páginas en el libro.	*There are **one hundred twenty** pages in the book.*

The other hundred forms, *doscientos, trescientos,* etc. do not drop the *-os* ending.

- *Santo* becomes *san* before masculine names of saints, except before those beginning with *To-* or *Do-*. *Santa* is invariable.

   San Miguel, **Santo** Tomás, **Santo** Domingo

- *Cualquiera* becomes *cualquier* before a singular noun.

   cualquier lección   **cualquier** ejercicio

EXERCISE

Complete the sentences with the correct forms of the adjectives in parentheses.

1. Sí, éste es un *(grande)* _____ país y ésta es una *(grande)*
_____ ciudad, pero hay otros *(grande)*
_____ países y otras *(grande)* _____
ciudades.

2. Mi padre tiene más de *(ciento)* _____ libros y casi
(ciento) _____ revistas. La biblioteca tiene más de
(ciento) _____ mil libros y *(cuatrocientos)*
_____ revistas.

3. El señor García es un hombre *(grande)* _____ La señora
García es una mujer *(grande)* _____ Los dos tienen
padres *(grande)* _____ .

4. Me gustaría conocer a *(cualquiera)* _____ torero. Pero ese señor no es un torero *(cualquiera)* _____ Es el primero. De todos modos es bastante antipático y debes tratar de estar de acuerdo con *(cualquiera)* _____ cosa que diga.

5. Visitamos *(Santos)* _____ Antonio, *(Santo)* _____ Bárbara, *(Santo)* _____ Rafael y *(Santo)* _____ Domingo.

GOAL 3

To use those adjectives that normally precede the nouns they modify.

A. Adjectives that in some way restrict or limit nouns generally precede the nouns.

- Numbers

  Note that with the exception of *uno* and numbers that include *uno*, *ciento* and numbers that include *ciento*, *mil*, and *millón*, all numbers are invariable.

Tengo **cuatro** clases.	*I have **four** classes.*
Tiene **veintiún** discos.	*He has **twenty-one** records.*
Visitamos **veintiuna** ciudades.	*We visisted **twenty-one** cities.*
Vendió **trescientas** cajas de semillas.	*He sold **three hundred** boxes of seeds.*
Yo compré **cien** cajas.	*I bought **one hundred** boxes.*
Pesa **ciento diez** libras.	*She weighs **one hundred ten** pounds.*

- The indefinites *alguno, cuantos, cualquiera, unos, unos cuantos, varios*

Algún día lo haré.	***Some day** I will do it.*
Estudia **varias materias.**	*He is studying **several subjects.***

- The articles *el, la, los, las, un, una*

La acción es emocionante.	***The action** is exciting.*
Una médica trabaja mucho.	***A doctor** works a lot.*

- The demonstratives *este, ese, aquel*

Este vaso es mio. **Ese vaso** es tuyo.	***This glass** is mine. **That glass** is yours.*
Aquella casa es de madera.	***That house** is made of wood.*

- Before noun possessives *mi, tu, su, nuestro, vuestro, su*

Mis clases son interesantes.	***My classes** are interesting.*
Nuestra escuela es moderna.	***Our school** is modern.*

E X E R C I S E

Write a new sentence using the appropriate form of the adjective in the proper position.

  1. *(diez)* Hay unas cartas en la mesa.

   Hay diez cartas en la mesa.
   _____

  2. *(varios)* Cada invierno leo novelas.

   _____

  3. *(ese)* La secadora de pelo es suya.

   _____

  4. *(su)* Los consejos son buenos.

   _____

  5. *(alguno)* Me trajo los calcetines.

   _____

  6. *(uno)* Hay flores en el jardin.

   _____

  7. *(este)* Los cepillos son de nilón.

   _____

  8. *(nuestro)* La reunión duró dos horas.

   _____

  9. *(cualquiera)* Me interesan las cosas científicas.

   _____

B. Adjectives that are used in exclamations generally precede the noun in the pattern *qué* + adjective + noun.

   ¡Qué buena idea!

E X E R C I S E

Respond to each sentence with an exclamation that expresses the speaker's feelings.

  1. José cree que el partido es emocionante.

   Exclama, "¡Qué emocionante partido!"
   _____

  2. María piensa que la blusa es bonita.

   _____

  3. Creo que las empanadas son deliciosas.

   _____

4. El señor observa que el empleado es descortés.

_____

5. La niña se da cuenta de que los edificios son altos.

_____

6. Mi madre cree que la minifalda es corta.

_____

GOAL 4

To place an adjective that differentiates the noun from others in its group after the noun.

In general, an adjective that describes the noun in such a way as to differentiate it from others of the same category follows the noun.

Vivimos en una **casa moderna.**   *We live in a **modern house.*** (Not all houses are modern.)

Es una **ópera italiana.**   *It is an **Italian opera.*** (Not all operas are Italian.)

An adjective preceded by an adverb also follows the noun.

Es un **quehacer muy desagradable.**   *It is a **very disagreeable chore.***

EXERCISE

Combine each pair of sentences into one.

1. El señor Martínez es un hombre. Es religioso.

   El señor Martínez es un hombre religioso.

2. Vamos a vivir en esta región. Es despoblada.

   _____

3. A la gente no le gusta esta ley. Es injusta.

   _____

4. Van a una película. Es divertida.

   _____

5. Juan y José son chicos. Son fuertes.

   _____

6. Sí, es abogado. Es muy conocido.

   _____

7. Sí, es un problema. Es realmente complicado.

_____

8. Bailan con las chicas. Son españolas.

_____

9. Admiro a una familia. Es trabajadora.

_____

10. Es una señorita. Es sumamente guapa.

_____

GOAL 5

To use those adjectives that may either precede or follow the nouns they modify.

Most descriptive adjectives may either precede or follow the noun. However, changing the position of the adjective changes the meaning or the emphasis that the speaker wishes to convey. Adjectives that follow the noun are generally more emphatic.

A. Descriptive adjectives precede the noun when they refer to a quality inherent in the basic characteristics of the noun itself. They follow the noun in order to distinguish it from others of its class.

La *blanca* **nieve** es hermosa.　　(All snow is white.)
Vivo en una **casa** *blanca.*　　(It is necessary to distinguish the color of the house, since houses may be almost any color.)

EXERCISE

Combine the ideas of the sentences into one sentence in which the adjective either precedes or follows the noun, according to the meaning being expressed.

1. (Estoy en Hot Springs, Arkansas.) Me baño en el agua. Es caliente.

_____

2. (Estoy en un restaurante cualquiera.) Me gusta el café. Está caliente.

_____

3. (Hablo de mis tíos.) Voy a visitar a mis tíos. Todos mis tíos son ricos.

_____

4. (Hablo de unos tíos míos que son ricos.) Voy a visitar a mis tíos. Voy a visitar sólo los que son ricos.

_____

5. (Los padres hablan de sus hijos.) Estamos orgullosos de nuestros hijos. Estamos orgullosos sólo de los que son buenos.

_____

6. (Los padres hablan de sus hijos.) Estamos orgullosos de nuestros hijos. Creemos que todos son buenos.

_____

B. In English we raise our voices to emphasize certain parts of a sentence. In Spanish the word order is changed.

The white snow is beautiful.   *La blanca nieve es hermosa.*
I live in a **white** house.   *Vivo en una casa blanca.*

EXERCISE

Express these contrasts in Spanish.

1. (Una señora ve un jardín de flores de muchos colores.) I like the *red* flowers.

   Me gustan las flores rojas.

2. (Una señora ve un jardín de flores de solo un color.) I like the red flowers of this garden.

   _____

3. (Consuelo habla de los platos típicos de México.) I like the hot *(picante)* dishes in Mexico.

   _____

4. (José habla de los platos favoritos hechos en su casa.) I like the *hot (picante)* dishes at our house.

   _____

5. (Los estudiantes hablan de unos profesores.) I like to study with *nice* teachers.

   _____

6. (Los estudiantes hablan de todos los profesores de su universidad.) I like to study with the nice teachers of the university.

   _____

C. Several adjectives have one meaning when used before the noun and another when used after the noun.

alguna posibilidad   *some possibility*
no hay posibilidad alguna   *there is no possibility*

antigua ley	*former law*
casa antigua	*old house*
cierto hombre	*certain man*
solución cierta	*definite solution*
diferentes problems	*various problems*
problemas diferentes	*different problems*
gran ciudad	*great city*
ciudad grande	*big city*
medio metro	*half a meter*
nota media	*average grade*
mismo hombre	*same man*
hombre mismo	*man himself*
nuevo coche	*new (to the owner) car*
coche nuevo	*(brand-) new car*
pobre mujer	*pitiable woman*
mujer pobre	*needy woman*
raras veces	*rarely*
niño raro	*strange boy*
único libro	*only book*
libro único	*unique book*
varios anuncios	*several ads*
anuncios varios	*miscellaneous ads*
viejo amigo	*long-time friend*
amigo viejo	*friend who is old*

EXERCISE

Use the cues to form sentences in which the adjective either precedes or follows the noun, according to the meaning being expressed.

1. ser/grande/señor

    a. Es famoso en el país.

    Es un gran señor.
    _____

    b. Tiene siete pies de altura y pesa doscientas cincuenta libras.

    Es un señor grande.
    _____

2. ser/único/moneda

    a. Es muy rara.

    _____

    b. Solamente hay una.

    _____

3. yo/visitar/viejo/amiga

   a. Ahora tiene más de ochenta años.

   _____

   b. Hace muchos años que la conozco.

   _____

4. pobre/mujer/estar/en casa

   a. Estuvo en un accidente horrible.

   _____

   b. No tiene ningún dinero.

   _____

5. mismo/chico/lo/hacer

   a. El chico lo hace solo, sin ayuda.

   _____

   b. Lo hizo ayer y él lo hace hoy.

   _____

D. Limiting adjectives, and demonstratives at times, may be placed after nouns if the speaker wishes to emphasize the information they carry. Similarly, the after-noun possessives are more emphatic than the before-noun possessives.

Tengo **dos libros.**	*I have **two books**.*
No, es **el libro dos.**	*No, it is **book two**.*
Su casa es grande.	***His house** is big.*
La casa suya es mejor.	***His house** is better.*

EXERCISE

Express these stress patterns in Spanish.

1. a. Do we study the second lesson?

   ¿Estudiamos _____?

   b. No, study the *third* lesson.

   No, estudien ustedes _____.

2. a. My sketch is well done.

   _____ está bien hecho.

   b. I agree, but *my* sketch is more artistic.

   De acuerdo, pero _____ es más artístico.

3. a. Your team is good. (Use *de ustedes*.)

   _____ es bueno.

b. But *our* team is the best.

Pero _____ es el mejor.

4. a. Do you like her room?

¿Te gusta _____ ?

b. Yes, but *your* room is prettier.

Sí, pero _____ es más bonito.

5. a. Do we have four exercises for tomorrow?

¿Tenemos _____ para mañana?

b. Are they on page five?

¿Están en _____ ?

c. Is the third exercise the most difficult?

¿Es _____ el más difícil?

d. No, the *first* exercise is the most difficult.

No, _____ es el más difícil.

e. Exercise three is easy.

_____ es fácil.

GOAL 6

To use phrases and clauses to describe nouns.

In some situations where an adjective may be used in English, a phrase or a clause is used in Spanish.

A. *De* and *para* are commonly used in Spanish to introduce adjectival phrases. This pattern is used because a noun may not ordinarily be used as an adjective in Spanish.

Es **el cuaderno de José.**	*It is **José's notebook.***
Es **el techo del edificio.**	*It is **the roof of the building.***
Es **una caja de metal.**	*It is **a metal box.***
Es **una caja para madera.**	*It is **a wood box (box for wood).***

EXERCISE

Combine each pair of sentences into one using a phrase with *de* or *para* to describe the noun. Give the English equivalent of the sentence.

1. Tengo el sacapuntas. Es de Juan.

   Tengo el sacapuntas de Juan.

   I have Juan's pencil sharpener.

2. Le dio un anillo. Era de oro.

_____

_____

3. Esto es un cuchillo. Se usa para la mantequilla.

_____

_____

4. La puerta es blanca. Es del garaje.

_____

_____

5. Están por terminar las paredes. Son del edificio.

_____

_____

6. Me gusta el helado. Es de chocolate.

_____

_____

7. Es comerciante. Trabaja en negocios de importación.

_____

_____

8. Hágame el favor de traer una taza. Se usa para café.

_____

_____

9. Una taza, por favor. Quiero café en la taza.

_____

_____

10. Asiste a una universidad. Es sólo para mujeres.

_____

_____

B. English phrases using "in," "on," "at," etc. to describe nouns are expressed in Spanish with clauses with *que* + *estar*. English phrases using "with" to mean "possessing" or "carrying" are expressed by *que* + *tener*.

la chica **que está en la piscina**   *the girl **in the pool***
el chico **que tiene la bandera**   *the boy **with the flag***

EXERCISE

Combine each pair of sentences into one using *que + estar* or *que + tener*. Give the English meaning of each new sentence.

1. La foto es mía. Está en el escaparate.

   La foto que está en el escaparate es mía.

   The photo in the display window is mine.

2. Los jóvenes son jugadores de fútbol. Están en la calle.

   _____

   _____

3. Las hojas son para la clase de biología. Están en la mesa.

   _____

   _____

4. Ese chico se llama Miguel. Está detrás de Rosita.

   _____

   _____

5. Es esa señorita. Tiene una bolsa roja.

   _____

   _____

6. Llegó un hombre distinguido. Tenía una cámara.

   _____

   _____

GOAL 7

To use the pattern article + adjective, adjectival phrase, or adjectival clause with the noun omitted.

A. If the word to which the adjective, the adjectival phrase, or the adjectival clause refers is clearly understood, it is quite common to drop the noun.

Me gustan los exámenes fáciles. Me gustan **los fáciles.**	*I like easy tests.* *I like **easy ones.***
Me gustan los exámenes del profesor Rodríguez. Me gustan **los del Profesor Rodríguez.**	*I like Professor Rodríguez's tests.* *I like **Professor Rodríguez's.***
Me gustan los exámenes que tienen preguntas orales. Me gustan **los que tienen preguntas orales.**	*I like tests that have oral questions. I like **those that have oral questions.***

EXERCISE   Answer each question affirmatively, omitting the noun in the answer.

1. ¿Prefiere Raúl el primer concierto?

   Sí, prefiere el primero.
   _____

2. ¿Trajo Pepita la máquina nueva?

   _____

3. ¿Salieron las amigas de Ana también?

   _____

4. ¿Rompió la raqueta que tenía?

   _____

5. ¿Es el mismo bombero?

   _____

6. ¿Es el profesor que estudió en España?

   _____

7. ¿Son los músicos de esta orquesta?

   _____

8. ¿Tiene algunos cheques viajeros?

   _____

9. ¿Quiere una naranja?

   _____

10. ¿Hay algún estudiante diligente aquí?

    _____

B. To express a generality, the neuter *lo* is used before an adjective, an adjectival phrase, or an adjectival clause.

lo típico	*the typical thing*
lo importante	*the important part*

EXERCISE   Give the Spanish equivalents of these English phrases using the pattern *lo* + adjective, adjectival phrase, or adjectival clause.

1. The good part is that we do not have a test.

   _____ es que no tenemos examen.

2. The curious thing is that I could not hear anything.

   _____ es que no podía oír nada.

3. What bothers me is your persistence.

_____ me molesta es tu insistencia.

4. That business yesterday worries me.

_____ me molesta.

5. The easy thing is to do nothing.

_____ es no hacer nada.

6. This business about the car irritates me.

_____ me irrita.

7. It is quite evident what interests him.

Es evidente _____ le interesa.

8. He told me the same thing.

Me dijo _____

Communication Pattern Exercises

I. Answer the questions in Spanish.

1. Este libro es fácil. ¿Y los ejercicios?

Los ejercicios son fáciles también.

2. El padre es alto. ¿Y la madre?

_____

3. Las hermanas son guapas. ¿Y los hermanos?

_____

4. La mensajera es rápida. ¿Y las recepcionistas?

_____

5. Los padres son amistosos. ¿Y José?

_____

6. Raúl es español. ¿Y María?

_____

7. Pierre es francés. ¿Y los otros?

_____

8. El apartamento es grande. ¿Y la casa?

_____

II. Read each paragraph and answer the questions.

1. María está preocupada. Tiene varios problemas que discute con varios profesores de la escuela. Todos los profesores son simpáticos. Rosa también está preocupada pero asiste a otra escuela. En esta escuela sólo hay unos cuantos profesores simpáticos. Rosa habla sólo con los simpáticos.

   a. ¿Cómo están María y Rosa? *(preocupado)*

   _____

   b. ¿Con quién habla María? *(simpático)*

   _____

   c. ¿Con quién habla Rosa? *(simpático)*

   _____

2. Esta ciudad tiene más de cinco millones de habitantes. La otra ciudad no tiene tantos habitantes pero es bien conocida y vienen muchos turistas para visitarla y conocerla.

   a. ¿Cómo es esta ciudad? *(grande)*

   _____

   b. ¿Cómo es la otra ciudad? *(grande)*

   _____

3. El señor Flores acaba de comprar un lavaplatos automático que tiene tres años. El señor García acaba de comprar uno directamente de la fábrica.

   a. ¿Qué acaba de comprar el señor Flores? *(nuevo)*

   _____

   b. ¿Qué acaba de comprar el señor García? *(nuevo)*

   _____

4. El psicólogo explica la lección para el próximo día. Juan pregunta si la clase tiene que leer el volumen dos. El psicólogo contesta que no, que el volumen tres.

   a. ¿Qué pregunta Juan? *(segundo)*

   _____

   b. ¿Qué contesta es psicólogo? *(tercero)*

   _____

III. Work with a partner. Take turns asking and answering the questions. Add any information you wish.

1. Tienes una caja. ¿Para qué es?

2. Puedes usar el libro. ¿El de tu amigo?

3. Llevas unos zapatos. ¿De qué son?

4. Quieres helado. ¿De vainilla o de fresa?

5. Hay que dejar algo: el dormir, la televisión o la lectura. ¿Cuál prefieres dejar?

6. Hay dos camisas. Una es roja y la otra es amarilla. ¿Cuál llevas?

7. Hay dos señoritas. Una está en la sala y la otra está en el comedor. ¿Cuál es tu amiga?

Actividades de comunicación

I. Prepara una descripción de 10 o 12 frases de la familia, la universidad y el pueblo o ciudad.

II. Escribe una conversación de media página en que dos estudiantes describen y comparan sus cuartos, los equipos de su escuela o universidad y sus coches.

III. Describe una clase ideal y compara la descripción con la de un(a) compañero(a) de clase.

IV. Describe un amigo ideal y compara la descripción con la de un(a) compañero(a) de clase.

V. Juega "¿Quién soy yo?" Imagínate que eres una persona bien conocida. Los compañeros de clase tratan de descubrir tu identidad haciendo preguntas que se pueden contestar con "sí" o "no".

Refrán

Tío rico tiene muchos sobrinos.
El amigo en la adversidad es amigo de verdad.
Tal padre, tal hijo.
A buen hambre no hay pan duro.
Explica el sentido. Da ejemplos de la vida.

---

6 Subject Pronouns

To use the appropriate pronoun to indicate the person referred to.

Subject Pronouns

	Singular	**Plural**
Person speaking	Yo *I*	nosotros, -as *we*
Person spoken to (familiar)	tú *you*	vosotros, -as *you* ustedes *you*
Person spoken to (formal)	usted *you*	ustedes *you*
Person spoken about	él *he* ella *she* ello *it*	ellos *they* ellas *they*

Since the ending added to the verb indicates person, the subject pronoun is not generally used with the verb in Spanish, except in the case of *usted* and *ustedes*.

A. Note that in Spanish one must choose between two ways of saying "you": the familiar—*tú* and *vosotros*—and the formal—*usted* and *ustedes*. *Tú* is used with one's family, friends, classmates, people of the same age or social position, children, pets, and sometimes servants. *Usted* is used with new acquaintances, strangers, or people whose position entitles them to a certain amount of respect, such as elders, teachers, bosses, officials, community leaders, etc. Although American society is less formal than Hispanic, the use of *tú* corresponds roughly to being on a first-name basis, while the *usted* relationship would be indicated by saying "Mr.," "Mrs.," "Ms.," "Miss," "Doctor," "Professor," etc. in English.

José, ¿tienes (tú) la lección para hoy?	*José, do you have today's lesson?*
Señor González, ¿sale usted hoy?	*Mr. González, are you leaving today?*

The *vosotros* form is used in Central Spain as the plural of *tú*, but the *ustedes* form is used generally in Hispanic America as the *plural* of both *usted* and *tú*.

Anita, ¿tienes una cuenta corriente? Y Raquel, ¿tienes una?	*Anita, do you have a checking account? And Raquel, do you have one?*
Bien, (vosotros) tenéis una cuenta corriente.	*Good, you (both) have a checking account.*

In Latin America, the answer would be the following:

Bien, ustedes tienen una cuenta corriente.

B. The neuter pronoun *ello* has no plural. It refers to no specific antecedent, but to an idea, opinion, event, etc.

Luis no me gusta, pero ello no importa.	*I do not like Luis, but it (that) does not matter.*

Usually the meaning "it" is indicated by the verb ending in Spanish.

Está roto.	*It is broken.*
¿Quién es?	*Who is it?*
Soy yo.	*It is I.*

EXERCISE

Indicate which subject pronoun would be used to identify correctly the person or persons the speaker wishes to indicate.

1. Juan y Carmen hablan y quieren referirse a sí mismos.

   Usan el pronombre de sujeto "nosotros".

2. Juan le habla al automovilista Gómez y quiere referirse al automovilista.

3. María le habla a Rosita y quiere referirse a Rosita.

4. María le habla a su prometido y quiere referirse a sus padres.

5. Juan le habla a María de su amigo Raúl y quiere referirse a Raúl.

6. Juan les habla a dos señoras y quiere referirse a las señoras.

7. María y Rosa hablan y quieren referirse a sí mismas.

8. Un español habla con tres amigos y quiere referirse a los tres.

9. Un colombiano habla con tres amigos y quiere referirse a los tres.

10. Manuel le habla a Violeta de su madre y quiere referirse a su madre.

11. María le habla a su madre de sus amigas y quiere referirse a sus amigas.

   _____

12. Juan tiene mucho que hacer y quiere referirse a la situación en total.

   _____

GOAL 2

To use subject pronouns alone.

At times a speaker may not use a verb. In such situations a subject pronoun is used.

JUAN:	¿Quién es?	*Who is it?*
MARÍA:	Yo.	*Me.*
JUAN:	Voy a comer.	*I'm going to eat.*
MARÍA:	Yo no.	*I'm not.*
	Yo también.	*Me too.*
JUAN:	No voy a comer.	*I'm not going to eat.*
MARÍA:	Yo sí.	*I am.*
	Yo tampoco.	*Me neither.*

EXERCISE

Respond to each question or statement with a subject pronoun and any necessary explanatory words. Do not use a verb.

1. (Fernando y Josefina hablan en la sala de Carlos y Ana. Fernando le pregunta a Josefina quién tuvo el accidente.)

   FERNANDO: ¿Quién tuvo el accidente? ¿Carlos o Ana?

   JOSEFINA: _El_.

2. (Jorge habla con sus amigos. Ellos van al partido de fútbol.)

   SUS AMIGOS: Vamos al partido.

   JORGE (no va): _____.

   JORGE (va): _____.

3. (Guillermo y Roberta les hablan a Pablo y Rosa. Pablo y Rosa no tienen hambre.)

   PABLO: No tenemos hambre.

   GUILLERMO (El y Roberta no tienen hambre.): _____.

   GUILLERMO (El y Roberta tienen hambre.): _____.

4. (Pepito y Juanito hablan de Rosita y Anita. Pepito ve a las dos chicas en la calle.)

   Juanito: ¿Quiénes son?

   Pepito: _____.

5. (Mamá está en la cocina. Entran sus hijos.)

   Mamá: ¿Quién es?

   Los hijos: _____.

6. (Catalina y su hermana hablan de la tarea en una clase.)

   Catalina: ¿Lo tengo yo que hacer todo?

   Su hermana (Sí, como los otros.): _____.

   Su hermana (No, porque está enferma.): _____.

7. (Carlos y Roberto hablan con el profesor.)

   Carlos y Roberto: ¿No hablamos mucho el español?

   El profesor (Cree que sí.): _____.

   El profesor (Cree que no.): _____.

GOAL 3

To use subject pronouns for emphasis.

In English we emphasize the subject of the verb by raising our voice. In Spanish the person is emphasized by using the subject pronoun.

Vamos.	*We are going.*
Nosotros vamos.	**We** *are going.*

EXERCISE

Give the Spanish equivalent of each English sentence. An italicized subject pronoun indicates emphasis.

1. We leave tomorrow.

   _____

2. *We* do not have a test.

   _____

3. I study every evening.

   _____

4. *I* study more than you.

   _____

5. Are you coming to the party, Elena?

_____

6. Mary, are *you* going out with him?

_____

7. He has room number 10.

_____

8. *He* is leaving now. *You* are staying.

_____

GOAL 4

To use subject pronouns for clarification.

When the subject of a Spanish sentence is either talking or being spoken to, there can be no confusion about who the subject is. The context always indicates the person very clearly, and, therefore, the subject pronoun is used only for emphasis. The third-person forms of the verb, however, may refer either to *él* or *ella, ellos* or *ellas*. Therefore, at times, the use of the subject pronoun may be necessary to specify the exact subject, as well as for emphasis.

Sí, son hermanos, pero son diferentes.	*Yes, they are brother and sister, but they are different.*
Ella estudia mucho y él juega.	*She studies a lot and he plays.*

EXERCISE

Write contrasts based on the sentences; select any characteristics you wish.

1. Sí, son novios, pero son diferentes.

   Ella es muy estudiosa; él es libre de cuidados. _____

2. Sí, son hermanos, pero son diferentes.

   _____

3. Sí, son amigos los chicos y las chicas, pero son diferentes.

   _____

4. Sí, son profesores los hombres y las mujeres, pero son diferentes.

   _____

5. Sí, son esposos, pero son diferentes.

   _____

Communciation Pattern Exercises

I. Answer the questions or statements using a subject pronoun but no verb. Then work with a partner. Take turns asking and answering the questions.

1. (Usted llama a la puerta.) ¿Quién es? _____*Yo*_____

2. (Carlos hace mucho ruido.) ¿Quién hace ruido? _____

3. (Ustedes quieren hacer camping.) ¿Quiénes quieren jugar?

   _____

4. (Las dos chicas van de compras.) ¿Quiénes van de compras?

   _____

5. (Los otros están de acuerdo.) ¿Y ustedes? (Sí) _____

6. (Los del cuarto año entran por aquí.) ¿Y los del tercero? (No)

   _____

7. (No vuelvo hasta las doce.) ¿Y tú? (No) _____

8. (No tomamos el desayuno.) ¿Y Rosa? (Sí) _____

9. (El profesor dice, "Nadie hace la tarea.") Usted responde con énfasis que usted sí la hace. _____

10. (Mamá dice, "Esos chicos nunca limpian sus cuartos.") Papá defiende con énfasis que los chicos sí los limpian. _____

11. (Papá dice, "Ustedes gastan demasiado dinero.") Ustedes responden con énfasis que ustedes no gastan demasiado dinero. _____

12. (Tu amiga dice, "Esa Rosa es antipática.") Usted responde con énfasis que ella no lo es. _____

II. Give the Spanish equivalents of the following sentences.

1. He arrives tonight and she leaves tomorrow.

   _____

2. Who knows? Me.

   _____

3. *I* believe what he says.

   _____

4. They (the girls) have the parties and they (the boys) come to the parties.

_____

5. *We* learn a lot.

_____

6. They are going up *(subir)* the mountain. We are, too.

_____

7. You are going to wait until tomorrow. I'm not.

_____

8. We do not walk to school. They do.

_____

9. I did not see the accident. She didn't either.

_____

10. Who is going with us? They are.

_____

Actividades de comunicación

Lee lo siguiente. Escribe el pronombre de sujeto que describa mejor la(s) persona(s) de tu familia.

yo
él (tu papá)
ella (tu mamá)
ellos (tus hermanos)
nosotros (todos)
X (nadie en tu familia)

1. Se levanta temprano. _____

2. No se queja nunca. _____

3. Es simpático. _____

4. Toma el desayuno cada día. _____

5. Mira la televisión más de tres horas cada día. _____

6. Trabaja todo el tiempo. _____

7. Cree en la democracia. _____

8. Le gustan los deportes. _____

9. Va al cine una vez por semana. _____

10. Tiene un estéreo o televisor en su cuarto. _____

11. Lee el periódico cada día. _____

12. Asiste a la iglesia los domingos. _____

13. Se divierte mucho. _____

14. Pasa mucho tiempo al aire libre. _____

15. Se acuesta antes de las diez. _____

16. Es inteligente. _____

17. Lleva blue jeans. _____

18. Habla poco. _____

19. Escucha la música mientras que trabaja. _____

20. Quiere tener mucho dinero. _____

Después de clasificar a los varios miembros de tu familia, entrevista a un(a) compañero(a) de clase para averiguar como son los miembros de su familia. Luego discutan ustedes dos las siguientes preguntas:

¿Cómo son semejantes y diferentes sus familias?
¿Hay diferencias entre los hombres y las mujeres?
¿Hay diferencias entre los jóvenes y los mayores?
¿Qué diferencias hay entre tú y tu compañero(a)?
¿Sabes describir las características principales de cada familia?

Refrán

Mal amigo y mal amor, olvidarlos es mejor.
Entre padres y hermanos no metas las manos.
Explica el sentido. Da ejemplos de la vida.

7 Pronouns Used as Objects of Prepositions

GOAL

To use the appropriate pronoun as the object of the preposition.

Pronouns Used as Objects of Prepositions

	Singular	Plural
Person speaking	cerca de **mí** *near **me***	cerca de **nosotros, -as** *near **us***
Person spoken to (familiar)	cerca de **ti** *near **you***	cerca de **vosotros, -as** *near **you***
Person spoken to (formal)	cerca de **usted** *near **you***	cerca de **ustedes** *near **you***
Person spoken about	cerca de **él** *near **him*** cerca de **ella** *near **her*** cerca de **ello** *near **it***	cerca de **ellos** *near **them*** cerca de **ellas** *near **them***

Note that the pronouns used as objects of prepositions are just like the subject pronouns except for *mí* and *ti* instead of *yo* and *tú*.

These forms are irregular when *mí* or *ti* is preceded by the preposition *con*.

Va **conmigo.**	*He is going **with me.***
Va **contigo.**	*He is going **with you.***

EXERCISE

Complete each sentence with the appropriate pronoun.

1. ¿José? Sí, vivo cerca de _____.

2. ¿Las abogadas? Sí, hablamos de _____.

3. ¿Tú? Sí, voy con_____.

4. ¿Yo? Sí, vas con_____.

5. ¿Yo? Sí, te sientas delante de _____.

6. ¿Tú? Sí, los lentes de contacto son para _____.

7. ¿El jefe? Sí, hablo con _____.

8. ¿Vosotros? Sí, vamos con _____.

9. ¿Usted? Sí, salió antes de _____.

10. ¿Nosotras? Sí, el paquete es para _____.

11. ¿Ustedes? Sí, es típico de _____.

12. ¿Los turistas? Sí, es típico de _____.

Communication Pattern Exercise

Answer the questions in the affirmative, using the appropriate pronouns in your answers. Then work with a partner. Take turns asking and answering the questions.

1. ¿Vives cerca de tus mejores amigos?

   Sí, vivo cerca de ellos.

2. ¿Vives cerca de tu profesor de español?

   _____

3. ¿Viven las chicas cerca de nosotros?

   _____

4. ¿Vives cerca de mí?

   _____

5. ¿Va Pedro al partido con las otras?

   _____

6. ¿Vas conmigo?

   _____

7. ¿Van ustedes con Catalina?

   _____

8. ¿Van Pedro y Pablo con ustedes?

   _____

9. ¿Va José con usted?

   _____

Actividades de comunicación

I. Completa las siguientes oraciones.

1. El profesor _____ de mí.

2. Yo _____ con ellos.

3. Mi amigo _____ antes de ella.

4. Anita _____ cerca de nosotros.

5. Los otros _____ después de ti.

6. Para mí _____.

II. Con cada una de las siguientes preposiciones, prepara una pregunta para hacer a un(a) compañero(a) de clase.

1. cerca de   4. antes de
2. de   5. después de
3. con   6. para

1. _____

2. _____

3. _____

4. _____

5. _____

6. _____

III. El día—Ten una entrevista con un(a) compañero(a) de clase para averiguar algunos de sus hábitos del día. Hazle las siguientes preguntas.

1. ¿A qué hora te levantas?

2. ¿Te levantas antes o después de tu(s) hermano(a)(s)?

3. ¿Quién se baña primero?

4. ¿Comes con tu familia?

5. ¿Quién prepara los comidas? ¿tú o él (ella)?

6. ¿Quién limpia la mesa y friega los platos?

7. ¿Caminas a clase con él (ella)?

8. ¿El profesor llega a clase antes de ustedes?

9. ¿Hablas individualmente con los profesores de tus clases?

10. ¿Tus amigos vuelven contigo después de las clases?

11. Al volver a tu casa, ¿hay mensajes o cartas para ti?

12. Cualquier otra pregunta que quieras hacer.

Refrán

Después de la tempestad viene la serenidad.
Explica el sentido. Da ejemplos de la vida.

PART II

Regular Verb Forms in the Indicative

Introduction

A sentence is made up of two basic components: a noun or noun phrase and a verb or verb phrase. Parts II through VI of this text deal with the verb and other words in the sentence associated with it. Although the verbs and verb phrases will generally be studied and practiced in complete sentences, the focus of attention will be on the verbs and the parts of the sentence related to the verbs.

Nouns name people and things. Verbs tell what these people and things do. For example, in the sentence "People walk," the speaker is talking about "people" who "walk." We can divide the world into things and their actions or existence. Language follows this same pattern.

Existence: They *are* at home in the evening.
Action: They *play* table tennis after dinner.

Verbs have various meanings according to their function in the sentence. For example, they may express mood: indicative, imperative, or subjunctive. The indicative states a fact: for example, "I have a car." The imperative mood gives a command or makes a request: "Buy me a car." The subjunctive mood describes an action that is not a fact: "I wish I had a car. If I had a car, we could go." (In both examples it is clear that I do not have a car.)

Verbs also carry information regarding verb class, tense, aspect, person, and number.

There are three verb classes in Spanish: *A, E,* and *I* verbs. The class is indicated by the vowel preceding the letter *r* in the infinitive.

A: habl*a*r **E:** com*e*r **I:** viv*i*r

Tense means time. In terms of time, an action may occur before, at, or after any given point in time. In general, verb forms can be divided into a *present* group and a *past* group.

Aspect of the verb relates to whether the action began at a point in time, continued through a point in time, or stopped at a point in time. For example, look at these three sentences: "I began at eight o'clock." "I was studying at nine o'clock." "I stopped at ten o'clock." Actions that begin or stop at a certain point in time are perfective (perfected) actions. This is an important concept in learning to use preterite verb forms in Spanish. Actions that continue through a point in time are imperfective (not perfected) actions. This is an important concept in learning to use imperfect verb forms in Spanish.

Person signifies whether the subject is speaking, spoken to, or spoken about.

I work, you save, and he spends.

Number refers to whether the subject is singular or plural.

I am more serious than she, but we have a good time together.

In order to comprehend fully the Spanish verb system, which is quite different from the English verb system, you must learn to understand and to manipulate the Spanish verb suffix system. Spanish verbs consist of a stem plus two suffixes.

The stem carries the meaning of the word. For example, in the verb *hablar* the letters *habl* convey the meaning "talk."

The stem of regular verbs can always be determined from the infinitive form, which is given in the dictionary, by removing the *r*, the sign of the infinitive, and the vowel, *a, e,* or *i,* that precedes it. What is left is the stem. Verb forms have two possible slots in which suffixes may be attached to the stem.

stem	1	2
cant	aba	s

The first column suffix indicates verb class, tense, and aspect. The second column indicates person and number.

Agreement is most important in fitting the parts of the noun phrase together. Agreement is also important in fitting the verb to the subject of the sentence. The verb must agree with the subject in person and number.

Juan es . . .	*Juan is . . .*
Juan y María son . . .	*Juan and María are . . .*
Yo soy . . .	*I am . . .*
Ellos son . . .	*They are . . .*

In each case, suffix number two must carry the same person and number as the subject of the verb in order to agree with it.

From the preceding discussion you have learned that each regular indicative verb form has three parts, a stem and two suffixes. Although there are several different forms, there is a similarity of suffixes that makes your learning task much easier.

The Present Set: An Overview

Verb forms in the present set are used to describe actions in some way related to the present. Since there are so many more verb forms in Spanish than in English, one of your principal tasks is learning to attach the correct endings to the stem of the verb. At the same time there is so much similarity between the endings that by comparing them you can make learning the verb system much easier. Compare the endings of the following forms of the present set:

Present

	A	E	I
stem +	o	o	o
	as	es	es
	a	e	e
	amos	emos	imos
	áis	éis	ís
	an	en	en

Present Perfect

All classes	
h + e	
h + as	
h + a	stem + a + do
h + emos	stem + i + do
hab + éis	
h + an	

Future

All classes	
stem + a + r +	é
stem + e + r +	ás
stem + i + r +	á
	emos
	éis
	án

Future Perfect

All classes	
habr + é	
habr + ás	
habr + á	stem + a + do
habr + emos	stem + i + do
habr + éis	
habr + án	

Starting with the present and proceeding through to the future perfect, you can easily see how similar each set of endings is to the preceding set. Once you learn the endings attached to *h* in the present perfect, the future and the future perfect are quite easy.

The Past Set: An Overview

Verb forms in the past set are used to describe actions in some way related to the past. Since there are so many more verb forms in Spanish than in English, one of your principal goals is learning to attach the correct endings to the stem of the verb. At the same time there is so much similarity between the endings that by comparing them you can make learning the verb system much easier.

Imperfect

	A	E and I
stem +	aba	ía
	abas	ías
	aba	ía
	ábamos	íamos
	abais	íais
	aban	ían

Past Perfect

All classes	
hab + ía	
hab + ías	
hab + ía	stem + a + do
hab + íamos	stem + i + do
hab + íais	
hab + ían	

Conditional   *Conditional Perfect*

All classes			All classes	
stem + a + r +	ía		habr + ía	
stem + e + r +	ías		habr + ías	
stem + i + r +	ía		habr + ía	stem + a + do
	íamos		habr + íamos	stem + i + do
	íais		habr + íais	
	ían		habr + ían	

Starting with the present endings of *A* class verbs, you can easily see that the imperfect adds either *ab* or *í* in front of the *A* endings. Once you learn the imperfect endings for *E* and *I* verbs, forming the past perfect, the conditional, and the conditional perfect is quite easy, since the same endings are used in each case.

The preterite is the most difficult to form, since it does not fit the very systematic pattern outlined above. It simply has to be memorized. However, there is some similarity within the preterite category itself.

Preterite

	A	E and I
stem +	é	í
	aste	iste
	ó	ió
	amos	imos
	asteis	isteis
	aron	ieron

Preterite (unaccented)

stem +	e
	iste
	o
	imos
	isteis
	(i)eron

Preterite Perfect
(Rarely used in modern Spanish)

All classes	
hub + e	
hub + iste	
hub + o	stem + a + do
hub + imos	stem + i + do
hub + isteis	
hub + ieron	

Note the similarities between the *A* and the *E* and *I* endings and between those endings and the unaccented preterite endings.

1 The Present

The present is generally used to describe a present action. The present can also be extended into the future, as in the sentence "I am going next year." Because the present is a moving point, present verb forms always describe an imperfective action, either a continuing action or a repeated action.

Continuing: I am studying
Repeated: I study every evening.

In Spanish, information about the present is carried in the suffixes that are attached to the stem. In the present there are two suffixes: the verb class vowel and the person-number suffix.

GOAL 1

To associate the proper person-number suffix with its subject.

Although the "I" *(yo)* form and the "he" *(usted, él, ella)* form of the verb do not require a person-number suffix, all other forms of a Spanish verb do. The suffixes must agree with the subject in person and number.

*Person-Number Suffixes for **A**, **E**, and **I** Verbs*

Singular		Plural	
yo	(no suffix)	nosotros,-as	mos
tú	s	vosotros,-as	is (ís for *I* verbs)
usted	(no suffix)	ustedes	n
él	(no suffix)	ellos	n
ella	(no suffix)	ellas	n

EXERCISE

For each verb, supply the suffix that agrees with the subject. Some verbs will not require a suffix.

1. Los chicos llama_____ por teléfono.

2. (Yo) como_____ en la cafetería.

3. ¿Sal_____ (vosotros) temprano?

4. Juan y yo camina_____ mucho.

5. ¿Comprende_____ ustedes?

6. (Tú) sufre_____ mucho.

7. José llega_____ pronto.

8. ¿Vendé_____ (vosotros) el coche?

9. Mi familia y yo vivi_____ aquí.

10. (Yo) limpio_____ mi cuarto.

GOAL 2
To use the correct vowel with each of the three verb classes.

The vowel suffix of a Spanish verb must agree with the class to which the verb belongs. If you do not know to which class a verb belongs, you can check the infinitive form in a dictionary.

Verb Class Vowel Suffixes for **A, E,** *and* **I** *Verbs*

Singular	A	E	I
yo	o	o	o
tú	a	e	e
usted	a	e	e
él	a	e	e
ella	a	e	e

Plural	A	E	I
nosotros,-as	a	e	i
vosotros,-as	á	é	no suffix
ustedes	a	e	e
ellos	a	e	e
ellas	a	e	e

EXERCISE

For each sentence, supply the appropriate vowel between the stem of the verb and the person-number suffix. In a few cases, no class vowel suffix will be needed.

1. *(llorar)* Los niños llor_____n a veces.

2. *(creer)* ¿Cre_____s tú la noticia?

3. *(escribir)* ¿La escrib_____mos en inglés?

4. *(vivir)* Mi amigo viv_____ cerca.

5. *(arreglar)* (Yo) arregl_____ mi cuarto.

6. *(comprender)* Sí, comprend_____mos.

7. *(reunirse)* ¿Os reun_____ís por la tarde?

8. *(estudiar)* Mi hermana y yo estudi_____mos mucho.

9. *(leer)* (Yo) le_____ muchos libros.

10. *(subir)* El viego sub_____ por ascensor.

11. *(subir)* Pero los jóvenes sub_____n por la escalera.

12. *(gritar)* Pepito grit_____ cuando está descontento.

13. *(nadar)* ¿Nad_____is aquí?

14. *(cumplir)* (Yo) cumpl_____ dieciséis años este mes.

15. *(esconder)* Escond_____is los huevos por todas partes.

GOAL 3

To change any present set verb form to the present indicative.

The present indicative in Spanish is formed by attaching two possible suffixes to the stem: the class vowel and the person-number suffix.

Class vowels: *a, e, i, o*

Person-number suffixes: *-s, -mos, -is, -n*

Forms of A, E, I Verbs in the Present

	A R	E R	I V
Singular	stem 1 2	stem 1 2	stem 1 2
Person speaking (yo)	habl o	com o	viv o
Person spoken to (familiar) (tú)	habl a s	com e s	viv e s
Person spoken to (formal) (usted)	habl a	com e	viv e
Person spoken about (él/ella)	habl a	com e	viv e
Plural			
Person speaking (nosotros,-as)	habl a mos	com e mos	viv i mos
Person spoken to (familiar) (vosotros,-as)	habl á is	com é is	viv ís
Person spoken to (formal) (ustedes)	habl a n	com e n	viv e n
Person spoken about (ellos/ellas)	habl a n	com e n	viv e n

The boxed forms indicate suffixes that do not follow the expected pattern.

Note that there are two "you" forms in Spanish, the familiar and the polite. In general, if you know a person well enough to use his or her first name, you should use the familiar. Otherwise, the *usted* form is the socially accepted form. In Spain, the *vosotros* form is used as the plural of *tú*, but generally in Hispanic America the *ustedes* form is used as the plural of *tú*.

EXERCISE

Look at the stem of each regular verb form in the present set and supply the corresponding form of the present indicative.

1. *dej*aremos

   dejamos _____

2. ha *beb*ido

   _____

3. yo *abr*iré

   _____

4. habrás *mont*ado

   _____

5. ha *suced*ido

   _____

6. Uds. *decid*irán

   _____

7. habréis *pregunt*ado

   _____

8. Ud. *cree*rá _____

9. hemos *viv*ido

   _____

10. habrás *vend*ido

    _____

11. yo *respond*eré

    _____

12. ha *bail*ado

    _____

13. habéis *aprend*ido

    _____

14. *escond*eremos

    _____

15. han *pag*ado

    _____

GOAL 4

To give the English equivalents of Spanish verbs in the present indicative.

In English we distinguish in the present indicative between the common form, "I work," the emphatic form, "I *do* work," and the progressive form, "I am working." Although in Spanish there are specific ways to express the emphatic form and the progressive, normally the present indicative is used for all three English forms.

Trabajo.	*I work, am working.*
No trabajo.	*I am not working, do not work.*
¿Trabajo?	*Am I working? Do I work?*

EXERCISE

Give the possible English equivalent(s) for each italicized sentence. Use the translations that seem most appropriate to the context.

1. ¿Vas al baile este fin de semana? *No, porque no bailo bien.*

   _____

2. José está de visita en la casa de su amigo Manuel. Cuando es hora de comer, la mamá de Manuel le pregunta, *"¿Bebes leche con la comida?"*

   _____

3. Mi papá es hombre de negocios. *Recibe muchas cartas.*

_____

4. Mi padre es científico. *Trabaja para el gobierno.*

_____

5. *Juana lee mucho. Esta semana lee un libro de cuentos cortos.*

_____

6. *¿Salen ustedes este mes o el próximo?*

_____

7. *¿Compras discos en esa tienda? Sí, compro algunos allí.*

_____

8. *¿Aprenden ustedes mucho en el laboratorio? Sí, aprendemos mucho.*

_____

9. *El agricultor vive en el campo. ¿Dónde vive usted?*

_____

10. *¿Para qué ahorras el dinero?*

_____

GOAL 5

To add the correct verb suffixes to the stem.

EXERCISE

Supply the correct form of the verb. Remember that the vowel must agree with the class to which the verb belongs and the person-number suffix must agree with the subject.

1. (Yo) *(tomar)* _____*tomo*_____ un refresco después de los partidos.

2. Mis padres y yo *(vivir)* _____ en un barrio antiguo.

3. Cuando mis padres no están en casa, mis hermanos *(preparar)*

    _____ la cena.

4. Mi familia y yo siempre *(comer)* _____ juntos por la noche.

5. (Yo) *(estudiar)* _____ desde las siete hasta las nueve.

6. ¿*(Aprender)* _____ (tú) las nuevas teorías de la genética?

7. Sí, (yo) *(aprender)* _____ muchas fórmulas nuevas, pero son complicadas.

8. ¿(Vender) _____ ustedes los libros al fin del semestre?

9. Ana y Rosa, (vosotros) no (deber) _____ hacer eso.

10. ¿Usted no (beber) _____ nada con el almuerzo?

11. Los González (producir) _____ adornos hechos a mano.

12. María no (salir) _____ sola por la noche.

13. ¿Señor, (hablar) _____ usted español?

14. Entonces, ¿por qué no (hablar) _____ (nosotros) en español?

15. (Tú) (patinar) _____ muy bien.

Communication Pattern Exercises

I. Answer each question affirmatively, using the appropriate form of the verb in your answer. Then work with a partner. Take turns asking and answering the questions.

1. ¿Compra usted verduras congeladas?

   Sí, compro verduras congeladas. _____

2. Pepe, ¿vives tú en una pensión?

   _____

3. Señor, ¿ahorra usted dinero?

   _____

4. Anita, ¿comes alimentos naturales?

   _____

5. Juana, ¿estudio estos problemas para mañana?

   _____

6. Profesor, ¿escribo todos los ejercicios?

   _____

7. José, ¿leo todo?

   _____

8. Señora, ¿camino por aquí?

   _____

II. Answer the questions in the negative. Then work with a partner. Take turns asking and answering the questions.

1. Amigos, ¿vendéis boletos para el baile?

   No, no vendemos boletos para el baile.
   _____

2. Señores, ¿trabajan ustedes en la municipalidad?

   _____

3. Señores, ¿cuidan ustedes a sus niños?

   _____

4. Profesor, ¿estudiamos toda la lectura?

   _____

5. Profesor, ¿escribimos las respuestas a las preguntas?

   _____

6. Pablo y Rodrigo, ¿volvemos con vosotros?

   _____

7. Juana y Susana, ¿subimos con vosotras?

   _____

III. Answer the questions in the affirmative or the negative. Then work with a partner. Take turns asking and answering the questions.

1. ¿Come su familia en casa?

   _____

2. ¿Toca tu amigo la guitarra?

   _____

3. ¿Vive tu amiga cerca de aquí?

   _____

4. ¿Toma tranquilizantes el hombre?

   _____

5. ¿Miran sus amigos telenovelas de amor?

   _____

6. ¿Creen los republicanos lo que dicen los demócratas?

   _____

7. ¿Salen los dos los viernes por la noche?

_____

8. ¿Visitan tus vecinos el parque de atracciones?

_____

IV. Work with a partner. Read each statement, then take turns asking and answering the questions.

1. No miro mucho la televisión.
   ¿Miro mucho la televisión? ¿Miras mucho la televisión? ¿Mira tu papá las noticias del día? ¿Miráis tú y él los partidos de fútbol? ¿Qué miráis? ¿Escucha tu mamá los programas de música? ¿Qué escucha? ¿Miran ella y tu papá los programas de amor?

2. Mis hermanos y yo recibimos muchos regalos para la Navidad.
   ¿Recibimos muchos regalos? ¿Cuándo recibimos muchos regalos? ¿Recibe tu familia muchos regalos? ¿Reciben tus padres muchos? ¿Recibes tú también muchos? ¿De quién recibes regalos?

3. Los españoles comen a los ocho o a las nueve de la noche.
   ¿A qué hora comen los españoles? ¿A qué hora comemos nosotros los norteamericanos? ¿A qué hora come tu familia? ¿Comes en casa con tu familia? ¿Comen allí todos juntos por la noche?

Actividades de comunicación

I. Imagínate una conversación entre un visitante de otro planeta y un estudiante de tu clase. Haciendo preguntas, cada uno trata de aprender tanto como sea posible de la vida del otro.

II. Prepara una lista de tus veinte actividades favoritas. Después de terminar, escribe "$" al lado de las que cuestan dinero, "S" al lado de las que se hacen solo, "P" al lado de las que se hacen con otras personas y "SP" al lado de las que se hacen solo o con otras personas. Discute tus actividades favoritas y las de un(a) compañero(a) de clase con él (ella).

III. ¿Cuántas horas pasas cada día en las siguientes actividades?

1. Dormir

2. Estar en clase

3. Trabajar

4. Divertirse hablando con amigos o jugando con amigos

5. Estudiar

6. Leer, jugar, escuchar música o ver la televisión solo

7. Hacer quehaceres

8. Pasar tiempo con la familia incluso las comidas

9. Otras actividades

Compara tus respuestas con las de un(a) compañero(a) de clase.

Refrán   El hombre propone, y Dios dispone.
Explica el sentido. Da ejemplos de la vida.

---

2 The Present Perfect

In general, the present perfect in Spanish is formed and used in the same way as it is formed and used in English. One difference between the two languages is that the helper verb and the main verb are inseparable in Spanish.

No hemos tomado el almuerzo. *We **have not had** our lunch.*
¿Han tomado ustedes el almuerzo? ***Have you had** your lunch?*

GOAL 1
To supply the correct class vowel for each verb used in the present perfect.

The verb *haber* has two stems in the present perfect, and its various forms use both an *a* and an *e* in the class vowel slot. However, the person-number suffixes are regular.

Haber

Singular	1 2	Plural	1 2
yo	h e	nosotros,-as	h e mos
tú	h a s	vosotros,-as	hab é is
usted	h a	ustedes	h a n
él/ella	h a	ellos/ellas	h a n

The "-ed" form of the verb, the perfective participle, is formed in the following manner: stem + class vowel *(a or* i) + aspect

Perfective Participle Forms

	stem	class vowel	aspect
hablar	habl	a	do
comer	com	i	do
vivir	viv	i	do

EXERCISE

Supply the appropriate vowel in the class vowel slot for both the helper verb and the perfective participle of the present perfect tense.

1. *(mandar)* ¿H_____s mand_____do la carta?

2. *(echar)* (El) h_____ ech_____do la carta en el buzón.

3. *(dormir)* Sí, h_____mos dorm_____do bien.

4. *(colocar)* (Yo) h_____ coloc_____do la ropa en el guardarropa.

5. *(defender)* Los soldados h_____n defend_____do con valor el pueblo.

6. *(decidir)* ¿Qué hab_____is decid_____do vosotros?

7. *(encontrar)* ¿H_____ encontr_____do usted los anteojos?

8. *(conocer)* Marta y yo h_____mos conoc_____do a muchos otros jóvenes sudamericanos.

GOAL 2

To change present set verbs to the present perfect.

The present perfect in Spanish is formed by adding the present of *haber* to the perfective participle.

Present Perfect

Singular	1 2	stem 1 2	
yo	h e	com i do	*I have eaten*
tú	h a s	com i do	*you have eaten*
usted	h a	com i do	*you have eaten*
él/ella	h a	com i do	*he (she) has eaten*

Plural			
nosotros,-as	h e mos	com i do	*we have eaten*
vosotros,-as	hab é is	com i do	*you have eaten*
ustedes	h a n	com i do	*you have eaten*
ellos/ellas	h a n	com i do	*they have eaten*

Note that the *vosotros* form has a different stem from the other forms of *haber*.

EXERCISE

Look at each verb form, then give the same person form of the present perfect.

1. quedamos

   hemos quedado

2. (él) será

   _____

3. habrán seguido

   _____

4. peleas

   _____

5. (yo) protegeré

   _____

6. reúnen

   _____

7. habréis tratado

   _____

8. (él) matara

   _____

9. ofreces

   _____

10. (yo) dormiré

    _____

11. pesco

    _____

12. entenderéis

    _____

13. permitimos

    _____

14. dejas

    _____

15. venden

    _____

GOAL 3

To attach correct endings to verbs used in the present perfect.

EXERCISE

Give the present perfect form of the verb.

1. ¿(Lavar) _____ usted los vasos?

2. Estos pobres (tener) _____ demasiadas dificultades.

3. Pepe, ¿(salir) _____ ya tu mamá?

4. Mi familia y yo (dar) _____ mucho a los pobres.

5. (Yo) (aceptar) _____ consejos.

6. ¿(Recoger) _____ (vosotros) los anuncios?

7. Tú (decidir) _____ ya, ¿no?

8. ¿(Preguntar) _____ ustedes el precio?

9. ¿Nos (ofrecer) _____ Josefina y tú vuestros boletos para el concierto?

10. (Nosotros) (nacer) _____ en una nación democrática.

GOAL 4

To distinguish between the uses of *tener* and *haber*.

There are two verbs in Spanish that can be translated "to have" in English: *tener* and *haber*. The Spanish verb *tener* is used to indicate possession. The Spanish verb *haber* is used primarily as a helper verb; for example, it is used in front of the perfective participle: *he estudiado*; "I have studied."

He preparado los ejercicios.   *I have prepared* the exercises.
Tengo los ejercicios preparados.   *I have* the exercises prepared.

EXERCISE

Supply the appropriate form of *haber* or *tener*.

1. (Yo) _____ una raqueta de tenis.

2. (Yo) _____ preparado mi disertación.

3. (Yo) _____ todos los ejercicios preparados.

4. ¿No _____ llamado (tú) todavía?

5. No, (nosotros) no _____ llamado.

6. Por fin, mamá lo _____ preparado todo.

7. ¿_____ aprendido ustedes a practicar karate?

8. Sí, nosotros _____ dos pares de zapatos de tenis.

9. ¿(Tú) _____ contado el dinero?

10. Sí, (yo) _____ todo el dinero.

GOAL 5

To shift the aspect of a sentence from present to present perfect.

EXERCISE

Complete the second sentence of each pair with the present perfect form of the verb in the first sentence.

1. Todos los domingos la llevo a la iglesia. Muchas veces la

   _____ a la iglesia.

2. Mis amigos y yo tomamos hoy un taxi en esa esquina. Pero

   _____ muchas veces un autobús.

3. Los García viven aquí ahora. _____ en muchas otras

   ciudades.

4. ¿Pescas mucho? ¿_____ en ese lago?

5. ¡Qué rápido crece Pablo! _____ mucho este año.

6. Nuestros padres no nos permiten hacer nada. Ni nos

_____ tener una fiesta en casa este semestre.

7. Chicos, ¿escucháis esto? Sí, lo _____ todo.

8. Señora, ¿vende usted *El diario?* Sí, pero ya los _____

todos esta mañana.

9. ¿Reciben los oficiales muchas cartas de protesta? Sí, y en el pasado

_____ muchas también.

10. ¿Solicita José un empleo en el centro? _____ tres más

también.

Communication Pattern Exercises

I. Answer the questions, using the appropriate form of the verb in your answer. Then work with a partner. Take turns asking and answering the questions.

1. Manual, ¿has estado enfermo?

   Sí, he estado enfermo, or *No, no he estado enfermo.*
   _____

2. Juana, ¿has escuchado las noticias?

   _____

3. Señora, ¿ha perdido usted algo?

   _____

4. Berta, ¿he respondido bien?

   _____

5. Señor, ¿no he sufrido bastante?

   _____

6. Miguel, ¿he contestado tu pregunta?

   _____

7. Chicos, ¿habéis dormido bien?

   _____

8. Muchachos, ¿han terminado ustedes?

   _____

9. Amigos, ¿habéis seguido las direcciones?

_____

10. Susana, ¿hemos limpiado bien el cuarto?

_____

11. Papá, hemos salido bien en las clases, ¿no?

_____

12. Señores, ¿hemos tenido buena suerte?

_____

13. ¿Ha tocado Anita esa pieza antes?

_____

14. ¿Ha pedido una autopsia?

_____

15. ¿Ha gastado la ganancia?

_____

16. ¿Han cumplido los hombres treinta años?

_____

17. No han cantado los músicos toda la hora, ¿verdad?

_____

18. Han corrido cinco millas, ¿no?

_____

II. Work with a partner. Read each statement, then take turns asking and answering the questions.

1. Juana y yo hemos recibido una beca para estudiar en la universidad.

   ¿Qué hemos recibido? ¿Ha recibido usted una beca? Y sus amigos, ¿han recibido una beca? ¿Ha recibido alguien dos becas?

2. José ha vendido su estéreo.
   ¿Qué ha vendido José? ¿Has vendido algo? ¿Qué has vendido? ¿Ha vendido algo tu papá? ¿Qué? ¿Qué han vendido tu mamá y tu hermana?

3. Carlos y Rosa han estudiado mucho para la clase de inglés.
   ¿Para qué clase han estudiado mucho Carlos Y Rosa? ¿Has estudiado mucho este semestre? ¿Para qué clase has estudiado más? Y tu mejor amigo, ¿para qué clase ha estudiado más? ¿Habéis estudiado juntos? ¿Dónde habéis estudiado? ¿Para qué clase has estudiado menos?

Actividades de comunicación

I. Dile a un(a) amigo(a) cinco cosas que has hecho esta semana.

II. Dile a la clase tres cosas que has aprendido a hacer este año. ¿Hay algunas cosas que todavía no has hecho o aprendido que quieras aprender o hacer?

III. ¿Qué cosas has hecho de las que estás muy orgulloso(a)? Compáralas con las de un(a) compañero(a) de clase.

Refrán

No devuelvas el mal que te han hecho.
No hay mal que por bien no venga.
Explica el sentido. Da ejemplos de la vida.

---

3 The Future

In English we may use four different verb forms to describe an action that is to occur after the present.

John **arrives** tomorrow.
John **is arriving** tomorrow.
John **is going to arrive** tomorrow.
John **will arrive** tomorrow.

In Spanish only three verb forms are used to describe an action that is to occur after the present.

Juan **llega** mañana.
Juan **va a llegar** mañana.
Juan **llegará** mañana.

In this section you will be studying the last form, the future.

The principal difference between the formation of the future in English and in Spanish is that in English a helper verb, "shall" or "will," is used. There is no helper verb in Spanish.

GOAL 1

To use the correct tense-aspect marker to form the future.

The future suffix for *A* verbs is the class vowel *a* plus *ré* or *rá (-aré, -ará)*. The future suffix is the same for *E* and *I* verbs except that the class vowels are *e* and *i*, respectively *(-eré, -erá and -iré, -irá)*.

Future Suffixes

Singular	Tense suffix			Plural	Tense Suffix		
	A	*E*	*I*		*A*	*E*	*I*
yo	aré	eré	iré	nosotros,-as	are	ere	ire
tú	ará	erá	irá	vosotros,-as	aré	eré	iré
usted	ará	erá	irá	ustedes	ará	erá	irá
él/ella	ará	erá	irá	ellos/ellas	ará	erá	irá

EXERCISE

For each sentence, supply the appropriate class vowel and tense marker for the future.

1. *(acabar)* (Ellos) acab_____n el bachillerato este verano.

    Acabarán el bachillerato este verano.

2. *(traer)* José tra_____ su tocadiscos.

3. *(ir)* Sí, nosotras _____mos juntas.

4. *(dar)* (Yo) le d_____ la propina al mesero.

5. *(aparecer)* (Vosotros) aparec_____is en ese momento.

6. *(partir)* (Tú) part_____s a las ocho de la mañana.

7. *(encontrar)* Usted encontr_____ el dinero en una caja.

8. *(tomar)* (Nosotros) tom_____mos el tren en Chicago.

9. *(dormir)* (Yo) dorm_____ menos en la universidad.

GOAL 2

To derive the future from any other present set verb.

The future in English is formed by adding the helper verb "shall" or "will" to the verb. In Spanish the future is formed by adding the person-number suffixes to the stem plus class vowel and tense suffix.

    Pattern: stem + class vowel and tense marker + person-number suffix

Future

Singular				
yo	volv	eré		*I will (shall) return*
tú	volv	erá	s	*you will return*
usted	volv	erá		*you will return*
él/ella	volv	erá		*he (she) will return*

Plural				
nosotros,-as	volv	ere	mos	*we will (shall) return*
vosotros,-as	volv	eré	is	*you will return*
ustedes	volv	erá	n	*you will return*
ellos/ellas	volv	erá	n	*they will return*

EXERCISE

Read each verb form. Then write the corresponding form of the future tense.

1. ayuda

   _____ayudará_____

2. han creído

   _____

3. abro

   _____

4. habrá cortado

   _____

5. recoges

   _____

6. hemos sufrido

   _____

7. habréis esperado

   _____

8. cae

   _____

9. escribo

   _____

10. has olvidado

   _____

11. habrá respondido

   _____

12. han servido

   _____

13. estudiamos

   _____

14. han perdido

   _____

15. abrís

   _____

GOAL 3

To change a verb implying future to the future.

EXERCISE Change the verb in each sentence from a form using *ir a* + infinitive to the future tense.

1. Voy a pasar dos semanas en un viaje en canoa.

   Pasaré dos semanas en un viaje en canoa.
   _____

2. Vamos a nadar en un lago cercano.

   _____

3. Pepe va a vender su colección de sellos.

   _____

4. ¿Vais a acabar pronto?

   _____

5. Van a escribir los ejercicios en la pizarra.

   _____

6. ¿Va usted a seguir esta dieta?

   _____

7. ¿Vas a pintar tu escritorio?

   _____

8. Ustedes van a perder la libertad.

   _____

9. Mi familia y yo vamos a conseguir bebidas dietéticas.

   _____

10. Vosotros vais a cantar.

    _____

GOAL 4

To change a present perfect verb to the future.

EXERCISE

Change the verbs from the present perfect to the future.

1. Han bailado en la fiesta.

   Bailarán en la fiesta.

2. Has defendido bien tus creencias.

   _____

3. Ha faltado un gran número de estudiantes.

   _____

4. He ido muchas veces a esa discoteca.

   _____

5. ¿Habéis estado aquí antes?

   _____

6. Hemos vendido muchos sistemas de alarmá.

   _____

7. ¿Han gozado ustedes?

   _____

8. ¿Ha subido usted a la pirámide?

   _____

Communication Pattern Exercises

On the line, write the form of the verb that would be used to answer each of the questions. Then, work with a partner. Take turns asking and answering the questions.

1. Raúl, ¿ayudarás a Miguel con la tarea? _____ *ayudaré* _____

2. ¿Verá usted el programa de juegos, señor Gil? _____

3. Susana, ¿aprenderás primeros auxilios en ese programa?

   _____

4. Señor García, ¿oirá usted la música animada del concierto?

   _____

5. Mamá, ¿trabajaré con Pepe? _____

6. Josefina, ¿iré a la fiesta con José? _____

7. Señorita, ¿abriré la ventana? _____

8. Señores, ¿irán ustedes a la luna en naves especiales?

_____

9. Amigos, ¿ganaréis más dinero con esa compañía? _____

10. Señoritas, ¿volverán ustedes a las doce? _____

11. Marta, ¿comeremos con el agente de bienes raíces? _____

12. Señor, ¿veremos a los astronautas desde aquí? _____

13. Juan, ¿hablaremos al gerente? _____

14. ¿Le dará el médico unas inyecciones? _____

15. ¿Cambiará el banquero las acciones? _____

16. ¿Pedirá permiso? _____

17. ¿Cantarán los músicos en la televisión? _____

18. ¿Ocurrirán otros accidentes allí? _____

19. ¿Seguirán el horario de clases hoy? _____

II. Work with a partner. Read each statement. Then take turns asking and answering the questions.

1. Este verano mi amigo y yo iremos a Costa Rica.
   ¿Adónde iremos este verano? ¿Irás a México este verano? ¿Adónde irás? ¿Quién irá contigo? ¿Irán los otros miembros de tu familia también? ¿Cómo iréis?

2. Jugaré al baloncesto después de las clases.
   ¿Qué jugaré después de las clases? ¿Jugarás después de las clases? ¿Con quién jugarás? ¿Qué jugaréis? ¿Jugarán tus hermanos? ¿Jugará tu papá (mamá) también?

3. Todos cenarán con nosotros.
   ¿Quiénes cenarán con nosotros? ¿Cenará su familia con nosotros? ¿Cenará usted con nosotros? ¿Cenarán usted juntos?

Actividades de comunicación

I. Describe lo que piensas hacer el verano que viene.

II. Habla a un(a) compañero(a) de clase de lo que vas a hacer este fin de semana.

III. Escribe 10 oraciones sobre como será la vida para el año 2000. ¿Será diferente la universidad de como lo es actualmente?

IV. Con un compañero de clase, haz planes para una excursión en bicicleta durante la semana de las vacaciones de primavera. Díganle a la clase lo que uds. van a hacer.

V. Describe lo que piensas hacer con tu vida. Dile a la clase.

Refrán

Más vale pájaro en mano que cien volando.
Nunca digas: "De esa agua no beberé."
Explica el sentido. Da ejemplos de la vida.

4 The Future Perfect

The future perfect in Spanish is formed by combining the future of *haber* and the perfective participle.

Nosotros **habremos hablado.**   We ***will have talked.***

GOAL 1

To change verb forms from the present perfect to the future perfect.

The formation of the future perfect is very much like the formation of the present perfect.

Pattern: future of *haber* + perfective participle

Future Perfect

	stem 1 2	stem 1 2	
yo	hab ré	estudi a do	*I will have studied*
tú	hab rá s	estudi a do	*you will have studied*
usted	hab rá	estudi a do	*you will have studied*
él/ella	hab rá	estudi a do	*he (she) will have studied*
nosotros,-as	hab re mos	estudi a do	*we will have studied*
vosotros,-as	hab ré is	estudi a do	*you will have studied*
ustedes	hab rá n	estudi a do	*you will have studied*
ellos/ellas	hab rá n	estudi a do	*they will have studied*

Note that the verb *haber* is irregular in the future in that the verb class vowel, *e,* is omitted. Otherwise, it is like any other future verb.

EXERCISE

Change the verb in the first part of the sentence to the future perfect in the second part.

1. Juan no ha contestado todavía pero ___habrá contestado___ para las seis.

2. No se han vestido todavía pero se _____ antes de salir.

3. No he subido aquel pico pero lo _____ para mañana por la noche.

4. No has caminado mucho todavía pero antes de llegar _____ muchísimo.

5. No habéis respondido bien pero antes de terminar _____ mejor.

6. No hemos salido todavía pero _____ para esta noche.

GOAL 2

To change any verb form in the present set to its corresponding future perfect form.

EXERCISE

Read each of the verb forms. Then give the corresponding form of that verb in the future perfect.

1. pinto
   habré pintado

2. ha podido
   _____

3. recibiremos
   _____

4. visitan
   _____

5. comprenderás
   _____

6. habéis producido
   _____

7. pagamos
   _____

8. ha tenido
   _____

9. subiréis
   _____

10. he arreglado
    _____

11. esconden
    _____

12. permites
    _____

13. hemos llevado
    _____

14. aprende
    _____

15. cumpliré
    _____

GOAL 3

To give the appropriate form of the future perfect.

EXERCISE

Write the appropriate future perfect form of the verb. Note the type of sentence in which the future perfect is used.

1. Mi amigo y yo *(empezar)* _____ para las seis.

2. Para mañana los ciudadanos *(tener)* _____ la oportunidad de elegir un presidente.

3. Dentro de tres años (tú) *(completar)* _____ la obra.

4. (Yo) *(arreglar)* _____ todo dentro de dos semanas.

5. ¿*(Salir)* _____ (ellos) a tiempo?

6. ¿*(Ganar)* _____ (vosotros) bastante dinero antes de matricularos en la universidad?

7. Tú y yo *(vivir)* _____ aquí diez años el veinte de abril.

8. ¿*(Decidir)* _____ Juana para mañana?

9. ¿*(Acostar)* _____ (ellos) a los niños para las once?

10. Para el fin del verano ustedes *(aprender)* _____ a jugar al tenis.

Communication Pattern Exercises

On the line, write the form of the verb that would be used to answer each of the following questions. Then take turns asking and answering the questions.

1. José, ¿habrás llamado para las seis? ___*habré llamado*___

2. Juana, ¿habrás venido más temprano? _____

3. Señor, ¿lo habrá enseñado usted a los otros? _____

4. Profesor, ¿habrá hablado a mi padre para mañana? _____

5. Señorita, ¿habré trabajado bastante? _____

6. Señor, ¿habré bebido demasiado? _____

7. Teresa, ¿habré comenzado para las diez? _____

8. Tomás, ¿habré conocido a muchas personas? _____

9. Amigos, ¿habréis practicado para las ocho? _____

10. Señores, ¿habrán pensado ustedes en eso para la medianoche?

   _____

11. Marta y Mariana, ¿habréis cumplido todo antes del verano?

   _____

12. Señoras, ¿la habrán preparado antes de salir? _____

13. Señores, ¿habremos caminado diez millas? _____

14. Amigos, ¿habremos protegido el pueblo? _____

15. Señores, ¿habremos conseguido el objetivo para el fin de este mes?

   _____

16. Raúl y Rosa, ¿habremos jugado bastante bien para ganar la serie?

   _____

17. ¿Habrá estudiado bastante en dos horas? _____

18. ¿Habrá comido antes de llegar? _____

19. ¿Habrá salido bastante temprano para llegar a tiempo?

   _____

20. ¿Habrá regresado para el sábado? _____

21. ¿Habrán descansado bastante para esta tarde? _____

22. ¿Se habrán mudado antes de julio? _____

23. ¿Habrán decidido antes de la reunión? _____

II. Read each statement. Then work with a partner. Takes turns asking and answering the questions.

1. Tenemos una tarea larga y difícil para la clase de matemáticas pero habremos terminado todo antes de ir a la clase.
   ¿Habremos terminado la tarea antes de la clase? ¿Habrán terminado ustedes la tarea? ¿Habrán terminado los otros alumnos también? ¿Habrás terminado todo el trabajo antes del examen?

2. Habré aprendido a bailar antes de la fiesta.
   ¿Habré aprendido a bailar antes de la fiesta? ¿Habrás aprendido algo nuevo para el fin de este semestre? ¿Qué habrá aprendido a hacer? ¿Habrá aprendido algo nuevo su mamá?

3. Raúl es un joven español. Visitará a sus amigos este sábado por la noche pero antes de salir habrá pedido permiso a sus padres.
¿A quiénes habrá pedido permiso antes de salir? ¿Habrá pedido usted permiso antes de salir este sábado por la noche? ¿Habrá pedido permiso su amigo?

Actividades de comunicación

I. ¿Qué habrás hecho para las diez esta noche? Prepara una lista de 10 oraciones como mínimo.

II. Sueña un poco y luego di a la clase algunas cosas que crees que habrás hecho cuando tengas treinta años.

III. Di la fortuna de tres miembros de tu clase empleando las expresiones *you will* y *you will have* en español. Cada fortuna debe tener tres oraciones como mínimo. A ver si tus compañeros de clase pueden adivinar para quienes son.

Refrán   No ensucies el agua que has de tomar.
Explica el sentido. Da ejemplos de la vida.

---

5 The Imperfect

The imperfect in Spanish is formed by adding a class vowel, a tense-aspect marker, and a person-number suffix to the verb stem.

The imperfect is used to describe imperfective actions in the past. These actions may be *continuing* actions or *repeated* actions.

One difference between the use of the imperfect in Spanish and in English is that in Spanish one does not distinguish between continuing and repeated action. In English, however, we do make that distinction, and we have various ways of expressing the two types of actions, including the use of helper verbs.

Estudiaba.	*I would study* (every day). *(repeated)*
Estudiaba.	*I used to study.* (repeated)
Estudiaba.	*I was studying.* (continuing)

At times, additional words are used to indicate a repeated action.

Muchas veces comíamos en casa.	*We often ate* at home.
Los jueves comíamos en casa.	*We ate* at home **on Thursdays.**
Siempre comíamos en casa.	*We always ate* at home.
Todas los días comíamos en casa.	*We ate* at home **every day.**

At other times the continuing nature of the action is inherent in the meaning of the verb itself.

La casa **estaba** sucia.	*The house **was** dirty.*
Eran las diez.	*It **was** ten o'clock.*
Tenía cuarenta años.	*He **was** forty years old.*
Juan **era** inteligente.	*Juan **was** intelligent.*
Estábamos tristes.	*We **were** sad.*

GOAL 1

To use the correct class vowel and tense-aspect marker with each of the three verb classes.

The imperfect suffix for *A* verbs is *ab* plus *a (aba)*. For *E* and *I* verbs the imperfect suffix is *í* plus *a (ía)*.

EXERCISE

Write the appropriate imperfect suffix for each verb.

1. (Yo) esper___ en la esquina.

2. Juan y yo corr___mos juntos.

3. Dorm___is bien todas las noches.

4. Mi hermano y yo acompañ___mos a nuestra madre

5. ¿Nad___s mucho en el verano?

6. Las llantas est___n desinfladas.

7. ¿Sal___n ustedes tempraro?

8. José us___ mi boleto.

9. (Yo) viv___ en San Antonio.

10. Los chicos ayuda___n al agente secreto.

GOAL 2

To change present verbs to the imperfect.

Combining *ab* and *a* for *A* verbs and *í* and *a* for *E* and *I* verbs with the person-number suffixes leads to the following patterns for the imperfect:

Patterns: stem + ab + a + person-number suffixes
              stem + í + a + person-number suffixes

camin	aba	n	*they were walking*
com	ía	mos	*we were eating*

Imperfect

Singular	A-stem	1 2	E and I-stem	1 2
yo	llam	aba	ten	ía
tú	llam	aba s	ten	ía s
usted	llam	aba	ten	ía
él/ella	llam	aba	ten	ía

Plural				
nosotros,-as	llam	ába mos	ten	ía mos
vosotros,-as	llam	aba is	ten	ía is
ustedes	llam	aba n	ten	ía n
ellos/ellas	llam	aba n	ten	ía n

Note that the *yo* form of the verb is the same as the *él* form and that the *nosotros* form of an *A* verb has a written accent.

EXERCISE

Change the present verb in the first part of the sentence to the imperfect in the second part.

1. Los jóvenes no lloran, pero cuando tenían menos años

   _____ a veces.

2. (Yo) trabajo bastante ahora, pero cuando era niño no

   _____ mucho.

3. No recordamos todos los detalles ahora, pero antes los

   _____ todos muy bien.

4. Josefina nunca toca el piano ahora, pero antes lo _____

   todos los días.

5. Ganáis más de lo que _____ en el otro empleo, ¿no?

6. ¿Compras ahora tanto como _____ antes?

7. María no come mucho ahora, pero antes _____ a todas

   horas.

8. Tú escribes novelas ahora, pero al principio _____ artículos para el periódico, ¿no?

9. Este semestre leen los editoriales, pero antes no los

_____ .

10. Vivimos lejos de la escuela ahora, pero antes _____ muy cerca.

GOAL 3

To derive the imperfect form of a verb from any other form in the past set.

EXERCISE

Look at each verb form. Then write the corresponding form of the imperfect.

1. yo sacaría

   yo sacaba
   _____

2. habían vendido

   _____

3. habríais subido

   _____

4. informaríamos

   _____

5. comprendería

   _____

6. construirían

   _____

7. habías entrado

   _____

8. usted habría tenido

   _____

9. yo había recibido

   _____

10. habrían evitado

    _____

11. esconderías

    _____

12. partiríamos

    _____

13. (ella) bailaría

    _____

14. habíais comido

    _____

15. yo habría seguido

    _____

GOAL 4

To use the correct form of the imperfect.

EXERCISE

Write the correct imperfect form of the verb.

1. Cuando (yo) era joven, *(vivir)* _____ en la ciudad.

2. Mi padre *(trabajar)* _____ en una estación de gasolina.

3. Yo *(tener)* _____ diez años y todos mis hermanos eran menores.

4. Ellos y yo *(jugar)* _____ mucho todos los días. A veces íbamos al parque para jugar allí.

5. Por la tarde, mientras mis hermanos menores *(dormir)* _____ una siesta yo *(visitar)* _____ a mis amigos.

6. Nosotros *(vivir)* _____ en un suburbio de clase media y *(asistir)* _____ una escuela cercana.

7. La escuela *(estar)* _____ a unas seis manzanas de nuestra casa. Todos nosotros *(caminar)* _____ a la escuela.

8. Pero cuando *(llover)* _____o *(nevar)* _____, mis padres nos *(llevar)* _____ en coche.

9. Mamá siempre *(preparar)* _____ la cena y mi familia y yo *(comer)* _____ a eso de las seis.

10. Papá *(volver)* _____ a casa generalmente a las cinco y media. *(Hablar)* _____ con nosotros hasta la hora de cenar.

11. ¿Dónde *(vivir)* _____ tú? ¿*(Estudiar)* _____ en una escuela grande or pequeña?

GOAL 5

To distinguish between the uses of the present and the imperfect.

EXERCISE

Complete each sentence with the appropriate form of either the present or the imperfect, depending upon the context.

1. *(tomar)* El chico _____ jugo ahora, pero antes

   _____ leche solamente.

2. *(conocer)* El alumno nuevo _____ a muchos alumnos

   ahora, pero al principio no _____ a nadie.

3. *(dormir)* (Nosotros) _____ bien antes, pero con este

   resfriado no _____ bien ahora.

4. *(pasar)* Antes los aviones _____ por aquí todos los días,

   pero ahora nunca _____ sobre nuestra casa.

Communication Pattern Exercises

I. Answer the questions using the appropriate form of the verb.

1. Pepita, ¿dormías tú en el mismo dormitorio de tus hermanas?

   Sí, dormía en el mismo dormitorio de mis hermanas. **or**

   No, no dormía en el mismo dormitorio de mis hermanas.

2. Señor, ¿tenía usted una casita en un árbol?

   _____

3. Señorita, ¿lloraba usted mucho?

   _____

4. Catalina, ¿hablaba (yo) de esto antes?

   _____

5. Señor, ¿estaba sentado (yo) aquí?

   _____

6. ¿Cruzaban ustedes la calle solos?

   _____

7. ¿Veíais mucho a vuestros abuelos?

   _____

8. ¿Creíais en Santa Claus?

_____

9. Señores, ¿andábamos en esta dirección?

_____

10. Amigos míos, ¿pedíamos papas fritas y hamburguesas?

_____

11. Ana, ¿almorzábamos en el centro?

_____

12. ¿Llegaba de repente la lluvia?

_____

13. ¿Veía Pablo todos los partidos?

_____

14. ¿Llamaba Pedro los fines de semana?

_____

15. ¿Trabajaban ellos en el campo?

_____

16. ¿Comprendían la percepción extrasensorial?

_____

II. Work with a partner. Read each statement, then take turns asking and answering the questions.

1. Cuando era niño (yo) vivía en el campo.
   ¿Dónde vivía yo cuando era niño? ¿Dónde vivía tu familia cuando eras niño? ¿Vivían ustedes en una casa grande? ¿Vivían cerca todos tus parientes? ¿Dónde vivías cuando tenías diez años?

2. En la escuela elemental hablábamos mucho en clase.
   ¿Dónde hablábamos mucho? ¿Hablaba usted mucho en la escuela elemental? ¿En qué clase hablaban más los alumnos? ¿En qué clase hablaba usted más? ¿Hablaban ustedes más en clase o fuera de clase?

3. Cuando era niño (yo) tenía un perrito y un gatito.
   ¿Qué tenía? ¿Tenías un animal doméstico? ¿Qué tipo de animal doméstico tenías? ¿Tenía otros animales domésticos tu familia? ¿Qué animales domésticos tenían tus hermanos? ¿Teníais un animal diferente? ¿Qué animal diferente teníais?

Actividades de comunicación

I. Prepara una descripción de media página como mínimo de lo que hacías, comenzando con lo siguiente: Cuando era niño(a) . . .

II. Contrasta lo que eras, hacías y te gustaba con lo que eres, haces y te gusta actualmente. ¿Has cambiado mucho? Antes . . . Ahora . . . Escribe 10 oraciones como mínimo.

III. Trata de acertar lo que hacían los otros miembros de la clase anoche a las 6:00, 8:00 y 10:00, haciendo preguntas que se puedan contestar con "sí" o "no."

Refrán

La letra con sangre entra.
La luz de adelante es la que alumbra.
Explica el sentido. Da ejemplos de la vida.

6 The Past Perfect

In general, the past perfect in Spanish is formed and used in the same way as the past perfect is formed and used in English. In Spanish the past perfect is formed by using the imperfect of *haber* with the *-ado* or *-ido* form of the verb, the perfective participle. One difference between the two languages is that the helper verb and the main verb are never separated in Spanish.

No habíamos comido.   *We had not eaten.*
¿Habían comido ustedes?   *Had you eaten?*

GOAL 1

To change any verb form in the past set to the past perfect.

The past perfect is formed in Spanish by combining the imperfect of *haber* with the perfective participle.

Pattern: English: "had" + perfective participle
             Spanish: imperfect of *haber* + perfective participle

Past Perfect

Singular	stem 1 2	stem 1 2	
yo	hab ía	gan a do	*I had earned*
tú	hab ía s	gan a do	*you had earned*
usted	hab ía	gan a do	*you had earned*
él/ella	hab ía	gan a do	*he (she) had earned*

Plural			
nosotros,-as	hab ía mos	gan a do	*we had earned*
vosotros,-as	hab ía is	gan a do	*you had earned*
ustedes	hab ía n	gan a do	*you had earned*
ellos/ellas	hab ía n	gan a do	*they had earned*

EXERCISE   Look at each verb form, then supply the corresponding form of the past perfect.

1. yo jugaba   *yo había jugado*

2. vendíamos

   _____

3. él recibía

   _____

4. habríais visitado

   _____

5. habrían recogido

   _____

6. Ud. escribiría

   _____

7. cuidaríamos

   _____

8. comerías

   _____

9. yo habría servido

   _____

10. bajaríais

    _____

11. él escondía

    _____

12. habríamos sufrido

    _____

13. habrías salido

    _____

14. correrían

    _____

15. buscábamos

    _____

G O A L   2

To give the correct form of the past perfect.

EXERCISE   Supply the appropriate past perfect form of the verb given.

1. ¿*(Lavar)* _____ usted el coche?

2. Los pobres *(tener)* _____ poca ropa.

3. Pepe, ¿qué *(pedir)* _____ a tu mamá?

4. Mi familia y yo les *(dar)* _____ caramelos a los festejados.

5. (Yo) *(aceptar)* _____ un regalo, pero dinero no.

6. ¿*(Entender)* _____ (vosotros) la película?

7. Tú te *(decidir)* _____, ¿no?

8. ¿*(Preguntar)* _____ ustedes el precio?

9. ¿*(Conseguir)* _____ Josefina y tú una lavadora de ropa?

10. (Nosotros) no *(pasar)* _____ antes por esa compañía electrónica.

G O A L   3

To change verbs from the imperfect to the past perfect.

EXERCISE   Change the verb in the first sentence to the past perfect in the second.

1. Todos los domingos (yo) la llevaba a la iglesia.

   Muchas veces la _____ a la iglesia.

2. Mis amigos y yo tomábamos un taxi en esa esquina.

   Pero también _____ muchas veces un autobús.

3. Los García vivían en esa casa entonces.

   _____ antes en una casa más grande.

4. ¿Pescabas mucho? Sí, pero nunca _____ antes de ese verano.

5. ¡Qué rápidamente crecía Pablo! _____ mucho ese año.

6. Nuestros padres no nos permitían hacer nada.

   Hasta entonces no nos _____ tener ni una fiesta en casa.

7. Chicos, ¿escuchabais eso? _____ hasta la última parte.

8. Señora, ¿vendía usted revistas? Sí, _____ muchas esa mañana.

9. ¿Recibían los oficiales muchas cartas de protesta? Sí, _____ muchas.

10. ¿Solicitaba José un empleo ese verano? No, no _____ ninguno ese verano.

GOAL 4

To use the present perfect and the past perfect in context.

EXERCISE

Complete each sentence with the appropriate form of either the present perfect or the past perfect, depending upon the context.

1. *(dibujar)* Mi marido _____ bastante este año, pero en el

   pasado no _____ mucho.

2. *(perder)* El niño lloraba porque se le _____ su juguete.

   ¿Por qué llora ahora? Porque lo _____ otra vez.

3. *(recibir)* (Ella) estaba contenta porque _____ una carta

   de su novio. Hoy está más contenta que nunca porque

   _____ dos.

4. *(solicitar)* Juana _____ este mes una beca de la

   Universidad de Texas. Antes de solicitar ésta _____ tres

   más.

Communication Pattern Exercises

I. Write the form of the verb that would be used to answer each of the questions.

1. Pepito, ¿habías saludado a tus amigos? _*había saludado*_

2. ¿Ya había cenado usted?_____

3. Juana, ¿habías leído la sección de anuncios? _____

4. ¿Había cometido usted un error, señorita? _____

5. Señor, ¿había recordado (yo) todos mis deberes? _____

6. Andrés, ¿había dejado (yo) la raqueta en tu coche? _____

7. Señorita, ¿no había pedido (yo) un bistec? _____

8. Susana, ¿había ido (yo) antes que mamá? _____

9. Señores, ¿habían cerrado ustedes la puerta con llave?

   _____

10. Juan y Pablo, ¿habíais regresado a esa hora? _____

11. Ana y Patricia, ¿habíais mentido a vuestros padres? _____

12. Señores, ¿habían pasado mucho tiempo afuera? _____

13. José, ¿habíamos terminado el juego? _____

14. Señora, ¿habíamos permitido eso? _____

15. Carolina, ¿habíamos hablado a José? _____

16. Señora, ¿habíamos pagado la cuenta? _____

17. ¿Había tomado el bebé la medicina? _____

18. ¿Había solicitado el joven una beca? _____

19. ¿Habían conocido a muchas personas? _____

20. ¿Habían visitado México? _____

II. Work with a partner. Read each statement. Then take turns asking and answering the questions.

1. Cuando yo tenía diez años ya había viajado por avión.
   Cuando tenía yo diez años, ¿había viajado por avión? ¿Habías viajado por avión a esa edad? Y tu papá, ¿había viajado por avión a esa edad? ¿Habían viajado tus abuelos por avión a esa edad? Cuando tenías diez años, ¿ya había viajado mucho tu familia? ¿Adónde habían viajado ustedes?

2. Al salir de casa esta mañana mi hermano y yo habíamos comido huevos con tocino y tostada.
   ¿Qué habíamos comido esta mañana? ¿Qué había comido usted al salir de casa? ¿Habían comido todos para las siete? ¿Había comido más su padre? ¿Qué había comido su madre?

3. Antes de clase (yo) no había aprendido el vocabulario.
   ¿Qué no había aprendido? ¿Lo habías aprendido? ¿Lo habían aprendido los otros alumnos? ¿Lo habían aprendido ustedes antes del último examen?

Actividades de comunicación

Habla con tus padres du sus experiencias cuando eran jóvenes. Describe algunas coasa que habían hecho y que no habían hecho cuando tenían 13 años en un párrafo de media página. En otro párrafo, contesta las siguientes preguntas:

¿Cuántas de estas cosas habías hecho tú cuando tenías 13 años? ¿Cuántos no habías hecho? ¿Qué habías hecho que tus padres no habían hecho? Compara tus experiencias con las de un(a) compañero(a) de clase.

Refrán   El árbol se conoce por su fruta.
Explica el sentido. Da ejemplos de la vida.

---

7 The Conditional

The conditional is sometimes described as the past future, since it is used to designate actions that are to occur after some point in the past. (Remember that the future is used to describe actions that are to occur after the present.)

Ayer **creía** que **terminaría** a tiempo.	*Yesterday he **thought** he **would finish** on time.*
Hoy todavía **cree** que **terminará** a tiempo.	*Today he still **believes** he **will finish** on time.*

The conditional is also used to describe something not being done. Typically, an explanation follows immediately.

Le **enseñaría,** pero no es posible.	*I **would teach** him, but it is not possible.*
Lo **leería,** pero no hay tiempo.	*I **would read** it, but there is not time.*
Lo **compraría,** pero no tengo el dinero necesario.	*I **would buy** it, but I do not have the necessary money.*

The conditional is also used to express a certain degree of courtesy.

Me **gustaría** ir con usted.	*I **would like**[1] to go with you.*
Me **haría** el favor . . .	***Would** you please . . .*

---

1. Contrast "I would like" with "I want," which is more brusque.

GOAL 1

To add the correct class vowel and tense marker for each verb used in the conditional.

The suffix that marks the conditional is *a* plus *ría* for *A* verbs *(aría)*, *e* plus *ría* for *E* verbs *(ería)*, and *i* plus *ría* for *I* verbs *(iría)*.

Pattern: stem + class vowel + *ría* + person-number suffix

EXERCISE

Supply the appropriate conditional suffix for each verb.

1. Pepe y usted empez_____n primero.

2. Julio cre_____ todo.

3. No viv_____s aquí, ¿verdad?

4. Elena y yo pas_____mos por tu casa.

5. (Yo) lo recog_____ antes del mediodía.

6. ¿Jug_____is en la cancha publica?

GOAL 2

To change any past verb form to the conditional.

The conditional in English is formed by using the helper verb "would," or possibly "should." In Spanish the conditional tense is formed in the following manner:

Pattern: stem + *a, e,* or *i* + *ría* + person-number suffix

viaj	aría	mos	*we would travel*
comprend	ería	s	*you would understand*
abr	iría	n	*they would open*

Conditional

Singular	stem	1	2	
Yo	volv	ería		*I would return*
tú	volv	ería	s	*you would return*
usted	volv	ería		*you would return*
él/ella	volv	ería		*he (she) would return*

Plural				
nosotros,-as	volv	ería	mos	*we would return*
vosotros,-as	volv	ería	is	*you would return*
ustedes	volv	ería	n	*you would return*
ellos/ellas	volv	ería	n	*they would return*

EXERCISE

Look at each regular verb in the past set and supply the corresponding form of the conditional.

1. (yo) mandaba ___*yo mandaría*___

2. esperábamos

   _____

3. bailabas

   _____

4. vendíais

   _____

5. escribía

   _____

6. perdían

   _____

7. yo había partido

   _____

8. habíamos dormido

   _____

9. habías ido

   _____

10. él habría informado

    _____

11. habrían establecido

    _____

12. habríais conseguido

    _____

13. miraban

    _____

14. habías crecido

    _____

15. habríamos sentido

    _____

GOAL 3

To change a sentence implying future from the past to the conditional.

To form the conditional, the endings of the imperfect for *E* and *I* verbs, *-ía, -ías, -ía, -íamos, -íais,* and *-ían,* are attached to the infinitive form of the verb.

EXERCISE

Change the verb in each sentence from a form using *ir a* + infinitive to the conditional.

1. Iban a volver temprano.   ___*Volverían temprano.*___

2. Iba a ganar más dinero.   _____

3. Ibamos a escribir a máquina.   _____

4. ¿Ibais a montar a caballo?   _____

5. ¿Ibas a recoger las listas?   _____

6. Usted iba a dirigir el tráfico. _____

GOAL 4

To change sentences in the present set to the past set.

An *r* in the tense-aspect marker of a Spanish verb indicates the future or the conditional. The future refers to some action future to the present, and the conditional refers to some action future from a point in the past.

EXERCISES

I. Rewrite each sentence, changing the time of the sentence from the present to the past.

1. El sabe que se levantará dentro de poco.

   El sabía que se levantaría dentro de poco.

2. Cree que ganarán el partido.

   _____

3. Sabes que me darás otra pluma.

   _____

4. Creen que veremos a los músicos.

   _____

5. Sabemos que escribirá pronto.

   _____

6. Creo que volveréis a la agencia de turismo.

   _____

7. Sabéis que llegaré temprano.

   _____

II. Rewrite each sentence in the past, changing *si* to *pero no* and making other necessary changes.

1. Leeré las historietas cómicas si hay tiempo.

   Leería las historietas cómicas, pero no hay tiempo.

2. Venderán el tocadiscos si es posible.

   _____

3. Comprará las entradas si tiene la oportunidad.

   _____

4. Irás al banquete si tienes dinero, ¿no?

   _____

5. Visitaréis la biblioteca si hay tiempo, ¿no?

   _____

6. Jugaremos a las cartas si es posible, ¿no?

_____

GOAL 5

To distinguish between the use of the future and the use of the conditional in context.

EXERCISE

Complete each sentence with the appropriate form of either the future or the conditional. Remember the contexts in which each may occur.

1. *(estar)* (Yo) _____ allí mañana si hay un vuelo.

   _____ allí mañana, pero no es posible.

2. *(correr)* Jorge y yo _____ contigo, pero no tenemos

   tiempo. Mañana _____ contigo si tenemos tiempo.

3. *(abrir)* No creía que los _____ María. ¿Crees tú que los

   _____ más tarde?

4. *(preparar)* ¿Saben que (nosotros) nos _____

   cuidadosamente? ¿Sabia el juez que (nosotros) nos _____

   todo el testimonio?

Communication Pattern Exercises

I. Write the form of the verb that would be used to answer each of the questions.

1. Marta, ¿irías el jefe? _____*iría*_____

2. Señora, ¿visitaría usted Bogotá? _____

3. Raúl, ¿le darías las respuestas a un amigo? _____

4. Señorita, ¿enseñaría usted en un barrio pobre? _____

5. Ana, ¿esperarías en el auditorio? _____

6. Señor, ¿leería su horóscopo? _____

7. Pablo, ¿correrías en otra carrera? _____

8. Señora, ¿preguntaría las opiniones de los otros? _____

9. Mariana y Susana, ¿trabajaríais juntas? _____

10. Amigos, ¿hablaríais en voz más baja? _____

11. Señor, ¿dormiríamos mejor en otro sitio? _____

12. Señorita, ¿aprenderíamos más en otro libro? _____

13. José, ¿recibiríamos mejor precio en otra librería? _____

14. ¿Escucharía Sergio unos discos? _____

15. ¿Creería el público que hay una crisis de energía? _____

16. ¿Volverían ellos para las doce? _____

17. ¿Escribirían los vándalos en las paredes? _____

18. ¿Escucharían los alumnos el concierto? _____

II. Work with a partner. Read each statement, then take turns asking and answering the questions.

1. Yo iría a España este verano, pero no es posible.
   ¿Adónde iría yo? ¿Adónde iría usted? ¿Adónde iría su familia? ¿Irían ustedes en coche o por avión? ¿Irían sus padres solos o con sus hijos?

2. Yo compraría más ropa, pero no tengo dinero.
   ¿Qué compraría yo? ¿Qué comprarías tú? ¿Compraría tu mamá más ropa? ¿Qué compraría tu papá? ¿Compraríais unos libros? ¿Qué comprarían tus amigos?

3. Jugaría al tenis cada tarde después de las clases, pero no puedo.
   ¿Qué jugaría yo? ¿Cuándo jugaría? ¿Cuándo jugaría usted? ¿Qué jugaría? ¿Con quién jugaría? ¿Dónde jugarían ustedes? ¿Jugarían otros muchachos?

Actividades de comunicación

I. Completa las siguientes oraciones.

1. Yo _____, pero no tengo tiempo.

2. Mis amigos y yo _____, pero no es posible.

3. Mi mejor amigo _____, pero no puede.

II. Contesta las siguientes preguntas con un párrafo corto.

1. Si tuvieras (had) $5,000.00, ¿para qué usarías este dinero?

2. Si no tuvieras que (had to) asistir a clases, ¿cómo pasarías el tiempo?

3. Si fueras (were) profesor, ¿cómo cambiarías las clases?

4. Si pudieras (could) ¿qué harías para ayudar a tus padres?

5. Si fuera *(were)* posible, ¿querrías saber lo que va a pasar en el futuro? ¿Por qué sí? o ¿por qué no? ¿Qué querrías saber? ¿Qué no querrías saber?

Discute tus respuestas con los otros de la clase.

Refrán

Donde está más hondo el río, hace menos ruido.
Cuidado con el agua mansa.
Explica el sentido. Da ejemplos de la vida.

---

8 The Conditional Perfect

The conditional perfect in Spanish is formed with the conditional of *haber* and the perfective participle.

Habríamos hablado.   *We would have talked.*

The conditional perfect describes an action that, from a past point of view, would have been completed by a certain point in time in the future or one that was not being done.

Habría terminado para las seis,   *I would have finished by six, but*
   pero no fue posible.   *it was not possible.*

GOAL 1
To change verb forms in the past perfect to the conditional perfect.

The suffixes of the conditional perfect are very similar to those of the past perfect.

Pattern: conditional of *haber* + perfective participle

Conditional Perfect

	stem 1 2	stem 1 2	
yo	hab ría	grit a do	*I would have shouted*
tú	hab ría s	grit a do	*you would have shouted*
usted	hab ría	grit a do	*you would have shouted*
él/ella	hab ría	grit a do	*he (she) would have shouted*
nosotros,-as	hab ría mos	grit a do	*we would have shouted*
vosotros,-as	hab ría is	grit a do	*you would have shouted*
ustedes	hab ría n	grit a do	*you would have shouted*
ellos/ellas	hab ría n	grit a do	*they would have shouted*

Note that the verb *haber* is irregular in the conditional tense in that the verb class vowel, *e*, is omitted. Otherwise, it is formed exactly as any other conditional verb. The only difference between the past perfect tense and the conditional perfect is that the forms of *haber* have an *r* before the *í*.

EXERCISE

Change the verb found in the first part of the sentence to the conditional perfect in the second part.

1. Juan no había llegado todavía, pero _____ para las seis.

2. No lo habían encontrado todavía, pero lo _____ antes de salir.

3. No había subido aquel monte, pero lo _____ para el próximo día.

4. No habías caminado mucho, pero antes de llegar _____ muchísimo.

5. No habíais respondido bien, pero antes de terminar

   _____ mejor.

6. No nos habíamos decidido todavía, pero nos _____ para esa noche.

GOAL 2

To change past set verb forms to the conditional perfect.

EXERCISE

Read each verb form. Then give the same person form of the conditional perfect tense.

1. yo pintaba *yo habría pintado*

2. había podido

    _____

3. recibiríamos

    _____

4. visitaban

    _____

5. comprenderías

    _____

6. habíais producido

    _____

7. pagábamos

    _____

8. usted había tenido

    _____

9. subiríais

    _____

10. yo había arreglado

    _____

11. escondían

    _____

12. permitías

    _____

13. habíamos llevado

    _____

14. él aprendía

    _____

15. cumpliría

    _____

GOAL 3

To give the correct forms of the conditional perfect.

EXERCISE

Supply the appropriate conditional perfect form of the verb. Note the type of sentence in which the conditional perfect is used.

1. Mi amigo y yo *(regresar)* _____ para las seis.

2. Para el día siguiente, la clase *(tener)* _____ tiempo para repasarlo todo.

3. Dentro de tres años (tú) *(completar)* _____ la obra.

4. (Yo) *(arreglar)* _____ el asunto en dos semanas.

5. ¿*(Ir)* _____ Ana y tú sin pedir permiso?

6. Los Ramos *(vivir)* _____ aquí diez años el veinte de abril.

7. (Yo) me *(quedar)* _____ con ellos por unos días.

8. (Ellos) no *(preguntar)* _____ sin razón.

9. Juan *(venir)* _____ más temprano.

10. María y yo la *(esconder)* _____ en otro lugar.

11. Tú no *(tener)* _____ tanto éxito como yo.

12. ¿*(Manejar)* _____ vosotros en la nieve?

GOAL 4

To use the future perfect and the conditional perfect in context.

EXERCISE

Complete each of the following sentences with the appropriate form of either the future perfect or the conditional perfect. Remember that future perfect refers to an action completed before some point in the future and that the conditional perfect describes an action completed prior to some future point viewed from the past.

1. *(tener)* Mañana (yo) lo _____ por una semana. Lo _____ más tiempo, pero mi amigo lo quiere.

2. *(estudiar)* ¿_____ (tú) bastante para el examen de mañana? (Yo) _____ más, pero fui a visitar a algunos parientes.

3. *(salir)* Mi familia y yo _____ hoy, pero nos fue imposible.

   ¿ _____ (vosotros) para el primero del próximo mes?

4. *(reservar)* Ricardo _____ las entradas para hoy, pero creo que José

   las _____ para mañana por la noche.

5. *(poder)* ¿ _____ (ustedes) terminar para mañana si no tienen otra

   tarea? (Nosotros) _____ terminar para hoy, pero hubo un partido

   de básquetbol anoche.

6. *(saber)* Y ellos no _____ nada. Los otros _____ lo que pasaba,

   pero estaban mirando la televisión.

Communication Pattern Exercise

Work with a partner. Read each statement, then take turns asking and answering the questions.

1. Yo habría ido a España el verano pasado, pero no fue posible.
   ¿Adónde habría ido yo? ¿Adónde habría ido usted? ¿Adónde habría ido su familia? ¿Habrían ido ustedes en coche o por avión? ¿Habrían ido sus padres solos o con sus hijos?

2. El año pasado, yo habría comprado más ropa, pero no tuve dinero.
   ¿Qué habría comprado yo? ¿Qué habrías comprado tú? ¿Habría comprado tu mamá más ropa? ¿Que habría comprado tu papá? ¿Habríais comprado unos libros? ¿Qué habrían comprado tus amigos?

Actividades de comunicación

Completa las siguientes oraciones.

1. Mi familia _____ el verano pasado, pero no fue posible.

2. Yo _____ anoche, pero no tuve bastante dinero.

3. Mis amigos y yo _____, pero no pudimos.

Refrán

La codicia rompe el saco.
Explica el sentido. Da ejemplos de la vida.

9 The Preterite

The preterite in Spanish has two suffixes: class vowel plus tense-aspect marker, as well as the person-number endings. All are irregular to some extent, although some similarity between classes does exist.

The preterite is used to describe a singular action in the past.

El señor Gómez **salió** de su casa a las ocho. **Llegó** a su trabajo a las ocho y veinte.	*Mr. Gómez **left** home at eight. He **arrived** at work at eight twenty.*

The preterite is also used to describe a continued action as a whole or from the point of view of its beginning or end.

Vivieron diez años en Texas.	*They **lived** ten years in Texas.*
Le **gustó** la pintura.	*He **liked** the painting. (This was his immediate reaction.)*
Se **quedó** hasta las seis.	*She **stayed** until six.*

GOAL 1

To give the correct class vowel and tense-aspect marker for verbs in the preterite.

In the preterite the class vowel and tense-aspect markers are as follows:

Singular	A	E and I
yo	é	í
tú	aste	iste
usted	ó	ió
él/ella	ó	ió

Plural		
nosotros,-as	a	i
vosotros,-as	aste	iste
ustedes	aro	iero
ellos/ellas	aro	iero

EXERCISE   Write the appropriate preterite tense-aspect marker for each verb.

1. Mamá y yo nos reun_____mos en el centro.

2. Yo le escrib_____ una vez.

3. Mis primos v_____n el lanzamiento del cohete.

4. María, ¿le habl_____ al columnista?

5. (Yo) us_____ mucho el diccionario.

6. ¿Vend_____ usted billetes de lotería?

7. ¿Observ_____n los estudiantes la manifestación politica?

8. ¿Os reun_____is (vosotros) con los otros jugadores?

9. Juan trat_____ de disminuir los prejuicios.

10. ¿Pregunt_____is a vuestros maridos?

GOAL 2

To change any past set verb form to the preterite.

The vowels in the preterite suffixes are *é, ó,* or *a* for *A* verbs and *í, i, ió,* or *ie* for *E* and *I* verbs. The remaining letters are the same for all three verb classes. The person-number endings are the same as in all other tenses except for the *tú* form, which drops the *s.*

Preterite

Singular	A— stem 1 2		E and I— stem 1 2	
yo	cant é	*I sang*	com í	*I ate*
tú	cant aste	*you sang*	com iste	*you ate*
usted	cant ó	*you sang*	com ió	*you ate*
él/ella	cant ó	*he (she) sang*	com ió	*he (she) ate*
Plural				
nosotros,-as	cant a mos	*we sang*	com i mos	*we ate*
vosotros,-as	cant aste is	*you sang*	com iste is	*you ate*
ustedes	cant aro n	*you sang*	com iero n	*you ate*
ellos/ella	cant aro n	*they sang*	com iero n	*they ate*

Note that the only differences between the two groups of endings are in the class vowel. Note, too, that the *nosotros* form for *A* and *I* verbs is the same in both the present and the preterite, i.e., there is no tense-aspect marker.

EXERCISE

Read each verb form. Then supply the corresponding form of the preterite.

1. lavo _____*lavé*_____

2. has cogido

_____

3. usted recibirá

_____

4. habremos visitado

_____

5. respondíais

_____

6. habían decidido

_____

7. (yo) bebería

_____

8. habrías contestado

_____

9. vive

_____

10. hemos vendido

_____

11. perderéis

_____

12. ustedes se habrán olvidado

_____

13. yo tomaba

_____

14. habías conocido

_____

15. Ud. volvería

_____

GOAL 3

To change present verbs to the preterite.

EXERCISE

Change the verb in the first part of the sentence to the preterite in the second part.

1. Lo ven en la unión estudiantil hoy pero ayer lo _____ en otro lugar.

2. Generalmente entro por la puerta principal, pero esta mañana _____ por la puerta de atrás.

3. Esta vez escribo una carta corta, pero la última vez _____ una carta larga.

4. Este año trabaja en el Pentágono, pero el año pasado _____ en la embajada en Suiza.

5. Ves este libro ahora, pero no lo _____ antes de la clase, ¿verdad?

6. Usted y yo limpiamos el cuarto ahora porque no lo _____ anoche.

7. Sí, comprendemos la amenaza ahora, pero no la _____ durante la Segunda Guerra Mundial.

GOAL 4

To use the present and the preterite in context.

EXERCISE

Complete each sentence with the appropriate form of either the present or the preterite, depending upon the context.

1. *(coser)* (Yo) _____ ahora porque no _____ ayer.

2. *(aprender)* Los alumnos no se _____ los reglamentos ayer. Por eso se los _____ hoy.

3. *(discutir)* Sí, la profesora _____ la discriminación esta tarde, porque no la _____ ayer por la tarde.

4. *(nadar)* ¿ _____ (tú) en la playa este verano? Pero el verano pasado _____ en la piscina, ¿no?

Communication Pattern Exercises

Write the form of the verb that would be used to answer each of the following questions.

1. María, ¿llenaste la canasta anoche? _____*llené*_____

2. Señor, ¿vivió usted en aquella casa? _____

3. José, ¿sufriste complejo de inferioridad? _____

4. Señora, ¿habló usted con el dueño? _____

5. Catalina, ¿volví antes que mamá? _____

6. Profesor, ¿contesté esa misma pregunta en la última clase?

_____

7. Mamá, ¿vendí mí libro de matemáticas? _____

8. Señorita, ¿lo recibí todo? _____

9. Señores, ¿perdieron ustedes el campeonato? _____

10. Mariana, ¿viajaste a todas partes del país? _____

11. Raúl, ¿aprendiste algo de sus costumbres? _____

12. Señoras, ¿visitaron ustedes catedrales famosas? _____

13. Amigos, ¿regresamos a las once o a las doce? _____

14. Señor, ¿establecimos colonias en aquel territorio? _____

15. Mamá, ¿abrimos todos los regalos? _____

16. Profesora, ¿limpiamos bien el cuarto? _____

17. ¿Dirigió Manuela el programa de recreación? _____

18. ¿Trabajó José en esa tienda el verano pasado? _____

19. ¿Tomó (ella) todo el desayuno? _____

20. ¿Los acompañó al centro? _____

21. ¿Cantaron muchas canciones mexicanas los socios del club español?

_____

22. ¿Vieron (ellos) a los dos conferencistas después de la reunión?

_____

23. ¿Escogieron los chicos el desodorante X? _____

II. Read each statement. Then take turns asking and answering the questions that follow.

1. (Yo) estudié en la biblioteca anoche.
¿Dónde estudié? ¿Dónde estudiaste tú? ¿Estudiaste con un amigo? ¿Qué lección estudiaron los alumnos de esta clase de hoy? ¿Estudiaron ustedes mucho? ¿Estudió tu papá anoche?

2. Mis amigos y yo vimos una película este fin de semana.
¿Quiénes vieron una película este fin de semana? ¿Cuándo vimos la película? ¿Viste una película este fin de semana? ¿Vieron tus padres una película? ¿Visteis la misma película? ¿Vio tu mejor amigo una película?

3. En la clase de salud física Roberto escribió un informe sobre las enfermedades cardiovasculares.
¿Qué escribió Roberto? ¿Para qué clase lo escribió? ¿Sobre qué tema escribió? ¿Estudió ústed la salud física? ¿Escribieron ustedes un informe? ¿Escribió un informe en otra clase? ¿Para qué clase?

Actividades de comunicación

I. Describe a la clase lo que hiciste en compañía de tus amigos el pasado fin de semana.

II. Escribe un párrafo de media página sobre lo que hiciste anoche.

III. Juego de acertar—Con un(a) compañero(a) de clase, piensa en un viaje o unas vacaciones memorables. El objeto es hacer preguntas que se contesten con "sí" o "no" hasta que el que hace preguntas sepa—¿Quién?, ¿Cuándo?, ¿Dónde?, ¿Qué pasó?, ¿Cómo fuiste?, etc.

Refrán

Quien sabe que no sabe, algo sabe.
Explica el sentido. Da ejemplos de la vida.

10 Imperfect vs. Preterite

In thinking about any action, we may think of that action from four possible points of view. We may focus our attention on the action as a whole, or we may focus on its beginning, its middle, or its ending. If we think of the beginning, the end, or the entire action, we are thinking of a perfective action, one that is complete.

Whole (entire action):   *I studied math three years.*

Beginning: *When he saw the evidence, he believed what I had told him.*

Ending: *They talked until dinner.*

If we think about the middle of an action, we are thinking of an imperfective action, one that is progressing and is therefore not complete. This type of action may be a continuing action or a repeated action.

Continuing: *We are talking.*
She was thirsty.
They understood the many problems involved.
The house had a fireplace.

Repeated: *I went every Saturday.*
I often studied.
I would call (every evening).
I used to play golf.

The present is a continuously moving point in time. We cannot stop it. Therefore, a present verb form always describes an imperfective action. This action may be a continuing action.

Are you reading the paper? Not now.

or the verb may describe a repeated or habitual action

Do you go to church? Yes, I go every Sunday.

In either case, the present describes something that is going on, as opposed to a completed action.

The past of the present—in other words, the past form that focuses on the middle of an action—is the imperfect. This form is used to describe continuing or repeated actions in the past.

Continuing:	*Were you reading the paper?*
Repeated:	*Did you go to church when you were younger?*
	Yes, I went every Sunday. My parents used to go, too.

In addition to imperfective actions, in the past, we can also mentally stop time and focus either on the beginning or the ending of an action or on the event as a whole. This description of specific points or units of time in the past is the function of the preterite.

Whole:	*I lived in Arizona six months.*
	The punter kicked the ball.
Beginning:	*He immediately knew the answer.*
Ending:	*We walked until dark.*

As you can see from the preceding discussion and examples, the concept of perfective and imperfective actions is basic to the way we view actions in the world around us. Both English and Spanish express these viewpoints. The difference between the two languages is that English uses helper verbs or other words in the sentence to communicate these ideas, while Spanish uses two separate verb forms. Since the present describes only imperfective actions, the problem of using the correct form to describe either an imperfective action or a perfective action is limited to the past, either the imperfect or the preterite.

Imperfect: **comía**	*I was eating.*
	I used to eat.
	I would eat (regularly).
	I ate (often).
Preterite: **comí**	*I ate.*
	(When the bell rang,) I ate.
	I ate (until I was full).
	I did eat.

Another difference between the two languages is that in English we distinguish between continuing actions and repeated actions. Spanish does not. Spanish distinguishes only between perfective and imperfective actions.

Present:	Continuing:	¿Estudias? *Are you studying?*
	Repeated:	¿Estudias? *Do you study?*
Past:	Continuing:	¿Estudiabas? *Were you studying?*
	Repeated:	¿Estubiabas? *Did you study (often)?*
	Repeated:	¿Estudiabas? *You used to study?*

GOAL 1

To change a present sentence to the imperfect.

The past of the present is the imperfect. Both the present and the imperfect are used to describe continuing or repeated actions. In addition to the fact that both describe the same types of actions, the imperfect endings are very similar to the present endings of *A* verbs: *ab* or *í* plus *a* endings.

	Present Endings	Imperfect Endings	
	A	*A*	*E* and *I*
yo	o	ab*a*	í*a*
tú	as	ab*as*	í*as*
usted	a	ab*a*	í*a*
él/ella	a	ab*a*	í*a*
nosotros,-as	amos	áb*amos*	í*amos*
vosotros,-as	áis	ab*ais*	í*ais*
ustedes	an	ab*an*	í*an*
ellos/ellas	an	ab*an*	í*an*

EXERCISE

Change the verbs in each sentence from the present to past (imperfect).

1. Respetamos a nuestro padres. _____*respetábamos*_____

2. Creen que (ella) está en el hospital. _____ _____

3. Sale a cada rato. _____

4. ¿Molestas a tus vecinos? _____

5. ¿Sabéis el nombre de esa muchacha? _____

6. Vivo al sur de la ciudad universitaria. _____

7. ¿Siempre pagan la cuenta? _____

8. ¿Gozáis de vuestras vacaciones? _____

GOAL 2
To use the present and the imperfect in context.

The present and the imperfect both describe imperfective actions, but they refer to different times.

EXERCISE

Complete each sentence with the appropriate form of either the present or the imperfect of the italicized verb, depending upon the context.

1. Ahora mi padre *trabaja* en casa. Antes _____ en una fábrica.

2. Ahora mi mamá _____ las comidas. Antes las *preparaba* una criada.

3. Este año los alumnos *leen* ficción. En los años anteriores

   _____ biografías.

4. Este semestre mis amigos _____ en su apartamento. Antes siempre *comían* en la casa de sus padres.

5. Tú le *escribías* a Raúl, pero ahora le _____ a Miguel, ¿no?

6. Sí, la anciana _____ la escalera, pero ahora *sube* en ascensor.

GOAL 3
To use the present and the preterite in context.

The present and the preterite describe different types of actions at different times.

EXERCISE

Complete each sentence with the appropriate form of either the present or the preterite of the italicized verb, depending upon the context.

1. No *llamas* a Jorge ahora. ¿Ya lo _____?

2. No _____ mi cumpleaños hoy porque lo *celebré* ayer.

3. *Bebemos* agua en la cena porque nos _____ toda la leche esta mañana en el desayuno.

4. La semana pasada vio bastante material sobre la sensualidad en la

   televisión, pero esta semana no _____ nada.

5. No *cumplen* con sus contratos ahora y parece que tampoco
_____ con ellos el mes pasado.

6. El discurso de hoy *trata* sobre los transplantes del corazón, pero el de
ayer _____ sobre la fisiología del corazón.

GOAL 4

To give the English equivalents of preterite and imperfect verb forms.

In any given sentence, the speaker may use the imperfect, the preterite, or a combination of the two in order to say what he or she wants to. If the speaker wants to talk about two things going on at the same time in the past, he or she uses the imperfect.

Continuing: Yo **estudiaba** mientras que él **miraba** la televisión.
*I **was studying** while he **was watching** television.*

Repeated: Los fines de semana María **estudiaba** y yo **miraba** la televisión.
*On weekends María **would study** and I **would watch** television.*

If the speaker wants to talk about two single or whole actions, he or she uses the preterite.

Salí cuando **llegó.**   *I **left** when he **arrived.***

Dormí y (él) **estudió.**   *I **slept** and he **studied.***

If the speaker wishes to talk about one action going on that is interrupted by another action, he or she uses both tenses: the imperfect to describe the continuing action and the preterite to describe the interrupting action.

Hablábamos cuando **sonó** el   *We **were talking** when the phone*
  teléfono.   ***rang.***

Salía cuando lo **vi.**   *He **was leaving** when I **saw** him.*

Note that the action in progress, represented by the imperfect, is interrupted by the preterite.
     Contrast these examples with the following:

Comíamos mientras **sonaba** el   *We **were eating** while the phone*
  teléfono.   ***was ringing.** (two continuing*
                                        actions)

Salía cuando lo **veía.**   *I (always) **left** when(ever) I **saw***
                                        him. (two repeated actions)

Salí cuando lo **vi.**   *I **left** when I **saw** him. (two single*
                                        actions)

EXERCISE

For each group of sentences, write the letter of the English sentence next to the number of the equivalent Spanish sentence.

_____   1. Cuando llamé a Juan, salía.

_____   2. Cuando llamaba a Juan, salía.

_____   3. Cuando llamé a Juan, salió.

A. Whenever I called Juan, he was always leaving.

B. When I called Juan, he was leaving.

C. When I called Juan, (last night), he left.

_____   4. ¿No notaste que salía tu abuela?

_____   5. ¿No notaste que salió tu abuela?

_____   6. ¿No notabas que salía tu abuela?

D. Didn't you notice that your grandmother left?

E. Didn't you notice that your grandmother was leaving?

F. Didn't you notice (ever) that your grandmother was leaving?

_____   7. Escribieron diciendo que vivían con amigos.

_____   8. Escribieron diciendo que vivieron con amigos.

_____   9. Escribían diciendo que vivían con amigos.

G. They wrote (from time to time) that they were living with friends.

H. They wrote (once) that they were living with friends.

I. They wrote that they lived with friends (for a period of time).

GOAL 5

To use the imperfect in a paragraph.

In a paragraph, just as is true in a sentence, the speaker may focus his or her attention on continuing or repeated past actions.

EXERCISE

Complete each paragraph with the appropriate imperfect form of the verbs given in parentheses. Note the contexts in which the imperfect occurs: continuing and repeated actions.

1. Continuing actions or conditions

Mi familia y yo *(1. vivir)* _____ cerca de la escuela. La

casa *(2. estar)* _____ en un barrio al norte de la escuela.

Me *(3. gustar)* _____ la casa. *(4. Tener)*

_____ muchas habitaciones grandes y *(5. haber)*

_____ mucho espacio para jugar detrás de la casa.

También mis hermanos y yo *(6. tener)* _____ varios

amigos que *(7. vivir)* _____ en ese barrio.

2. Repeated, habitual actions

Todos los días (yo) *(1. salir)* _____ de casa a las ocho y

(2. caminar) _____ . Mis amigos me *(3. acompañar)*

_____ a la escuela. Cuando *(4. hacer)*

_____ mal tiempo, mamá nos *(5. llevar)*

_____ en coche. Siempre *(6. llegar)* _____

con anticipación y *(7. pasar)* _____ unos momentos

hablando con nuestros amigos antes de las clases. Cuando *(8. sonar)*

_____ el timbre, todos *(9. entrar)* _____

para empezar el día.

GOAL 6

To use the preterite in a paragraph.

The speaker may use only the preterite in a paragraph, if he or she wishes to focus on perfected or completed actions.

EXERCISE

Complete the paragraph with the appropriate preterite forms of the verbs in parentheses. Note the contexts in which the preterite occurs: singular or whole actions in the past.

Anoche (yo) *(1. comer)* _____ a las seis y luego *(2. estudiar)*

_____ dos horas. *(3. Leer)* _____ dos capítulos

para la clase de español. A las ocho me *(4. llamar)* _____

Manuel y *(5. hablar)* _____ quince minutos. Después mi

hermano y yo *(6. mirar)* _____ la televisión y *(7. discutir)*

_____ el partido de fútbol del viernes. (Yo) me *(8. acostar)*

_____ a las diez y media.

GOAL 7

To distinguish between the imperfect and the preterite, according to the context.

The imperfect and the preterite may also be used together in the same paragraph. When both are used, the preterite describes what happened, and the imperfect is used to describe the setting and the other continuing or repeated actions that serve as a background to the narrative. Study the following paragraph and its translation carefully.

Generalmente (1) *llegaba* a la oficina a las ocho. Pero esta mañana (2) *hacía* buen tiempo y (3) *caminé* más despacio. Mi compañero ya (4) *estaba* cuando (5) *entré*. (6) *Leía*. Le (7) *saludé* y (8) *empecé* a trabajar.

Usually (1) I *arrived* at the office at 8:00. But this morning the weather (2) *was* so nice that (3) I *walked* more slowly. My office mate (4) *was* already then when (5) I *came* in. (6) He *was reading*. (7) I *greeted* him and (8) *began* to work.

Note the form and aspect of each verb in the preceding paragraph.

1. Imperfect: a repeated, habitual action
2. Imperfect: description of a continuing condition
3. Preterite: a singular action in the narration of what I did this morning.
4. Imperfect: a continuing past action
5. Preterite: a singular action in the narration
6. Imperfect: a continuing past action
7. Preterite: a singular action in the narration
8. Preterite: a singular action in the narration

EXERCISE

Keeping in mind the difference between imperfective actions and perfective actions and how they fit together in a paragraph, complete the paragraphs with either the imperfect form or the preterite form of the verbs in parentheses.

Cuando (yo) *(1. vivir)* _____ en el este, mi familia siempre *(2. hacer)* _____ un viaje durante las vacaciones de mi padre. Generalmente (nosotros) *(3. viajar)* _____ a un lago o a las montañas.

El verano pasado mi madre *(4. decidir)* _____ que ella *(5. querer)* _____ visitar la capital de los Estados Unidos, Washington, D.C. Todos nosotros *(6. estar)* _____ de acuerdo con eso.

(Nosotros) *(7. salir)* _____ en el auto a las tres de la mañana. (Yo) *(8. tener)* _____ mucho sueño y no *(9. poder)*

_____ ver nada en la obscuridad. (Yo) me *(10. dormir)*

_____ otra vez dentro de poco.

Cuando (yo) me *(11. despertar)* _____, *(12. ver)*

_____ que todavía *(13. dormir)* _____ mis

hermanos. Mis padres *(14. hablar)* _____. El sol *(15. brillar)*

_____ y *(16. hacer)* _____ buen tiempo.

Cuando mis hermanos se *(17. despertar)* _____ (nosotros)

(18. comer) _____ en un restaurante.

Después *(19. seguir)* _____ el viaje. El paisaje era

magnífico. (Nosotros) *(20. mirar)* _____ lo que *(21. pasar)*

_____.

Una vez Pepe *(22. ver)* _____ unas vacas. María *(23.*

notar) _____ una flor grandísima y una casa de estilo antiguo

me *(24. llamar)* _____ la atención.

Más tarde (nosotros) *(25. tener)* _____ hambre y *(26.*

comer) _____ otra vez.

Por fin, después de pasar el día entero en el viaje *(27. llegar)*

_____ a la capital. *(28. Estar)* _____ cansados

pero muy contentos.

Communication Pattern Exercise

Work with a partner. Take turns asking and answering the questions about the paragraphs from the preceding exericse.

1. ¿Dónde vivía el narrador anteriormente?
2. ¿Viajaba mucho cuando vivía allí?
3. ¿Con quién viajaba?
4. ¿Cuándo viajaba la familia?
5. ¿Dónde pasaban las vacaciones generalmente?
6. ¿Qué pasó el verano pasado?
7. ¿Adónde decidieron ir?
8. ¿Quién decidió ir a la capital primero?
9. ¿Qué pensaban los otros?
10. ¿A qué hora salieron?
11. ¿Qué tenía el narrador?
12. ¿Qué tiempo hacía cuando se despertaron ellos?
13. ¿Había sol?
14. ¿Qué hacían mamá y papá?
15. ¿Qué hicieron cuando los niños se despertaron?
16. ¿Dónde comieron?
17. ¿Qué miraron?
18. ¿Qué vieron los ninos?
19. ¿Cuándo comieron otra vez?
20. ¿Cuánto tiempo tardaron en el viaje?
21. ¿Cómo estaban al llegar a la capital?

Actividades de comunicación

I. Escribe un párrafo de media página como mínimo comenzando así.

Anoche estaba en mi cuarto . . .

II. Escribe un cuento corto de una página como mínimo comenzando así.

La noche era oscura . . .

Lo (la) vi por primera vez en la playa . . .

III. Busca un compañero. Imagínense que uno es reportero y otro testigo.

El reportero le hace preguntas al testigo de un accidente que ocurrió en frente de la escuela o universidad ayer por la tarde. Preparen una entrevista de tres minutos.

Refrán

Más vale callar lo que se sabe que decir lo que no se sabe.
Explica el sentido. Da ejemplos de la vida.

PART III

Irregular Verb Forms in the Indicative

Introduction

Given the fact that each conjugated verb form has a stem and two suffixes, each verb could theoretically be irregular in any or all of the three parts. However, the number of irregular forms is actually quite small compared to the total number of verbs.

Although the number of verbs with irregular forms is small, their importance cannot be ignored, since often the most commonly used verbs are those that tend to have irregular forms. The *yo* form of the verb is the form most likely to be irregular.

In spite of the problems associated with learning irregular verbs, you should look for patterns and similarities even in verb forms that are labeled as irregular. To begin with, most irregularities occur in the stem. These irregularities fall into four categories.

Vowel changes in the stem:	entender—entiendo
	dormir—duermo
	pedir—pido
Verbs that add consonants or accents to the stem:	salir—salgo
	reunir—reúno
Verbs that have both a vowel change and add a consonant or an accent:	caer—caigo
Verbs with different spellings to represent the same sound:	coger—cojo

1 Verbs with Vowel Changes in the Stem

Due to the historical development of Spanish, certain verbs have a change in the main vowel of the stem in some forms. *O* may change to *ue*, *e* to *ie*, or *e* to *i*. In the present these changes occur when the syllable containing the vowel is stressed. *A* and *E* verbs have a stem vowel change only in certain forms of the present. *I* verbs have a stem vowel change in forms of the present and a stem vowel change in the preterite and in the imperfective participle. The above-mentioned stem vowel changes are the only ones that occur in the indicative mood.

> **GOAL 1**
>
> To give the correct stem vowel or stem vowel change for class 1 verbs in the present.

A and *E* verbs with a stem vowel change can be classified into one group of verbs; these are called class 1 verbs. These verbs have a stem vowel change only in the present.

Yo recuerdo ahora pero no recordé ayer.

Vive recordando el pasado.

The stem vowel change for class 1 verbs takes place when the emphasis falls on the o (in the case of *jugar, u*) or *e* of the main part of the verb stem. For example, as the conjugated forms of *recordar* or *entender* are pronounced, the emphasis falls on the second syllable except in the *nosotros* and *vosotros* forms. If the emphasis falls on the main stem vowel, *o* becomes *ue* and *e* becomes *ie*.

Pattern: stem (with vowel change in all forms except *nosotros* and *vosotros*) + class vowel + person-number suffix.

Class 1 Verbs

Singular	A (recordar [ue])	E (entender [ie])
yo	rec**ue**rd o	ent**ie**nd o
tú	rec**ue**rd a s	ent**ie**nd e s
usted/él/ella	rec**ue**rd a	ent**ie**nd e

Plural		
nosotros,-as	record a mos	entend e mos
vosotros,-as	record á is	entend é is
ustedes/ellos/ellas	rec**ue**rd a n	ent**ie**nd e n

EXERCISE

Complete each of the verb forms by adding the correct vowel or vowel change in the stem.

1. *(encender)* Las autoridades enc_____nden las luces a las seis.

2. *(extender)* Pedro ext_____nde los pies.

3. *(jugar)* Sí, yo j_____go al golf.

4. *(pensar)* ¿Qué p_____nsas de la educación sexual?

5. *(poder)* Josefina y tú no p_____déis acompañarnos.

6. *(probar)* Sí, él y yo pr_____bamos todo.

7. *(querer)* Tú qu_____res fumar pero nosotros no qu_____remos fumar.

8. *(soler)* ¿S_____len ustedes leer mucho?

9. *(volver)* Ellos v_____lven a las tres pero nosotros v_____lvemos más tarde.

10. *(cerrar)* Vosotros no c_____rráis la puerta con llave pero yo sí

    c_____rro la mía con llave.

GOAL 2

To give the correct stem vowel or stem vowel change for class 3 verbs in the present, the preterite, and the imperfective participle.

Class 3 verbs include *I* verbs that have a stem vowel change in which the main stem vowel *e* changes to *i*. The *e* changes to *i* in the present when the emphasis falls on the syllable in which the *e* would occur. This happens in all forms except the *nosotros* and *vosotros* forms.

Class 3 Verbs (repetir)

Singular		**Plural**	
yo	repit o	nosotros,-as	repet i mos
tú	repit e s	vosotros,-as	repet ís
usted/él/ella	repit e	ustedes/ellos/ellas	repit e n

In Class 3 verbs the *e* also changes to *i* in the *él* and *ellos* forms of the preterite and in the imperfective participle.

Class 3 Verbs (repetir)

Singular		**Plural**	
yo	repet í	nosotros,-as	repet i mos
tú	repet iste	vosotros,-as	repet iste is
usted/él/ella	repit ió	ustedes/ellos/ellas	repit iero n
Imperfective participle: repitiendo			

EXERCISES

I. Complete each sentence by adding the correct vowel change in the stem.

1. *(pedir)* Mis hijos nunca me p_____den dinero.

2. *(repetir)* (Yo) no rep_____to obscendidades.

3. *(seguir)* María s_____gue trabajando en la oficina.

4. *(servir)* (Nosotros) s_____rvimos pastel con helado.

5. *(conseguir)* Tú cons_____gues más que yo.

6. *(impedir)* ¿Imp_____dís (vosotros) el progreso?

7. *(repetir)* El bebé anda por la casa rep_____tiendo los sonidos.

8. *(servir)* ¿Estás s_____rviendo la cena ahora?

II. Change the verb in each of the sentences from the present to the past.

1. Los alumnos repiten las palabritas. _____*repitieron*_____

2. Servimos como intérpretes. _____

3. Siempre pide permiso antes de usar el coche. _____

4. Este trabajador impide la línea de producción. _____

5. ¿Sigo con la dieta? _____

GOAL 3

To give the correct stem vowel or stem vowel change for Class 2 verbs in the present and preterite and the imperfective participle.

Class 2 stem vowel changing verbs are *I* verbs that are like Class 1 verbs in the present and like Class 3 verbs in the preterite and the imperfective participle. That is, in the present *o* changes to *ue* and *e* changes to *ie*. In the preterite and in the imperfective participle, *e* changes to *i*. The new factor is that in the preterite and in the imperfective participle *o* changes to *u*.

Class 2 Verbs

	sentir		dormir	
Singular	*Present*	*Past*	*Present*	*Past*
yo	si**e**nt o	sent í	d**ue**rm o	dorm í
tú	si**e**nt e s	sent iste	d**ue**rm e s	dorm iste
usted/ él/ella	si**e**nt e	sint ió	d**ue**rm e	durm ió

Plural				
nosotros,-as	sent i mos	sent i mos	dorm i mos	dorm i mos
vosotros,-as	sent ís	sent iste is	dorm ís	dorm iste is
ustedes/ ellos/ellas	si**e**nt e n	sint iero n	d**ue**rm e n	durm iero n

Imperfective participle	sintiendo	durmiendo

EXERCISES

I. Complete each sentence with the appropriate form of the verb: the present or the imperfective participle.

1. Juana *(sentir)* _____ compasión por sus amigas que sufren.

2. Muchos animales *(morir)* _____ de hambre en el invierno.

3. Rodrigo y yo *(preferir)* _____ el ajedrez.

4. José y Ana siempre *(divertir)* _____ a sus amigos.

5. ¿*(Convertir)* _____ la casa en apartamento?

6. A veces (yo) los *(advertir)* _____ de mis planes.

7. ¿*(Mentir)* _____ a tus padres?

8. La madre pasa el día *(divertir)* _____ a su niño.

9. Pasa el día entero *(dormir)* _____ allí.

10. *(Sentir)* _____ frío y se puso la bufanda.

II. Change the sentences from the present to the past.

1. ¿Dormís ocho horas?

_____

2. Divertimos mucho al viejo.

_____

3. ¿Sientes compasión por el secuestrador?

_____

4. Muere en la guerra.

_____

5. Convierten el carbón en electricidad.

_____

6. Prefiero el servicio militar.

_____

GOAL 4

To give the correct stem vowel or stem vowel change for all classes in all forms.

In the indicative mood, verbs with stem vowel changes have a change only in the following cases:

- *A* and *E* verbs—present *(yo, tú, él, ellos)*
- *I* verbs—present *(yo, tú, él, ellos)*
  preterite *(él, ellos)*
  imperfective participle

EXERCISES

I. Write the infinitive for each verb.

1. demuestra ____demostrar____
2. despertaron _____
3. encenderías _____
4. han impedido _____
5. habíamos pedido _____
6. repitió _____
7. pedí _____
8. recordáis _____
9. confesaste _____
10. resolverá _____

11. confieso _____
12. perdieron _____
13. contaremos _____
14. puedes _____
15. cierro _____
16. volvió _____
17. sirvió _____
18. habéis repetido _____
19. durmieron _____
20. duermes _____

II. Change the verb in each sentence from the present to the past.

1. No vuelvo más. _____

2. Almuerzan en casa. _____

3. ¿Comienzas con este cuarto? _____

4. ¿Defendéis vuestros derechos? _____

5. Demostramos un aparato garantizado. _____

6. Resuelve el problema mejor la próxima vez. _____

7. Siempre pide helado. _____

8. No repetimos la entrevista. _____

9. Todos siguen por el camino. _____

10. ¿Sirves café con leche? _____

11. ¿Qué conseguís en aquel pueblo? _____

12. No impido sus actividades. _____

13. Lo siento. _____

14. Duerme en una cama grande. _____

15. Advertimos a nuestros clientes. _____

16. Divierten a sus huéspedes. _____

17. ¿Sentís lo suave que es? _____

18. ¿Te mueres de miedo en esa situación? _____

GOAL 5

To use stem vowel changing verbs in context.

EXERCISE

Complete each of the sentences with the appropriate form of the verb. Use the present except where the preterite is clearly indicated.

1. Mis padres *(preferir)* _____ ir a las fiestas. Nosotros

   (preferir) _____ reuniones pequeñas, pero no *(perder)*

   _____ una ocasión de ir a fiestas extravagantes.

2. ¿*(Cerrar)* _____ ustedes los libros en clase? Nosotros

   también los *(cerrar)* _____, pero el profesor nunca

   (cerrar) _____ el suyo. Ayer Josefina tampoco *(cerrar)*

   _____ el suyo.

3. Cada semana (yo) *(pedir)* _____ mi dinero a mi amigo y
él me *(pedir)* _____ más tiempo. Por eso él y yo *(pedir)*
_____ dinero continuamente a nuestros padres. El último
fin de semana él *(pedir)* _____ tres dólares y yo *(pedir)*
_____ cinco.

4. Aunque los padres los *(acostar)* _____ temprano, a veces
mis hermanos menores no *(poder)* _____ dormirse. A
veces yo tampoco *(querer)* _____ dormirme y los
(divertir) _____. (Nosotros) *(contar)* _____
cuentos de horror. Los estamos *(contar)* _____ ahora.
Anoche mis padres *(acostar)* _____ temprano a mis
hermanos y (ellos) *(contar)* _____ mucho cuentos.

5. ¿A qué hora los *(despertar)* _____ tu mamá? Pués, el
domingo pasado los *(despertar)* _____ a las siete, pero
ayer (ellos) *(dormir)* _____ hasta las diez. (Ellos) estan
(dormir) _____ ahora. Pero no importa la hora. Nunca
(querer) _____ levantarse.

6. ¿*(Servir)* _____ usted huevos con jamón para el
desayuno? Sí, señor, nosotros *(servir)* _____ desayuno al
estilo americano porque los turistas siempre lo *(pedir)*
_____. ¿Por qué *(almorzar)* _____ ustedes
tanto? El jueves pasado un gordo *(almorzar)* _____ aquí
y comió mucho.

7. Rodolfo nunca *(entender)* _____ bien lo que pasa en
clase. Pero ayer *(entender)* _____ perfectamente la
explicación y yo no la *(entender)* _____. Después de la
clase (yo) no *(perder)* _____ ni un momento en hablarle
al profesor.

8. ¿Cuánto *(costar)* _____ esto? Dos dólares. Pero ayer sólo
(costar) _____ un dólar. Pues, chicos, así es la vida.
¿*(Querer)* _____ ustedes comprar unos? Con este sistema
no *(poder)* _____ comprar nada.

Communication Pattern Exercises

I. Write the correct form of the verb to answer the question. Then work with a partner. Take turns asking and answering the questions.

1. ¿Cierra usted las ventanas por la noche? _____*cierro*_____

   ¿Y las cerró anoche? _____*cerré*_____

2. ¿Vuelves temprano los domingos? _____

   ¿Y volviste temprano el domingo pasado? _____

3. Ana, ¿lo despierto? _____

   ¿Lo desperté anoche? _____

4. ¿Encontráis los libros? _____

   ¿Y encontrasteis los otros ayer? _____

5. ¿Comenzaron ustedes a tiempo? _____

6. Profesor, ¿volvimos la última vez con el director? _____

7. ¿Pueden ustedes votar si tienen dieciocho años? _____

8. Señor, ¿cerramos la puerta con llave? _____

9. Señora, ¿podemos salir a las doce? _____

10. ¿Sirves como guía? _____

    ¿Serviste como guía la última vez? _____

11. ¿Pedís tortillas? _____

    ¿Y las pedisteis para la cena de ayer? _____

12. ¿Consigue más este chico? _____

    ¿Y consiguió más anteayer? _____

13. ¿Pide usted permiso? _____

14. ¿Señor, ¿lo sirvo bien? _____

15. ¿Piden ustedes leche? _____

16. Señorita, ¿lo servimos ahora? _____

17. ¿Pidió usted más? _____

18. Señor, ¿seguí a ese señor? _____

19. ¿Consiguieron ustedes la información? _____

20. Señoritas, ¿lo servimos con tostada? _____

II. Work with a partner. Read each statement. Then take turns asking and answering the questions.

1. Cada verano mis amigos y yo servimos como intérpretes.
   ¿Cómo servimos? ¿Sirves este verano como intérprete? ¿Serviste como intérprete el verano pasado? ¿Sirven tus amigos como intérpretes a veces? ¿Cuándo sirvo yo como intérprete? ¿Sirvió tu padre como intérprete durante la guerra?

2. Siempre duermo bien.

¿Cómo duermo yo? ¿Dormiste bien anoche? ¿Cuántas horas duermen tus padres? ¿Durmieron ustedes más o menos durante las últimas vacaciones? Durante las vacaciones, ¿duermen ustedes al aire libre o en un motel? ¿Duermes bien siempre? ¿Cuántas horas duermes generalmente?

3. Mi familia y yo perdemos muchas cosas.

¿Qué perdemos? ¿Perdió usted algo ayer? ¿Pierden usted y sus hermanos muchos lápices? ¿Qué perdieron ustedes la semana pasada? ¿Perdieron sus hermanos algo de valor? ¿Qué pierde usted?

Actividades de comunicación

I. Conoce a tus compañeros de clase—Prepara 10 (por lo menos) preguntas que contengan estos verbos. Usalas en clase para tener una entrevista con un(a) compañero(a) de clase. Está preparado(a) para decirle a tu profesor(a) o a otro(a) estudiante lo que aprendiste. ¿Cuáles son algunas cosas que ustedes dos hacen? ¿Qué no hace ninguno de ustedes?

Los siguientes verbos son unos que ustedes han estudiado.

Class 1		Class 2	Class 3
recordar	soler	sentir	pedir
entender	volver	dormir	repetir
encender	cerrar	morir	seguir
jugar	almorzar	preferir	servir
pensar	despertar	divertir	conseguir
poder	costar	mentir	
probar	encontrar		
querer	comenzar		

II. Empleando verbos de la misma lista, escribe un párrafo de 10 oraciones como mínimo en el que describes a un(a) estudiante típico(a).

Refrán

Dios aprieta pero no ahoga.
De la mano a la boca, se pierde la sopa.
La caridad empieza con nosotros mismos.
Explica el sentido. Da ejemplos de la vida.

---

2 Verbs That Add Consonants or Accents to the Stem

GOAL 1
To form and use verbs that add a consonant to the stem.

In the indicative mood there are a number of verbs that add either a *z* or a *g* to the stem of the *yo* form in the present.

Those verbs that add a *z* have a vowel followed by *-cer* or *-cir* in the infinitive form.

Pattern: vowel + *-cer* or *-cir* becomes vowel + *z* + *co*

agradecer (yo) agradezco
conocer   (yo) conozco
obedecer   (yo) obedezco
reducir   (yo) reduzco

Those verbs that add a *g* to the stem in the *yo* form of the present indicative are less easy to recognize. Some of the more common cases include the following:

hacer   (yo) hago
salir   (yo) salgo
poner   (yo) pongo
valer   (yo) valgo

Note that with the verb *hacer,* the *g* is substituted for the *c.* All other forms of these verbs are regular in the present.

EXERCISE

Choose a verb from the list that correctly completes each sentence and supply the necessary present form.

agradecer	pertenecer	obedecer	conducir	salir
crecer	conocer	permanecer	hacer	valer
desaparecer	merecer	producir	poner	

1. Yo _____ todas las leyes de mi patria, pero hay unas que

   no _____.

2. Yo le _____ toda la ayuda y toda la información. Mi

   mamá también le _____ todo.

3. Yo _____ la ropa en el armario, pero tú no

   _____ la tuya allí.

4. Es la primera vez que he visto a ese señor. No lo _____.

   ¿Lo _____ vosotros?

5. _____ mis lecciones antes de mirar la televisión.

   ¿_____ las tuyas antes de mirar la televisión?

6. Yo _____ cuando hay trabajo que hacer en la casa. Mis

   hermanos _____ también.

7. Con este amplificador eléctrico yo _____ sonidos

   fantásticos. ¿_____ ustedes lo mismo.

8. Yo _____ aquí durante los veranos para trabajar con mi

   padre. ¿_____ José aquí?

9. Siempre yo _____ de la casa por la noche con un amigo,

   nunca solo, pero (nosotros) no _____ mucho.

10. _____ una "A" pero recibo una "B" en esa clase. ¿Qué

    nota _____ tú?

GOAL 2

To form and use stem vowel changing verbs that add a *g* to the stem
of the *yo* form.

Some verbs have a vowel change in the stem as well as an added consonant. The
endings are regular.

The following are common examples:

decir: digo, dices, dice, decimos, decís, dicen
tener: tengo, tienes, tiene, tenemos, tenéis, tienen
venir: vengo, vienes, viene, venimos, venís, vienen

Note that in the *yo* form of *decir,* the *g* is substituted for the *c.* A few verbs add
an *i* before the *g.*

caer: caigo, caes, cae, caemos, caéis, caen
traer: traigo, traes, trae, traemos, traéis, traen
oír: oigo, oyes, oye, oímos, oís, oyen

EXERCISE   Choose a verb from the list that correctly completes each sentence and supply
the necessary present form.

detener   mantener   tener   caer   oír
decir   obtener   venir   traer

1. Yo _____ cenicero en la mesita. Los obreros

   _____ la condición de la carretera.

2. Yo _____ dos dólares. ¿Cuántos _____ tú?

3. (Yo) _____ refrescos a la fiesta.

4. Yo _____ permiso del profesor y ella

   _____ permiso del director.

5. Estoy escuchando, pero no _____ nada. ¿Qué

   _____ tú?

6. Yo _____ a pie a la escuela pero mis amigos

   _____ en coche.

7. Cuando no _____ nada en casa mis padres me

   _____ que hable.

8. _____ mi coche fácilmente pero tú _____
   el tuyo con dificultad porque los frenos no funcionan bien.

GOAL 3

To form and use verbs that add *y* to the stem.

I verbs in which the stem ends in *u* add a *y* in the present tense before all suffix vowels except *i*. The stem adds *y* in all forms except *nosotros* and *vosotros*.

construir: construyo, construyes, construye, construimos,
             construís, construyen

EXERCISE

Choose a verb from the list that correctly completes each sentence and supply the appropriate present form.

construir   huir
destruir   influir

1. _____ de mi perro cuando está irritado y mis hermanas

   también _____ de él.

2. Yo _____ carreteras y puentes de juguetes, pero mi padre

   _____ los verdaderos.

3. _____ las revistas que no quiero. ¿_____

   ustedes las revistas? Sí, las _____.

4. Te _____ mucho. También me _____ tú
   mucho.

GOAL 4
To give those forms that require a written accent.

Some *A* verbs in which the stem ends in *i* or *u* have an accent over that vowel in all the forms of the present except *nosotros* and *vosotros*.

continuar: continúo, continúas, continúa, continuamos, continuáis, continúan

It is important to remember that many *A* verbs in which the stem ends in *i* do not follow this pattern. For example: *anunciar, cambiar,* and *iniciar*.

EXERCISE

Choose a verb from the list that correctly completes each sentence and supply the appropriate present form.

continuar   enviar
actuar   guiar
acentuar   confiar

1. María no _____ en sus padres. Por eso no les dice sus deseos secretos.

2. (Yo) _____ una carta a Juan todos los lunes.

3. (Nosotros) _____ a los turistas por el museo.

4. Los políticos _____ sus planes para las elecciones.

5. Tú no _____ la sílaba apropiada.

6. ¿_____ (vosotros) con el mismo sindicato?

Communication Pattern Exercises

I. Write the correct form of the verb to answer the question. Then work with a partner. Take turns asking and answering the questions.

1. ¿Conduces con cuidado? _____*conduzco*_____

2. ¿Conoce usted a ese personaje de televisión? _____

3. Ana, ¿me parezco a Michael Jordan? _____

4. Señor, ¿reduzco bastante los precios? _____

5. ¿Tiene el número de teléfono? _____

6. ¿Vienes a la meditación transcendental? _____

7. ¿Oyes los chismes? _____

8. ¿Dice usted la verdad? _____

9. Mamá, ¿tengo tiempo para comer más? _____

10. Rosa, ¿vengo con Rafael? _____

11. Manuela, ¿traigo el video? _____

12. Señora, ¿digo más? _____

13. ¿Influye usted en sus amigos? _____

14. ¿Destruyen ustedes las emisiones tóxicas? _____

15. Señores, ¿huimos juntos Miguel y yo? _____

16. ¿Continúas en el mismo apartamento? _____

17. Señora, ¿envío este paquete? _____

18. ¿Actúan ustedes todos los planes? _____

II. Work with a partner. Read each statement, then take turns asking and answering the questions.

1. Me parezco a mi abuelo.
   ¿A quién me parezco yo? ¿A quién te pareces tú? ¿Se parecen ustedes a sus padres? ¿A quiénes se parecen tus hermanos? ¿A quién se parece tu padre?

2. Mi hermano y yo tenemos una motocicleta.
   ¿Qué tenemos? ¿Tienen usted y sus hermanos una motocicleta? ¿Tiene su padre una motocicleta o una bicicleta? ¿Tienen ustedes una bicicleta? ¿En qué andan sus amigos?

Actividades de comunicación

I. Conoce a tus compañeros de clase—Prepara 10 (por lo menos) preguntas que contengan estos verbos. Usalas en clase para entrevistar a un(a) compañero(a) de clase.

Está preparado para decirle a tu profesor(a) o a otro(a) estudiante lo que aprendiste.

Los siguientes verbos son unos que has estudiado.

conocer	hacer	caer	construir	continuar
obedecer	salir	oír	destruir	enviar
agradecer	poner	traer	influir	guiar
conducir	decir			
parecer	tener			
	venir			

II. Empleando verbos de la misma lista, escribe un párrafo de 10 frases como mínimo que trate de ti mismo(a). Yo . . .

Refrán

La pobreza tiene por amiga la tristeza.
Explica el sentido. Da ejemplos de la vida.

3 Verbs with Different Spellings to Represent the Same Sound

In Spanish most words are spelled just the way they sound, although there are a few exceptions to this rule. At times a letter, or combination of letters, may have a different sound depending upon the following vowel. The same thing is true in English. For example, the pronunciation of the letter *c* in "cite" and "cede" is different from the *c* in "cut," "cat," and "cot." The letter *g* in "general" and "giraffe" is different from the *g* in "got," "gut," and "gate." An understanding of spelling and pronunciation is the key to learning to write verbs with different spellings.

GOAL 1

To spell the "s," "k," "g," "h," and "gw" sounds in Spanish.

The sounds that you must learn to spell correctly in order to learn to write spelling-changing verbs are discussed below.

A. The "s" sound (in Latin American pronunciation) is represented by

- the letter *c* before *e* or *i:*
  cereal   cinta

- the letter *s* before all vowels:
  salsa   sé   sino   solo   su

- the letter *z* before all vowels except *e* or *i:*
  zapato   zorro   zumbido

B. The "k" sound is represented by

- the letter *c* before *a, o,* or *u:*
  cada   con   curar

- the letters *qu* before *e* or *i:*
  que   quien

C. The "h" sound is represented by

- the letter *g* before *e* or *i:*
  gente   gimnasio

- the letter *j* before all vowels:
  jamás   jefe   jinete   joven   jugar

D. The "g" sound is represented by

- the letter *g* before *a, o,* or *u:*
  gato   gordo   gusto

- the letters *gu* before *e* or *i:*
  guerra   guiar

E. The "gw" sound is represented by

- the letters *gu* before *a* or *o:*
  guantes   averiguo

- the letters *gü* (with a dieresis) before *e* or *i*
  (These forms are rather rare.):
  vergüenza

EXERCISE

Pronounce and spell the words with a partner.

1. cama	6. general	11. suelo	16. guiar
2. sabio	7. cielo	12. centro	17. corto
3. zona	8. sombra	13. zapato	18. quinto
4. ganar	9. quemar	14. cuento	19. joven
5. siete	10. jamón	15. goma	20. sed

GOAL 2

To apply spelling rules to spelling changes in verb conjugations.

The spelling rules you have just reviewed become important in learning to write the correct forms of certain verbs as the vowel in the verb ending changes with the different persons and tenses. In the indicative mood these changes occur in the *yo* form of the present and the *yo* form of the preterite. There are many verbs that require these changes, so they are very important in learning to write Spanish.

Those verbs that have a spelling change in the *yo* form of the present indicative are as follows:

- Verbs ending in *-ger* and *-gir*
  In order to represent the "h" sound before an *o*, the *g* becomes *j* before *o:*

  escoger > (yo) escojo

- Verbs ending in *-guir*
  In order to represent the "g" sound before *o*, the *gu* becomes *g* before *o:*

  distinguir > (yo) distingo

All other written forms of *-ger, -gir,* and *-guir* verbs in the present indicative correctly represent the spoken sound without changing the spelling.

Those verbs that have spelling changes in the *yo* form of the preterite are as follows:

- Verbs ending in *-car*
  In order to represent the "k" sound before an *e*, the *c* becomes *qu* before *e:*

  tocar > (yo) toqué

- Verbs ending in *-gar*

  In order to represent the "g" sound before an *e,* the *g* becomes *gu* before *e:*

  llegar > (yo) llegué

- Verbs ending in *-guar*

  In order to represent the "gw" sound before an *e,* the *gu* becomes *gü* before *e:*

  averiguar > (yo) averigüe

- Verbs ending in *-zar*

  In order to represent the "s" sound before an *e,* the *z* becomes *c* before *e:*

  almorzar > (yo) almorcé

All other written forms of the verbs in the preterite correctly represent the spoken sound without changing the spelling.

EXERCISE

Pronounce and spell each verb with a partner.

1. toco	5. almorcé	9. cogemos	13. averiguo
2. toqué	6. almorzó	10. pagan	14. averigua
3. consigo	7. almuerza	11. pagué	15. dirijo
4. consiguen	8. cojo	12. averigüé	16. dirige

GOAL 3

To give the form of the *i* ending in the preterite for *E* and *I* verbs.

Spanish does not permit an unaccented *i* between two vowels in verb endings. In forms in which such a combination would occur, the *i* is changed to a *y.* This change takes place with *E* and *I* verbs that end in *a, e,* or *u* with the following suffixes: *-ió, -ieron,* and *-iendo.*

caer: cayó, cayeron, cayendo

There is one additional irregularity with verbs whose preterite stems end in *a* or *e.* All the forms that have an *i* plus a consonant in the suffix have an accent mark over that vowel. This is done so that the *i* will have a separate sound in the verb form.

leí, leíste, (leyó), leímos, leísteis, (leyeron), leído

EXERCISES

I. Complete each of the verb forms by adding *i, í,* or *y.*

1. Constru_____eron una carretera magnífica.

2. Tú te ca_____ste tres veces.

3. El científico destru_____ó su invención.

4. Todos nosotros hu_____mos sin hacer ni una pregunta.

5. Los ciudadanos o_____eron las noticias pronto.

6. ¿O_____steis la decisión de la corte?

II. Change the verb from the present to the preterite.

1. Destruyen las computadoras. _____

2. Leen autobiografías. _____

3. Construyo un aparato mecanizado. _____

4. No oigo muchos chistes. _____

5. Huye con su marido. _____

6. Cae en el lago. _____

7. Influimos en nuestros amigos. _____

8. Leemos en voz alta. _____

9. Huyes de la responsabilidad. _____

10. Crees en la disciplina. _____

GOAL 4

To use these forms in context with correct spelling.

EXERCISE

Complete each sentence with the correct spelling of the verb.

Present

1. *(recoger)* Yo _____ los periódicos aquí ahora pero mi
amigo los _____ en otra esquina.

2. *(seguir)* ¿_____ tú a la derecha? Yo _____
a la izquierda.

Preterite

3. *(sacar)* El semestre pasado mi hermana _____ una "B"
en esa clase pero yo _____ una "A".

4. *(pagar)* (Yo) no _____ lo que el vendedor me pidió.
¿_____ (vosotros) tanto?

5. *(averiguar)* (Yo) _____ la verdad antes que los otros.
(Ellos) no la _____ hasta mucho más tarde.

6. *(comenzar)* ¿_____ ustedes ayer? Yo no

_____ hasta esta mañana.

7. *(huir)* (Nosotros) _____ delante del enemigo. Mariana

_____ con Roberto y yo _____ con Ana.

Communication Pattern Exercises

I. Supply the form of the verb that would be used to answer each question.

1. ¿Proteges a la víctima o al criminal? _____*protejo*_____

2. Anita, ¿lo recojo ahora? _____

3. ¿Sigue usted estudiando para ser psiquiatra? _____

4. Señor, ¿distingo bien los cambios significativos? _____

5. ¿Secaste la ropa? _____

6. Pedro, ¿toqué con sentimiento esa pieza? _____

7. ¿Rogaste al líder de los terroristas? _____

8. Señorita, ¿llegué a tiempo? _____

9. ¿Empezó usted al amanecer? _____

10. Papá, ¿almorcé demasiado temprano? _____

11. ¿Construyó usted un garaje nuevo? _____

12. ¿Oíste quien ganó el Premio Nobel? _____

13. Profesor, ¿leí bien el estudio de María? _____

14. ¿Destruyeron ustedes las librerías pornográficas? _____

15. ¿Leísteis el artículo sobre la sobrepoblación? _____

16. Amigos míos, ¿oímos bien? _____

II. Work with a partner. Read each statement, take turns asking and answering the questions that follow.

1. Yo escojo mi propia ropa.
   ¿Qué escojo yo? ¿Escogen tus hermanos su propia ropa? ¿Escogéis el estilo de pelo? ¿Quién escoge la casa en que vivís? ¿Escoges tú tu propia ropa? ¿Quién escoge las comidas?

2. Mis amigos y yo sacamos buenas notas en las clases.
   ¿Qué sacamos en las clases? ¿Sacan buenas notas sus amigos? ¿Sacó usted buena nota en esta clase el semestre pasado? ¿Sacaron sus hermanos buenas notas el semestre pasado? ¿Sacaron ustedes mejores notas que sus padres? ¿Saca usted buenas notas? ¿En qué clase sacó usted la mejor nota?

Actividades de comunicación

Conocer a tus compañeros de clase—Prepara 10 (por lo menos) preguntas que contengan estos verbos. Usalas en clase para entrevistar a un(a) compañero(a) de clase.

Está preparado(a) para decirle a tu profesor(a) o a otro(a) estudiante lo que aprendiste.

Los siguientes verbos son unos que ustedes han estudiado.

tomar	sacar	oír	proteger
recoger	pagar	caer	secar
seguir	averiguar	leer	rogar
conseguir	comenzar	creer	llegar

Refrán

Hay que escuchar los consejos de los sabios y los viejos.
Explica el sentido. Da ejemplos de la vida.

4 Other Verbs with Irregular Forms in the Present

Some common verbs have forms that do not fit into any general pattern. These verbs must be learned individually. In the next five sections, these irregular forms in the indicative mood are studied.

Although these forms do not follow a general pattern, in many cases they have a great deal of similarity to those of regular verbs. At times there is a pattern within these irregular forms even though it may differ from the pattern of regular verbs. Look for these similarities and contrasts as you study these irregular verbs. For example, you can expect most of the person-number suffixes to be fairly regular.

GOAL 1

To give the irregular present forms and to use them in context.

Several Spanish verbs are irregular only in the *yo* form of the present.

caber	(yo) quepo, cabes, etc.
saber	(yo) sé, sabes, etc.
ver	(yo) veo, ves, etc.
dar	(yo) doy, das, etc.
ir	(yo) voy, vas, etc.

Ir is listed with this group because it has the same forms as the verb *dar*.

Estar has an irregular *yo* form plus accent marks; *haber* and *ser* are completely irregular.

estar: estoy, estás, está, estamos, estáis, están
haber: he, has, ha, hemos, habéis, han
ser: soy, eres, es, somos, sois, son

E X E R C I S E   Choose a verb from the preceding lists of irregular verbs that will correctly complete each of the sentences and supply the correct present form.

1. (Yo) _____ en la sala y Pepito _____ en su cuarto.

2. ¿_____ (tú) dónde están los anteojos de papá? (Yo) no _____.

3. Los otros ya _____ salido y (yo) _____ pasado la tarde estudiando. ¿_____ terminado (tú) la tarea?

4. (Yo) _____ primero a su casa y luego nosotros _____ juntos al baile.

5. Mi padre y yo _____ buenos amigos. (El) _____ siempre justo. Cuando _____ yo buen chico, (él) me _____ bastante dinero para comprar lo que quiero.

6. Yo les _____ el dinero a los oficios y (ellos) se lo _____ a los pobres.

7. Yo no _____ muy grande. Yo _____ en un espacio tan pequeño pero un mayor no _____ aquí.

Communication Pattern Exercises

I. Supply the form of the verb that would be used to answer each question.

1. ¿Cabes allí? _____*quepo*_____
   ¿Y quepo yo también? _____*cabes*_____

2. ¿Sabe usted la dirección de Rosa? _____
   Profesor, ¿sé bien los hechos más importantes? _____

3. ¿Ves los letreros de luces de neón por la noche? _____
   Marta, ¿lo veo todo? _____

4. ¿Les da usted dinero a los pobres? _____

Señor, ¿les doy bastante tiempo a los alumnos? _____

5. ¿Vas con los otros? _____

José, ¿voy con ustedes? _____

6. ¿Estás enojado? _____

7. ¿Ha saludado al señor Gil? _____

8. ¿Eres miembro de esta sociedad? _____

9. Señor, ¿estoy listo ahora? _____

10. Rafael, ¿he estado equivocado? _____

11. Señora, ¿soy demasiado ambicioso? _____

12. ¿Están ustedes deprimidos? _____

13. ¿Habéis pensado en el resultado? _____

14. ¿Son ustedes de México? _____

15. Manuel, ¿estamos de acuerdo? _____

16. Señorita, ¿hemos completado todo? _____

17. Catalina, ¿somos demasiado pequeños? _____

18. ¿Es conformista Roberto? _____

19. ¿Es de algodón esta camisa? _____

20. ¿Son de California esas chicas? _____

21. ¿Son derechos civiles? _____

II. Work with a partner. Read each statement, then take turns asking and answering the questions that follow.

1. Los padres no van a trabajar los sábados y los domingos.
¿Qué días no van los padres a trabajar? ¿Qué días van ustedes a trabajar? ¿Adónde va su familia los domingos? ¿Adónde va usted los sábados? ¿Va usted al trabajo de noche?

2. Yo sé jugar al tenis.
¿A qué sé yo jugar? ¿A qué otros deportes sabes jugar? ¿Saben tus padres jugar al ping-pong? ¿Sabes jugar al tenis? ¿A qué deportes sabe jugar tu papá? ¿Saben ustedes esquiar?

3. Mis amigos y yo somos alumnos de una prestigiosa universidad del este. ¿En qué universidad somos alumnos? ¿Son todos tus amigos alumnos de la misma universidad? ¿Es tu mejor amigo alumno de la misma universidad? ¿Es una buena universidad? ¿En qué universidad eres alumno? ¿Son ustedes buenos alumnos?

Actividades de comunicación

Completa las siguientes oraciones.

1. Yo sé _____.

2. Mis padres saben _____.

3. Mis padres no saben _____.

4. Yo soy _____.

5. Mi amigo es _____.

6. Les doy a mis padres _____.

7. Mi familia y yo vamos _____.

Refrán

Quien con lobos anda, a aullar aprende.
Explica el sentido. Da ejemplos de la vida.

---

5 Irregular Verb Forms in the Imperfect

GOAL

To give the correct imperfect forms of irregular verbs and to use them in context.

There are only two verbs with irregular stems in the imperfect and one that has an extra vowel. These verbs are *ir, ser,* and *ver.*

ir:	iba, ibas, iba, íbamos, ibais, iban
ser:	era, eras, era, éramos, erais, eran
ver:	veía, veías, veía, veíamos, veíais, veían

EXERCISES

I. Complete each sentence with the appropriate imperfect form of *ir, ser,* or *ver.*

1. Cuando (yo) _____ niño mis padres _____ al cine todos los sábados por la noche y (yo) _____ con ellos.

2. (Nosotros) _____ muchas películas de vaqueros y del oeste de los Estados Unidos. Especialmente mis hermanos _____ todas esas películas.

3. De los niños (yo) _____ el mayor pero mis hermanos _____ más grandes que yo.

4. Durante las vacaciones _____ (nosotros) a muchos lugares pintorescos. Todos esos sitios _____ muy interesantes.

II. Change each sentence from the present to the imperfect.

1. Voy a casa.

   _____

2. Vemos los cohetes.

   _____

3. Es mi secretaria ejecutiva.

   _____

4. Van por laca y champú natural.

   _____

5. ¿Lo ves en la cola?

   _____

6. ¿Sois ciclistas en la carrera?

   _____

Communication Pattern Exercises

I. Answer the questions.

1. ¿Ibas a pie?

   Sí, iba a pie. or *No, no iba a pie.* _____

2. ¿Era usted el menor?

   _____

3. ¿Veías las demostraciones de yoga?

   _____

4. Señor, ¿iba yo demasiado lento?

   _____

5. Pablo, ¿era yo la más bonita?

   _____

6. Señorita, ¿veía yo los más baratos?

   _____

7. ¿Iban ustedes muchas veces a la peluquería?

   _____

8. ¿Erais introvertidos o extravertidos?

_____

9. ¿Veían ustedes unas carreras de caballos?

_____

10. Josefina, ¿íbamos con ellos?

_____

11. Señor, ¿éramos los mejores?

_____

12. Ricardo, ¿veíamos los Juegos Olímpicos en la televisión?

_____

13. ¿Eran buenos jugadores?

_____

14. ¿Iba Pepe al cine los sábados?

_____

15. ¿Veían a sus amigos?

_____

II. Work with a partner. Read the statement. Then take turns asking and answering the questions that follow.

Desde niño mi familia y yo íbamos al campo para visitar a mis abuelos durante los veranos.

¿Adónde íbamos? ¿Cuándo íbamos? ¿Iban sus padres también? ¿A quiénes visitábamos? ¿Adónde iba usted durante los veranos? ¿Iban ustedes al campo?

Actividades de comunicación

Discute las siguientes preguntas con un(a) compañero(a) de clase. Cuando eras niño(a),

1. ¿Cómo eras?
2. ¿A quién veías más?
3. ¿Qué veías más?
4. ¿Adónde ibas?

Refrán

No hay regla sin excepción.
Explica el sentido. Da ejemplos de la vida.

6 Irregular Verb Forms in the Preterite

GOAL 1

To give the correct preterite forms of irregular verbs and to use them in context.

Several commonly used verbs are irregular in the preterite. The stems are quite irregular, but the endings are only slightly different from those of regular verbs.

	stem
andar	anduv-
estar	estuv-
tener	tuv-

	stem
hacer	hic-[1]
venir	vin-

	stem
poner	pus-
querer	quis-
caber	cup-
saber	sup-
haber[2]	hub-
poder	pud-

Preterite Suffixes

	Regular Verbs		**Irregular Verbs**
	A	*I*	
yo	é		e
tú		iste	iste
usted/él/ella	ó		o
nosotros,-as		imos	imos
vosotros,-as		isteis	isteis
ellos/ellas		ieron	ieron

Note that the *e* and *o* lose their accents with the preterite of irregular verbs.

In one group of irregular verbs, the stem ends with the letter *j*.

	stem
decir	dij-
producir	produj-
traer	traj-

---

1. *C* becomes *z* before *o: hizo*
2. The preterite forms of *haber* may be used with a perfective participle to form the preterite perfect tense. This usage is rather rare and is usually restricted to literary usage. When this form is used, it is normally introduced by an adverb of time.

With these stems the *ellos* ending loses the *i*.

dijeron   trajeron   produjeron

The verb *dar* is irregular in that although it is an *A* verb, *E* and *I* preterite endings are used to form the preterite.

Dar

di	dimos
diste	disteis
dio	dieron

The verbs *ser* and *ir* are different from the preterite of the other irregular verbs. Both verbs have the same forms in the preterite tense. The context makes the meaning of each clear.

Fui pintor.   *I was a painter.*
Fui a esa escuela.   *I went to that school.*

Ser / Ir

fui	fuimos
fuiste	fuisteis
fue	fueron

As you can see, even these verbs, with the exception of the *yo* and *él* forms, are regular except for the stem.

EXERCISES

I. Complete each sentence by adding the appropriate preterite ending to the verb.

1. Cuando entré, papá no dij_____ nada.

2. Sí, (nosotros) anduv_____ al parque ayer.

3. (Yo) pus_____ la jaula en el coche.

4. Los otros traj_____ los refrescos.

5. Todos estuv_____ de pie.

6. Mis amigos fu_____ a la procesión.

7. ¿Hic_____ (tú) estas galletas?

8. ¿Adónde fu_____ Pepe?

9. Sí, le d_____ una afeitadora eléctrica.

10. ¿Vin_____ (vosotros) por avión?

II. Write the appropriate preterite form of the verb.

1. Juan *(andar)* _____ a la casa de su novia.

2. Los llamé pero no *(querer)* _____ aceptar.

3. (Yo) *(venir)* _____ para visitarte.

4. Ese señor es muy amable. Me *(dar)* _____ un billete de cinco.

5. ¿No te *(decir)* _____ (yo) eso antes?

6. ¿*(Tener)* _____ (tú) más que hacer?

7. Mi hijo lo *(hacer)* _____ solo.

8. (Nosotros) lo *(saber)* _____ anoche.

9. Querían venir pero no *(poder)* _____ salir a tiempo.

10. (Yo) *(ser)* _____ piloto por diez años.

III. Change the verb in each sentence from the present to the preterite.

1. Voy ahora mismo. _____

2. Trae su guitarra. _____

3. Sí, caben todos. _____

4. ¿Pones esto aquí? _____

5. No, (vosotros) estáis cansados. _____

6. Producimos muchas calculadoras. _____

7. Es hombre de negocios. _____

8. No lo dan gratis. _____

9. Vengo solo. _____

10. No quieren portarse bien. _____

GOAL 2

To give the specific meanings of certain verbs in the imperfect and preterite.

The imperfect describes imperfective actions, in other words, actions that are continuing or being repeated. The preterite focuses on the beginning, the end, or the action as a whole. With a few verbs like *conocer, hacer, poder, querer, saber, estar, tener,* and *creer,* the concept is such that in English we may need to use different words to make the distinction made in Spanish by using either the imperfect or preterite of the same verb.

Claro, yo **conocía** a su hermano.	*Of course, **I knew** your brother. (I was acquainted with him.)*
Lo **conocí** en una fiesta en la casa de Pablo.	***I met** (first knew) him at Pablo's party.*

EXERCISE

On the line, write the letter of the English sentence that correctly expresses the idea of the Spanish sentence.

_____   1. Mamá sabía que (yo) había ido al cine.

_____   2. Mamá supo que había ido al cine.

A. Mom found out that I had gone to the movie.

B. Mom knew that I had gone to the movie.

_____   3. El bandido no podía escaparse.

_____   4. El bandido no pudo escaparse.

C. He was unable to escape. (It was impossible.)

D. He did not succeed in his escape. (He tried and failed.)

_____   5. Los García no querían aceptar la invitación.

_____   6. Los García no quisieron aceptar la invitación.

E. The Garcías refused to accept the invitation.

F. The Garcías did not want to accept the invitation.

_____   7. Cuando lo vimos teníamos miedo.

_____   8. Cuando lo vimos tuvimos miedo.

G. When we saw him, we were afraid.

H. When we saw him, we became frightened.

_____   9. Hacía frío anoche.

_____ 10. Hizo frío anoche.

I. It got cold last night.

J. It was cold last night.

_____ 11. Creía que yo le diría la verdad.

_____ 12. Cuando le dije, me creyó.

K. He believed that I would tell him the truth.

L. When I told him, he believed me.

Communication Pattern Exercises

I. Answer the questions in the negative.

1. ¿Anduviste por la casa de los García?

   No, no anduve por la casa de los García.

2. ¿Estuvo usted en el centro ayer?

3. Señor, ¿tuvo un paquete en su cuarto?

4. Mamá, ¿hice todo lo necesario?

5. ¿Hizo Juan esto para su mamá?

6. ¿Vino María al baile el último fin de semana?

7. ¿Pusieron ustedes la máquina en el garaje?

8. ¿No quisisteis ayuda profesional?

9. Marta, cupimos en el asiento de atrás, ¿no?

10. Señorita, ¿supimos todo lo que pasó?

11. ¿Pudieron alcanzar su meta?

12. ¿Dijeron lo que creían?

13. ¿Trajiste los trajes de baño?

14. ¿Le dio usted las llaves al mecánico?

15. ¿Fuisteis al ensayo de la banda anoche?

_____

16. ¿Fuiste tú director cinematográfico?

_____

II. Work with a partner. Read each statement. Then take turns asking and answering the questions.

1. Mi novia y yo fuimos al cine el viernes por la noche.
   ¿Adónde fuimos mi novia y yo? ¿Adónde fuiste tú? ¿Fuisteis a comer después? ¿Con quién fuiste? ¿Fuisteis otros amigos con ustedes? ¿Vais mucho al cine?

2. Anoche le dije a mi familia todo lo que había pasado durante el día.
   ¿Qué le dije a mi familia? ¿Qué dijo su mamá? ¿Dijeron ustedes muchas cosas durante la comida? ¿Qué dijo su papá anoche? ¿Qué dijeron sus hermanos?

3. Mi abuela y yo anduvimos por el parque el domingo por la tarde.
   ¿Cuando anduvimos por el parque? ¿Anduvo su familia por el parque o por las calles el último fin de semana? ¿Anda mucho su familia? ¿Andan mucho los americanos?

Actividades de comunicación

Escribe un párrafo de media página como mínimo empleando sólo los verbos de las páginas 157–158 y los verbos "ir" y "ser" para describir algunas cosas que hiciste el verano más memorable de tu vida.

Refrán

En tierra de ciegos, el tuerto es rey.
Explica el sentido. Da ejemplos de la vida.

7 Irregular Verb Forms and Uses in the Future and Conditional

To give the correct irregular future and conditional verb forms and to use them in context.

Irregular verb forms in the future and conditional fall into three groups.

Group 1: E *verbs that drop the verb class vowel*

	Future	Conditional
caber	cabré, etc.	cabría, etc.
haber	habré, etc.	habría, etc.
poder	podré, etc.	podría, etc.
querer	querré, etc.	querría, etc.
saber	sabré, etc.	sabría, etc.

Note the *rr* in the stem of *querer*.

Group 2: E *and* I *verbs in which the verb class vowel is replaced by the letter d*

	Future	Conditional
poner	pondré, etc.	pondría, etc.
salir	saldré, etc.	saldría, etc.
tener	tendré, etc.	tendría, etc.
valer	valdré, etc.	valdría, etc.
venir	vendré, etc.	vendría, etc.

Group 3: Decir *and* hacer *drop most of the stem*

	Future	Conditional
decir	diré, etc.	diría, etc.
hacer	haré, etc.	haría, etc.

Note that in all the forms the *r,* which signals futurity, is maintained throughout. As is true in most other cases, these irregular verb forms are only slightly different from the regular verb forms.

EXERCISES

I. Complete each verb stem. In some cases, no letter will be needed.

1. No sab_____remos hasta mañana.

2. Ten_____ré más tiempo la semana que viene.

3. ¿H_____rás lo que te diga?

4. El señor González ven_____rá con su mujer.

5. Pod_____rán interrogar al asesino.

6. Yo hab_____ría arreglado todo pero no era posible.

7. ¿Querr_____íais eliminar toda la burocracia?

8. Daniel d_____ría la verdad.

9. Ese señor val_____ría más pero perdió una fortuna durante la revolución.

10. ¿Pon_____rías tú esta mesa allí?

II. Change the verb form from "I am going to" to "I will" or from "I was going to" to "I would."

1. Vamos a salir pronto. _____*saldremos*_____

2. ¿Me vas a hacer una torta de cumpleaños? _____

3. Van a poner el piano en la sala. _____

4. Va a caber en este espacio. _____

5. Voy a querer hablar contigo. _____

6. (Yo) iba a poder investigar la energía solar. _____

7. Iban a hacer todo lo posible. _____

8. ¿Ibais a venir después del partido? _____

9. ¿Ibas a saber los gustos del público? _____

10. Ibamos a tener una fiesta. _____

III. Choose a verb from the list on page 163 of irregular verbs in the future and conditional tenses and supply its appropriate form in each sentence. Remember that the future tense is future from the present and the conditional tense is future from the past.

1. Me dicen que le _____ a la policía todo lo que saben.

2. Me dijeron que le _____ a la policía todo lo que sabían.

3. María y yo _____ una reunión en mi casa este fin de semana si es posible.

4. No, no _____ una huelga este año. _____ una, pero el sindicato está satisfecho con lo que les ofrece la compañía a los obreros.

5. Juan, yo _____ ir contigo pero José me invitó primero.

    Si me invitas más temprano la próxima vez _____ ir

    contigo.

6. No, (él) no _____ la respuesta hasta mañana.

    _____é_____ hoy pero el jefe no está.

7. Si hay bastante tiempo, _____ (tú) a mi casa.

    _____ (yo) pero tengo que ayudar a mi mamá.

8. Si nieva, ¿_____ (vosotros) el coche en el garaje? Lo

    _____ en el garage pero no cabe.

GOAL 2

To use the future and conditional to express probability.

In addition to expressing futurity, future and conditional forms may also be used to express probability. This change in meaning occurs when the future tense is used in the present and the conditional in the past. Note the time in the English translations.

¿Dónde está Rosa?   *Where is Rosa? I don't know.*
   No sé. **Estará** en su cuarto.   *She **must be** in her room.*
                                 *(She **is probably** in her room.)*

¿Dónde estaba Rosa?   *Where is Rosa?*
   No se. **Estaría** en su cuarto.   *I don't know. She **must have been** in her room.*
                                 *(She **was probably** in her room.)*

Write an equivalent English meaning for each sentence.

1. ¿Qué come ese chico? _____

    Comerá un sandwich. _____

2. ¿Qué hacían los dos? _____

    Estudiarían las lecciones. _____

3. ¿Qué hora es ahora? _____

    Serán las dos o tres. _____

4. ¿Qué tenía la pobre cuando llamó? _____

    Tendría dolor de cabeza. _____

5. ¿Cómo se siente Marta? _____

    Estará bien. Va al partido. _____

6. ¿Quién es ese joven? _____

    Será la hermana de Pepe. _____

7. ¿Dónde consiguió esa camisa? _____

   ¿La compraría en México? _____

8. ¿Cuando se casaron? _____

   Se casaron _____

GOAL 3

To give the Spanish equivalents of "will" and "would."

A. Quite often in English the verbs "will" or "would" are not used to express futurity but to indicate willingness. This meaning is quite common, especially in questions. When "will" in English indicates willingness, the equivalent form in Spanish requires the verb *querer*.

¿**Quieres** cerra la ventana?	***Will** you close the window?*
¿**Quieres** poner el radio?	***Will** you turn on the radio?*

EXERCISE

Give the English equivalent of each sentence.

1. ¿Quieres ayudarme?

   _____

2. Sí, y te ayudaré mañana también.

   _____

3. ¿Saldrás a la medianoche?

   _____

4. Sí, ¿quieres acompañarme?

   _____

5. Sí, ¿me acompañarás?

   _____

6. Juana, ¿quieres tener la reunión en tu casa?

   _____

7. No, no puedo porque mis padres no me darán permiso.

   _____

8. Rafael, ¿tendrás la reunión en tu casa?

   _____

9. Sí, el club decidió eso anoche.

   _____

10. Pepito, ¿me quieres decir lo que te molesta?

   _____

B. The word "would," which is used in English to express an action future from the past and to express a conditional statement, is also used to express a repeated action in the past. You must be careful to distinguish between the meanings of "would" in English as you try to express the same ideas in Spanish.

Futurity:	Dijo que lo **haría.** (conditional)	*He said he **would do** it.*
Contrary to fact:	Lo **haría** si tuviera tiempo.	*I **would** do it if I had time.*
Past repeated:	Lo **hacía** muchas veces. (imperfect)	*He **would** often **do** it.*

The conditional is often used in Spanish, as we use "would" in English, as a softer or more courteous way of asking a favor or making a request.

Preferiría ir contigo.   *I **would prefer** to go with you.*

EXERCISE

Underline the verb form in parentheses, conditional or imperfect, that correctly expresses the italicized English verb.

1. **(iría/iba)** When I was a boy, *I would go* to the movies alone on Saturday evenings.

2. **(iría/iba)** *I would go* if I had the time.

3. **(haríamos/hacíamos)** You said that *we would make* a snowman.

4. **(haríamos/hacíamos)** Whenever it snowed down on the farm, *we would* always *make* a big snowman.

5. **(diría/decía)** Wasn't he funny? *He would* always *tell* the same stories over and over.

6. **(diría/decía)** We weren't afraid. We knew that *he would* not tell.

7. **(vendría/venía)** When he was lonely, *he would come* to our house to talk.

8. **(vendría/venía)** *He would come* right now if you called him.

9. **(pondrías/ponías)** María, *would you put* the napkins on the table?

10. **(querría/quería)** *I would like* to leave at ten.

Communication Pattern Exercises

I. Write the form of the verb that would be used to answer each of the following questions. Then work with a partner. Take turns asking and answering the questions.

1. ¿Me dirás la solución? _____ *diré* _____

2. ¿Tendrá usted las ayudas audio-visuales? _____

3. Señor, ¿cabré en este asiento? _____

4. Manuel, ¿saldré a la una? _____

5. ¿Podrías regatear en español? _____

6. Señorita, ¿sabría yo bastante para explicarlo? _____

7. ¿Querrán ustedes comer inmediatamente al llegar? _____

8. ¿Haréis todo a mano? _____

9. Manolo, ¿vendremos a tu casa? _____

10. Señora, ¿sabremos las causas de la enajenación? _____

11. ¿Le diríais todo? _____

12. Señor, ¿tendríamos más prestigio en otro empleo? _____

13. ¿Los pondrá (él) en mi cuarto? _____

14. ¿Lo haría el mecánico ahora? _____

15. ¿Querrán un ambiente tranquilo? _____

16. ¿Vendrán antes de la hora de cenar? _____

17. ¿Saldrían sin visitarnos? _____

II. Work with a partner. Read each statement. Then take turns asking and answering the questions that follow.

1. Saldré de la escuela esta tarde a las tres y media.
   ¿A qué hora saldré de la escuela? ¿A qué hora saldrás tú? ¿Siempre sales a esta hora? ¿Saldrá tu padre de su trabajo más temprano o más tarde? ¿Saldrán tus amigos de la escuela a la misma hora? ¿Saldréis tu compañero de cuarto y tú del apartamento después de cenar?

2. Mi amigo y yo haríamos un viaje en bicicleta a California pero nuestros padres dicen que no.
   ¿Adónde haríamos un viaje? ¿Cómo lo haríamos? ¿Haría usted un viaje en bicicleta? ¿Adónde haría un viaje? ¿Harían sus padres un viaje por bicicleta? ¿Harían ustedes un viaje por avión?

Actividades de comunicación

I. Conoce a tus compañeros de clase—Prepara 10 (por lo menos) preguntas que contengan los verbos de la página 163. Usalas para practicar con un(a) compañero(a) de clase.

Está preparado(a) para decirle a tu profesor(a) o a otro(a) estudiante lo que aprendiste.

II. Empleando verbos de la misma lista, escribe un párrafo corto en el que describes lo que no harás cuando seas independiente de tus padres.

Refrán   Bien predica quien bien vive.
                Explica el sentido. Da ejemplos de la vida.

8 Irregular Verb Forms in the Perfect

The perfect verb forms follow the pattern *haber* + perfective participle. A perfect verb may have an irregular form of *haber,* as it does in the present perfect, the preterite perfect, the future perfect, and the conditional perfect, or it may have an irregular perfective participle.

The most common verbs having irregular perfective participles are the following:

abrir	abierto	*opened*
cubrir	cubierto	*covered*
morir	muerto	*dead*
resolver	resuelto	*resolved*
volver	vuelto	*returned*
poner	puesto	*placed, put*
ver	visto	*seen*
escribir	escrito	*written*
romper	roto	*broken*
decir	dicho	*said*
hacer	hecho	*made, done*

EXERCISE

Choose the appropriate verb from the preceding list that will correctly complete each of the following sentences, then supply its perfective participle.

1. Es un autor famoso. Ha _____ muchos libros.

2. Yo tengo frío. ¿Has _____ una ventana?

3. Ahora (ella) va a tener mala suerte por siete años porque ha

   _____ un espejo.

4. Papá, estoy preocupada. Ya son las doce y Lola y Susana todavía no han

   _____ del gimnasio.

5. Este programa es muy emocionante. ¿Lo ha _____ usted?

6. No tenemos que esperar mucho más. Papá ha _____ la comida en la mesa.

7. Hijo mío, todos los perritos se han _____ sin abrir los ojos.

8. Antes de entrar en la catedral nos habíamos _____ la cabeza con una pañuelo.

9. Todavía no sabemos que hacer. No hemos _____ todos los problemas.

10. Pablo, ¿has _____ todos los quehaceres esta mañana?

11. No puedo ir. Mamá me ha _____ que no.

Communciation Pattern Exercise

Work with a partner. Read each statement. Then take turns asking and answering the questions.

1. Mis padres y yo hemos visto el edificio Empire State.
   ¿Qué hemos visto? ¿Lo ha visto usted?
   ¿Qué otros puntos de interés ha visto usted?
   ¿Han visto ustedes, por ejemplo, los árboles redwood de California?
   ¿Qué sitios famosos ha visto su mejor amigo?

2. He hecho una tarjeta para mi mamá.
   ¿Qué he hecho yo? ¿Para quién he hecho una tarjeta?
   ¿Has hecho algo para alguien? ¿Ha hecho tu papá algo para tu mamá?
   ¿Qué ha hecho tu mamá para la familia?
   ¿Han hecho ustedes regalos de Navidad para sus abuelos?

Actividades de comunicación

Empleando los participios pasivos irregulares, escribe 10 (por lo menos) oraciones, unas de las cuales sean ridículas y otras de las cuales sean posibles. Leélas a tus compañeros de clase.

Ejemplos: Un elefante ha escrito su nombre en el techo del edificio Empire State.

El paciente ha abierto la boca, y el dentista le examina los dientes.

Refrán

Más sabe el diablo por viejo, que por diablo.
Explica el sentido. Da ejemplos de la vida.

PART IV

Uses of Selected Verbs

Introduction

Estar, ser, haber, hacer, tener, gustar, conocer, saber, pedir, preguntar, and verbs meaning "to become" have been selected for special consideration and practice for several reasons. First, they are often needed to express common ideas. Trying to get along in a Spanish-speaking environment without knowing how to express such basic ideas as "I'm hungry," "It's hot," or "I like chicken and rice" would be rather difficult. Second, they have a variety of uses and meanings. Attempting to relate *Hay diez billetes en la mesa, hay que venderlos,* and *había luna anoche* to *haber* and to decipher the meaning of each would be impossible without some attention to the many uses and meanings of this verb. Third, the contrasts in Spanish or with English are such that you may have difficulty using each correctly. Not knowing how to use the two different verbs for "to be" can be a frustrating and perhaps embarrassing experience.

In this part of the text these verbs, along with their various uses, are studied in context and practiced in communicative patterns.

1 Estar vs. Ser

GOAL 1

To use *estar* and *ser* before the preposition *de.*

A *de* phrase after *estar* is used to tell position or place.

Estamos aquí de visita.	*We are here on a visit.*
Estoy de pie.	*I am standing.*

A *de* phrase after *ser* is used to indicate material, origin, or possession.

El suéter es de lana.	*The sweater is made of wool.*
José es de México.	*José is from Mexico.*
El reloj es de María.	*The watch is María's.*

EXERCISES

I. Complete each sentence with *está* or *es*.

1. Mi reloj _____ de oro.

2. El señor Rodríguez _____ en Washington de representante.

3. Mi padre _____ de Nueva York.

4. Esta chaqueta _____ de Mario.

5. La profesora _____ de pie enfrente de la clase.

6. El juguete _____ de plástico.

II. Form complete sentences using either *están* or *son* plus *de* and the words given.

1. Mariana y su amigo/visita.

   Mariana y su amiga están de visita.
   _____

2. señoritas/Colombia

   _____

3. zapatos/Manolo

   _____

4. aficionados/pie

   _____

5. vestidos/algodón

   _____

6. escritorios/madera

   _____

GOAL 2

To use *estar* and *ser* to express the location of an entity or an event.

If the subject is an entity, the verb *estar* is used to indicate place.

El disco está en la mesa.   *The record is on the table.*

If the subject is an event, the verb *ser* is used to indicate place.

La reunión es en el cuarto tres.   *The meeting is in room three.*

EXERCISES

I. Complete each sentence with *están* or *son.*

1. Los jugadores _____ en el estadio ahora.

2. Los partidos _____ en el estadio nuevo.

3. Los partidos _____ a las dos.

4. Las chicas _____ cerca del coche.

5. Ya _____ aquí los invitados.

6. Sí, _____ aquí las conferencias.

7. Las fiestas _____ los viernes y los sábados por la noche.

8. Las luces _____ sobre tu escritorio.

II. Form complete sentences using *está* or *es* with the words given. Use any other words as necessary.

1. boda/en/iglesia

La boda es en la iglesia. _____

2. casa/en/campo

_____

3. clase/a/diez

_____

4. gimnasio/cerca de/dormitorios

_____

5. concierto/aquí

_____

6. director de orquesta/allí

_____

GOAL 3
To use *estar* and *ser* before a perfective participle.

If the speaker wishes to describe a condition, he or she uses *estar* before the perfective participle.

El pobre **está muerto.**   *The poor fellow **is dead.***

La casa **está construida** de piedras.   *The house **is built** with stones.*

Ser plus a perfective participle is used to describe an action. In Spanish this pattern is more common in the past.

Fue matado por un ladrón.	He **was killed** by a robber.
Fue construida por los colonos alemanes.	It **was built** by the German colonists.

EXERCISES

I. Complete each sentence with *está, fue, están,* or *fueron.*

1. ¿_____ abierta la ventana? Yo tengo frío.

   Sí, _____ abierta por Anita.

2. ¿_____ escrito en español ese libro?

   No, ese libro _____ escrito por un portugués.

3. ¿_____ resueltos todos los problemas?

   Sí, _____ resueltos por el jefe y el representante de los obreros.

4. ¿_____ pagados los gastos?

   Sí, _____ pagados por sus padres.

II. Rewrite each sentence, changing it into two separate sentences using the perfective participle.

1. Cortés destruyó la ciudad. *(destruída)*

   La ciudad está destruída. Fue destruída por Cortés.
   _____

2. El campesino sembró el grano. *(sembrado)*

   _____

3. Matilde sirvió la comida. *(servida)*

   _____

4. El profesor escribió los ensayos. *(escritos)*

   _____

5. El agente de la aduana cerró las maletas. *(cerradas)*

   _____

GOAL 4

To use *estar* and *ser* before descriptive words.

Estar is used to describe a temporary condition or change from the expected norm.

> Mrs. Gómez is an excellent housekeeper, but her friend Sofía arrives early one morning before she has had time to clean things up. *¡Qué sucia está la casa hoy!* she thinks to herself.

> Diego dwells among a seemingly uninhabitable jumble of clothes, games, pictures, etc. But one day he decides to clean up his room to surprise his mother. *¡Qué limpio está tu cuarto!* exclaims his mother upon seeing the room.

Ser describes a characteristic or the expected norm. The people who know Mrs. Gómez and Diego would say:

> La casa de la señora Gómez es limpia.
> El cuarto de Diego es sucio.

EXERCISE

Complete each sentence with the appropriate form of either *estar* or *ser*, depending upon the situation described.

1. Mi hermano aprende muy rápidamente. Mi hermano

   _____ inteligente.

2. Mis hermanitos tienen dos años y tres años. Mis hermanitos

   _____ muy jóvenes.

3. Mamá ha trabajado todo el día en una fábrica. Mamá

   _____ muy cansada ahora.

4. Rosa tiene una personalidad muy alegre, pero acaba de salir mal en un

   examen. Rosa _____ triste.

5. El señor González no tiene muchos años pero ha sufrido un ataque de

   corazón. Cuando lo vi después del ataque pensé, "¡Qué viejo

   _____ él!"

6. Todos los miembros de la familia están sentados en la mesa comiendo

   torta. "¡Qué rica _____ esta torta!" dice Pepito. "Sí,"

   responde mamá, "esta clase de torta de chocolate _____

   sabrosa."

7. Dorotea va a un baile. Cuando sale, papá le dice a su mamá, "¡Qué

   bonita _____ esta noche con ese vestido!"

8. Joselito sabe que la nieve _____ blanca. Por eso cuando va al centro y ve la nieve sucia exclama, "Mira, mamá, ¡la nieve aquí _____ negra!"

9. No voy a tomarme este café. _____ frío.

10. Las aguas de Hot Springs _____ calientes.

GOAL 5

To use *estar* with the imperfective participle to form the progressive and to use *ser* with nouns, time, dates, and impersonal expressions.

Estar combines with verbs ending in *-ando* or *-iendo* to form the progressive.

Estoy escribiendo.   *I am writing.*
Estábamos esperando.   *We were waiting.*

Ser is used in most other cases, such as the following:

- Telling who or what
  El señor Fernández es médico.

- Telling time
  ¿Qué hora es? Son las diez.

- Telling the date
  ¿Cuál es la fecha? Es el tres de diciembre.

- Impersonal expressions
  Es necesario comer para vivir.

EXERCISE

Complete each sentence with the appropriate form of *estar* or *ser*.

1. _____ interesante viajar a países extranjeros.

2. Hoy _____ el veinte de noviembre.

3. ¿Qué hora _____ cuando ustedes regresan?

4. Ahora (ellos) _____ discutiendo el voto.

5. Esto no _____ legal.

6. Yo _____ alumno de la universidad.

7. (Nosotros) _____ discutiendo la eutanasia.

8. ¿Qué hora _____? _____ las tres. No, perdón. _____ la una.

9. _____ difícil subirles el salario a todos los obreros.

10. Ayer _____ martes.

Communication Pattern Exercise

Work with a partner. Takes turns asking and answering the questions.

1. ¿Estás sentado o de pie?

2. ¿Eres de Arizona? ¿De dónde eres?

3. ¿Cómo se le pregunta a Pablo si está sentado o de pie?

4. ¿Cómo se le pregunta a una señora si es de los Estados Unidos?

5. ¿Qué tienes que sea de plástico? ¿De algodón? ¿De lana?

6. ¿Es del profesor el libro que tienes?

7. ¿Está tu casa cerca de aquí?

8. ¿Dónde son los partidos de básquetbol? ¿Cuándo son?

9. ¿Está cerrada la puerta? ¿Por quién fue cerrada?

10. ¿Estás enojado? ¿Cansado? ¿Triste? ¿Feliz?

11. ¿Es americano el profesor? ¿Alto? ¿Modesto? ¿Pesimista? ¿Optimista?

12. ¿Están ustedes hablando ahora? ¿Escribiendo? ¿Comiendo?

13. ¿Estás durmiendo? ¿Mirando la televisión? ¿Caminando?

14. ¿Eres alumno bueno? ¿Regular? ¿Diligente? ¿Mediocre?

15. ¿Es fácil recibir una "A" en esta clase? ¿En qué clases es fácil?

16. ¿Es fácil dormir en clase y recibir una "A"?

17. ¿Es la una? ¿Qué hora es?

18. ¿Qué día es hoy? ¿Cuál es la fecha?

Actividades de comunicación

Contesta las siguientes preguntas. Amplifica tus respuestas para dar una presentación oral, para conversar con un(a) compañero(a) de clase or para escribir un párrafo.

1. Tu familia—¿Cuántos son ustedes? ¿Cómo son ustedes? ¿Qué son ustedes? ¿De dónde son ustedes? ¿Dónde están todos ahora? ¿Cómo están todos ahora?

2. Tus clases y tu cuarto o apartamento—¿Dónde son? ¿Cómo son? ¿Dónde está? ¿De qué color es? ¿De qué es?

3. La hora y la fecha—¿Qué hora es? ¿Cuál es la fecha? ¿En qué día es su cumpleaños? ¿A qué hora son sus clases? ¿A qué hora son las comidas?

Refrán

En la tardanza suele estar el peligro.
Más vale estar solo que mal acompañado.
Explica el sentido. Da ejemplos de la vida.

2 Haber

To use *haber* as a helper verb.

In Spanish perfect forms are used to describe actions completed by a certain time. The helper verb *haber* indicates the time.

- Action is completed at the present (present perfect)

  He comido.   *I have eaten.*

- Action will be completed by some point in the future (future perfect)

  Dice que **habrá comido** para las ocho.   *He says he **will have eaten** by eight.*

- Action was completed at some point in the past (past perfect)

  Había comido cuando llegaron.   *I **had eaten** when they arrived.*

- Action would be completed by some point future from the past (conditional perfect)

  Dijo que **habría comido** antes del partido.   *He said he **would have eaten** before the game.*

EXERCISES

Complete each sentence by supplying the appropriate form of *haber*.

I. *Present perfect*

1. ¿Cumples el semestre? No, ya lo _____*he*_____ cumplido.

2. ¿Llaman ustedes esta tarde? No, ya _____ llamado.

3. ¿Hacemos más? No, ustedes ya _____ hecho bastante.

4. ¿Digo más? No, tú ya _____ dicho demasiado.

5. ¿Vende Alejandro sus esquíes este verano? No, ya las _____ vendido.

6. ¿Escriben la tarea? No, ya la _____ escrito.

II. *Future perfect*

1. ¿Pedirán ustedes permiso? Sí, _____*habremos*_____ pedido permiso para mañana.

2. ¿Recogerás el alquiler? Sí, _____ recogido todo el alquiler para esta tarde.

3. ¿Comenzaremos pronto? Sí, ustedes _____ comenzado para las dos.

4. ¿Veré una corrida de toros? Sí, antes de volver usted _____ visto una corrida.

5. ¿Extenderán esa carretera? Sí, la _____ extendido hasta este punto.

6. ¿Conocerá a muchos españoles? Sí, dentro de dos semanas _____ conocido a muchos.

III. *Past perfect*

1. ¿Comió María con ustedes? No, ya ___*había*___ comido.

2. ¿Viste ese programa anoche? No, ya lo _____ visto.

3. ¿Hicieron ustedes lo que les pedi? _____ hecho bastante.

4. ¿Llevamos toda la basura? Sí, ustedes _____ llevado toda.

5. ¿Indiqué la ruta mejor? Sí, _____ indicado la mejor.

6. ¿Huyeron con el dinero? Sí, _____ huído con todo.

IV. *Conditional perfect*

1. ¿Dijo que esperaría dos horas? No, o ___*habría*___ esperado más.

2. ¿Dijeron que saldrían el veinte? No, o _____ salido ayer.

3. ¿Dijeron ustedes que pondrían el tocadiscos? No, o lo _____ puesto en seguida.

4. ¿Dijiste que vendrías a la reunión anoche? No, o _____ venido.

5. ¿Dijimos que subiríamos la escalera? No, o ustedes _____ subido sin quejarse.

6. ¿Dije que sabría la respuesta? No, o tú la _____ sabido sin duda.

GOAL 2

To use *haber* as a main verb.

- *Haber* is used to describe weather conditions that are seen.

¡Qué luna tan romántica **hay** esta noche!	*What a romantic moon **there** **is** tonight!*
Había un sol brillante.	*There **was** a bright sun.*

- *Haber* is used to express "there is," "there are," "there was," "there were," etc. In English we use both a singular and a plural form. In Spanish only the singular form is used. This structure may be used in any tense, but not with a definite article.

Hay un sofá en la sala.	*There is a sofa in the living room.*
También hay tres sillas.	*There are also three chairs.*
Hay un examen hoy.	*There is a test today.*
Hubo uno ayer y habrá otro mañana.	*There was one yesterday and there will be another tomorrow.*

- *Haber* is used with *que* followed by an infinitive to mean *es necesario*.

Hay que salir a las diez. Es necesario salir a las diez.

EXERCISE

Complete each sentence with the appropriate form of *haber*.

1. Juan mira por la ventana y grita, "Mamá, _____ sol. Podemos ir al parque para un picnic."

2. Hijo mío, entiendo tus dificultades. Yo sé que no es fácil pero _____ estudiar mucho para sacar buenas notas.

3. Según el horario _____ dos partidos aquí la semana que viene.

4. Juana, ¿_____ algo que comer?

5. Chico, leer es mi pasatiempo favorito. ¿_____ una biblioteca en esta ciudad?

6. No llueve mucho por aquí durante el verano, ¿verdad? Es verdad. _____ mucho polvo por todas partes.

Communication Pattern Exercise

Work with a partner. Take turns asking and answering the questions.

1. ¿Había luna anoche?
2. ¿Cree usted que habrá sol mañana?
3. ¿Hay nubes hoy?
4. ¿Hay que prestar atención en las clases?
5. ¿Hay que hablar español en esta clase?
6. ¿Hay que ganar dinero para vivir?
7. ¿Hay más de mil alumnos en esta escuela?
8. ¿Hay otra escuela en esta ciudad?

Actividades de comunicación

Contesta las preguntas. Amplifica tus respuestas tanto como sea posible.

I. En tu vida ¿qué tienes que hacer? ¿Antes de las clases? ¿Durante el día de clases? ¿Después de las clases? ¿Los fines de semana?

II. ¿Qué hay en tu cuarto, tu casa, tu escuela, tu ciudad? Dile a un(a) compañero(a) de clase lo que hay en un cuarto, un edificio o una calle para averiguar si sabe acertar qué es.

III. ¿Qué diversiones hay en tu comunidad? Prepara una lista de diversiones populares y entrevista a un(a) compañero(a) de clase según los ejemplos.
1. Hay un cine. ¿Has visto la película que dan ahora?
2. Hay una cancha de tenis. ¿Has jugado al tenis en ella?

Refrán

No hay atajo sin trabajo.
Nada hay oculto entre cielo y tierra.
Explica el sentido. Da ejemplos de la vida.

---

3 Hacer

To use the verb *hacer* to describe weather conditions.

Hacer is used impersonally to describe the weather.

¿Qué tiempo hace?	*How's the weather?*
Hace buen (mal) tiempo.	*It's good (bad) weather.*
Hace frío (calor).	*It's cold (hot).*

One problem in learning to use *hacer* with weather expressions is that speakers of English have difficulty expressing the concept of "very." For weather expressions, the equivalent Spanish word is *mucho*.

Hace mucho calor.	*It is very hot.*
Hace mucho viento en Pike's Peak.	*It is very windy on Pike's Peak.*

Hacer is not used with *llover* ("to rain") and *nevar* ("to snow").

Llueve en la primavera y nieva en el invierno.

EXERCISE

Answer the following questions in Spanish.
1. ¿Cómo te diviertes cuando hace mal tiempo?
2. ¿Qué haces cuando hace buen tiempo?
3. Donde vives tú, ¿Qué tiempo hace en la primavera?
4. ¿Qué tiempo hace en el verano?
5. ¿Qué tiempo hace en el otoño?
6. ¿Qué tiempo hace en el invierno?

GOAL 2

To use the verb *hacer* to describe continuing actions.

Hacer is used in a set pattern to express an action that began sometime in the past and that has continued.

- With a present verb form

  Hace una hora **que estudio** esta lección.

  Estudio esta lección **desde hace** una hora.

  I have been studying this lesson for an hour.

- With an imperfect verb form

  Hacía una hora **que estudiaba** esa lección.

  Estudiaba esa lección **desde hacía** una hora.

  I had been studying that lesson for an hour.

- With a preterite verb form (In this pattern *hace* means "ago.")

  Hace tres días **que salieron.**   *They **left** three days **ago.***

  Salieron desde hace tres días.

- Do not confuse these *hace* expressions with the use of *desde. Desde* is used to express a certain point in time at which the action began.

  Estudio desde las tres.   *I **have been studying since** three.*

  Estudiaba desde las tres.   *I **had been studying since** three.*

EXERCISE

Write sentences with *hace* or *desde* expressions to describe each situation.

1. Los candidatos empezaron el debate a la una menos quince. Ya es la una.

   a. *(Stress how long ago they began.)*

   _____

   b. *(Stress how long they have been talking.)*

   _____

   c. *(Stress the point from which they have been talking.)*

   _____

2. Manuel empezó a enfrentarse a la realidad cuando estaba en el primer año de la universidad. Ya está en el cuarto año. Sigue ejerciendo esa actitud.

   a. *(Stress how long he has been facing reality.)*

   _____

    b. *(Stress the point from which he has had that attitude.)*

---

    c. *(Stress how long ago he began.)*

---

3. Nosotros fuimos a la biblioteca a las siete para leer la tarea. Pero era una tarea muy larga. A las nueve y media todavía leíamos.

    a. *(Stress the point from which we had been reading.)*

---

    b. *(Stress how long we had been reading).*

Communication Pattern Exercise

Work with a partner. Take turns asking and answering the questions.

1. ¿Hace buen tiempo hoy?
2. ¿Hacía mal tiempo ayer?
3. ¿Hace calor hoy?
4. ¿Hacía fresco ayer?
5. ¿Hay sol hoy?
6. ¿Había luna anoche?
7. ¿Hace dos años que estudias el español?
8. ¿Hace una hora que estudias esta lección?
9. ¿Vives en esta ciudad desde hace diez años?
10. ¿Eres estudiante en esta escuela desde hace un año?
11. ¿Estudian ustedes este libro desde septiembre?
12. ¿Están ustedes aquí desde las ocho y media?
13. ¿Hace cuatro horas que saliste de tu cuarto?
14. ¿Hace una hora que hablaste con tu mejor amigo?

Actividades de comunicación

Contesta las siguientes preguntas.

1. ¿Qué tiempo hace hoy?
   ¿Qué tiempo hace en tu ciudad en la primavera? ¿En el verano? ¿En el otoño? ¿En el invierno? ¿Qué tiempo hacía ayer?

2. ¿Cuánto tiempo hace que estudias español? ¿Eres alumno(a) de esta escuela? ¿Vives en esta ciudad? ¿Sigues con otros intereses y actividades que tienes?

3. Describe el clima ideal para ti.

Refrán
Quien siembra vientos recoge tempestades.
Explica el sentido. Da ejemplos de la vida.

4 Tener

GOAL 1

To use expressions with *tener*.

The verb *tener* is used in many Spanish idioms. Some common ones include:

tener—años	*to be—years old*	tener gracia	*to be funny*
tener buena cara	*to look good*	tener gusto	*to have the pleasure of*
tener calor	*to be hot*	tener hambre	*to be hungry*
tener la culpa	*to be to blame*	tener lugar	*to take place*
tener la costumbre	*to be used to*	tener miedo	*to be afraid*
		tener prisa	*to be in a hurry*
tener en cuenta	*to take into consideration*	tener razón	*to be right*
		no tener razón	*to be wrong*
tener cuidado	*to take care*	tener sed	*to be thirsty*
tener éxito	*to be successful*	tener sueño	*to be sleepy*
tener frío	*to be cold*	tener vergüenza	*to be ashamed*

With *tener* expressions, the Spanish equivalent for "very" is *mucho*.

Tengo mucho sueño.   *I am very sleepy.*

EXERCISE

Explain each of the following statements using the appropriate *tener* expression.

1. Quieres tomar un refresco.

   Tienes sed.

2. El niño quiere dormirse.

   _____

3. Abro la ventana porque hace fresco afuera.

   _____

4. Las chicas están muy nerviosas porque andan solas de noche.

   _____

5. Salimos tarde de la casa. Queremos llegar pronto a la estación.

   _____

6. Me molestaba lo que había hecho y no quería decir a nadie lo que pasó.

   _____

7. El alumno dice que dos y dos son tres.

_____

8. Tú debes aceptar la responsabilidad.

_____

9. Vamos a comer inmediatamente.

_____

10. Ellos tienen mucho dinero y posición importante en su pueblo.

_____

11. El niño no es muy grande. Para cruzar la calle mira en las dos direcciones varias veces y corre al otro lado.

_____

GOAL 2

To use *tener deseos de, tener ganas de,* and *tener que* plus an infinitive.

In the following cases the *tener* expression has a different meaning from those previously presented and is followed by an infinitive.

Tenemos deseos de cantar.	*We feel like singing.*
Tengo ganas de ir al cine.	*I feel like going to a movie.*
Tiene que salir para las doce.	*She has to leave by twelve.*

EXERCISE

Complete each sentence using the *tener* expression that corresponds to the cue in parentheses.

1. *(querer)* Berta _____ mirar la televisión.

2. *(es necesario)* Los hijos _____ volver a casa antes de las diez.

3. *(es necesario)* Yo _____ estudiar para un examen mañana.

4. *(querer)* (Nosotros) _____ descansar ahora.

5. *(querer)* ¿_____ (tú) protestar los precios altos?

6. *(es necesario)* Ustedes _____ estacionar el coche al otro lado de la calle.

Communication Pattern Exercise

Work with a partner. Take turns asking and answering the questions.

1. ¿Cuántos años tienes?
2. ¿Tienes frío ahora?
3. ¿Tiene gracia tu amigo?
4. ¿Tienes mucho gusto en conocer a otros estudiantes?
5. ¿Tienen razón siempre tus amigos?
6. ¿Tiene buena cara tu comida?
7. ¿Tienes la costumbre de llegar a tiempo para una cita?
8. ¿Tienen ustedes miedo antes de un examen?
9. ¿Tienen ustedes hambre al mediodía?
10. ¿Tienen ustedes sueño en las clases a veces?
11. ¿Tienes vergüenza cuando sales mal en un examen?
12. Si sales mal en un examen, ¿quién tiene la culpa?
13. ¿Tienes calor ahora?
14. ¿Tienes sed?
15. A veces tu padres no tienen razón, ¿verdad? ¿Y tú también?

Actividades de comunicación

I. Empleando las expresiones de "tener", di tanto como puedas de ti mismo(a), de tu mejor amigo(a) y de los otros estudiantes.

II. Empleando "tener ganas (deseos) de" y "tener que", di tanto como puedas de lo que te gusta hacer y lo que tienes que hacer en la escuela o universidad, por la tarde y los fines de semana.

III. Empleando "estar", "ser" y "tener", describe a alguien de la clase o de la escuela o universidad; luego, a ver si los otros estudiantes pueden averiguar quién es. Haz sólo preguntas que se puedan contestar con "sí" o "no".

Refrán

Tenemos que bailar al son que se toca.
Explica el sentido. Da ejemplos de la vida.

5 Gustar

To use the appropriate form of *gustar*.

In English we say:

I like the movie. **I like** science-fiction movies.

In Spanish one says:

Me gusta la película. **Me gustan** las películas de ciencia ficción.

Note the English and the Spanish patterns. In English we say "I like," and in Spanish one says the equivalent of "It pleases me" or "they please me." There is at least one verb in English that functions in the same way as the *gustar* construction in Spanish. For example, if someone asks us what we think of some work, we may say, "It seems OK to me." If someone asks us what we think of the plans, we may say, "They seem fine to me." The Spanish verb *parecer* expresses the equivalent idea.

¿Qué **le parece** el trabajo?	*What **do you think** of the work?*
Me parece bien.	*It seems fine to me.*
¿Qué **le parecen** los planes?	*What **do you think** of the plans?*
Me parecen bien.	*They seem fine to me.*

The verb *gustar* functions in exactly the same pattern.

¿Te gusta la película?	*Do you like the movie?*
*Si, **me gusta** mucho.*	*Yes, I like it a lot.*
¿Te gustan las películas de ciencia ficción?	*Do you like science-fiction movies?*
Sí, me gustan mucho.	*Yes, I like them a lot.*
¿Te gusta jugar al golf?	*Do you like to play golf?*
Sí, **me gusta** jugar al golf y esquiar.	*Yes, I like to play golf and ski.*

Note that the use of the *él* or *ellos* form of the verb is determined by the word that indicates what is liked.

Other verbs that follow the same pattern include:

doler(ue) *to hurt—*
    duele/duelen

hacer falta *to need—*
    hace/hacen

encantar *to delight—*
    encanta/encantan

parecer *to seem—*
    parece/parecen

quedar *to have left—*
    queda/quedan

interesar *to interest—*
    interesa/interesan

fascinar *to fascinate—*
    fascina/fascinan

gustar *to like—*
    gusta/gustan

EXERCISE

Complete each sentence with the appropriate form of the verb.

1. ¿Te *(gustar)* _____ manejar el auto?

2. Sí, y me *(gustar)* _____ más manejarlo cuando papá no está.

3. ¿Le *(parecer)* _____ pequeños los cuadros?

4. Cuando a Luisa le *(doler)* _____ los pies, se sienta.

5. ¿Cuánto dinero les *(hacer falta)* _____ para comprar un coche?

6. Sí, a ellos les *(gustar)* _____ ir de paseo.

7. Sólo nos *(quedar)* _____ unos minutos antes del timbre.

8. ¿Les *(gustar)* _____ los deportes?

9. ¿A ellos les *(gustar)* _____ esta universidad? Sí, les *(gustar)* _____.

10. ¿A tí te *(gustar)* _____ los dulces? Sí, sí me *(gustar)* _____.

GOAL 2

To use the appropriate indirect object pronoun with the *gustar* pattern.

Indirect object pronouns are used to indicate the person liking, thinking, hurting, needing, etc.

yo	**Me** falta un libro.	*I need a book.*
tú	¿**Te** hace falta un lápiz?	*Do **you** need a pencil?*
usted	¿**Le** hacen falta servilletas?	*Do **you** need napkins?*
él	*Le* hacen falta más.	**He** *needs more.*
ella	**Le** hacen falta dos.	***She** needs two.*
nosotros, -as	**Nos** hace falta un coche.	***We** need a car.*
vosotros, -as	¿**Os** hacen falta éstos?	*Do **you** need these?*
ustedes	**Les** hace falta una bicicleta.	***You** need a bike.*
ellos	**Les** hacen falta cinco.	***They** need five.*
ellas	**Les** hace falta dinero.	***They** need money.*

Complete each sentence with the appropriate indirect object pronoun to refer to the person indicated.

1. *(vosotros)* Sí, _____ queda una hora más.

2. *(tú)* ¿_____ duelen los dientes?

3. *(María)* Sí, _____ gusta patinar sobre el hielo.

4. *(ellos)* No, no _____ hace falta nada.

5. *(yo)* Sí, _____ quedan dos cosas que hacer.

6. *(ustedes)* No, no _____ gustan los programas.

7. *(Los García)* Si, _____ hace falta dinero.

8. *(él)* No, no _____ duele el estómago.

9. *(usted)* Sí, _____ parecen justos los castigos.

10. *(nosotros)* No, no _____ gusta el arte moderno.

GOAL 3

To use a noun with the *gustar* pattern.

When the name of the person or persons liking, needing, having left, etc. is included in a *gustar* construction, it must be preceded by *a*. A pronoun used as the object of a preposition may be used for emphasis.

Le quedan cinco minutos.	*He has five minutes left.*
A Pedro le quedan cinco minutos.	***Pedro** has five minutes left.*
Me gusta.	*I like it.*
A mí me gusta.	***I** like it.*

EXERCISE

Write complete sentences in Spanish using the person, verb, and object indicated. A noun used in a general sense must be preceded by a definite article.

1. todos/gustar/vacaciones

   A todos les gustan las vacaciones.

2. Lola/hacer falta/tiempo

3. nuestra familia/parecer/interesante/religión

4. chico/doler/dientes

5. mí/gustar/filosofia oriental

6. Raúl y Pepe/quedar/semana

_____

7. señorita Fernández/hacer falta/empleo

_____

GOAL 4

To reply in agreement or disagreement to a *gustar* statement.

To respond in agreement or disagreement to a statement containing a *gustar* construction, one uses the pattern *a* + a pronoun to refer to the person.

Positive statement	*Negative statement*
Me falta dinero.	No le gusta el yoga.
a. A mí también. *Me too.*	a. A mí tampoco. *Me neither.*
b. A mí no. *Not me.*	b. A mí sí. *I do.*

EXERCISE

Respond to each statement using *a* + *mí, ti, usted, él, ella, nosotros, vosotros, ustedes, ellos,* or *ellas.*

1. No me gusta leer. ¿Y a ti? *(No te gusta leer.)*

   A mí tampoco. _____

2. No me gusta levantarme. ¿Y a sus padres? *(Les gusta levantarse.)*

   _____

3. Me hace falta una oportunidad. ¿Y a Mariano? *(No le hace falta una oportunidad.)*

   _____

4. Te queda otro. ¿Y a mí? *(Me queda otro.)*

   _____

5. No nos parece mentirosa. ¿Y a ustedes? *(No les parece mentirosa.)*

   _____

6. Me duelen los pies. ¿Y a los otros? *(Les duelen los pies.)*

   _____

7. No les queda nada. ¿Y a nosotros? *(Nos queda algo.)*

   _____

8. Me gusta la música clásica. ¿Y a tu amiga? *(No le gusta.)*

   _____

Communication Pattern Exercise

In answering questions one may or may not repeat the thing liked, needed, etc.

¿Le gusta el programa?
Sí, me gusta.   *Yes, I like it.*
Sí, me gusta el programa.   *Yes, I like the program.*

¿Le gustan los discos?
No, no me gustan.   *No, I do not like them.*
No, no me gustan los discos.   *No, I do not like the records.*

Work with a partner. Take turns asking and answering the questions.

1. ¿Te gusta ir al cine?
2. ¿A usted le gusta viajar?
3. ¿Te parece justo hacer chuletas?
4. ¿Le quedan más ejercicios que hacer?
5. Profesor, ¿me queda más tiempo?
6. Profesora, ¿me hacen falta más papeles?
7. Mamá, ¿me gustaban las legumbres?
8. Mamá, ¿me dolía la cabeza?
9. ¿Le parece bueno el apartamento a ella?
10. ¿Le gustan los muebles a él?
11. ¿Les gusta a ustedes dar un paseo por el parque?
12. ¿Os gusta jugar a las cartas?
13. ¿Les gustan a ustedes las playas de la costa?
14. ¿Os gusta el café con leche?
15. Profesor, ¿nos quedan otros ejercicios que escribir?
16. Señora, ¿nos hará falta un abrigo en la cueva?
17. Papá, ¿nos parecía posible la reencarnación?
18. Carlota, ¿nos gustaba disfrazarnos para las fiestas de Carnaval?
19. ¿Les duele la cabeza a Juan y a José?
20. ¿Les gustan los vestidos a las señoritas?

Actividades de comunicación

Escribe un párrafo de media página o una conversación de una página o discute con un(a) compañero(a) de clase lo siguiente:

- Lo que te gusta y no te gusta
- Lo que le gusta y no le gusta a tu familia
- Lo que les gusta y no les gusta a tus amigos
- Lo que te hace falta y no te hace falta
- Lo que le hace falta y no le hace falta a tu familia
- Lo que les hace falta y no les hace falta a tus amigos

Refrán   Ojos que no ven, corazón que no siente.
Explica el sentido. Da ejemplos de la vida.

6 Verbs Meaning "to Become"; Conocer vs. Saber; Pedir vs. Preguntar

GOAL 1
To understand Spanish equivalents of "become."

The meaning of the common English expression "to become" varies considerably from one context to another.

They became friends.   He became (got) lost.

She became a lawyer.   We became sad.

The decision became a public issue.

Instead of using one word, Spanish speakers tend to use different words, each with a specific usage.

The Spanish equivalents for the most common English uses of "become" are as follows:

- *llegar a ser*—used to describe the culmination of a lengthy process
  Llegó a ser presidente.   *He **became** president.*

- *hacerse*—used to describe the result of one's desires or efforts
  Se hizo abogada.   *She **became** a lawyer.*

- *ponerse*—used with an adjective to describe an emotional or physical change
  Te pusiste roja.   *You blushed (**became** red).*

- *volverse*—used with an adjective to describe a drastic, a lasting, an unexpected, or a sudden change
  Se volvió loco.   *He **became** demented.*

- *convertirse en*—used to describe change in nature
  Se convertirá en un gas.   *It will **become** a gas.*

- *ser de* or *hacerse de*—used to ask what happened to something or someone
  ¿Qué **es de** Juan?   *What **has become** of John?*
  (¿Qué **se ha hecho de** Juan?)

- *reflexives*—used to describe a physical or phychological change
  Se enfermaron en el viaje.   *They got (**became**) sick
  on the trip.*

EXERCISES

I. Study the following sentences, and give the English "become" equivalent of each of the cued verbs on the line.

1. Despues de la operación mi padre *se cansó* rápidamente.

   _____

2. Mamá, ¿qué *se ha hecho* de la guía de teléfono? _____

3. Resultado de mucho entrenamiento *se hizo* uno de los mejores jugadores del equipo. _____

4. No importa lo que pasa. Mi amiga *se pone* deprimida.

   _____

5. Sí, *se puso* enfermo anoche durante la fiesta. _____

6. El pobre *se volvió* incapaz de pensar claramente. _____

7. Las hojas *se vuelven* rojas en octubre. _____

8. Pasó ocho años de vicepresidente antes de *llegar a ser* el Presidente del país. _____

9. Ghandi *llegó a ser* muy famoso, pero nunca *se hizo* rico.

   _____   _____

10. El agua *se convirtió* en hielo. _____

11. Inmediatamente, todo *se volvió* silencioso. _____

12. El jugo de las uvas *se ha hecho* vino. _____

13. Claro, todos *se entristecen* a veces, pero pronto *nos ponemos* contentos.

    _____   _____

14. *Se quedó* ciego a causa de la enfermedad. _____

15. Mi hermana *cumplirá* 21 años la semana que viene.

    _____

16. Las orugas *se transforman* en mariposas. _____

17. El principe *subió* al trono. _____

18. ¿Qué *ha sido de* los demás? _____

II. Complete the following synopsis of the rise and fall of Mr. López, an insurance agent, using the appropriate Spanish words and phrases to say "become."

El señor López era muy pobre, pero tenía un apetito tremendo para el dinero. Era tímido y le costaba trabajo hablar con desconocidos. Al ser presentado a alguien, siempre _____ turbado y no sabía que decir. Sin embargo, tomó un curso para darse a sí mismo mucha confianza. Aprendió todo y en su corazón creyó lo que le dijeron. Con mucha práctica y dedicación _____ un excelente agente de seguros. Vendió pólizas que valían más de un millón de dólares cada año. Fue miembro del "Million Dollar Club." Despacio pero sin duda comenzó a subir en la jerarquía administrativa de la compañía. Un día, después de quince años de trabajo superior, _____ director de la compañía. Estaba orgulloso de su éxito, pero sentía la presión de su posición. Comenzó a tomar más y más alcohol. En un año _____ alcohólico y perdió su posición. ¡Pobre señor López pobre!

GOAL 2

To distinguish between uses of *conocer* and *saber*.

"To know" is another common expression in English that may be used with different meanings and in different contexts.

We know this town like the back of our hand.

We know how to take care of ourselves.

Do you know the leader of the labor party?

Do you know where to get help if you are in trouble?

In Spanish *conocer* is used with people, places, or things with which one can be acquainted. *Saber* is used with nouns about which one can have information or with verbs to mean "to know how to" do something. The Spanish equivalents of the verbs in the previous English examples would be as follows:

Conocemos esta ciudad . . .

Sabemos cuidarnos . . .

Conocen ustedes al líder . . .

Saben ustedes dónde conseguir socorro . . .

EXERCISES

I. Read each sentence carefully. Then write the appropriate form of *saber* or *conocer* to express the idea of the English verb "know".

1. Do you know who is in charge of the meeting this evening?

   _____

2. Do you know the chairman of this meeting? _____

3. They know the bureaucratic system very well. _____

4. They know how to get what they want. _____

5. Do you know the works of Cervantes? _____

6. Do you know the name of Don Quijote's squire? _____

7. Do you know what the squire symbolizes? _____

8. We know the central region of Spain, but we have not traveled in the

   southern part. _____

9. I don't know how it works. _____

10. I know they love me. _____

II. Write eight complete sentences in Spanish using each subject twice, once with the appropriate form of *conocer* and once with the appropriate form of *saber*. Pick any objects from the list to complete the sentences.

yo
los mayores
nosotras
mi amigo
ese libro
dónde están las llaves
las teorías de los terroristas
llevarse bien con los vecinos
a los otros miembros del comité
bien el centro

su dirección
jugar al golf
quienes son los vándalos
a la autora
la Ciudad de México
el objeto de las manifestaciones
lo que quieren los otros
los planes de los espías
a Raúl y a Berta

1. _____

2. _____

3. _____

4. _____

5. _____

6. _____

7. _____

8. _____

GOAL 3

To distinguish between uses of *pedir* and *preguntar*.

Pedir and *preguntar* both mean "to ask." *Pedir* means to order or to ask for something. *Preguntar* means to ask in the sense of asking someone for information. *Hacer una pregunta* means to ask a question.

Piden hamburguesas, papas fritas y batidos.	They **order** hamburgers, french fries, and shakes.
Siempre me **piden** el coche los viernes por la noche.	The always **ask** me **for** the car on Friday nights.
Cuando no sabe, **pregunta** a los profesores.	When she does not know, she **asks** the professors.
El niño le **hace** muchas **preguntas** a su madre.	The child **asks** his mother a lot of questions.

EXERCISE

Underline the phrase that correctly expresses the meaning of the sentence.

1. No sé. (Pide/Pregunta/Haz una pregunta) a esa señora.

2. ¿Qué responden tus padres cuando les (pides/preguntas/haces una pregunta) más dinero?

3. Creía que ustedes iban a (pedir/preguntar/hacer una pregunta) una comida mexicana.

4. ¿Por qué no (piden/preguntan/hacen preguntas) en la conferencia si no comprenden lo que quiere decir el conferenciante?

5. Vamos a (pedirle/preguntarle/hacerle una pregunta) si es periodista.

6. Se dice que es más difícil y más importante (pedir/preguntar/hacer una pregunta) que contestar.

7. Me (pidió/preguntó/hizo una pregunta) dónde viven mis padres.

8. Siempre te doy lo que me (pides/preguntas/haces una pregunta), ¿no?

Communication Pattern Exercise

Work with a partner. Take turns asking and answering the questions.

1. ¿Quieres llegar a ser Presidente de los Estados Unidos? ¿De una universidad? ¿De una compañía grande? ¿Qué quieres llegar a ser?

2. ¿Quieres hacerte una persona intelectual? ¿Popular? ¿Simpática? ¿Independiente?

3. A veces ¿te pones deprimido? ¿Confundido? ¿Enojado? ¿Irritado? ¿Celoso? ¿Cuándo?

4. ¿Te cansas fácilmente? ¿Te enfermas mucho? ¿Te enojas a veces?

5. ¿A quién conoces mejor? ¿Te conoces bien a ti mismo? ¿Te conocen bien a tus padres?

6. ¿Sabes lo que quieres ser en el futuro? ¿Qué quieres ser?

7. ¿Sabes jugar al golf? ¿Al tenis? ¿Al básquetbol? ¿Al fútbol?

8. ¿Sabes la diferencia entre el capitalismo y el socialismo? ¿Un presidente y un rey? ¿Un senador y un representante? ¿Un conservador y un liberal?

9. ¿Haces muchas preguntas? ¿A quiénes? ¿De qué?

10. ¿Que pides cuando vas a un restaurante? ¿Qué piden tus hermanos? ¿Tus padres?

Actividades de comunicación

I. ¿Qué es el éxito? ¿Qué significa tener éxito? Parece que hay tantas definiciones como hay individuos. Define que es el éxito, en tu opinión, y luego selecciona las siete posibilidades que te atraen más y las siete que no te interesan nada. Compara tus selecciones con las de un(a) compañero(a) de clase. Hablen ustedes de los elementos más básicos del éxito.

A. Descubrir una cura para una enfermedad como el cáncer.

B. Inventar un aparato beneficioso como un motor que use una energía inagotable y que no dañe el ambiente.

C. Ser un líder político.

D. Tener muchísimo dinero posiblemente ganando el premio gordo de una lotería.

E. Ser alguien famoso.

F. Escribir un libro clásico.

G. Poder hacer algo mejor que nadie como correr una milla en tres minutos y treinta segundos.

H. Ser feliz.

I. Tener un cuerpo sano y una mente sana.

J. Obtener el doctorado en tu especialidad académica.

K. Vivir por cien años.

L. Ser popular y no tener enemigos.

M. Asistir a muchas fiestas.

N. Ayudar a los otros como a los pobres.

O. Vivir en una casa grande con una piscina.

P. Casarme con un hombre, o mujer, simpático(a) que me ame.

Q. No tener ninguna preocupación nunca.

R. Obtener un empleo en que haya muchas oportunidades y muchos desafíos.

S. No tener que trabajar nunca.

T. Ir al cine o mirar la televisión todos los días.

U. Mantener la fe religiosa.

V. Trabajar para mantener, o cambiar, el sistema político y económico.

W. Tener hijos que sean responsables y que tengan éxito.

X. Siempre tener amigos interesantes y fieles.

Y. Viajar por todo el mundo.

Z. (Otros que escojas tú.)

¿En qué es diferente tu lista de la de los otros miembros de la clase? ¿Cuáles son algunas posibilidades populares que no te parecen importantes? ¿Cuáles son algunos objetivos relacionados específicamente con la vida estudiantil?

II. Escribe una composición de media página sobre los consejos.
¿A quiénes les pides consejos? ¿Qué preguntas haces más? ¿Quién te pide consejos? ¿Qué preguntas te hacen más? ¿Cuáles son los problemas más difíciles de los estudiantes y con quiénes hablan para resolver o aliviar estas dificultades?

Refrán

No hay peor ciego que el que no quiere ver.
Explica el sentido. Da ejemplos de la vida.

PART V

Verb Phrases

Introduction A sentence consists of a noun phrase and a verb phrase. The verb phrase is made up of a verb plus any words that tell something about the verb. The basic patterns are as follows:

1. Verb	Juan **habla.**
2. Verb + noun	Juan **habla español.**
	Juan **es estudiante.**
3. Verb + adjective	Juan **es inteligente.**
4. Pronoun + verb	Juan **lo habla.**
5. Verb + verb form	Juan **desea hablar.**
6. Verb + verb form + pronoun	Juan **desea hablarlo.**
7. Verb + adverb	Juan **habla rápidamente.**
8. Verb + prepositional phrase	Juan **habla en casa.**
9. Verb + clause	Juan **habla cuando sabe.**

Two important considerations must be kept in mind while studying verbs and verb phrases. First, word order is important. Second, agreement is necessary. The verb changes suffixes to agree with the subject of the sentence. Adjectives and pronouns change suffixes and forms to agree with the words to which they refer. Words that describe verbs—adverbs—and words used to connect one part of the sentence to another do not follow the basic pattern of agreement. Generally, they have only one form.

This part of the text deals with indirect objects, object pronouns, adverbs and adverbial phrases, and prepositions.

Indirect object:	Lo di *a mi hermanito.*	*I gave it **to my little brother.***
Object pronoun:	*Nos* llevaron a casa.	*They took **us** home.*
Adverb:	Estudian *con cuidado* el mapa.	*They're studying the map **carefully.***
Preposition:	Están *en* la sala.	*They're **in** the living room.*

1 Indirect Objects

GOAL 1

To use the pattern *a* + noun to refer to an indirect object.

There may be two objects in a sentence: a direct object and an indirect object. The direct object receives the action of the verb. The indirect object indicates the person or object interested in the verb and the direct object.

	d.o.	
Pepe escribió	**una carta.**	*Pepe wrote **a letter**.*

	d.o.	**i.o.**	
Pepe escribió	**una carta**	**a su madre.**	*Pepe wrote **a letter to his mother**.*

In the above examples, "a letter" is what Pepe wrote and "mother" is the person interested in the letter he wrote.

Indirect object pronouns are commonly used with these verbs:

comprar	explicar
dar	mandar
decir	pedir
enseñar	preguntar
entregar	quitar
escribir	robar

EXERCISES

I. Form complete sentences using the cues given and adding any other necessary words.

1. profesor/enseñar/libro/estudiantes

    El profesor enseña el libro a los estudiantes.

2. Juan/dar/regalo/novia

    _____

3. chico/quitar/juguetes/hermanos

    _____

4. madre/escribir/carta/hijo

    _____

5. Marta/comprar/discos/José

    _____

6. bandido/robar/acciones/señor

    _____

II. Using the words in the chart in any combination, write at least six sentences according to the following pattern: noun phrase + verb + direct object + indirect object.

Noun phrase	Verb	Direct object	Indirect object
dentista	explicar	problema	María
profesores	dar	coche	clase
nosotros	sacar	diente	señor
yo	enseñar	bicicleta	señora
papá	comprar	tarea	amigos
hermanos	vender	regalo	chicas
tú	escribir	tarjeta postal	padres

1. _____

2. _____

3. _____

4. _____

5. _____

6. _____

GOAL 2

To substitute *le* or *les* for *a* + noun.

Le is the indirect object pronoun used to refer to a singular object of interest, and *les* is used to refer to a plural object of interest. Note that indirect object pronouns usually precede the verb.

¿Al profesor? Sí, **le** di la tarea.   Yes, I gave him the homework.

¿A la profesora? Sí, **le** di la tarea.   Yes, I gave her the homework.

¿A los profesores? Sí, **les** di la tarea.   Yes, I gave them the homework.

¿A las profesoras? Sí, **les** di la tarea.   Yes, I gave them the homework.

EXERCISES

I. Complete each sentence with the appropriate indirect object pronoun.

1. ¿A mis amigos?   Sí, _____ enseñé mi cuarto.

2. ¿A su madre?   Sí, _____ dimos las flores.

3. ¿A ustedes?   Sí, _____ trajo algo.

4. ¿A las chicas?   Sí, _____ quitamos la pasta dentífrica.

5. ¿Al señor?   Sí, _____ robaron el dinero.

6. ¿A Manuela?   Sí, _____ quité la loción para las manos.

7. ¿A usted?   Sí, _____ arregla la cama.

8. ¿A José y a usted? Sí, _____ cambió los boletos.

II. Rewrite each sentence, changing the italicized phrase to an indirect object pronoun and placing it in its proper position in the sentence.

1. El joven robó la cartera *al viejo.*

El joven le robó la cartera.

2. María explicó la situación *a su amiga.*

_____

3. El dentista limpia los dientes *a los pacientes.*

_____

4. Mamá lava la cara *al bebé.*

_____

5. Los padres compraron los muebles *a sus hijas.*

_____

6. El profesor dio una "A" *a Pepe.*

_____

GOAL 3

To use the pattern *le* or *les* with *a* + noun or pronoun in the same sentence.

In English one uses either an indirect object or an indirect object pronoun.

Mother wrote a letter **to Jim.**
She wrote a letter **to him.**
She wrote **him** a letter.

In Spanish both may be used in the same sentence.

Mamá **le** escribió una carta.
Mamá **le** escribió una carta **a Diego.**
Mamá **le** escribió una carta **a él.**

EXERCISE

Answer each question using both an indirect object pronoun and an indirect object.

1. ¿Enseñar la escuela? ¿A los visitantes?

Sí, nosotros ___*Sí, nosotros les enseñamos la escuela a los visitantes.*___

2. ¿Dar esperanza? ¿A los pobres?

Sí, el proyecto _____.

3. ¿Mandar los paquetes? ¿A la familia?

   Sí, Berta _____.

4. ¿Explicar las posibilidades? ¿A él?

   Sí, el director _____.

5. ¿Comprar un boleto? ¿A usted?

   Sí, mi padre _____.

6. ¿Dar la nota? ¿A María?

   Sí, José _____.

7. ¿Arreglar la ropa? ¿A ellos?

   Sí, la criada _____.

Communication Pattern Exercise

Work with a partner. Take turns asking and answering the questions. Answer using both an indirect object pronoun and an indirect object.

1. ¿A quién le enseñas tu cuarto?
2. ¿A quiénes les das regalos?
3. ¿A quién le entregas las tareas?
4. ¿A quiénes les dices tus problemas?
5. ¿A quién le hablas más por teléfono?
6. ¿A quiénes les vendes tus libros?
7. ¿A quién le escribes cartas?

Actividades de comunicación

I. Escribe un párrafo de media página que trate de lo que les compras y les das a los otros. Piensa en los cumpleaños, la Navidad, el Día del Padre, el Día de la Madre y el Día de los Novios. ¿A quiénes les compras regalos? ¿Hay algo típico que les compras? ¿Cuándo y cómo les das los regalos?

II. La comunicación habitual—Muchas veces todos nosotros solemos contestar lo mismo en ciertas situaciones. ¿Qué le dices a la otra persona en las siguientes situaciones?

1. ¿Qué le dices a un(a) amigo(a) cuando te saluda?
2. ¿Qué les dices a tus padres por la mañana?
3. ¿Qué dices al contestar el teléfono?
4. ¿Qué dices al terminar una conversación por teléfono?
5. ¿Qué le dices a tu padre cuando te dice que manejes con cuidado?
6. ¿Qué le dices a tu mamá cuando te pide que te portes bien?

7. ¿Qué le dices a un policía si te pregunta adónde vas tan rápido?

8. ¿Qué les dices a los profesores si te dicen que no estudias bastante?

9. ¿Qué le dices a tu novio(a) si se queja de que no lo (la) llamas bastante?

Refrán   A caballo regalado no hay que mirarle el diente.
Explica el sentido. Da ejemplos de la vida.

---

2 Object Pronouns

GOAL 1

To use the correct object pronoun to refer to *yo, tú, nosotros,* and *vosotros.*

The object pronouns used to refer to *yo, tú, nosotros,* and *vosotros* are as follows:

yo	**me**	*me, to me, for me, from me, myself*
tú	**te**	*you, to you, for you, from you, yourself*
nosotros,-as	**nos**	*us, to us, for us, from us, ourselves*
vosotros,-as	**os**	*you, to you, for you, from you, yourselves*

No distinction is made in Spanish between direct object pronouns, indirect object pronouns, and "self" pronouns referring to *you, tú, nosotros,* and *vosotros.*

Direct object pronoun	**Me** ve.	*He sees **me.***
Indirect object pronoun	**Me** escribió una carta.	*He wrote **me** a letter. (He wrote a letter **to me.** He wrote a letter **for me.**)*
	Me robó el dinero.	*He stole the money **from me.***
"Self" pronoun	**Me** presento.	*I introduce **myself.***

EXERCISE

Complete each sentence with the appropriate pronoun to refer to the person indicated. Give the English equivalent of each sentence.

1. *(tú)* ¿_____*Te*_____ dieron un empleo?

2. *(tú)* ¿_____ hablas a veces?

3. *(tú)* ¿_____ llamó Ana anoche?

4. *(nosotros)* _____ vieron en el supermercado.

5. *(yo)* Carlos _____ trajo un sandwich.

6. *(vosotros)* ¿_____ preparáis para el torneo?

7. *(yo)* Sí, Rodrigo _____ llevó a la fiesta.

8. *(nosotros)* No, no _____ explicaron nada.

9. *(vosotros)* Sí, _____ conozco. ¿Cómo estáis?

10. *(yo)* _____ acuesto cuando estoy cansado.

11. *(vosotros)* ¿_____ habla en español?

12. *(nosotros)* _____ compramos mucha ropa.

GOAL 2

To place *me, te, nos,* and *os* correctly in a sentence.

In English an object pronoun always follows the verb. In Spanish the position varies. The possible positions in the sentence are as follows:

A. With commands

- Positive commands: Díga**nos**   *Tell us.*
- Negative commands: No **nos** diga.   *Don't tell us.*

B. With infinitives and imperfective participles.

Quiere decir**nos**. *or* **Nos** quiere decir.   *He wants to tell us.*

Está diciéndo**nos**. *or* **Nos** está diciendo.   *He is telling us.*

C. With other verb forms

Nos dice.   *He tells us.*

No **nos** dice.   *He doesn't tell us.*

EXERCISE

The object pronouns have been omitted in the following sentence fragments. Complete each sentence by providing the appropriate object pronoun to refer to the person in parentheses and place it in its appropriate position in the sentence.

1. *(nosotros)*   divertimos aquí   _____*Nos divertimos aquí.*_____

2. *(nosotros)*   habla (tú) en inglés   _____

3. *(nosotros)*   Juan no habla mucho   _____

4. *(nosotros)*   el chico no puede decir   _____

5. *(yo)*   explica (tú) este problema   _____

6. *(tú)*   levantas temprano   _____

7. *(tú)*   ¿ayuda María con las tareas?   _____

8. *(vosotros)*   podéis sentar ahora   _____

GOAL 3

To relate these pronouns to the third-person forms.

Me, te, nos, and *os* may function either as direct objects, indirect objects, or "self" pronouns. However, when talking about other people, the system is more differentiated. First, each type of pronoun is expressed by a different word. Second, direct object pronouns have different endings to agree with males and females and to show number.

Object Pronouns

yo	**me**	*me, to me, for me, myself*
tú	**te**	*you, to you, for you, yourself*
nosotros,-as	**nos**	*us, to us, for us, ourselves*
vosotros,-as	**os**	*you, to you, for you, yourselves*

	Direct object pronoun		**Indirect object pronoun**		**"Self" pronoun**	
usted	**lo,**[1] **la**	*you*	**le**	*to or for you*	**se**	*yourself*
él	**lo**[1]	*him*	**le**	*to or for him*	**se**	*himself*
ella	**la**	*her*	**le**	*to or for her*	**se**	*herself*
ustedes	**los,**[2] **las**	*you*	**les**	*to or for you*	**se**	*yourselves*
ellos	**los**[2]	*them*	**les**	*to or for them*	**se**	*themselves*
ellas	**las**	*them*	**les**	*to or for them*	**se**	*themselves*

1. In many parts of the Spanish-speaking world, *le* is also used as a direct object pronoun to refer to *usted* (male) and *él. Lo* will be used throughout this text.
2. *Les* is used as a direct object pronoun in many parts of the Spanish-speaking world to refer to *ustedes* (male) and *ellos. Los* will be used throughout this text.

EXERCISES

I. Answer each question based on the sample sentence.

A. Me llamó anoche.

1. ¿Y a Juan? _____ *Lo llamó también* _____

2. ¿Y a los otros? _____

3. ¿Y a María? _____

4. ¿Y a mí? _____

5. ¿Y a nosotros? _____

6. ¿Y a ellas? _____

B. No me trajo nada.

1. ¿Y al hermano? _____ *No le trajo nada tampoco.* _____

2. ¿Y a vosotros? _____

3. ¿Y a sus amigos? _____

4. ¿Y a mí? _____

5. ¿Y a ella? _____

6. ¿Y a José y a Raúl? _____

C. Me escribo notitas.

1. ¿Y él? _____ *El no se escribe notitas.* _____

2. ¿Y usted? _____

3. ¿Y yo? _____

4. ¿Y sus padres? _____

5. ¿Y Anita? _____

6. ¿Y las chicas? _____

7. ¿Y ustedes? _____

8. ¿Y nosotros? _____

II. Based on the meaning of the verb, the context of the sentence, and the person referred to, complete each sentence with the appropriate object pronoun.

1. *(María)* María _____ presenta al desconocido.

2. *(José)* María _____ presenta a su tío político.

3. *(ellos)* Ellos _____ ven en el espejo.

4. *(ellos)* El profesor _____ explica la diferencia.

5. *(ellos)* El policía _____ vio en el coche.

6. *(tú)* Tú _____ castigas siempre.

7. *(tú)* ¿_____ arregló mamá el asunto?

8. *(tú)* ¿_____ hablaron con cortesía?

9. *(ella)* No _____ diste una calculadora nueva, ¿verdad?

10. *(ella)* Ella _____ compró un vestido anoche.

11. *(ella)* _____ vi en el restaurante anoche.

12. *(usted)* ¿_____ divirtió usted en México?

13. *(usted)* ¿_____ entregan el periódico?

14. *(usted)* ¿_____ llamó anoche?

G O A L   4

To use two object pronouns in the same sentence.

When any two object pronouns are combined in the same sentence, they are arranged in the following order: (1) "self" pronoun; (2) indirect object pronoun; (3) direct object pronoun.

The indirect object pronouns *le* and *les* become *se* when they precede any object pronoun beginning with the letter *l*.

¿Le diste el libro al profesor? Sí, **se lo** di.

¿Le diste las tarjetas a tu mamá? Sí, **se las** di.

¿Le diste los periódicos a los Jiménez? Sí, **se los** di.

¿Les diste la noticia a las señoras? No, no **se la** di.

EXERCISE

Give the English equivalent of the model sentence, then continue writing sentences of the same pattern using object pronouns to refer to the persons and things indicated.

1. Me lo dio ayer.

   He (she) gave it to me yesterday. _____

   a. (a él/los papeles)

   Se los dio ayer. _____

   b. (a ellos/la bandera)

   _____

   c. (a nosotros/las flores)

   _____

   d. (a ti/el mapa)

   _____

   e. (a usted/la posición)

   _____

   f. (a mí/el lápiz)

   _____

2. Me lo presentó.

_____

   a. (a mí/la chica)

_____

   b. (a nosotros/los recién llegados)

_____

   c. (a ti/yo)

_____

   d. (a vosotros/nosotros)

_____

   e. (a ella/el chico)

_____

   f. (a los estudiantes/la señora González)

_____

3. Se me olvidaron las llaves.

_____

   a. (a él)

_____

   b. (a ustedes)

_____

   c. (a nosotros)

_____

   d. (a ti)

_____

   e. (a Juana y a María)

_____

   f. (a mí)

_____

Communication Pattern Exercise

Work with a partner. Read each statement, then take turns asking and answering the questions.

1. Esta mañana se me olvidaron los libros.
   ¿Qué se me olvidó esta mañana? ¿Qué se les olvidó a tus hermanos?
   ¿Se os olvidó apagar las luces? ¿Qué se le olvida más a tu mamá? ¿Se

te olvidaron los libros esta mañana? ¿Qué se le olvidó a tu papá? ¿Qué se olvida más? ¿Qué se les olvida más a tus amigos?

2. Para la Navidad mis padres me dieron diez dólares.
¿Qué me dieron mis padres? ¿Qué le dieron sus padres? ¿Qué les dieron sus padres a sus hermanos? ¿Qué les dieron sus abuelos a ustedes?

3. El dentista me limpió los dientes.
¿Me limpió los dientes el dentista? ¿Te los limpió también? ¿Se los limpió a su madre? ¿Se los limpió a sus hermanos? ¿Se los limpió a ustedes?

4. Hay cinco regalos bajo el árbol de Navidad.
¿Cuántos regalos hay bajo el árbol de Navidad? ¿Quién le dio la bata a mamá? ¿Quién les dio el dinero a sus hermanos? ¿Quién les dio la fruta a ustedes? ¿Quién le dio las camisas a usted? ¿Quién le dio los calcetines a papá?

Actividades de comunicación

I. Entrevista a un(a) compañero(a) de clase sobre el recibir y el dar regalos de Navidad.

1. ¿Qué compraste?
2. ¿A quién se los diste?
3. ¿Qué compraste con tu propio dinero? ¿A quién se lo diste?
4. ¿Qué recibiste? ¿Quién te lo dio?

II. Haz un inventario de algunas posesiones tuyas. ¿Cuántos te compraste? ¿Cuántos te dio alguien? ¿Quiénes te los dieron?

1. camisas
2. pantalones
3. chaquetas
4. zapatos
5. vestidos
6. discos compactos
7. tocadiscos estereofónico
8. carteles
9. dinero
10. cartera/bolsa

Refránes

A quien madruga, Dios le ayuda.
Quien tiene tienda, que la atienda.
Explica el sentido. Da ejemplos de la vida.

3 Adverbs and Adverbial Phrases

GOAL 1

To add the adverbial endings to the adjectival forms.

In both English and Spanish an adverb may be derived from an adjective by adding an adverbial suffix.

Pattern: adjective (feminine singular) + *mente*

| **lento** | **lentamente** | *slow, slowly* |
| **fácil** | **fácilmente** | *easy, easily* |

When there is a series of adverbs that end in *-mente*, *-mente* is used only with the last.

lenta, fácil y cortésmente—*slowly, easily,* and **courteously**

EXERCISE

Complete each sentence with the adverbial form of the given adjective.

1. El rey se vestía *(rico)* _____.
2. Estaba enojado y lo miró *(frio)* _____.
3. Con mi perro yo andaba *(alegre)* _____.
4. Mi papá *(general)* _____ tiene prisa.
5. Me gusta escucharla. Habla *(dulce)* _____.
6. Trabajaban *(desesperado)* _____ como locos.

GOAL 2

To distinguish between words functioning as adverbs and adjectives.

Adverbs have only one form. The endings of adverbs are not changed to agree with the words they modify. Most adjectives, on the other hand, change suffixes to show number,[1] and four-ending adjectives change suffixes to show gender. This contrast presents problems in using the correct word form when the same word or a similar word may be used as an adverb or as an adjective.

- Adjective

  Cuando tiene **muchos** libros que leer tiene **mucha** dificultad.

  *When he has **many** books to read, he has a **lot of** difficulty.*

  Es una cura **rápida.**

  *It is a **fast** cure.*

- Adverb

  No nos habla **mucho.**

  *She doesn't talk to us **much.***

  Corre **rápido.**

  *He runs **fast.***

---

1. *Más* and *menos* used as comparative adjectives are a common exception to the typical adjectival suffix system. They do not change.

EXERCISE

Complete each pair of sentences with the correct forms of the word indicated in parentheses.

1. *(poco)* María tiene _____ actividades. Ella sale

   _____ de su casa.

2. *(mejor)* Los González hablan _____ que sus vecinos. Pero

   los vecinos tienen _____ recursos económicos.

3. *(demasiado)* No estudio _____. Pero yo tengo

   _____ tareas que hacer.

4. *(más)* Los otros sí tienen _____ tiempo que él. Pero él

   estudia _____ que ellos.

5. *(menos)* Tienes _____ dinero que tu hermano. Pero él

   gasta _____ que tú.

6. *(malo/mal)* Sí, Juan juega _____. Pero él no es un chico

   _____.

7. *(bueno/bien)* Sí, ellas son _____ chicas y cantan

   _____.

GOAL 3
To use the pattern *con* + noun to modify a verb.

The pattern *con* + noun is often used in Spanish in a situation where we would use an adverb in English.

Escribe **lentamente.**   *She writes **slowly.***
Escribe **con lentitud.**

EXERCISE

Complete each sentence using the pattern *con* + noun to express the idea of the adjective.

1. Los padres se despiden de sus hijos *(cariñoso).*

   Los padres se despiden de sus hijos con cariño.

2. Los vecinos siempre se saludan *(amistoso).*

   _____

3. Los novios se miraban *(amoroso).*

   _____

4. Los dos discutían *(emocional)* sus varios problemas.

_____

5. El pobre anciano andaba *(triste)* por la lluvia.

_____

6. Los habitantes luchaban *(valiente)* para defender a su patria.

_____

GOAL 4

To use adverbs and adverbial phrases of time and order, place and direction, manner and means, cause, goal, accompaniment, extent, duration, and frequency.

A. Adverbs of time and order are used to answer the question *¿cuándo?*

Time: ahora, hoy, ayer, mañana, ya, de noche, por la mañana, a las tres, el primero de septiembre

¿Cuándo sale? Sale **ahora.**

Order: después, antes, primero, esta vez, más tarde, luego

Lo hacemos **después.**

B. Adverbs of place and direction are used to designate *dónde.*

Place: aquí, acá, ahí, allí, allá, adentro, afuera, abajo, arriba, lejos, cerca, en mi cuarto

¿Dónde viven? Viven **aquí.**

Direction: acá, ahí, a, a la escuela, por aquí, para abajo, hacia arriba, para atrás

Van **a Madrid.**

C. Adverbs of manner and means are used to designate *cómo.*

Manner: bien, perfectamente, mejor que tú, así, a prisa, como la última vez, como un profesor, fácilmente, por favor, sólo

¿Cómo escribo? Escribes **bien.**

Means: por la puerta, leyendo el periódico, por medio de sus amigos

Mira **por la ventana.**

D. Adverbial phrases of cause are used to designate *por qué* or *por quién.*

Cause: por agradecer a sus amigos, por la Navidad, por María, por eso

Por eso no les dice nada.

E. Adverbial phrases of goal are used to designate *para qué* or *para quién*.

Goal: para ayudarla, para profesor, para mejorar la situación, para llegar a tiempo, para las dos, para eso, para sus padres

Trabajamos **para mejorar la situación.**

F. Adverbial phrases of accompaniment are used to designate *con quién*.

Accompaniment: con ella, con un español, con mis amigos

Nunca sale **con él.**

G. Adverbs of extent, duration, and frequency are used to designate *cuánto*.

Extent: poco, mucho, demasiado, más, menos, apenas, por lo menos, dentro de una hora

Comemos **dentro de quince minutos.**

Duration: un año, cinco minutos, tres días, durante la semana, todo el día

¿Pasas **tres meses** allí?

Frequency: a menudo, muchas veces, a veces, cada día, todos los días

¿Corres **todos los días?**

EXERCISE

Work with a partner. Take turns asking and answering the questions. Answer with an adverb or adverbial phrase.

1. ¿Cuándo estás más contento?
2. ¿Dónde estás más contento?
3. ¿Adónde vas de compras cuando quieres comprar una ganga?
4. ¿Cómo manejas?
5. ¿Por qué, o por quién, viniste a clase?
6. ¿Para qué viniste a clase?
7. ¿Con quién compartes tus sueños más íntimos?
8. ¿Cuánto miras la televisión? ¿Escuchas la música? ¿Hablas por teléfono? ¿Pierdes el tiempo?

GOAL 5
To use adverbs to modify other adjectives or adverbs.

Some adverbs are used to modify other adjectives or adverbs. The following are examples of this type of adverb:

muy	algo	mucho
tan	nada	bastante
más	demasiado	igualmente
menos	medio	especialmente
bien	poco	

Note that these words are placed directly in front of the words they modify.

Esa clase es **muy difícil.**	*That class is **very difficult.***
Esa generación es **demasiado seria.**	*That generation is **too serious.***

EXERCISE

Give the English equivalent of each sentence.

1. Somos muy felices.

   _____

2. Habla tan rápido que no puedo entenderlo.

   _____

3. Come más despacio ahora.

   _____

4. Es menos callada en casa.

   _____

5. Está bien preparado.

   _____

6. Estamos algo cansados.

   _____

7. No es nada importante.

   _____

8. Come demasiado rápido.

   _____

9. Está medio dormido.

   _____

10. Es poco interesante.

    _____

11. Tienen muchas flores.

    _____

12. Lo hace bastante fácilmente.

    _____

13. Esto es igualmente improbable.

_____

14. Eso es especialmente difícil.

_____

G O A L   6

To place an adverb in its proper position in a sentence.

Although in general the placement of Spanish adverbs is quite similar to that of English, there are some differences.

  A. In Spanish the adverb usually is placed as close to the verb as possible.

    Van mucho al cine.   *They **go** to the movies **a lot.***

  B. In Spanish the adverb never comes between the main verb and its helper.

    Ya han salido.   *They **have already left.***

    Siempre está estudiando.   *She **is always studying.***

  C. In Spanish it is not necessary to follow the word order of English with such verbs as "come," "go," and "be."

    Ayer vino **temprano.**   *She came **early yesterday.***

    Ya es hora de comer.   *It is **already** time to eat.*

    Yo estaba **allá.**   ***There** I was.*

  D. In Spanish if the verb has no expressed subject, the adverb usually precedes it.

    Ahora salgo.   *I'm **leaving now.***

  E. In Spanish *no* precedes the verb. The negative follows the helper verb and the verb "to be" in English.

    No soy médico.   *I am **not** a doctor.*

    No trabajamos aquí.   *We do **not** work here.*

    Note, however, that with an adverb by itself *no* follows.

    Ahora no.   *Not now.*

    Ayer no.   *Not yesterday.*

  F. In Spanish *poco* may be preceded by *muy*, but *mucho* may not. Instead, one uses the form *muchísimo* to say "very much."

    Come **muy poco** pero bebe **muchísimo.**   *He eats **very little** but he drinks **very much.***

G. In Spanish, *que* may be used with adverbs of manner and adverbs of time, not with adverbs of extent.

¡**Qué** bien toca!   ***How*** *well he plays!*

¡**Qué** temprano se levantaron!   ***How*** *early they got up!*

¡**Cuánto** hablan!   ***How*** *much they talk!*

EXERCISE

Form complete sentences using the cues. Then give the English equivalents. Note those sentences in which the word order is different in Spanish and English.

1. trabaja/muchísimo/poco/pero/gana/muy

   Trabaja muchísimo pero gana muy poco. He works very much,

   but earns very little.

2. coma/con/nosotros/usted/hoy/aquí

   _____

   _____

3. ya/ha/el/empezado/partido

   _____

   _____

4. todavía/debe/me/dólares/diez

   _____

   _____

5. prepara/lecciones/bien/las

   _____

   _____

6. por qué/clase/vino/ayer

   _____

   _____

7. estudia/en/mucho/cuarto/su

   _____

   _____

Communication Pattern Exercise

Work with a partner. Take turns asking and answering the questions.

1. ¿Juegan con determinación los jugadores de fútbol?
2. ¿Y salen del campo con tristeza cuando pierden?
3. ¿Y gritan los aficionados con emoción durante el partido?
4. ¿Escucha usted con interés lo que dice el anunciador por la mañana?
5. ¿Se levanta Ud. alegremente por la mañana?
6. ¿Les habla mamá dulcemente a los niños cuando se portan mal?
7. ¿Habla rápido o despacio el profesor en la clase?
8. ¿Hablan más o escuchan más los alumnos en las clases?
9. ¿Está su casa cerca o lejos de la escuela?
10. ¿Se sientan ustedes bajo un árbol cuando hace calor?
11. ¿Gastan ustedes mucho o poco dinero cada semana?

Actividades de comunicación

I. Empleando adverbios de posición y dirección, di donde está tu casa con respecto a la escuela, el centro y donde viven tus amigos.

II. Empleando los adverbios de tiempo y orden, describe tu horario diario en casa y durante las clases.

III. Completa las siguientes oraciones.

1. Mi abuelo habla _____.
2. Aprendemos _____.
3. Como _____.
4. Bailas _____.
5. Trabajan para _____.
6. Sale con _____.

IV. Es interesante el enojo. Piensa un poco en el enojo y luego contesta las siguientes preguntas. Después discute el enojo con tus compañeros de clase.

1. ¿Cuándo y por qué te enojas? ¿Cuándo se enojan tus padres? ¿Tus hermanos? ¿Tus profesores? ¿Tus amigos?
2. ¿Cómo te enojas? ¿Cómo se enojan tus padres? ¿Tus hermanos? ¿Tus profesores? ¿Tus amigos? ¿Qué hace cada uno?
3. ¿Cuáles son las características del enojo?

Refrán

Más vale tarde que nunca.
Explica el sentido. Da ejemplos de la vida.

4 Prepositions

Prepositions show relationships in space (length, width, height), and time.

G O A L   1

To use prepositions to show relationships in space.

The following are prepositions that are used to indicate relationships:

Depth	
delante de	*in front of*
detrás de	*behind*
en frente de	*in front of, facing, opposite*

Length	
a la derecha (de)	*to the right (of)*
a la izquierda (de)	*to the left (of)*

Height	
abajo	*down, downstairs*
arriba	*up, upstairs*
en	*on*
sobre	*over*
encima de	*above*
debajo de	*underneath*
bajo	*below*

Location within or without	
en	*in*
en casa	*at home*
adentro	*inside*
afuera	*outside*
dentro de	*inside*
fuera de	*outside*
alrededor de	*around*
por	*through*

Physical contact or distance	
contra	*against*
cerca de	*near*
lejos de	*far from*

GOAL 2

To use the preposition *a*.

If something or someone occupies a position at the same plane in space or in time, *a* is used to indicate this relationship.

Está **a** la puerta.	*He is **at** the door.*
Está **al** nivel del mar.	*It is **at** sea level.*
Se fue **a** la una.	*She left **at** one.*
¿**A** cómo se venden?	***At** what price do they sell?*

When one of the objects involved in the relationship is moving, *a* is used to indicate its destination.

Voy **a** México.	*I am going **to** Mexico.*
Los tira **al** suelo.	*He throws them **to** the floor.*
Se acerca **al** altar.	*He approaches the altar.*

This same relationship holds for movement toward doing something.

Aprenden **a** jugar.	*They are learning to play.*
Se deciden **a** salir.	*He decides to leave.*
Se pone **a** llorar.	*She begins to cry.*

Any type of psychological adjustment that leads to some resultant activity is an extension of the same pattern. In some cases these verbs may be followed by an object noun as well as an action.

Me acostumbro **a** vivir aquí.	*I am getting used to living here.*
Me acostumbro **a** mis circunstancias.	*I am getting adjusted to my circumstances.*

EXERCISE

Form complete sentences using the words given. Remember to include the preposition *a* in each.

1. turistas/llegar/estación

   Los turistas llegan a la estación.

2. mamá/los/invitar/quedarse/aquí

3. Juan/resignarse/estudiar/más

4. jugadores/determinar/ganar/partido

5. tú/subir/autobus/en/esquina

6. mis amigos/venir/jugar

_____

7. yo/aprender/tocar/guitarra

_____

8. nosotros/empezar/entender/ahora

_____

9. otros/no/atreverse/decir/nada

_____

10. niño/correr/su/mamá

_____

11. nosotros/salir/medianoche

_____

12. mi/hijo/estar/izquierda

_____

GOAL 3

To use the preposition *en*.

The preposition *en* is used to describe a relationship in which one thing is on, surrounded by, enclosed in, or contained in something else.

El libro está **en** la mesa.	*The book is **on** the table.*
La casa está **en** el bosque.	*The house is **in** the woods.*
La señora está **en** casa.	*The lady is **at** home.*
María está **en** el cine.	*María is **at** the movies.*
Lo pone **en** la caja.	*He puts it **into** the box.*
Se divierten **en** la Florida.	*They have a good time **in** Florida.*
Se divierten **en** el partido.	*They have a good time **at** the game.*
Entra **en** el cuarto.	*She enters the room.*

EXERCISE

Form complete sentences using the words given. Remember to include the preposition *en* in each.

1. Juan/confiar/sus/amigos

   Juan confía en sus amigos. _____

2. coche/estar/garaje

3. yo/tener/placer/hablar/contigo

_____

4. mamá/insistir/quedarse/casa

_____

5. papá/estar/oficina/ahora

_____

6. chicos/ocuparse/mirar/televisión

_____

7. su/abrigo/estar/sofá

_____

8. nosotros/entrar/escuela/temprano

_____

9. este/chico/nunca/pensar/sus/problemas

_____

10. estudiantes/estar/clases/ahora

_____

G O A L   4

To use the preposition _de._

The preposition _de_ is used to describe the idea of a moving subject going away from some point or object.

Salí **de** la casa.	_I left (moved away **from**) the house._
Corrió **del** accidente.	_He ran **from** the accident._

This same relationship exists with verbs that express the idea of separation such as getting rid of something, being free of something, doing without, forgetting, stopping some activity, etc.

Está libre **del** sentido de culpa.	_He is free **from** the feeling of guilt._
Se olvidó **de** hacerlo.	_He forgot to do it._
Dejó **de** escribirle.	_She stopped writing to him._

This same idea is the basis for the use of _de_ to show origin, either physical, emotional, or psychological.

Esta cartera es **de** México.	_This wallet is **from** Mexico._
Me alegro **de** estar aquí.	_I am happy to be here._
El niño se asusta **del** ruido.	_The child is afraid **of** the noise._

EXERCISE

Form complete sentences using the words given. Remember to include the preposition *de* in each.

1. Juan/estar/enamorado/Anita

   Juan está enamorado de Anita.

2. ellos/llegar/Los Angeles/anoche

3. nosotros/despedirse/nuestros/amigos

4. María/venir/España

5. devoto/arrepentirse/sus/pecados

6. tú/quejarse/todo

7. papá/enojarse/eso

8. obreros/cesar/hacer/ruido

9. niñera/cuidar/niños

10. jóvenes/cansarse/bailar

GOAL 5

To distinguish between the uses of *a, en,* and *de.*

In order to distinguish between the use of *a, en,* and *de,* you should remember that *a* indicates a time of day, a position in space, or motion toward or in the direction of the object; *en* means on, surrounded by, enclosed in, or contained in the object; and *de* refers to going away from the object following the preposition.

EXERCISE

Complete each sentence with *a, en,* or *de,* depending upon the context.

1. Mi padre trabaja _____ una oficina lujosa.

2. Sale _____ la casa bastante temprano.

3. Llega _____ su destino _____ las ocho.

4. Un águila puede volar _____ una altura tremenda.

5. Salen _____ aquí el sábado y llegan _____ San Diego el lunes por la tarde.

6. ¿Haces un papel _____ el drama?

7. Siempre asisto _____ mis clases.

8. Y participo _____ las actividades.

9. Le obligan _____ volver inmediatamente después del partido.

10. Persiste _____ hacer lo mismo cada día.

11. José es _____ Texas pero sus padres vienen _____ México.

12. Los profesores y los estudiantes están avergonzados _____ lo que pasó.

13. Se acercan _____ María.

14. Me limito _____ comer legumbres.

15. Se prepara _____ ser abogado.

16. El orador incitó a la muchedumbre _____ rebelarse.

17. Se empeña _____ continuar el trabajo.

18. Esa señora se place _____ ayudar a los otros.

19. Mi padre es aficionado _____ el fútbol.

20. Sí, ella se conforma _____ los deseos de sus padres.

GOAL 6

To use the preposition *por.*

The preposition *por* has many of the same meanings as the two Latin words *per* and *pro.* In order to be able to use *por* correctly, you must be aware that *por* has several clusters of meanings.

A. From the Latin word *per*

- Movement through space or time including what remains to be done, said, completed, etc.

Anda **por** el parque.	*He walks **through** the park.*
Va a quedarse allí **por** tres semanas.	*She is going to stay there **(for)** three weeks.*
Les queda una hora **por** estudiar.	*They have an hour left to study.*

- Actions and their cause, motivation, or means, either physical or psychological

Fue roto **por** Juan.	*It was broken **by** Juan.*
Fueron **por** avion.	*They went **by** plane.*
Lo hace **por** sus padres.	*He does it **for** his parents.*
Van **por** detergente.	*They are going **for** detergent.*

- Ideas of intensity, completeness, thoroughness, etc.

Vamos **por seguro.**	*We are going **for sure.***
Por radical que sea, no es descortés.	***However radical** he may be, he is not discourteous.*

B. From the Latin word *pro*

- In the place of, or representation

Un dólar **por** el libro.	*A dollar **for** the book.*
Juan va **por** Carlos.	*Juan goes **for** Carlos.*
Pasa **por** nativo.	*He passes **for** a native.*

- For the sake or benefit of

Lo hizo **por** su familia.	*He works **for** his family.*
Votaron **por** Manuela.	*They voted **for** Manuela.*

EXERCISE

Form complete sentences using the words given. Remember to include the preposition *por* in each.

1. dos/salir/puerta de atrás

_____

2. casa/ser/destruida/huracán

_____

3. eso/nosotros/no/poder/ir

_____

4. Lincoln/se/distinguir/su/honradez

_____

5. equipo/perder/partido/falta de tiempo

_____

6. mucho/dinero/ser/posible/comprar/Cadillac

_____

7. novios/hablar/dos/horas

_____

8. que/hacer/Raúl/sus/padres

_____

9. mamá/ir/dos/veces/semana

_____

10. mucho/tráfico/pasar/aquí

_____

11. estos/obreros/trabajar/noche

_____

GOAL 7

To use the preposition *para*.

The preposition *para* is used to indicate purpose, goal, or destination.

Salgo **para** Nueva York mañana.   *I leave **for** New York tomorrow.*

Estudiamos **para** aprender.   *We study **in order to** learn.*

Es un regalo **para** mi novio.   *It is a gift **for** my sweetheart.*

EXERCISE

Form complete sentences using the words given. Remember to include the preposition *para* in each.

1. vendo/éste/comprar/otro

_____

2. madre/preparar/torta/familia

_____

3. mis/padres/salir/ocho/Texas

_____

4. estudiantes/estudiar/sacar/nota/buena

_____

5. Jorge/llegar/ocho

_____

6. hay/algo/mí

_____

GOAL 8

To distinguish between the uses of *por* and *para.*

EXERCISE

Complete each sentence with *por* or *para,* according to the context.

1. Sí, salimos el martes _____ España.

2. Viajaremos _____ avión.

3. Pasaremos _____ varios países europeos antes de llegar a España.

4. Nos quedaremos en Madrid _____ una semana.

5. Llegaremos allí _____ el veinte del mes.

6. _____ supuesto vamos a visitar el sur de España también.

7. _____ cansados que estemos vamos a ver lo más posible.

8. Tenemos mucho tiempo _____ visitar muchos lugares interesantes.

9. Vamos _____ visitar a nuestros amigos en España también.

10. Llevaremos regalos _____ ellos.

11. Nos quedan varios quehaceres _____ hacer.

12. El viaje fue sugerido _____ Pepe.

13. El habla español muy bien y a veces pasa _____ hispano.

14. Vamos _____ nuestro hijo que estudia español.

15. Cada día hay muchas cartas _____ nosotros.

16. Al llegar cambiaremos nuestros dólares _____ pesetas.

GOAL 9

To use Spanish verbs not followed by a preposition.

Many Spanish verbs may be followed by an object without a preposition.

No puedo venir.	*I cannot come.*
Busca su libro.	*He is looking **for** his book.*
Esperan el autobús.	*They are waiting **for** the bus.*
Pensamos salir temprano.	*We intend to leave early.*

EXERCISE

Give the English equivalent of each sentence.

1. Mi padre siempre mira los partidos de fútbol.

_____

2. La policía buscaba un coche robado.

_____

3. Nosotros debemos ayudar a nuestros amigos.

_____

4. Pablo nunca recuerda escribir a sus padres.

_____

5. Mis amigos prefirieron ir al cine.

_____

6. ¿Piensas tomar este curso?

_____

7. La familia estaba esperando el principio del concierto.

_____

8. Los profesores nos hicieron estudiar.

_____

9. Mi hermano y yo queremos pasar las vacaciones aquí.

_____

10. Mi hermanito sabe nadar bien.

_____

GOAL 10

To use the personal _a_ in Spanish.

In Spanish an _a_ precedes the object of the verb in a number of cases.

A. An _a_ must be used with a definite person.

¿Ve Carlos **a** Rosa?	_Does Carlos see Rosa?_
Llamo **a** mis amigos.	_I call my friends._

- _A_ is not used with things.

    Veo el pico.   _I see the peak._

- With indefinite persons, the _a_ may be omitted.

    Vimos muchos niños a lo largo   _We saw many children along the_
    de las calles.   _streets._

- At times _a_ may be used to distinguish between definite and indefinite objects.

    Busco **a** un amigo.   _I am looking for a (certain)_
                                        friend.

    Busco un amigo.   _I am looking for a (any) friend._

- An *a* is not used with the verb *tener*.

  El señor Méndez tiene dos hijos.   *Mr. Méndez has two children.*

- Of course, an *a* is also used with an indirect object, and you should not confuse the two patterns.

Direct object

Hace un mes que no veo **a Marta.**   *I have not seen **Marta** for a month.*

Indirect object

Cada noche ella le escribe una carta **a Juan.**   *She writes a letter **to Juan** every night.*

B. An *a* is used with a personification of an abstract noun or an animal.

No veo **a Fortunato,** mi perro.   *I do not see **Fortunato,** my dog.*

Amo **a mi patria.**   *I love **my native country.***

C. An *a* is used before the indefinites *(alguien, nadie, alguno, ninguno)* used as objects of the verb.

No veo **a nadie.**   *I don't see **anyone.***

D. An *a* may be used with geographical names, except those that are preceded by an article.

He visitado (a) México pero nunca he visitado el Canadá.   *I have visited Mexico, but I have never visited Canada.*

EXERCISE

Complete each sentence with *a* when necessary.

1. Los profesores saludan _____ los estudiantes.

2. Los estudiantes escriben _____ los ejercicios.

3. Los estudiantes entregan _____ la tarea _____ la profesora.

4. Tengo _____ un tío que vive allí.

5. Admiramos _____ la belleza.

6. Juan no habla _____ nadie esta mañana.

7. Mi profesor conoce bien _____ México.

8. Observamos _____ muchos jóvenes allí.

9. No puedo encontrar _____ Félix, mi gatito.

10. Los turistas visitan _____ todas las catedrales.

Communication Pattern Exercise

Work with a partner. Take turns asking and answering the questions.

1. ¿Dónde está el patio?
2. ¿Dónde está el sótano?
3. ¿Adónde van ustedes para las vacaciones?
4. ¿A qué hora es tu clase de español?
5. ¿A qué te aplicas más?
6. ¿A qué te resistes más?
7. ¿Dónde estás ahora?
8. ¿En qué calle está tu casa?
9. ¿Qué te place más?
10. ¿Qué te molesta más?
11. ¿De dónde eres?
12. ¿De dónde vienen tus padres?
13. ¿De qué te cansas más?
14. ¿De qué te enojas más?
15. ¿Por qué calles vuelves a casa?
16. ¿Por qué cualidades te distingues?
17. ¿Por qué estudias?
18. ¿Para qué estudias?
19. ¿Para qué hora habrás terminado?
20. ¿Qué te gusta hacer más?
21. ¿Qué necesitas estudiar más?
22. ¿Qué quieres hacer algún día?
23. ¿A quién visitas más?
24. ¿Qué programas miras en la televisión?

Actividades de comunicación

I. Describe en dónde está tu cuarto y la posición de otras cosas, personas y sitios con respecto a tu casa.

II. Con las preposiciones "por" y "para" y otras necesarias, escribe una descripción de un viaje que has hecho.

Refránes

Come para vivir y no vivas para comer.
Por la boca muere el pez.
Para el mal de amores no hay doctores.
Explica el sentido. Da ejemplos de la vida.

PART VI

Non-Finite Verbs

Introduction A finite verb requires a subject and can appear in any tense. The action of the verb is performed by a specified subject at a specified time. In this sense, the verb is finite, or limited, to the given subject and time.

My father knows.	Subject: father	Time: present
I told him last night.	Subject: I	Time: past
You will be punished later.	Subject: you	Time: future

Non-finite verbs name actions that are not finite. In other words, they are not limited to a certain subject at a certain time. In fact, a non-finite verb names an action just as a finite verb does, but it has no person-number suffix and no tense marker. A non-finite verb form may be used as main verb or to serve another function in the sentence.

There are three types of non-finite verbs: infinitives, imperfective participles, and perfective participles. Each has different functions in the sentence, and each has more than one use.

Infinitive:
  a. Noun—El **reír** es buena medicina. ***Laughter** is good medicine.*

  b. Verb—No **reír**. *No **laughing**.*

Imperfective participle:
  a. Adverb—Vive **riendo**. *He lives **laughing**.*

  b. Verb—Está **riendo** ahora. *He is **laughing** now.*

Perfective participle:
  a. Verb—Siempre ha **reído** mucho. *He has always **laughed** a lot.*

  b. Adjective—Su objetivo es una vida **gozada**. *His goal is an **enjoyed** life.*

The material in Part VI focuses on the uses of each type of non-finite verb.

1 The Infinitive

To recognize an infinitive in Spanish and to change any verb form to the infinitive.

An infinitive in English is marked by the word "to." "To work," "to eat," and "to live" are infinitives. In Spanish, the infinitive of the verb ends in the letter *r*. A Spanish infinitive has two suffixes, one to indicate verb class and one to indicate the infinitive.

Pattern: stem + class vowel + r

1st class	habl	a	r
2nd class	com	e	r
3rd class	viv	i	r

Note that there is no suffix to indicate person or number in a non-finite verb form.

EXERCISE   Indicate the stem of each regular verb form. Then give the infinitive.

1. estado   *est-, estar*

2. comes   _____

3. servíamos   _____

4. pasando   _____

5. leen   _____

6. salís   _____

7. ayudaba   _____

8. volviendo   _____

9. vivo   _____

10. miro   _____

11. creo   _____

12. llevaste   _____

13. vendemos   _____

14. recibiendo   _____

15. compramos   _____

To give the infinitive in Spanish for its English counterparts.

An infinitive is generally used as a noun in a sentence. A noun in general names a thing; an infinitive names an action.

A. An infinitive phrase in Spanish may be followed by a verb and may serve as the subject of a sentence.

Hablar español es interesante.   *Speaking Spanish* is interesting.

EXERCISE

Write the Spanish equivalent of the English word in parentheses.

1. *(Running)* _____ es buen ejercicio.

2. *(Looking at)* _____ la televisión no me interesa.

3. *(Opening)* _____ la puerta es una cortesia.

4. *(Preparing)* _____ las lecciones no es difícil.

5. *(Leaving)* _____ tan temprano me irritaba.

6. *(Learning)* _____ es necesario.

7. *(Dancing)* _____ es agradable.

8. *(Going up)* _____ la escalera fatiga.

9. *(Losing)* _____ el partido fue un desastre.

10. *(Forgetting)* _____ el libro me irritó.

B. An infinitive in Spanish may be the object of a conjugated verb.

Quiere aprender español.	*He **wants to learn** Spanish.*
Lo **vi salir.**	*I **saw** him **leave(ing).***
Lo **oí cantar.**	*I **heard** him **sing(ing).***

At times the nominalization of this verb form is made even more evident by the addition of an article.

Prefiere **el jugar al trabajar.**	*He prefers **playing to working.***
Prefiere **jugar.**	*He prefers **to play.***

EXERCISE

Supply the Spanish equivalent of each English sentence.

1. Seeing is believing.

_____

2. I saw them laugh(ing).

_____

3. I like to ski.

_____

4. They like writing.

_____

5. It is not possible to sleep well here.

_____

6. Do you want to study?

_____

7. I see them throwing rocks.

_____

8. He likes talking on the phone.

_____

C. An infinitive is the verb form used in Spanish as the object of a preposition. Often, the "-ing" form is used in English.

Antes de comer, se lavó las manos.	*Before eating, he washed his hands.*
No hay nada **que hacer.**	*There is nothing to do.*
Al ver a su papá, el niño empezó a correr.	*On seeing his father, the child began to run.*
Insisten en salir.	*They insist on leaving.*
Aprenden a leer.	*They are learning to read.*

EXERCISE

Supply the Spanish equivalent of the English word in parentheses.

1. La niña empezó a (cry) _____.

2. Después de (finishing) _____, se acostó.

3. Al (hearing) _____ la noticia, volvió a casa.

4. Juan trató de (answer) _____ la pregunta.

5. Vino a clase sin (reading) _____ la lectura.

6. ¿Insistes en (selling) _____ tu creación?

7. Fue a Nuevo México antes de (writing) _____ la carta.

8. Al (finding) _____ el dinero, se puso contento.

9. Aprende a (play) _____ al fútbol.

10. Estudian mucho para (receive) _____ una buena nota.

D. Many impersonal expressions in Spanish are followed by the infinitive.

Es importante **estudiar.**	*It is important to study.*

EXERCISE

Combine each pair of sentences into one sentence using the impersonal expression and the infinitive form of the verb.

1. Todos estudian mucho. Es importante.

   Es importante estudiar mucho.

   _____

2. Los estudiantes hacen la tarea. Es necesario.

   _____

   _____

3. La maestra no abre la ventana. Es imposible.

   _____

   _____

4. La madre cuida del bebé. Es preciso.

_____

5. Todos ven el sol cuando no hay nubes. Es posible.

_____

6. El niño corre de un perro grande. Es natural.

_____

7. Ella rompió un espejo. Es mala suerte.

_____

8. El escucha música popular. Es interesante.

_____

9. Los García viven en la Florida. Es agradable.

_____

10. Ese joven maneja demasiado rápido. Es peligroso.

_____

E. It is possible to use an infinitive as the main verb in a sentence. When it is used this way, it is used as a command or in a short question showing surprise.

No hablar.	*No talking.*
Callarse.	*Be quiet.*
¿Hacerlo yo?	***I do it?***

EXERCISE

Supply the Spanish equivalent of the English word in parentheses.

1. No *(running)* _____ en los pasillos.

2. No *(walking)* _____ en la hierba.

3. *(Smoke)* _____ afuera.

4. *(Enter)* _____ por la otra puerta.

5. No *(eating)* _____ adentro.

6. *(Study)* _____ en voz baja.

7. No *(writing)* _____ en las paredes.

8. No *(opening)* _____ las ventanas.

9. *(We study?)* _____

GOAL 3

To distinguish between the use of finite and non-finite verbs in context.

EXERCISE   Complete each sentence using the appropriate form of the verb indicated.

1. *(hablar)* Generalmente ella _____ de sus amantes, pero esta noche no desea _____.

2. *(estudiar)* ¿_____ tú mucho para los exámenes comprensivos? Sí, pero ahora no es posible _____ más.

3. *(comer)* Antes mi mamá _____ mucho, pero ahora desea _____ menos.

4. *(regresar)* ¿_____ usted tarde anoche? Sí, y al _____ estaba fatigado.

5. *(llegar)* Generalmente ellos _____ temprano. Después de _____ leen un rato.

6. *(aprender)* ¿Le gusta _____? Sí, es fácil _____ aquí, y yo _____ mucho.

7. *(escribir)* _____ los ejercicios es buena manera de aprender. Nosotros siempre los _____ todos.

8. *(salir)* El señor García siempre _____ temprano. Lo oigo _____ a eso de las seis.

9. *(hablar)* Chicos, vosotros _____ mucho en casa, pero aquí en la biblioteca hay una regla: Prohibido _____ en voz alta.

10. *(comprar)* Yo _____ un helado. ¿Vas a _____ tú uno también?

11. *(viajar)* ¿ _____ mucho? Yo pienso _____ algún día pero antes de _____ debo ganar suficiente dinero.

Communication Pattern Exercise

Work with a partner. Take turns asking and answering the questions.

1. ¿Deseas jugar al baloncesto esta tarde?
2. ¿Deseas ir al partido mañana?
3. ¿Debes practicar en el piano ahora?
4. ¿Debes conseguir la licencia para conducir?
5. ¿Tratas de mejorar la nota?
6. Antes de acostarse, ¿leen ustedes el periódico?
7. Después de estudiar, ¿miran ustedes la televisión?
8. ¿Es agradable visitar a tus amigos?
9. ¿Es el correr un buen ejercicio?
10. ¿Es el leer un placer?
11. ¿Es más importante el hablar o el escuchar?

Actividades de comunicación

Abajo hay una lista de actividades. Favor de examinar esta lista y discutir con tus compañeros de clase las siguientes preguntas.

fumar	ir de compras	hablar con amigos
correr	aprender	montar a caballo
mirar (la) televisión	reír	esquiar
estudiar	dormir	caminar en las montañas
comer	bailar	creer
obedecer	escuchar (la) música	leer
manejar	jugar	(otra actividad favorita)

1. ¿Cuáles son tus actividades favoritas?
2. ¿Cuáles son los mejores ejercicios?
3. ¿Cuáles son más necesarias?
4. ¿Hay unas peligrosas?
5. ¿Cuáles son las actividades favoritas de tus amigos?

Refránes

Querer es poder.
Ver es creer.
Oír, ver y callar son cosas de gran preciar.
Explica el sentido. Da ejemplos de la vida.

2 The Imperfective Participle

GOAL 1

To recognize the imperfective participle in Spanish and to change any verb form to the imperfective participle form.

An imperfective participle in English ends in "-ing." "Walking," "running," and "jumping' are imperfective participles. An imperfective participle in Spanish is marked by -ndo. A Spanish imperfective participle has two suffixes, one to indicate verb class and one to indicate the imperfective participle.

Pattern: stem + class vowel + *ndo*

1st class	habl	a	ndo
2nd class	com	ie	ndo
3rd class	viv	ie	ndo

Note that there is no suffix to indicate person or number in a non-finite verb form.

EXERCISE

Supply the imperfective participle for each regular verb.

1. enseñar _____enseñando_____

2. bebes _____

3. vivido _____

4. daba _____

5. cubrió _____

6. correr _____

7. bailamos _____

8. aprendido _____

9. cogía _____

10. escribir _____

11. perdiste _____

12. rompen _____

13. llegado _____

14. subíamos _____

15. llamó _____

GOAL 2

To use the imperfective participle as the main verb.

An imperfective participle may be used as the main verb in the sentence.

A. The imperfective participle is used with the progressive verb forms.

Pattern: helper verb + imperfective participle

Singular	
estoy cantando	*I am singing*
estás comiendo	*you are eating*
usted está saliendo	*you are leaving*
está hablando	*he (she) is talking*

Plural	
estamos cantando	we are singing
estáis comiendo	*you are eating*
ustedes están saliendo	*you are leaving*
están hablando	*they are talking*

Certain other verbs such as *andar, ir, seguir,* and *venir* may be used in this pattern instead of the helper verb *estar*.

Siguen comiendo.   ***They keep on*** *eating.*

EXERCISE

Complete each sentence with the imperfective participle of the verb.

1. ¿Comer?   Estoy _____ ahora.

2. ¿Hablar?   Sí, están _____ en su despacho.

3. ¿Salir?   Sí, está _____ en este momento.

4. ¿Buscarlo? Sí, estamos _____.

5. ¿Escribir? Sí, estoy _____ en español.

6. ¿Pintar?   Sí, sigue _____.

7. ¿Aprender? Es muy listo. Lo está _____ todo.

8. ¿Abrir?   El niño anda _____ todas las puertas.

B. This pattern (*estar* + perfective participle) may be used with any verb form.

Estaba cantando.   *He was singing.*

Estarán comiendo.   *They will be eating.*

Hemos estado sufriendo.   *We have been suffering.*

E X E R C I S E

Change the verb in each sentence to the pattern *estar* + imperfective participle in the same verb form.

1. Mirábamos el canal.

    Estábamos mirando el canal.

2. El niño rompe la lámpara.

3. Los dos pedirán fondos del gobierno.

4. ¿Has contado el dinero?

5. ¿Vendían ustedes libros?

6. Había recibido muchos paquetes.

7. ¿Sales con Héctor?

8. Celebraré mi cumpleaños con mi novio.

9. Peleamos mucho.

10. Las muchachas preparan la merienda.

C. This pattern is used much less frequently in Spanish than in English. Normally, the regular tense form is used in Spanish.

Trabaja en una oficina.   *He **is working** in an office.*

At times, this form of the verb is used in English to express a planned action in the future. In Spanish a form of the expression *ir a* or the simple present is used.

Van a salir mañana.	*They **are leaving** tomorrow.*
Salen mañana.	*They **are leaving** tomorrow.*

However, in Spanish, progressive forms are used to indicate a change from the normal or to emphasize the fact that the action is going on at a particular moment.

Trabaja en la oficina, pero hoy **está trabajando** en casa.	*He works at the office, but today he **is working** at home.*
Ahora **está buscando** un libro.	*Right now he **is looking** for a book.*

EXERCISE

Complete each sentence using either the present or the progressive form of the verb, according to the meaning of the sentence.

1. *(tomar)* Generalmente, los jóvenes _____ Coca-Cola pero en estos días _____ Gatorade.

2. *(poner)* Cuando está en casa, Rosa _____ la mesa, pero hoy la _____ María.

3. *(salir)* Ay, María. No es posible hablar ahora. En este momento yo _____ para el cine. Sí, mi marido y yo siempre _____ a esta hora los sábados.

4. *(viajar)* El señor González _____ mucho. La próxima semana *(volar)* _____ a Madrid.

5. *(aprender)* Por lo general (yo) no _____ mucho en esta clase, pero en los últimos días _____ más.

6. *(producir)* Los japoneses _____ muchos productos y los _____ baratos.

7. *(tocar)* Sí, es muy buen guitarrista. _____ en nuestra casa a veces y mañana por la tarde _____ en un programa de la escuela.

8. *(proteger)* ¡Cuidado con esa gallina, niño! Tiene pollitos ahora, y los _____ de esa manera. Las gallinas siempre _____ así a sus pollitos.

G O A L   3

To use the imperfective participle as an adverb.

An imperfective participle may also be used to modify the verb in the sentence.

Volviendo a case, tuve un
   accidente.

Returning home, I had an
   accident.

Estudiando mucho, uno aprende
   más.

(By) studying a lot, one learns
   more.

Often the Spanish phrase beginning with an imperfective participle is equivalent to a clause in English.

Estando allí, comimos con ellos.

**Since (as, when, while) we
   were there,** we ate with them.

Salió **cantando.**

He left **singing.**

Encontré a los estudiantes
   hablando en el pasillo.

I found the students **talking** in the
   corridor.

E X E R C I S E

Complete each of the following sentences with the correct form of the verb in parentheses.

1. *(Encontrar)* _____ la pelota perdida, regresó a casa.

2. *(Abrir)* _____ el libro, comencé a leer.

3. *(Volver)* _____ a la librería, pedí otro libro.

4. *(Cerrar)* _____ la puerta, vi el papel.

5. *(Subir)* _____ la montaña, podíamos ver unos paisajes maravillosos.

6. Los niños salieron *(correr)* _____ de la casa.

7. Todos llegan *(hablar)* _____ a la vez.

8. Dejó a sus amigos *(discutir)* _____ la esquizofrenia.

9. Encontró a los chicos *(adornar)* _____ el postre.

10. Siempre venimos *(esperar)* _____ lo mejor.

G O A L   4

To distinguish between the use of the infinitive and the imperfective participle.

EXERCISE

Complete each sentence with the correct form of the English verb in parentheses.

1. Estoy *(working)* _____ aunque no quiero *(work)*
_____.

2. Al *(returning)* _____ del supermercado vi a mi
amiga. *(Talking)* _____ de las clases, supe que
hacemos una excursión mañana.

3. Pepe, antes de *(going)* _____ al estadio debes
arreglar tu cuarto. Sí, mamá. Estoy *(straightening up)*
_____ todo ahora.

4. *(Studying)* _____ es muy importante. *(Studying)*
_____ mucho, uno saca buenas notas. Pero, no
me gusta *(studying)* _____.

5. ¿Sigues *(walking)* _____ a las clases? Sí, *(walking)*
_____ es un buen ejercicio.

6. *(We leave?)* ¿_____? Ahora no, estamos *(learning)*
_____ a *(dance)* _____ un
baile nuevo.

7. En la biblioteca hay una regla. *(No talking.)*
_____. Pero, ¿por qué no podemos *(talk)*?
_____? Queremos *(to know)*
_____ la dirección de Juana. Porque están ustedes
(bothering) _____ a los otros que están aquí.

8. Sí, él estaba *(accompanying)* _____ a Anita. Los vi
(dancing) _____ juntos.

9. Debes *(go in)* _____ por la puerta principal. Los
obreros están *(painting)* _____ la otra.

10. Voy a *(read)* _____ ahora. Pero es imposible *(to
read)* _____ cuando los chicos están *(making)*
_____ tanto ruido.

Communication Pattern Exercise

Work with a partner. Take turns asking and answering the questions. Use imperfective participles in your answer.

1. ¿Estás escribiendo ahora?
2. ¿Estás esperando a tu amigo?
3. Señor, ¿estoy pidiendo demasiado?
4. Juana, ¿estoy ganando el juego?
5. ¿Llegó (ella) llorando?
6. ¿Están ustedes sembrando trigo?
7. ¿Estáis prestando atención?
8. Señor, ¿estamos ensuciando la atmósfera?
9. Rosa, ¿estamos descubriendo alternativos de energía?
10. ¿Están engañando al público los políticos?
11. ¿Aprendes mucho hablando a tus amigos?
12. Estando en el centro, ¿viste la manifestación?
13. ¿Lo encontró paseando por las calles desiertas?
14. ¿Las encontró cultivando las plantas?
15. ¿Lo encontró tocando el piano?
16. ¿Salió (él) corriendo?

Actividades de comunicación

I. Con participios imperfectos, describe una noche típica en tu casa y un sábado por la mañana. (Imagínate que eres un(a) reportero(a) de televisión que describe la vida de una familia famosa.) Compara lo que pasa en tu casa con lo que pasa en la casa de un(a) compañero(a) de clase.

II. Charadas—Imita una acción o una escena. Tus compañeros de clase van a tratar de averiguar lo que estás haciendo. Por ejemplo, ¿Estás comiendo, lavándote los dientes, etc.?

Refrán

Más vale pájaro en mano que cinto volando.
Explica el sentido. Da ejemplos de la vida.

3 The Perfective Participle

GOAL 1

To recognize a perfective participle in Spanish and to change any verb form to the perfective participle.

A perfective participle in English is marked by an *-ed* for most verbs. "Walked," "jumped," and "talked" are perfective participle forms in English. (These forms should not be confused with the past tense forms in English. For example, there is a difference between the word "walked" in "I walked" and "I have walked." This difference must be shown in Spanish.) A perfective participle in Spanish ends in *-do*. A regular perfective participle in Spanish adds two suffixes to the verb stem, one to indicate verb class and one to indicate the perfective participle.

	stem +	class vowel +	do
1st class	habl	a	do
2nd class	com	i	do
3rd class	viv	i	do

EXERCISE

Write the perfective participle for each regular verb form.

1. saliendo ___*salido*___

2. jugar _____ 9. vivo _____

3. aprendiste _____ 10. tenías _____

4. busco _____ 11. entrando _____

5. veníamos _____ 12. comer _____

6. vendiendo _____ 13. recibió _____

7. subir _____ 14. corro _____

8. ganaron _____ 15. cantaba _____

GOAL 2

To use the perfective participle as an action word after a form of *haber* or *ser*.

A perfective participle may be used in a sentence as a main verb.

A. The perfective participle is used in perfect verb forms.

Pattern: form of *haber* + perfective participle

Present perfect	he llegado	*I have arrived*
Future perfect	habrás llegado	*you will have arrived*
Past perfect	había llegado	*he had arrived*
Conditional perfect	habrían llegado	*they would have arrived*

B. The perfective participle is also used after a form of *ser* in the passive voice. After the verb *ser,* the perfective participle changes its ending to agree with the word to which it refers.

Pattern: form of *ser* + perfective participle

Singular: El edificio **fue destruido.**   *The building **was destroyed.***
La casa **fue destruida.**   *The house **was destroyed.***

Plural: Los edificios **fueron destruidos.**
Las casas **fueron destruidas.**

EXERCISE

Complete each sentence with the appropriate form of the perfective participle.

1. Mamá, Pepe ha *(usar)* _____ mi pluma.

2. ¿Habrás *(tener)* _____ tiempo para bañarte?

3. Ya habían *(venir)* _____ cuando salí.

4. La comida fue *(preparar)* _____ por mi hermana.

5. Los informes fueron *(meter)* _____ en la caja por los estudiantes.

6. El bolígrafo fue *(dejar)* _____ por Juan.

7. ¿Has *(pagar)* _____ la cuenta?

8. No, fue *(pagar)* _____por mi tío.

9. ¿Ha *(conseguir)* _____ usted el puesto?

10. Los antigüedades fueron *(comprar)* _____ por la señora de Virginia.

GOAL 3

To use the perfective participle as a describing word.

When the perfective participle is used as an adjective, the suffix of the perfective participle uses four endings just as any other adjective ending in *-o.*

Pattern: *estar* + perfective participle ending in *-o, -a, -os,* or *-as*

	Masculine	**Feminine**
Singular	El libro está **cerrado**.	La puerta está **cerrada**.
Plural	Los libros están **cerrados**.	Las puertas están **cerradas**.

Pattern: stem + perfective participle + noun

Terminada la tarea, María se acostó.

When (as soon as) she finished *her homework, María went to bed.*

Pattern: noun + perfective participle

Tengo la lección **preparada**.

*I have the lesson **prepared**.*

EXERCISE

Complete each sentence with the appropriate form of the perfective participle.

1. Las fábricas están *(cerrar)* _____ ahora.

2. Tengo los ejercicios *(preparar)* _____.

3. En las composiciones *(entregar)* _____ ayer hay muchos errores.

4. El hombre *(perder)* _____ es mi abuelo.

5. *(Acabar)* _____ la novela, la cerró lentamente.

6. Es una canción popular *(cantar)* _____ por todos.

7. *(Bañar)* _____ los niños, la madre podía descansar un poco.

8. Ese señor está *(casar)* _____.

9. *(Contestar)* _____ las preguntas, escuchó la radio.

10. La construcción está *(terminar)* _____.

GOAL 4

To distinguish between the uses of the infinitive, the imperfective participle, and the perfective participle in context.

EXERCISE

Complete each sentence with either an infinitive, an imperfective participle, or a perfective participle of the verb in parentheses, depending upon the context.

1. ¿Has *(acabar)* _____ la lectura? Estoy *(acabar)*

_____ la última página ahora. Me fue difícil *(acabar)*

_____ esta lectura porque no me gusta *(leer)*

_____ cuentos de este tipo.

2. Mamá, Manolo está *(correr)* _____ y dice en la pared
   "Prohibido *(correr)* _____ en los pasillos." Eduardo, es
   sábado y está bien *(correr)* _____ si no hay nadie en
   el edificio. Le gusta *(correr)* _____. ¿No has *(correr)*
   _____ tú nunca por los pasillos?

3. *(Servir)* _____ la comida, Raúl comió inmediatamente.
   (Salir) _____ de la casa después, vio a Teresa que
   también estaba *(salir)* _____. Le preguntó si ya había
   (comer) _____. Cuando ella dijo que sí, sabía que
   podían *(jugar)* _____ juntos.

4. ¿*(Contestar)* _____ él? Nunca ha *(contestar)*
   _____ ninguna pregunta en esta clase. No le gusta
   (contestar) _____ en clase porque no quiere
   (contestar) _____ mal.

5. ¿Aprendes a *(tocar)* _____ la guitarra? Sí, me gusta
   mucho *(tocar)* _____. Ya he *(aprender)*
   _____ cinco canciones. *(Tocar)* _____
   la guitarra uno puede descansar. ¿Deseas *(tocar)* _____
   ahora? No es posible *(tocar)* _____ en este momento
   porque mi hermano está *(tocar)* _____.

6. Después de *(perder)* _____ el suéter fuimos al
   despacho de los artículos *(perder)* _____ y le dije a la
   señora lo que yo había *(perder)* _____. *(Buscar)*
   _____ en una caja grande, lo encontró.

7. Volvimos a casa para *(encontrar)* _____ a los jóvenes
   (bailar) _____ en la cocina y *(comer)*
   _____ en la sala. Mi mujer estaba *(irritar)*
   _____. Pero después con la casa *(arreglar)*
   _____, estaba más calmada.

8. ¿Quieres *(escuchar)* _____ unos discos nuevos?
   ¿Podemos *(bailar)* _____ también? *(Escuchar)*
   _____ es agradable, pero *(bailar)*
   _____ es más agradable.

9. *(Entrar)* _____ en la casa, vimos que papá estaba

   (mirar) _____ la televisión y que mamá estaba *(hablar)*

   _____ por teléfono. Subimos a mi cuarto y bajamos

   cuando estaba *(servir)* _____ la cena.

10. ¿Fue *(asesinar)* _____ por un joven? No, lo mató un

    viejo que no podía *(ver)* _____ bien. Estaba *(manejar)*

    _____ sin los anteojos.

Communication Pattern Exercise

Work with a partner. Take turns asking and answering the questions. Use perfective participles in your answers.

1. ¿No has terminado todavía?
2. ¿Ha cuidado María a su hermana?
3. ¿Han conocido ustedes a muchos otros jóvenes?
4. ¿Han vivido los Rodríguez en Nuevo México?
5. ¿Fue pintada esta obra por Picasso?
6. ¿Son visitadas las pirámides por muchos turistas?
7. ¿Fue conquistada la civilización azteca por Cortés?
8. ¿Fueron completados los proyectos por los obreros?
9. ¿Está usted casado?
10. ¿Están ustedes enamorados?
11. ¿Está cerrada la puerta?
12. ¿Están despiertos los chicos?
13. Servida la comida, ¿comieron?
14. Callado el público, ¿empezó a hablar?
15. Recogidos los papeles, ¿entró?
16. ¿Tienes la lista preparada?
17. ¿Tienes todas las cosas escondidas?
18. ¿Es el camino indicado en el mapa?

Actividades de comunicación

Completa las siguientes oraciones.

1. Terminado el examen, nosotros _____.
2. Este semestre he _____.
3. Este semestre no he _____.

4. _____ fue atacado por _____.

5. Los estudiantes seleccionados _____.

6. _____ es admirado de _____.

Refránes

En boca cerrada no entra moscas.
Afortunado en el juego, desgraciado en amores.
Explica el sentido. Da ejemplos de la vida.

Simple Sentence Transformations

Introduction Grammatical concepts can be divided into two broad categories. First, rules of sentence formation are applied to create basic, simple sentences; second, rules of transformation are used to transform basic sentences into different and/or more complex patterns.

Parts I through VI of this text treat the rules of sentence formation. Knowledge of the forms and order of nouns and the words that go into noun phrases plus a knowledge of the verb suffix system and the forms and order of words that go into verb phrases enable the speaker to create basic sentences in Spanish.

Part VII of this text focuses on grammatical changes that can be made in the basic sentence patterns of the language. The purpose of these rules and patterns is not to enable the speaker to create a completely new sentence but to convert an existing sentence into one with a different emphasis or meaning. Much of the material in this part treats word order and manipulation of sentence parts. Topics treated include negatives, interrogatives, commands, positions of pronouns, passive voice, and *se*.

Negative	No me saludó.
Interrogative	¿Es de Texas tu novia?
Position of pronouns	Se los escondieron.
Passive voice	El campeón fue derrotado por el joven.
Se	No se ven mucho.

1 Negation

A Spanish sentence is made negative by placing *no* before the verb.

Come mucho.	**No** come mucho.	*He does **not** eat a lot.*
Está leyendo.	**No** está leyendo.	*She is **not** reading.*
Ha comido.	**No** ha comido.	*He has **not** eaten.*

The only words that may come between *no* and the verb it negates are object pronouns.

Le da el libro a María.	*He gives the book to María.*
No le da el libro a María.	*He **does not give** the book to María.*
Se lo da.	*He gives it to her.*
No se lo da.	***He does not give it to her.***

To make a noun negative, a form of *ninguno* is used. *Ningún* is used with masculine singular nouns and *ninguna* with feminine singular nouns. The plural forms, *ningunos* and *ningunas,* are used only with nouns that appear only in the plural.

Ningún alumno sabe eso.	***No student** knows that. (**No students** know that.)*
Ninguna chica va.	***No girl** is going. (**No girls** are going.*
No veo **ningunas tijeras.**	*I don't see **any scissors.***

EXERCISES

I. Rewrite each of the following sentences in the negative.

1. Este libro es mío.

   Este libro no es mío.

2. Esa familia ha gozado del verano.

   _____

3. En ese momento estaba mirando el mismo programa.

   _____

4. A los chicos les gusta jugar.

   _____

5. Le di el menú al mesero.

   _____

6. Me los dará a mí.

   _____

II. Rewrite each sentence, making the italicized noun negative.

1. Muchos *sabios* tienen orientación práctica.

   Ningún sabio tiene orientación práctica.
   _____

2. Todas las *azafatas* son simpáticas.

   _____

3. Unas *amigas* la ayudaban.

   _____

4. La *producción* de los pueblos es mayor cada año.

   _____

5. *Mi* compañero de cuarto es siempre amable.

   _____

6. Los *profesores* saben todas la respuestas.

   _____

GOAL 2

To give a negative reply to a question or a negative statement.

There are several patterns that you should learn in order to answer a question negatively or reply to a negative statement.

A. In Spanish one frequently repeats the negative *no*. The first *no* answers the question and the second makes the verb negative.

   ¿Va usted?   *Are you going?*

   No, no voy.   *No, I am **not** going.*

B. If there is no verb in the reply, *no* often follows the reply.

   ¿Quieres ir? Gracias, **no.**   *No, thanks.*

   No, gracias.   *No, thanks.*

   ¿Va usted? **Yo no.**   *Not I.*

C. *Tampoco* is used to show agreement with a negative statement.

   Juan no va al cine este fin de semana.

   Ni yo **tampoco.**   *Nor I **either.***

   Yo **tampoco.**   *Me **neither.***

   Tú **tampoco.**   *You **neither.***

   Nosotros **tampoco.**   *We **neither.***

   Note that *tampoco* may be used with any person subject pronoun.

D. With a verb in the *gustar* pattern, the negative structure is changed slightly.

A Juan no le gusta nadar.

A mí tampoco.   *Me neither.*

A ti tampoco.   *You neither.*

This structure also may be used with any person.

EXERCISES

I. Give a negative answer to each of the following questions.

1. ¿Es usted astronauta? _____ *No, no soy astronauta.* _____

2. ¿Vive usted en la escuela? _____

3. ¿Saltas rascacielos como Superhombre? _____

_____

4. ¿Entiendes la teoría de Einstein? _____

5. ¿Vuelas a la luna? _____

6. ¿Has dirigido una orquesta sinfónica? _____

_____

7. ¿Le das dinero al señor Rockefeller? _____

_____

8. ¿Estás durmiendo ahora? _____

II. Give a negative reply to each of the following statements.

1. ¿No quieres comer ahora? _____ *Ahora no.* _____

2. Yo no tengo hambre. ¿Y tú? _____

3. A mí no me gusta comer cuando no tengo hambre. _____

_____

4. No, a nosotros no nos gusta ir al cine. _____

5. Nosotros no tenemos que estudiar esta noche. _____

_____

6. ¿No va ella? _____

7. ¿No tenemos examen mañana? _____

GOAL 3

To give the negative of indefinite words.

In order to be able to use negative words correctly, you must be able to contrast them with their indefinite counterparts. The following are the most common:

algo	*something*	nada	*nothing*
alguien	*someone*	nadie	*no one*
alguno	*some*	ninguno	*none*
siempre	*always*	nunca *or* jamás	*never*
a veces	*sometimes*	nunca *or* jamás	*never*
muchas veces	*often*	nunca *or* jamás	*never*
o . . . o	*either . . . or*	ni . . . ni	*neither . . . nor*
también	*also, too*	tampoco	*neither, not either*

EXERCISES

I. Supply the opposite of each italicized word.

1. *Siempre* se acuesta temprano.   _____

2. No veo *nada*.   _____

3. *Alguien* me asustó.   _____

4. Caridad nació allí *también*.   _____

5. *Ninguna* persona lo sabía.   _____

6. *A veces* cantamos en la clase.   _____

7. No es *ni* justo *ni* correcto.   _____

II. Complete each sentence with the appropriate indefinite or negative word, depending upon the English meaning given in parentheses.

1. Sí, ese chico tiene *(something)* _____ en el bolsillo.

2. No, no tengo confianza en *(no one)* _____.

3. *(Either)* _____ vas conmigo *(or)*

   _____ sales solo.

4. Nosotros no lo hemos reconocido *(either)* _____.

5. *(Never)* _____ termina lo que empieza.

6. *(Some)* _____ productos son mejores.

GOAL 4

To use the double negative in Spanish.

A. In Spanish either one negative or a double negative is used, depending upon the position of the negative word in the sentence.

- Single negative—negative word before the verb

Nunca ayuda.   *He **never** helps.*

- Double negative—negative word after the verb, *no* before the verb

No ayuda **nunca.**   *He does **not ever** help. (He **never** helps.)*

EXERCISES

I. Rewrite each of the following sentences, negating the idea expressed in the sentence.

1. Tienes algo.   *No tienes nada.*

2. Toca muchas veces.   _____

3. O usted o Mario va a perder.   _____

4. Ellos celebraron también.   _____

5. Alguien me llamó.   _____

6. Algunos aeropiratas me asustan.   _____

II. Rewrite each of the following sentences, changing the negative statement to an affirmative statement.

1. No oigo nada.   *Sí, oigo algo.*

2. Jamás despertamos a mamá.   _____

3. Tampoco sabían.   _____

4. Nadie quiere prestármelo.   _____

5. Ni ellos lo creen, ni nosotros lo creemos.   _____

6. Ningún animal doméstico vale tanto.   _____

B. There are additional, related uses of negative words.

- More than one negative word may occur in a sentence.

Nunca veo a **nadie.**   *I **never** see **anyone.***

Tampoco veo **nunca** a **nadie.**   *I **never** see **anyone either.***

Note that only one negative word is used in English.

- In Spanish a negative is used after a comparative.

Roberto tiene más que **nadie.**   *Roberto has more than **anyone.***

Me siento peor que **nunca.**   *I feel worse than **ever.***

- In Spanish the expression *¿no es verdad?* (often shortened to *¿verdad?* or *¿no?)* is often added to the end of a statement. In English we repeat the helper verb in the sentence.

Tú vas también. **¿no?**   *You're going, too, **aren't you?***

Tú no sabes, **¿verdad?**   *You don't know, **do you?***

EXERCISE   Give the English equivalent of each sentence.

1. Yo nunca tomo nada tampoco.

   _____

2. Ahora los policías preguntan más que nunca.

   _____

3. Me acompañarás, ¿no?

   _____

4. ¿Sabe (él) más que nadie?

   _____

5. El chico quería el potro más que nada.

   _____

6. Nadie le habla jamás a nadie.

   _____

7. No me diste las llaves, ¿verdad?

   _____

Communication Pattern Exercise

Work with a partner. Take turns asking and answering the questions.

1. ¿Escribes?
   Sí, escribo. No, no escribo.
2. ¿Les escribes a tus abuelos?
3. ¿Les has escrito esta semana?
4. ¿Les escribes algunas notas?
5. ¿Les escribes muchas veces?
6. Siempre les escribes algo importante, ¿no?
7. ¿También le escribes a algún otro pariente?
8. ¿Le escribes más que nadie?
9. ¿Escribes con tinta?

Actividades de comunicación

I. Escribe una oración con cada una de las siguientes palabras: ¿verdad?, más que nunca, alguien, ninguno, nada, a veces, o . . . o.

II. Piensa en tus amigos. Selecciona a uno(a) que sea optimista y otro(a) que sea pesimista. Escribe un diálogo entre los dos sobre un tema de interés.

Refránes

No es oro todo lo que reluce.
No hay rosa sin espinas.
No hay mal de que bien no venga.
Explica el sentido. Da ejemplos de la vida.

---

2 Interrogatives

GOAL 1

To convert a statement into a yes/no question.

A. In Spanish as well as in English there are two ways to convert a statement into a question. The first is by raising your voice at the end of the sentence instead of lowering it.

Statement: Juan tiene un coche.   *Juan has a car.*

Question: ¿Juan tiene un coche?   *Juan has a car?*

Note that in Spanish an inverted question mark must precede the question.

EXERCISE

Say each statement aloud, then say each as a question.

1. Me falta una bicicleta.
2. Los ancianos reconocieron a su hijo.
3. Abres la puerta.
4. Compraremos unas hamburguesas.
5. Pescabais en el lago.
6. El señor González dirigió las actividades.

B. In both Spanish and English it is also possible to invert the subject and the verb. In a Spanish question the subject comes after the complete verb. In English it comes between the helper verb and the main verb. Of course, there is still a rise in the voice at the end of the question.

Juan canta.   *Juan sings.*

¿Canta Juan?   *Does Juan sing?*

Los invitados han llegado.   *The guests have arrived.*

¿Han llegado los invitados?   *Have the guests arrived?*

There are two points to remember as you invert the subject and verb. First, the entire noun phrase used as the subject is inverted. Second, if the subject is short, it is placed immediately after the verb. If it is long, the rest of the sentence comes immediately after the verb, and the subject is placed at the end of the sentence.

Todos estos estudiantes viven aquí.	*All these students live here.*
¿Viven aquí todos los chicos?	*Do all the children live here?*
Juan vive en esa casa grande cerca de la piscina.	*Juan lives in that big house near the pool.*
¿Vive Juan en esa casa grande cerca de la piscina?	*Does Juan live in that big house near the pool?*

EXERCISE

Rewrite each of the following sentences, inverting the subject and verb in order to form a question.

1. Los ancianos roncan.

   _____

2. Los dos se miraban.

   _____

3. La pareja andaba lentamente por el vecindario.

   _____

4. Los turistas de los Estados Unidos ya habían visto la catedral.

   _____

5. Este grupo está construyendo un aparato para destruir el plástico sin contaminar nada.

   _____

6. Las flores que le trajo a su novia son rojas.

   _____

GOAL 2

To convert a yes/no question into an information question using the interrogative words and the proper intonation pattern.

A. An interrogative word naturally is used to ask a question. A question beginning with an interrogative word normally requires an information answer. You can always distinguish between a yes/no question and an information question by the intonation pattern of the speaker's voice. In a yes/no question the intonation of the voice rises. In an information question the intonation of the voice starts high and drops.

You can easily recognize an information question by noticing the interrogative words. They are always written with an accent mark.

EXERCISE

Say the following questions aloud to another student, paying special attention to the falling intonation pattern.

1. ¿Qué haces?
2. ¿Qué libro le gusta más?
3. ¿Cuál es la capital de México?
4. ¿Dónde están sus padres?
5. ¿Quién es su mejor amigo?
6. ¿Cómo está usted?
7. ¿Qué tal fueron las vacaciones?
8. ¿Cuánto cuesta este sarape?

B. The most commonly used interrogative word is *¿qué?* ("what?"). It may be used alone or with a noun.

¿Qué tiene en la mano?	**What** *does he have in his hand?*
¿Qué almacén le gusta más?	**What department store** *do you like best?*

When *¿qué?* is used alone, the answer will be a description, a definition, or an explanation. When *¿qué?* is used with a noun, the answer will be a discrimination or a selection.

Depending upon the verb with which it is used, *¿qué?* may be preceded by a preposition. If the verb is followed by a preposition in the answer, then that same preposition normally must precede the interrogative word in the question. Spanish speakers do not end a sentence with a preposition.

¿De qué hablabas?	*What were you talking **about?***
Hablaba **del** partido.	*I was talking **about** the football game.*

This same pattern is used in English, but not as frequently.

To what do I attribute this sudden burst of energy?
About whom were you talking?
Into which store did he go?

In English the position of the preposition varies with the speaker. However, in Spanish the preposition, if it is used, must precede the interrogative word.

EXERCISE

Change the yes/no questions into information questions using *¿qué?*

1. ¿Leíste algo ayer?   *¿Qué leíste ayer?*
2. ¿Es el león un animal?   _____
3. ¿Escogió Carmen el vestido azul?   _____
4. ¿Leías la novela corta?   _____
5. ¿Sueñas con monstruos horribles?   _____
6. ¿Quieres el televisor importado?   _____

C. *¿Cuál?* and *¿cuáles?* ("what," "which") have a similar meaning to the pattern *¿qué?* + noun. *¿Cuál?* may refer to people or to things. However, it is used in different patterns. The three patterns in which *¿cuál?* is used are as follows;

- *¿cuál?* + verb

  ¿Cuál visitaron ustedes la última vez?   ***Which did you visit** last time?*

- *¿cuál?* + de + noun + verb

  ¿Cuáles de las clases prefieres?   ***Which classes** do you prefer?*

- *¿cuál?* + ser

  ¿Cuál es su opinión?   ***What (which) is** your opinion?*

Contrast the sentence in the second pattern with the following question using *¿qué?*

¿Qué ciudad prefieres?   *What city do you prefer?*

EXERCISE

Change each yes/no question to information questions using *¿cuál?* or *¿cuáles?*

1. ¿Compraste las blandas o las duras?

   ¿Cuáles compraste?

2. ¿Sabes sus planes?

3. ¿Quieren los turistas uno nuevo o uno antiguo?

4. ¿Prefieres el coche grande o el pequeño?

5. ¿Busca las maletas negras o las pardas?

6. ¿Toman la hija menor o la mayor?

7. ¿Saben ustedes su nacionalidad?

8. ¿Sabe usted la fecha?

D. *¿Quién?* and *¿quiénes?* refer to persons. Note both the singular and the plural forms.

¿Quién es el profesor?   ***Who** is the teacher?*

¿Quiénes son sus amigos?   ***Who** are your friends?*

¿Quien? may also be preceded by a preposition.

¿A quiénes hablabas anoche?   ***To whom** were you talking last night?*

EXERCISE

Change each yes/no question to an information question using *¿quién?* or *¿quiénes?*

1. ¿Viene el embajador esta noche?   *¿Quién viene esta noche?*

2. ¿Destruyeron los García el coche?   _____

3. ¿Viajaron Ana y Rosa con sus padres? _____

4. ¿Damos el mensaje a su padre?   _____

5. ¿Son de él estos artículos?   _____

6. ¿Es de ellas este apartamento?   _____

E. *¿Cómo?* ("how?," "what?") refers to how something is done or to the condition or characteristics of someone or something. It has only one form and is never preceded by a preposition.

¿Cómo está usted?   ***How** are you?*

¿Cómo es Teresa?   ***What** is Teresa **like?***

EXERCISE

Form information questions using *¿cómo?* and the cues given.

1. estar/tú   *¿Cómo estás?*

2. ser/tu novia   _____

3. viajar/sus padres   _____

4. ser/esta clase   _____

5. llegar/los turistas   _____

6. escribirse/la palabra "cinco"   _____

7. ir/nosotros/al gimnasio   _____

F. A question using *¿qué tal?* is asking for an opinion. It has only one form and is never preceded by a preposition.

¿Qué tal le gusta el drama?   ***How do you like** the play? (**What do you think of** of play?)*

Hola, **¿qué tal?**   *Hi. **How are things?***

When followed by the verb *ser*, *¿qué tal?* and *¿cómo?* are interchangeable.

¿Cómo es el artículo?   ***How*** *is the article?*

¿Qué tal (es) la vida moderna?   ***What's*** *modern life like?*

However, in some patterns the meaning is different. In addition, *¿qué tal?* may not be used in some patterns in which *¿cómo?* is used.

¿Cómo le gusta el té?   *How do you like your tea?*

Con limón y azúcar.   *With lemon and sugar.*

¿Qué tal le gusta la película?   *What do you think of the movie?*

A mí me parece emocionante.   *I think it is exciting.*

EXERCISE

Change each yes/no question into an information question using *¿qué tal?* or *¿cómo?*

1. ¿Fue pesada la conferencia?   _____

2. ¿Son emocionantes los partidos?   _____

3. ¿Estás agitado?   _____

4. ¿Estaban desconcertados?   _____

5. ¿Es agradable el clima de la Florida?   _____

G. *¿Dónde?* means "where?". Its form does not change, but with certain verbs it is preceded by a preposition.

¿Dónde *está su padre?*   **Where** *is your father?*

¿De dónde es?   **Where** *is she* ***from?***

EXERCISE

Change each yes/no question into an information question using *¿dónde?*

1. ¿Están los barcos en el canal?_____

2. ¿Es el concierto en el auditorio?   _____

3. ¿Salieron por la puerta principal?   _____

4. ¿Saldremos para la Argentina mañana? _____

5. ¿Va a la feria del estado este fin de semana? _____

H. *¿Cuándo?* is used like its English counterpart, "when," except for the position of the subject in relation to the verb. *¿Cuándo?* has only one form, and it is not normally preceded by a preposition.

¿Cuándo sales?   **When** *are you leaving?*

EXERCISE

Change each yes/no question to an information question using *¿cuándo?*

1. ¿Nos dirá mañana?   _____

2. ¿Leyó este libro el verano pasado?   _____

3. ¿Quieres jugar ahora?   _____

4. ¿Lo escribió ayer?   _____

5. ¿Habían llegado temprano los otros? _____

I. *¿Cuánto, -a, -os, -as?* ("how much?," "how many?") refer to quantity or to number. *¿Cuánto?* has four forms, and it may be preceded by a preposition. It may be used with a noun or by itself.

¿Cuántos regalos haces?	***How many gifts** do you make?*
¿Cuánta nieve hay?	***How much snow** is there?*
¿Por cuánto me lo vendes?	***For how much** will you sell it to me?*
¿Cuántas quieres?	***How many** do you want?*

EXERCISE

Change each yes/no question into an information question using *¿cuánto?*

1. ¿Tengo yo veinte dólares?   _____

2. ¿Quieres todas las guías?   _____

3. ¿Quiere usted mucho dinero?   _____

4. ¿Le hace falta mucha ayuda?   _____

5. ¿Hablas con dos colegas?   _____

6. ¿Compras regalos para tres muchachas? _____

J. *¿Por qué?* ("why") is used to ask the reason why something happened. *¿Para qué?* is used to ask the purpose of an action.

¿Por qué llegaste tarde?	***Why** did you arrive late?*
Porque me perdí.	*Because I got lost.*
¿Para qué estudias tanto?	*Why do you study so much?*
Para sacar buenas notas.	*In order to get good grades.*

EXERCISE

Change each statement into information questions using *¿por qué?* or *¿para qué?*

1. Asistió a la universidad para obtener mejor empleo.

_____

2. Asistió a la universidad porque quería aprender.

_____

3. Lo compraste porque le gustaba.

_____

4. Lo compraste sólo para romperlo.

_____

5. Le hablan porque es su amigo.

_____

6. Le hablan para darle más confianza.

_____

Communication Pattern Exericse

Work with a partner. Take turns asking and answering the questions.

1. ¿Qué es su padre? ¿Ingeniero? ¿Y su madre?
2. ¿Qué equipo de fútbol es su favorito?
3. ¿Qué haces por la noche?
4. ¿Cuál es la fecha?
5. ¿Cuáles son sus cantantes favoritos?
6. ¿Cuáles de las diferentes marcas de coches prefieres?
7. ¿Cuál tiene su familia?
8. ¿A quién le hablas más?
9. ¿Con quiénes vas al museo?
10. ¿De quién es este libro?
11. ¿Quién es su actor favorito?
12. ¿Cómo está usted?
13. ¿Cómo es usted?
14. ¿Qué tal te gusta la ciudad en que vives?
15. ¿Adónde van ustedes para las vacaciones?
16. ¿Por qué trabajan sus padres?
17. ¿Para qué trabajan sus padres?

Actividades de comunicación

I. Prepara una pregunta, por lo menos, con cada una de las palabras interrogativas, y haz preguntas a tus compañeros de clase.

II. Imagina que tienes un/una visitante de Hispanoamérica en tu universidad. Escribe una conversación con muchas preguntas, como las que crees que haría tu visitante, y da respuestas que, en tu opinión, le serían más útiles.

Refrán

Quien mal anda mal acaba.
Explica el sentido. Da ejemplos de la vida.

3 Affirmative Familiar Commands

GOAL

To add the appropriate verb endings to give familiar commands.

The affirmative familiar (*tú* and *vosotros*) commands are quite easy to form. In the singular (*tú*) form these forms are the same as the *él* form of the verb in the present tense. The context in which each is used clarifies the meaning.

Habla.	*He talks.*	**Habla** *(tú) en voz baja.*	**Talk** *in a low voice.*
Come.	*She eats.*	**Come** (tú) *aquí.*	**Eat** *here.*
Abre.	*He opens.*	**Abre** *(tú) la boca.*	**Open** *your mouth.*

In the plural forms, the *r* after the class vowel is replaced by a *d*.

habl	a r	**Habl a d** (vosotros) en español.	**Speak** *in Spanish.*
com	e r	**Com e d** aquí.	**Eat** *here.*
abr	i r	**Abr i d** los ojos.	**Open** *your eyes.*

Note that when the pronoun is used, it follows the command form. Remember, too, that the *vosotros* form is used in Spain, while the *ustedes* form is used generally in Spanish America.

Eight common verbs do not follow this pattern in the familiar singular. These verbs are regular in the familiar plural. The irregular forms in the singular are as follows:

hacer	**Haz** (tú) los quehaceres.	**Do** *your chores.*
poner	**Pon** (tú) el libro aquí.	**Put** *the book here.*
tener	**Ten** (tú) paciencia.	**Have** *patience.*
venir	**Ven** (tú) acá.	**Come** *here.*
salir	**Sal** (tú) de aquí.	**Leave** *here.*
ser	**Sé** (tú) buen chico.	**Be** *a good boy.*
decir	**Di** (tú) todo.	**Tell** *everything.*
ir	**Ve** (tú) a tu cuarto.	**Go** *to your room.*

As you can see, *poner, tener, venir,* and *salir* use the stem for the familiar command, *ser* uses the stem plus the theme vowel, and the last two are completely irregular.

EXERCISE

I. Supply the affirmative familiar commands for these infinitives.

1. llegar   _llega, llegad_

2. leer   _____   8. enviar(í)   _____

3. escribir   _____   9. salir   _____

4. cerrar (ie)   _____   10. ver   _____

5. dormir (ue)   _____   11. hacer   _____

6. servir (i)   _____   12. decir   _____

7. oír (y)   _____

II. Change the verb in each sentence as indicated.

1. Cantad en voz alta. Y Pepe, _____ en voz alta también.

2. Poned los abrigos en la cama. Y Josefina, _____ el tuyo allí también.

3. Pensad en los recursos naturales. Y Carlos, _____ en ellos también.

4. Recordad que somos libres. Y Manuela, _____ lo mismo.

5. Sabed los nombres de los autores. Y Roberto, _____ lo mismo.

6. Marta, ven a mi oficina. Y _____ (vosotros) también.

7. José, empíeza aquí. Y _____ (vosotros) en la próxima fila.

8. Enrique, escribe la composición a máquina. Y _____ (vosotros) la vuestra de la misma manera.

9. Pepito, ten cuidado al cruzar la calle. Y _____ (vosotros) cuidado también.

10. Lola, mira ese traje. Y _____ (vosotros) ése también.

Communication Pattern Exercises

I. Write new sentences using affirmative commands to ask the people to do what they are not doing.

1. Carlos no ayuda a don Fernando.

   Carlos, ayuda a don Fernando.

2. Jorge no escribe con tinta.

   _____

3. Alicia no cree lo que dicen.

_____

4. Raúl no viene a la fiesta.

_____

5. Pepito no es buen muchacho.

_____

6. María Juana no dice la verdad.

_____

7. Susana no hace la tarea.

_____

8. Teodoro no sale ahora.

_____

9. Pedro no pone la ropa en la cesta.

_____

10. José y Juan no toman un taxi.

_____

11. Carlos y Conchita no tienen fe.

_____

12. María y Rodrigo no duermen más.

_____

II. Using the following chart, write ten sentences with singular affirmative familiar commands and five with plural forms.

Names	Verbs		Words and phrases	
hijo mío	abrir	leer	ventana	con Ana
amigo mío	cerrar	pagar	guitarra	en coche
querida mía	almorzar	salir	a las diez	quehaceres
Bernardo	decir	tocar	temprano	paquete
Catalina	escribir	venir	aquí	mañana
Papá	hacer	volver	en casa	libro
Raúl y Rosa	poner		carta	mesa
Susana y Carlos			lectura	cuarto
amigos míos			cuento	a pie
			verdad	

Actividades de comunicación

Escribe una conversación de una página en la que una madre o un padre dice a sus hijos lo que deben hacer. Emplee tantos imperativos, singulares y plurales, como sea posible.

Refránes

Haz bien y no mires a quien.
Haz lo que digo, no lo que hago.
Explica el sentido. Da ejemplos de la vida.

---

4 Polite Commands and Negative Familiar Commands

GOAL 1
To add the appropriate endings to the stem to form the present subjunctive.

The present subjunctive is formed by using an *e* class vowel for *A* verbs in all forms, and an *a* class vowel for *E* and *I* verbs in all forms. Thus, the *opposite* vowel sound signals the subjunctive.

A. The suffixes for present-tense verbs in the indicative and subjunctive are as follows:

Singular	Indicative			Subjunctive	
	A	E	I	A	E and I
yo	o	o	o	e	a
tú	a s	e s	e s	e s	a s
usted	a	e	e	e	e
él/ella	a	e	e	e	a

Plural					
nosotros,-as	a mos	e mos	i mos	e mos	a mos
vosotros,-as	á is	é is	ís	é is	á is
ustedes	a n	e n	e n	e n	a n
ellos/ellas	a n	e n	e n	e n	a n

EXERCISE

Complete each verb form by adding the correct class vowel to form the present subjunctive.

1. habl___*e*___mos
2. (yo) com_____
3. viv_____s
4. (usted) cant_____
5. escrib_____is

6. vend_____n
7. (yo) repit_____
8. (él) pierd_____
9. durm_____mos
10. almuerc_____n

11. dig_____is
12. conozc_____s
13. (yo) salg_____
14. (ella) coj_____
15. busqu_____n

B. Learning the suffixes of the present subjunctive is quite easy. The problem centers around learning the stems of the verbs that have irregular forms in the subjunctive. These irregularities can be divided into two types (1) those verbs in which the *yo* form of the present indicative ends in -*o* and (2) those verbs in which the *yo* form does not end in -*o*.

• Verbs in which the *yo* form ends in -*o*.

Stem-vowel changing verbs

Class 1 (A and E verbs) o➔ue, e➔ie	Class 2 (I verbs) o➔ue, e➔ie, i	Class 3 (I verbs) e➔i, i
encuentro	*duermo*	*sirvo*
encuentr e encuentr e s encuentr e	duerm a duerm a s duerm a	sirv a sirv a s sirv a
encontr e mos encontr é is	durm a mos durm á is	sirv a mos sirv á is
encuentr e n	duerm a n	sirv a n

Note the vowel in the stem of the boxed forms. In *A* and *E* verbs there is no vowel change. In the case of *I* verbs the *o* becomes *u* and the *e* becomes *i* in the *nosotros* and *vosotros* forms. All the other stem-vowel changing verbs follow the same pattern.

Other stem changes

conozco   conozca, conozcas, conozca, conozcamos, conozcáis, conozcan

salgo   salga, salgas, etc.

caigo   caiga, caigas, etc.

continúo   continúe, continúes, continúe, continuemos, continuéis, continúen

Note that in this type of verb the stem of the *yo* form in the present indicative is kept in all the forms of the present subjunctive.

Verbs with spelling changes

("k" sound)	buscar:	busco—bus*qu*e, bus*qu*es, etc.
("g" sound)	pagar:	pa*g*o—pa*gu*e, pa*gu*es, etc.
("h" sound)	coger:	co*j*o—co*j*a, co*j*as, etc.
("gw" sound)	averiguar:	averi*gu*o—averi*gü*e, averi*gü*es, etc.
("g" sound)	distinguir:	distin*g*o—distin*g*a, distin*g*as, etc.
("s" sound)	cruzar:	cru*z*o—cru*c*e, cru*c*es, etc.

Note that these are the same spelling changes to represent the same sound in front of different vowels as occur with the same verbs in the present and preterite. The sound of the stem in the *yo* form of the present indicative is maintained throughout.

- Those forms in which the *yo* form does not end in -o

	Indicative	Subjunctive
dar	doy	dé, des, dé, demos, deis, den
estar	estoy	esté, estés, esté, estemos, estéis, estén
haber	he	haya, hayas, etc.
ir	voy	vaya, vayas, etc.
saber	sé	sepa, sepas, etc.
ser	soy	sea, seas, etc.

Dar and *estar* actually form the subjunctive in the regular manner. (The accent of *dé* is to distinguish it from *de* meaning "of.") The others have irregular stems, but you will notice similarities between the forms of *haber* and *ir* and between *saber* and *ser*. The important point to note is that the opposite class vowel is maintained throughout.

EXERCISE

Complete each sentence with the appropriate subjunctive stem of the verb.

1. *(Resolver)* _____an ustedes sus propios problemas.

2. *(Contar)* Que _____e el paciente hasta ciento.

3. *(Dormir)* _____amos afuera esta noche.

4. *(Pensar)* _____emos en nuestros padres.

5. *(Tener)* _____an ustedes cuidado.

6. *(Construir)* _____a usted otro modelo.

7. *(Traer)* _____amos una frazada.

8. *(Llegar)* _____e usted a los ocho.

9. *(Recoger)* _____an ustedes todo aquí.

10. *(Buscar)* _____emos otro sitio.

11. *(Estar)* _____én ustedes aquí para los dos.

12. *(Ser)* _____amos más tolerantes.

13. *(Ir)* _____a usted a su laboratorio pronto.

14. *(Saber)* _____an ustedes mejor las fórmulas para el próximo experimento.

GOAL 2

To form polite affirmative commands.

The affirmative polite commands are the same as the *usted* and *ustedes* forms of the present subjunctive.

hablar	hable	(usted)	hablen	(ustedes)
comer	coma	(usted)	coman	(ustedes)
tener	tenga	(usted)	tengan	(ustedes)
cerrar	cierre	(usted)	cierren	(ustedes)
saber	sepa	(usted)	sepan	(ustedes)

If the pronoun *usted* is used, it follows the verb.

EXERCISE

Form new sentences using affirmative polite commands to ask the people to do what they are not doing.

1. La señorita García no compra leche.

   Señorita García, compre leche.

2. El señor Rodríguez no vende los boletos.

   _____

3. La señora Sánchez no sube la escalera.

   _____

4. La profesora no viene esta noche.

_____

5. La señora Gómez no va con los otros.

_____

6. La señora Alborg no almuerza.

_____

7. Los basureros no recogen los papeles.

_____

8. Los niños no cruzan con la luz verde.

_____

9. Las señoritas no siguen con el trabajo.

_____

10. Los señores no dicen la verdad.

_____

GOAL 3

To form polite negative commands.

The affirmative polite commands are made negative by putting *no* in front of the verb phrase.

Hable (usted).	No hable (usted).
Hablen (ustedes).	No hablen (ustedes).

EXERCISE

Form negative polite commands to ask the people not to do what they are doing.

1. La señorita Cibrián llama por teléfono.

   Señorita Cibrián, no llame por teléfono.

2. Los bebés comen con los dedos.

   _____

3. La señora Fernández llega cansada.

   _____

4. El señor González es exigente.

   _____

5. Mi amigo continúa el estudio de la astrología.

_____

6. Los bomberos hacen mucho ruido.

_____

7. Los jóvenes viajan por la noche.

_____

8. Las señoras están enojadas.

_____

9. Las abogadas cierran los casos.

_____

10. Los pintores piden más tiempo.

_____

GOAL 4

To respond to a question by telling the person what to do.

Note the following pattern:

Señora, ¿entro por aquí?	*Ma'am, do I go in here?*
No, señor, no entre usted por aquí. Entre por la otra puerta.	*No, sir, don't go in there. Go in the other door.*

EXERCISE

Complete the reply to each question based on the above pattern.

1. Maestro, ¿toco canciones peruanas?

_____ canciones francesas.

2. Señorita, ¿tomo éste?

_____ el otro.

3. Señor, ¿vuelvo con Jorge?

_____ con Juan.

4. Señora, ¿pongo los papeles aquí?

_____ en el escritorio.

5. Profesora, ¿abro todas las ventanas?

_____ una solamente.

6. Señor, ¿seguimos derecho?

_____ a la izquierda.

7. Profesor, ¿leemos todo el capítulo?

_____ la primera parte.

8. Señora, ¿dejamos los paquetes en el pasillo?

_____ en la cocina.

9. Señorita, ¿salimos antes de las ocho?

_____ después.

10. Profesora, ¿vamos por esta carretera?

_____ por ésa.

GOAL 5

To use familiar negative commands.

The negative familiar commands are the same as the *tú* and *vosotros* forms of the present subjunctive.

hablar	no hables	(tú)	no habléis	(vosotros)
comer	no comas	(tú)	no comáis	(vosotros)
tener	no tengas	(tú)	no tengáis	(vosotros)
cerrar	no cierres	(tú)	no cerréis	(vosotros)
saber	no sepas	(tú)	no sepáis	(vosotros)

Remember that in Hispanic America the *ustedes* forms are normally used instead of the *vosotros* forms.

EXERCISE

Form negative familiar commands to ask the people not to do what they are doing.

1. José lava el coche.

   José, no laves el coche. _____

2. Mariana corre por la cocina.

   _____

3. Raúl escribe en las paredes.

   _____

4. Pepe viene con nosotros.

_____

5. Catalina sube la escalera.

_____

6. Pedro despierta al bebé.

_____

7. Rosa y Alfredo van a la casa de Ramón.

_____

8. Pepita y Marta están tristes.

_____

9. Mi prima y José tocan el clarinete.

_____

10. Berta y Lola pierden los guantes.

_____

Communciation Pattern Exercises

I. Complete each of the following commands with the appropriate command forms.

1. Pepe, no *(dejar)* _____ la carne; y *(comer)*

_____ la ensalada también.

2. Ana, *(escribir)* _____ las tuyas en la pizarra.

3. Hija mía, no *(vivir)* _____ así.

4. Chiquito, *(salir)* _____ para jugar, por favor, pero no

(salir) _____ del patio.

5. José, *(ir)* _____ solamente a la casa de Roberto. No *(ir)*

_____ a la de Juan.

6. ¡Cuánto me gusta esta canción, amigos míos! Ahora, *(cantar)*

_____ la misma otra vez. Y luego no *(cantar)*

_____ más. Estoy cansado.

7. Niños, *(escribir)* _____ este poema para la semana que viene. Josefina *(escribir)* (tú) _____ el de la próxima página. Y Raúl, no *(escribir)* _____ ninguno. Puedes esperar hasta mañana.

8. Juana, Marta, no *(hacer)* _____ eso.

9. No *(gritar)* (vosotros) _____ tanto.

10. Adiós, hijos míos; *(ir)* _____ si queréis, pero no *(volver)* _____ demasiado tarde.

II. Answer each question according to the model.

1. Diego, ¿entro por aquí?

   No, no entres por aquí. Entra por la otra puerta. _____

2. Dorotea, ¿le pregunto al hotelero?

   _____ a Lola.

3. Roberto, ¿leo más?

   _____ sólo dos páginas.

4. Juan, ¿construyo un puente?

   _____ una casa.

5. Juana, ¿traigo éstos?

   _____ los otros.

6. Amigos míos, ¿servimos el postre ahora?

   _____ el postre más tarde.

7. Mamá, ¿jugamos el mismo otra vez?

   _____ otro ahora.

8. Papá, ¿le damos el premio a Guillermo?

   _____ el premio a Paco.

Actividades de comunicación

I. El objeto de esta actividad es decirles a otros que hacer o no hacer. (Esto es buena práctica para ser un(a) profesor(a) o un padre.) Preparar por lo menos tres imperativos en cada una de estas categorías.

Decirle a un(a) compañero(a) de clase que haga algo.

Decirle a un(a) compañero(a) de clase que no haga algo.

Decirles a todos que hagan algo.

Decirles a todos que no hagan algo.

Decirle al(a la) profesor(a) que haga algo.

Decirle al(a la) profesor(a) que no haga algo.

II. Escribe una conversación de media página como mínimo con tantos imperativos como sea posible. Puedes describir una escena en casa o en la escuela en la que tratas de tomar una decisión. Por ejemplo, ustedes toman un examen. Sabes que otro(a) compañero(a) de clase está mirando el libro de texto. ¿Vas a decirle al(a la) profesor(a) o no?

Refránes

No trates de cubrir el sol con un dedo.
No dejes para mañana lo que puedas hacer hoy.
Explica el sentido. Da ejemplos de la vida.

5 Other Command Forms

GOAL 1

To use the appropriate endings to form the *nosotros, él,* and *ellos* forms of the present subjunctive.

The present subjunctive is characterized by the "opposite" vowel, an *e* for *A* verbs and an *a* for *E* and *I* verbs. Since the *nosotros, él,* and *ellos* commands all use the subjunctive form, they also have the opposite class vowel. The person-number suffixes are regular.

	Nosotros			*El*		*Ellos*		
hablar	habl	e	mos	habl	e	habl	e	n
comer	com	a	mos	com	a	com	a	n
tener	teng	a	mos	teng	a	teng	a	n
cerrar	cerr	e	mos	cierr	e	cierr	e	n
dormir	durm	a	mos	duerm	a	duerm	a	n
saber	sep	a	mos	sep	a	sep	a	n

Note that the stem-vowel changing *I* verbs have a stem change in the *nosotros* form.

EXERCISE

Complete each of the following verb forms by supplying the correct class vowel to form the present subjunctive.

1. Sub_____mos este árbol.

2. Que llam_____ José.

3. Que vend_____n los otros los suyos.

4. Teng_____mos una fiesta en nuestro apartamento.

5. Que destruy_____n todas la fábricas.

6. Que cuelgu_____ ella la ropa.

7. Dig_____mos a Pepe.

8. Que hag_____ mamá los sandwiches.

9. Que se vay_____n a pie.

10. Sirv_____mos helado con fresas.

GOAL 2

To form commands with *nosotros*.

When one is in a group, it is quite common to hear someone say "let's" do something. In Spanish there are two ways to say "let's": with an *ir a* construction or with the present subjunctive.

jugar	Vamos a jugar. *or* Juguemos.
volver	Vamos a volver. *or* Volvamos.
salir	Vamos a salir. *or* Salgamos.

Of course, *vamos a jugar* can also mean "we are going to play." The context will make the meaning clear. The expression *ir a* is not used with verbs of motion. Therefore, "let's" with verbs like "go," "come," etc. must use the subjunctive form.

To say "let's not," one must use the subjunctive form of the verb.

No vamos a jugar.	*We are not going to play.*
No juguemos.	*Let's not play.*

EXERCISES

I. Write new sentences using a "let's" command to ask your group to do the opposite of what it is doing.

1. No abrimos los regalos.

   Abramos los regalos or *Vamos a abrir los regalos.*

2. Tomamos la máquina de escribir.

   _____

3. No compramos otro.

   _____

4. Damos el postre a papá.

_____

5. No vamos al partido.

_____

6. Despertamos a los otros.

_____

7. No prendemos las luces.

_____

8. Volvemos antes de la medianoche.

_____

II. Answer each question according to the model.

1. ¿Comemos?

   a. (Usted tiene hambre.)

   Sí, vamos a comer or _Comamos._

   b. (Usted no tiene hambre.)

   No, no comemos.

2. ¿Escuchamos discos?

   a. (Usted prefiere hablar.)

   _____

   b. (Usted quiere escuchar discos.)

   _____

3. ¿Abrimos las ventanas?

   a. (Usted tiene calor.)

   _____

   b. (Usted ya tiene frío.)

   _____

4. ¿Volvemos a casa?

   a. (Usted quiere esperar un poco.)

   _____

   b. (Usted está listo para volver.)

   _____

5. ¿Cruzamos aquí?

   a. (Usted está de acuerdo.)

   _____

   b. (Usted sabe que hay bastante tráfico aquí.)

   _____

G O A L 3

To give affirmative or negative indirect commands.

The indirect commands in Spanish are formed according to the following pattern:
Que + present subjunctive of *él* or *ellos* form of verb.

Que salga (él).	*Have (let) him leave.*
Que salgan (ellos).	*Have (let) them leave.*

EXERCISE

Write new sentences using indirect commands to ask the people to do the opposite of what they are doing.

1. Miran el boxeo.   *Que no miren el boxeo.*

2. No leen los anuncios. _____

3. Escriben en sus libros. _____

4. No cierran la puerta. _____

5. Duerme en el sofá. _____

Communication Pattern Exercise

Answer each question with an indirect command.

1. ¿Comes tú o come Roberto aquí?

   Que (no) coma él aquí.

2. ¿Contestas tú o contesta María?

   _____

3. ¿Sirves tú las galletas o las sirve Pepe?

   _____

4. ¿Vas tú de compras o va Susana de compras?

   _____

5. ¿Entregan ustedes los periódicos o entregan Pablo y Pepe los periódicos?

   _____

6. ¿Vienen ustedes o vienen los otros?

_____

7. ¿Juegan ustedes o juegan Carlos y Cristina?

_____

Actividades de comunicación

I. Escribe una conversación con tantos imperativos "let's" e imperativos indirectos como sea posible, basada en las siguientes situaciones.

- Tú y tus amigos están sentados en un "snack bar" tomando unas bebidas tratando de decidir algo interesante que hacer.
- La clase ha sido aburrida recientemente. Piensa en algunas actividades nuevas que hacer. Haz una colección y presenta las mejores al(a la) profesor(a).
- No es muy interesante esta noche en casa. Traten ustedes de pensar en algo que hacer.

II. Eres miembro(a) del "Student Senate," y los miembros quieren iniciar una campaña de propaganda para fomentar el orgullo y el _esprit de corps_ de los estudiantes. Prepara algunos "slogans" para la campaña.

III. Prepara una lista de los imperativos que oyes más en casa y en clase y que usas más. Compara tu lista con la de los otros estudiantes.

Refrán

Entre dos perros amigos, echa un hueso y los verás enemigos.
Explica el sentido. Da ejemplos de la vida.

6 Position of Object Pronouns with Commands

GOAL 1

To place object pronouns in the proper position in indirect commands.

With an indirect command, affirmative or negative, object pronouns are placed before the verb.

Que los acueste la niñera.   _Have the baby-sitter put them to bed._

EXERCISE

Form indirect commands, asking that the people do the opposite of what they are doing.

1. Juan no los prueba. _____ *Que Juan los pruebe.* _____

2. José las sube. _____

3. Los editores no lo leen. _____

4. El señor no los despierta. _____

5. Ellos no los traen. _____

6. Ellas lo hacen. _____

7. El no se lo dice. _____

8. Ella se sienta. _____

GOAL 2

To place object pronouns in the proper position in negative commands.

With a negative command, the object pronouns come before the verb.

Le habla.   *He speaks to him.*

No le hable (usted).   *Don't speak to him.*

Remember that negative commands use the present subjunctive forms of the verb.

EXERCISE

Write commands asking the people not to do what they are doing. The subject should be the same as in the original sentence.

1. Tú los llamas. _____ *No los llames.* _____

2. Tú la vendes. _____

3. Las abrís. _____

4. Usted las canta. _____

5. Ustedes se los dan. _____

6. Nosotros nos acostamos. _____

GOAL 3

To place accent marks on commands with attached pronouns.

A. The rules for learning which syllable of a spoken Spanish word to stress are very simple: If a word ends in a vowel, an *n*, or an *s*, the next to the last syllable is stressed. If a word ends in any other consonant, the last syllable is stressed. If the pronunciation of the word does not correspond to this rule, an accent mark is added in the written language to indicate which syllable is emphasized in the spoken language.

Next-to-last syllable

		Last syllable
ro pa	cul *tu* ra	mu *jer*
gen te	con ti *nen* te	le van *tar*
ca si	*ga* to	pen sa *dor*
le *van* tas	*tri* bu	a ni *mal*
pa gan	le van *ta* mos	a mis *tad*
		ne ce si *dad*

Accent required

a *llí*	*cá* ma ra
al *gún*	*chó* fer
a *sí*	es pec *tá* cu lo
ca *fé*	ja *más*
ló gi co	*lá* gri ma
mé di co	pa *pá*

EXERCISE

Each word has been divided into syllables and the stressed syllable italicized. Indicate where accent marks should be placed for these words whose pronunciation does not correspond to the general rules.

1. ca pi *tal*	6. pre si *den* te	11. mer *ca* do
2. *sa* ba do	7. *pe* rro	12. *ma* qui na
3. re *loj*	8. na vi *dad*	13. es pe *rar*
4. *sa* la	9. *mu* si ca	14. es *pe* ras
5. *pro* xi mo	10. na *riz*	15. es ta *cion*

B. Affirmative command forms, with the exceptions of *dé*, *sé*, and *esté*, do not have accent marks. Therefore, you know that the pronunciation of the affirmative command forms correspond to the general pronunciation rules.

EXERCISE

The command forms in the list have been divided into syllables. Underline the stressed syllable.

1. to ma	6. ex pli que mos	11. di	16. da
2. to mad	7. re pi te	12. de cid	17. dad
3. a pren de	8. re pe tid	13. di ga	18. dé
4. ex pli que	9. re pi ta	14. di gan	19. den
5. ex pli quen	10. re pi tan	15. di ga mos	20. de mos

C. Orthographic changes occur in written Spanish in order to represent as nearly as possible the pronunciation of the spoken language. Adding an object pronoun or two object pronouns does not change the pronunciation of the verb. If it did, communication would be very difficult. Therefore, the combination of the verb and pronoun(s) must be written to show that the verb is pronounced the same way even though the number of combined syllables has changed.

When an object pronoun, or pronouns, is added to a command form in Spanish, one of three possibilities occurs: (1) No accent mark is added. (2) An accent mark is deleted. (3) An accent mark is added. An accent mark is deleted when one object pronoun is added to a one-syllable command that has a written accent *(dé, deme)*. A written accent mark is always added when two object pronouns are attached to the command and when one object pronoun is added to a command form stressed on any syllable other than the one just before the object pronoun *(dígaselo, dígale)*. No accent mark is added to other combinations.

The combined word containing the command and the object pronoun(s) must retain the original pronunciation of the command and follow the rules in Spanish for accentuation. Saying the word to yourself without the object pronoun(s) is the best way to decide whether or not an accent mark is needed.

One-syllable commands

Command	One object pronoun	Two object pronouns
dé	*de*lo	*dé*selo
da	*da*lo	*dá*selo
dad	*dad*lo	*dád*selo

Two or more syllables

Command	One object pronoun	Two object pronouns
*com*pra	*cóm*pralo	*cóm*praselo
com*prad*	com*prad*lo	com*prád*selo
*com*pre	*cóm*prelo	*cóm*preselo
com*pre*mos	com*pré*moslo	com*pré*moselo

EXERCISE

The list contains the answers to the previous exercise. One or two object pronouns have been added to each. Indicate where accent marks should be added to the combined words that no longer fit the two basic accentuation rules.

1. *to*malo
2. to*mad*lo
3. a*pren*delas
4. ex*pli*queles
5. ex*pli*quenles
6. expli*que*mosles
7. re*pi*telos
8. repe*tid*los
9. re*pi*talos
10. re*pi*tanlos
11. *di*selo
12. de*cid*selo
13. *di*gaselo
14. *di*ganselo
15. di*ga*moselo
16. *da*lo
17. *dad*selo
18. *de*selo
19. *den*selo
20. demoselo

GOAL 4
To attach object pronouns to affirmative commands.

With a direct affirmative command, object pronouns follow and are attached to the verb. Remember that at times an accent mark is added to the command form itself to indicate that the pronunciation of the verb does not change.

Véndelo (tú).	Véndeselo (tú).
Vendedlo (vosotros).	Vendédselo (vosotros).
Véndalo (usted).	Véndaselo (usted).
Véndanlo (ustedes).	Véndanselo (ustedes).
Vendámoslo.	Vendámoselo.

Note that when the *nosotros* form is followed by *se*, one of the *s*'s is dropped.
    When the object pronoun is the same as the subject, you must remember to make it agree in the command form.

Lávate (tú).	Lávense (ustedes)
Lávese (usted).	Lavaos (vosotros).
Lavémonos.	

Note that in the plural forms *nosotros* and *vosotros* the last letter of the command form itself is dropped. This has happened over a period of time as the sound has disappeared in speech.

EXERCISES

Write new sentences using affirmative direct commands (*tú, vosotros, usted, ustedes,* or *nosotros,* depending upon the subject of the sentence) to ask the people to do what they are not doing. Attach the pronoun whenever possible. Remember that the affirmative forms of *tú* and *vosotros* do not use the present subjunctive forms. The *usted, ustedes,* and *nosotros* forms are the same as the present subjunctive.

A. *Tú* and *Vosotros*

1. Alicia no lo cree. _____ *Alicia, créelo.* _____

2. Carlos no la ayuda. _____

3. Marta no los cuelga. _____

4. Susana no lo hace. _____

5. María Juana no les dice. _____

6. José no se sienta en el banco. _____

7. Carlos y Concha no la aprenden. _____

8. Antonio y Nardo no hablan en voz alta. _____

B. *Usted* and *Ustedes*

1. La señorita no las escribe a máquina. _____

2. El doctor González no lo toma. _____

3. La señora Martínez no se levanta temprano. _____

4. Las señoritas no la escuchan ahora. _____

5. Los señores no lo buscan. _____

6. Las señoritas no se divierten. _____

C. *Nosotros*

1. No la defendemos. _____

2. No lo acompañamos. _____

3. No se la escribimos. _____

4. No nos dormimos. _____

G O A L   5

To use the appropriate command form in context.

EXERCISE

Complete each sentence with the appropriate command form and with the object pronoun in the correct position. Use the pronoun verb in parentheses.

1. *(la buscar)* ¿Has perdido la pelota? Pues, no ____*la busques*____ aquí.
   ____*Búscala*____ en otro jardin.

2. *(las aprender)* ¿Han aprendido ustedes las reglas? No. Pues,
   _____ para mañana. No, no _____ aquí
   en clase, en casa esta noche.

3. *(le decir)* ¿Ha hablado usted al jefe de policía? Pues,
   _____ lo que me dijo. ¿Cómo? No, no
   _____ eso.

4. *(ir)* ¿No puedes encontrar una ganga? Pues, no _____ a
   esa tienda. _____ a la del centro.

5. *(se lo dar)* ¿Tenemos todo ahora? No, no _____ a ellos.
   _____ a los Martínez.

6. *(la escribir)* Las instrucciones para la composición son las siguientes:
   _____ vosotros con tinta pero no _____
   sin tratar de corregir los errores.

7. *(divertirse)* Mañana sales para las montañas a esquiar, ¿no? Pues,
   _____ pero no _____ tanto que no tengas
   tiempo para aprender.

8. *(acostarse)* Ya son las once y tenemos que levantarnos temprano por la
   mañana. _____.

Communication Pattern Exercise

Answer the questions according to the model.

1. ¿Comemos aquí?

   No, no _____*comamos aquí*_____. _____*Comamos*_____ en otro restaurante.

2. Pablo, ¿la escribo en la postal?

   No, no _____. _____ en un papel.

3. Juana, ¿los llevo hoy?

   No, no _____. _____ mañana.

4. Roberto, ¿se lo vendemos al señor González?

   No, no _____. _____ al señor Gómez.

5. Señora, ¿se lo doy?

   No, no _____. _____ a Ana.

6. Señor, ¿las ponemos ahora?

   No, no _____. _____ más tarde.

7. Marta, ¿los levantamos temprano?

   No, no _____ (nosotros).

   _____ tarde mañana.

Actividades de comunicación

I. Como consejero(a) de recreación, prepara una lista de instrucciones para las actividades del día. Luego, lee la lista a la clase. Entonces, toda la clase puede escojer con quién desea pasar el día.

II. Explícale a un(a) compañero(a) de clase cómo se hace algo. Por ejemplo, una casita para pájaros, un modelo, un vestido. Trata de usar tantas formas diferentes del imperativo como sea posible.

Refrán

Lo que cuesta poco, se estima en menos.
Explica el sentido. Da ejemplos de la vida.

7 Passive Voice

GOAL 1

To use the appropriate form of the perfective participle to agree with the subject.

All perfective participles end in the letter *o*. When used after *ser* or *estar*, they change suffixes, just as any regular *o* adjective does, to agree with the word they describe. The verb suffix must also change, of course, to agree with the subject.

EXERCISE

Form new sentences with the given subjects, making any necessary changes in the remainder of the sentence.

1. La carta fue escrita por Juana. *(mensaje/anuncios/tarjetas)*

   El mensaje fue escrito por Juana. _____

   _____

   _____

2. Los quehaceres ya están terminados. *(tarea/investigaciones/voto)*

   _____

   _____

   _____

3. El español es hablado por aquí. *(lengua/dialectos/lenguas)*

   _____

   _____

   _____

GOAL 2

To change an active sentence to a passive one.

In active voice the subject acts. In passive voice the subject is the object of the action and the active voice subject becomes the agent.

Active: El enemigo **atacó** la ciudad.   *The enemy **attacked** the city.*
Passive: La ciudad **fue atacada**   *The city **was attacked** by the*
   por el enemigo.   *enemy.*

Normally, the passive voice is used only when the agent is expressed. In a sentence in which the verb is in the passive voice, *por* is used before the agent. (In Old Spanish *de* precedes the agent when the verb expresses emotion or sentiment.)

Fuimos invitados **por** Ana.   *We were invited **by** Ana.*
Es respetado **de** todos.   *He is respected **by** everyone.*

Passive voice is not used as much in Spanish as in English. It is used most commonly in the past in Spanish.

EXERCISE

Rewrite the following sentences, changing each from active voice to passive voice.

1. Un ladrón attacó a la pobre anciana.

   La pobre anciana fue atacada por un ladrón.

2. Jorge reparó mi coche.

   _____

3. El niño perdió las llaves.

   _____

4. Hablan español por aquí.

   _____

5. Todos estiman al director de esta escuela.

   _____

6. Los arquitectos admiran la catedral.

   _____

GOAL 3

To distinguish between the pattern *ser* + perfective participle and *estar* + perfective participle.

Ser + a perfective participle describes an action. *Estar* + a perfective participle describes a condition.

Un ladrón lo **mató.**	*A robber **killed** him.*
Sí, **fue matado** por un ladrón.	*Yes, **he was killed** by a robber.*
Sí, **está muerto.**	*Yes, **he is dead.***

EXERCISE

Complete each sentence with the appropriate form of either *ser* or *estar*, depending upon the context.

1. Mamá, no puedo salir. La puerta _____ cerrada.

2. Ay, se me olvidó. _____ cerrada por su papá cuando salió.

3. Las pinturas _____ robadas la semana pasada por gente desconocida.

4. ¡Cuánto me gustan estas pinturas! _____ pintadas en colores vivos.

5. ¿_____ escrita en inglés esa canción?

6. Sí, aunque _____ escrita en francés por un fraile italiano.

7. Manuela, ¿_____ invitada a la fiesta?

8. Sí, mi hermana y yo _____ invitadas ayer por Ana.

9. ¡Qué bien _____ preparado este plato!

10. Mario, tengo que confesarle que _____ preparado por me mamá.

Communciation Pattern Exercise

Answer the questions.

1. ¿Está abierto el puerto?

   _____

2. ¿Fue abierto el puerto por los comerciantes?

   _____

3. ¿Están preparados los soldados?

   _____

4. ¿Fueron preparados por el general Márquez?

   _____

5. ¿Están hechas las mantillas?

   _____

6. ¿Fueron hechas por su abuela?

   _____

7. ¿Está construida de cemento la carretera?

   _____

8. ¿Fue construida por la compañía Gómez?

   _____

Actividades de comunicación

Escribe por lo menos, cinco preguntas con la estructura "ser" + participio pasivo y, por lo menos, cinco preguntas con la estructura "estar" + participio pasivo, y pide a un(a) compañero(a) de clase que las conteste. Puedes usar palabras de la siguiente lista u otras que se te ocurran.

respetar	coche	muchachos
amar	ventanas	muchachas
ver	accidente	Juan
proteger	director	María
hacer	policía	paquete
enviar	caja	carta
cerrar	libros	puerta
abrir	político	casa
comprar		vender

Refrán

Mejor es ser corregido por los sabios que alabado por los necios.
Explica el sentido. Da ejemplos de la vida.

8 Uses of *Se*

GOAL 1

To convert a sentence containing a person subject but no object into a sentence with *se*.

When the verb in a Spanish sentence has no object, *se* may be used in front of the *él* form of that verb to signify an indefinite subject.[1]

Se come bien en los Estados Unidos.

People (you, they, one) eat(s) well in the United States.

EXERCISE

Substitute, whenever possible, the *se* pattern for the given verb and subject. In the sentence where the use of *se* is not possible, use *uno*. Give the English equivalent of each answer.

1. Uno estudia mucho en esta clase.

   Se estudia mucho en esta clase

   People study a lot in this class.

---

1. In order to make a sentence that already has *se* in front of the verb indefinite, *uno* is used. Uno se levanta tarde los domingos. *People (you, they, one) get(s) up late on Sundays.*

2. La gente gana mucho en los Estados Unidos.

_____

_____

3. Creen que ese señor es muy rico.

_____

_____

4. Uno ve bien desde este punto.

_____

_____

5. La gente se levanta tarde los días de fiesta.

_____

_____

6. Se divierten durante la celebración.

_____

_____

7. Uno entra por la puerta principal.

_____

_____

8. Salen por la puerta de atrás.

_____

_____

GOAL 2

To convert a sentence with a subject and an object into a sentence with *se*.

When the verb in a Spanish sentence has an object, *se* may be used in front of the *él* or *ellos* form of that verb to express a lack of any subject or to indicate an indefinite subject. The verb may be in any tense.

Se rompió el tocadiscos.	*The record player **broke**. (It just stopped. No one broke it.)*
Se vende leche en esa tienda.	***They sell** milk in that store. (Milk is sold in that store.)*
Se venden huevos allí.	***They sell** eggs there. (Eggs are sold there.)*

Note that the passive voice is used quite often in English to express the idea of an indefinite subject. This pattern is not possible in Spanish. Note, too, that the verb agrees with the noun in each sentence.

EXERCISE

I. Form sentences with *se* according to the model. Give the English equivalent of each answer.

1. Nadie rompió el tocadiscos.

   Se rompió.

   It just broke or got broken.

2. Nadie perdió las llaves.

   _____

   _____

3. Nadie olvidó la carne.

   _____

   _____

4. Nadie cerró la puerta.

   _____

   _____

5. Nadie enciende las velas.

   _____

   _____

II. Rewrite each of the following sentences, changing the given form to the *se* pattern. Give the English equivalent of each answer.

1. Ven las montañas a la distancia.

   _____

   _____

2. Venden mucho helado en el verano.

   _____

   _____

3. Oyen las campanas los domingos por la mañana.

   _____

   _____

4. Alguien tocará el himno nacional antes del partido.

   _____

   _____

5. Alguien ha pintado los cuartos.

_____

_____

6. Alguien publicó esa novela en Francia.

_____

_____

GOAL 3

To distinguish between the patterns *ser* + a perfective participle, *estar* + a perfective participle, and *se* with no subject.

A sentence that is, or appears to be, the passive voice in English may be expressed in three different ways in Spanish, depending upon the meaning.

- Describing a condition

  Le puerta **está cerrada.**   *The door **is closed.***

- Expressing an action (agent expressed)

  La puerta **fue** cerrada por el   *The door **was** closed by the*
  gerente.   *manager.*

- Expressing an action (agent not expressed)

  Se cierra la puerta a las diez.   *The door **is closed** at ten o'clock.*
                                               (They close the door at ten
                                               o'clock.)

In the first example *(La puerta está cerrada.)*, there is no movement or action. The door is shut. In the second example *(La puerta fue cerrada por el gerente.)*, the verb describes an action. The manager shut the door. By using the passive voice (putting "door" before the verb), the speaker emphasizes "door" instead of the person closing it. In the third example *(Se cierra la puerta a las diez.)*, the stress is on the action, shutting, rather than on the door or the manager.

EXERCISE

Complete each sentence using the appropriate form, according to the context, of one of the three patterns: *estar* + a perfective participle, *ser* + a perfective participle, or *se* + the *él* or *ellos* form of the verb.

1. Los puentes *(destruir)* _____ por las tropas.

2. Los puentes *(construir)* _____ otra vez por los habitantes del pueblo.

3. *(Construir)* _____ los puentes nuevos en 1970.

4. *(Construir)* _____ de piedras grandes.

5. Esposa mía, no vale la pena llorar. La casa *(vender)*

_____.

6. *(Vender)* _____ por el agente de bienes raíces hace dos días.

7. *(Vender)* _____ discos compactos muy baratos en esa tienda.

8. *(Cambiar)* _____ las sábanas con regularidad.

9. Las sábanas *(cambiar)* _____ por las criadas.

10. Sí, puede acostarse. Ya *(cambiar)* _____ las sábanas.

GOAL 4

To personalize the *se* pattern.

The sentence *Se perdieron las llaves* states "The keys were lost." No indication is given as to who lost the keys, nor whose keys they were. Of course, one of the functions of *se* is to express an action that has no agent. On the other hand, in expressions of this type, it can be made clear by adding indirect object pronouns.

Se perdieron las llaves.	*The keys got lost.*
Se **me** perdieron las llaves.	***My** keys got lost.*
Se **te** perdieron las llaves.	***Your** keys got lost.*
Se **le** perdieron las llaves.	***His (her) (your)** keys got lost.*
Se **nos** perdieron las llaves.	**Our** *keys got lost.*
Se **os** perdieron las llaves.	***Your** keys got lost.*
Se **les** perdieron las llaves.	***Their (your)** keys got lost.*

EXERCISE

Complete each sentence according to the model. Write the English equivalent of each answer.

1. No la perdí, pero _____ *se me perdió* _____ la llave.

I didn't lose it, but my key got lost

_____

2. No lo perdió, pero _____ el horario.

_____

_____

3. No la rompimos, pero _____ la lámpara.

_____

_____

4. No los olvidé, pero _____ los lápices.

_____

_____

5. No las dejaron caer, pero _____ las plantas.

_____

_____

6. No lo apagué, pero _____ el fuego, ¿verdad?

_____

_____

G O A L   5

To use *se* with the meaning of "self."

Se may also be used as a reflexive object of the verb.

(usted) **Se** presenta.	*You introduce **yourself.***
(él) **Se** presenta.	*He introduces **himself.***
(ella) **Se** presenta.	*She introduces **herself.***
(ustedes) **Se** presentan.	*You introduce **yourselves.***
(ellos) **Se** presentan.	*They introduce **themselves.***
(ellas) **Se** presentan.	*They introduce **themselves.***

Remember that in Spanish this pattern is used much more than in English. In fact, the equivalent English form often uses no reflexive form at all.

Se lava.	*He washes (himself).*
Se cortó el dedo.	*He cut his finger.*

You should also note that many of these verb forms may be used with other object pronouns as well.

Se levantaron.	*They got **(themselves)** up.*
Lo levantaron.	*They got **him** up.*
Se compra mucha ropa.	*She buys **herself** a lot of clothes.*
Les compra mucho ropa.	*She buys a lot of clothes **for them.***

EXERCISE

Give the English equivalent of each Spanish sentence.

1. Mira. El bebé se ve en el espejo.

_____

2. Se preparan comidas deliciosas.

_____

3. Mariá se compra muchos aretes.

_____

4. Mis amigos se levantan tarde.

_____

5. Carlos se presentó a la joven.

_____

6. Sí, se corta el pelo.

_____

GOAL 6

To use *se* to mean "each other."

Se, as well as *nos* and *os,* can also be used to express the idea of "each other."

Se escribieron.   *They wrote to **each other.***

Nos saludamos.   *We greeted **each other.***

These verbs are always in the plural, of course, since "each other" is a plural idea.

EXERCISE

Change each sentence to an equivalent sentence containing a pattern using *se.*
Give the English equivalent of each answer.

1. Escriben el uno al otro.

   _____

   _____

2. Esperábamos la una a la otra.

   _____

   _____

3. Ayudáis el uno al otro.

   _____

   _____

4. Soñaban el uno con el otro.

   _____

   _____

5. Tutean uno a otro.

   _____

   _____

6. Ustedes saludan el uno al otro, ¿no?

   _____

   _____

GOAL 7
To use *se* as a substitute for *le* or *les*.

The object pronouns *le* and *les* become *se* before *lo, la, los,* or *las.*

Le di el boleto.   *I gave **him** the ticket.*

Lo di a Juan.   *I gave **it** to Juan.*

Se lo di.   *I gave **it to him.***

EXERCISE

Answer each question using *lo, la, los,* or *las.*

1. ¿Le diste el regalo? (sí)

   Sí, se lo di.
   _____

2. ¿Les da permiso el director? (sí)

   _____

3. ¿Les explica el profesor lo que quiere? (no)

   _____

4. ¿Le sirvieron todos los platos? (no)

   _____

5. ¿Le abrió la puerta a la señorita? (sí)

   _____

6. ¿Les dijo las noticias? (no)

   _____

Communication Pattern Exercises

I. Give the English equivalent of each sentence.

1. Se trabaja mucho en esa fábrica.

   _____

2. Se entra por aquí.

   _____

3. Se ven los rascacielos a la distancia.

   _____

4. Se habla lento en el sur.

_____

5. Se rompió el disco.

_____

6. Se me rompieron los anteojos.

_____

7. La comida está servida.

_____

8. Se sirve la comida a las seis.

_____

9. La comida es servida por mamá.

_____

10. Se lava la cara.

_____

11. Lava la cara al niño.

_____

12. Nos vemos antes de la clase.

_____

13. Se saludan con cariño.

_____

14. Se observaron detenidamente.

_____

15. ¿Te acuestas antes de las doce?

_____

16. ¿Le dio el lápiz? Sí, se lo di.

_____

17. ¿Les pidió las flores? No, no se las pedí.

_____

18. Se quejó del ruido.

_____

II. Work with a partner. Take turns asking and answering the questions.

1. ¿Se come bien en los Estados Unidos?
2. ¿Se estudia mucho en esta clase?
3. ¿Se divierte uno mucho en esta ciudad?
4. ¿Se vende ropa en una lechería?
5. ¿Se compran huevos en una librería?
6. ¿Se hablan varias lenguas en la ciudad donde vives?
7. ¿Se te olvidaron las noticias esta mañana?
8. ¿Se te olvidaron los otros quehaceres?
9. ¿Al peatón se le olvidó cruzar en la esquina?
10. ¿A los otros alumnos se les olvidó el refrán?
11. ¿A ustedes se les acabó el cambio?
12. ¿Se compra su mamá mucha ropa?
13. ¿Se habla a sí mismo el profesor a veces?
14. El consejero y los pacientes, ¿se saludan en el pasillo?
15. Tú y tu novia, ¿se ven los sábados?
16. Las respuestas, ¿se las dio María a Juan?
17. El periódico, ¿se lo dio papá a Pepito?
18. ¿Se lavan los chicos antes de comer?

Actividades de comunicación

I. Con *se,* escribe una descripción de media página como mínimo de los habitantes de tu pueblo o cuidad. Describe donde se va de compras, para divertirse, por la noche, etc.

II. Con *se,* describe lo que pasa con una persona a quien siempre se le olvida todo.

III. Con *se,* escribe una conversación entre un padre y su hijo: El padre se queja del perder, olvidar, romper, dejar caer, etc., de su hijo. El hijo le responde que él no tiene la culpa, que simplemente ocurren estas cosas.

IV. Escribe un párrafo de diez oraciones como mínimo en el que describes lo que una persona hace generalmente por sí misma y lo que él o ella y un amigo hacen.

Refránes

Cuando una puerta se cierra, otra se abre.
Quien con perros se acuesta con pulgas se levanta.
Explica el sentido. Da ejemplos de la vida.

Complex Sentence Transformations

Introduction Grammatical rules are of two types: rules of sentence formation and rules of sentence transformation. Rules of sentence transformation can be further divided into those that apply to simple sentence transformations and those that apply to complex sentence transformation. Part VIII of this text treats rules covering complex sentence transformations.

Simple sentence transformation rules involve transformations on parts of the sentence that change its emphasis or meaning. However, in addition to making changes in basic sentences, the native speaker of a language also knows how to combine more than one sentence or idea into a single sentence. For example, "The man who just came in is my uncle." is a simpler and more efficient sentence than, "The man just came in. The man is my uncle."

In this part you will learn to use comparatives, relator words, dependent clauses as objects of the verb, dependent clauses used to describe nouns, and dependent clauses used to describe verbs. Much of the work in this part involves the transformation of basic sentence components as well as the manipulation of noun and verb suffixes.

1 Comparisons of Inequality

GOAL 1

To compare unequal qualities or characteristics of two different people or things.

Different qualities of two entities may be compared as follows:

Pattern: Spanish—más (or *menos*) + adjective or noun + *que*
English—"more" (or "less") + adjective or noun + "than"[1]

---

1. Note that English also uses the "-er" form with certain words.

Juan es **más gordo** (**que** Jaime).	*Juan is **heavier** (**than** Jaime).*
También es **más inteligente.**	*He is also **more intelligent.***
Sin embargo, es **menos cortés y** tiene **menos amigos.**	*However, he is **less courteous** and has **fewer friends.***

If both a noun and an adjective are included in the comparative phrase, the adjective follows the noun as in regular word order.

un chico más alto	*a taller boy*

EXERCISE

Rewrite each pair of sentences as one sentence, comparing the two. Choose an appropriate word from the list to use in the comparison:

alto	dinero	flor	hermano
cansado	grande	idioma	diligente

1. El señor González tiene un millón de dólares.

   El señor Fernández tiene diez millones de dólares.

   El señor Fernández tiene más dinero que el señor González.

2. Pepe trabaja ocho horas cada día.

   Raúl trabaja todo el tiempo.

   _____

3. María tiene ocho hermanos.

   José tiene dos hermanos.

   _____

4. Ramón tiene seis pies de altura.

   Susana tiene cinco pies de altura.

   _____

5. El chico está cansado.

   Las chicas están completamente fatigadas.

   _____

6. Pepito pesa 60 libras.

   Paquita pesa 80 libras.

   _____

7. Le señorita lleva siete flores.

   La señora lleva tres flores.

   _____

8. Mariana habla tres idiomas.

Rosa habla sólo un idioma.

GOAL 2

To compare unequal qualities of more than two people or things.

Different qualities of more than two entities may be compared as follows:

- Adjectives

    Spanish—*el, la, los, las, lo más* (or *menos*) + adjective + *de*

    English—"the most" (or "least") + adjective + "in"[2]

Juan es **más gordo que** Jaime, pero Guillermo es **el más gordo.**	*Juan is **heavier than** Jaime, but Guillermo is **the heaviest.***
María es **la más inteligente.**	*María is **the most intelligent.***
José y Pepe son **los menos corteses.**	*José and Pepe are **the least courteous.***

If a noun is included in the superlative phrase, it is placed after the article: *el chico más gordo, la estudiante más inteligente.*

- Nouns

    Spanish—*más* (or *menos*) + noun

    English—"the most" (or "least") + noun

    Raúl tiene veinte discos.

    José tiene cincuenta.

    Josefina tiene cien.

Josefina tiene **más (discos).**	*Josefina has **the most (records).***

Note that in Spanish *el más, la más* (or *menos*) etc., is not used with nouns. The context will make it clear whether *más discos* means "more records" or "the most records."

EXERCISE

Combine each group of sentences into one sentence, comparing the last sentence with the others. Choose an appropriate word from the list to use in the comparison:

alto	dinero	idioma	cansado
ocupado	hermano	flor	grande

---

2. Note that English also uses the "-est" form in certain cases.

1. El señor González tiene un millón de dólares.

   El señor Fernández tiene diez millones de dólares.

   La señora Gómez tiene más de veinte millones de dólares.

   La señora Gómez tiene más (dinero).
   _____

2. Pepito pesa 60 libras.

   Paquita pesa 80 libras.

   Ana pesa 95 libras.
   _____

3. María tiene ocho hermanos.

   José tiene cinco hermanos.

   Rodrigo tiene tres hermanos.
   _____

4. Papá tiene seis pies de altura.

   Pepe tiene casi seis pies de altura.

   Mamá tiene un poco más de cinco pies de altura.
   _____

5. Mi padre habla sólo un idioma.

   Yo hablo dos idiomas.

   El profesor habla tres idiomas.
   _____

6. Rafael tiene cinco horas para divertirse.

   Ana tiene tres horas para jugar.

   Manuel tiene una hora libre.
   _____

7. El chico no tiene mucha energía.

   Papá está cansado.

   Las chicas están completamente fatigadas.
   _____

8. La señora lleva una flor.

   La señora lleva dos flores.

   La presidente lleva tres flores.
   _____

It is not necessary to state the area under consideration in a comparison. However, if the area is stated, "in" is used in English; *de* is used in Spanish.

Es el (muchacho) más alto
   de la clase.

*He is the tallest (boy) **in** class.*

EXERCISE

Combine the ideas in each item into one sentence using the superlative comparison and *de*. Choose an appropriate adjective from the list to use in the comparison.

pequeño   grande   largo   rico
oscuro   alto   sabio

1. Hay seis muchachos en la clase. Jorge tiene seis pies y medio de altura. Todos los otros muchachos tienen menos.

   Jorge _____ *es el más alto de* _____ la clase.

2. Hay cuatro en la familia. Papá pesa doscientas libras, Mamá ciento treinta, Mariana noventa y Pepito cincuenta.

   Papá _____; Pepito _____.

3. Hay muchos miembros en el club. Todos tienen mucho dinero, pero el señor Rodríguez tiene más.

   El señor Rodríguez _____.

4. Hay tres tiendas en la vecindad. En la de la calle Florida hay menos espacio y menos mercancías para vender. Las otras dos tienen más.

   La de la calle Florida _____.

5. Hay cuatro habitaciones es este apartamento. La sala es de color verde oscuro. Una alcoba es de azul oscuro y la otra es de color rojo oscuro.

   La cocina _____.

6. Hay muchos profesores en esta universidad, pero el que sabe más es el señor Fulano.

   El señor Fulano _____.

GOAL 3

To use irregular comparatives.

There are four common adjectives that have irregular forms in the comparative and superlative patterns. The word *más* is not used with these irregular forms.

Instead, the comparative ending is part of the word itself much the same as in the English pattern "new*er*," "whit*er*," etc.

Positive	*Comparative*	*Superlative*
bueno *good*	mejor *better*	el mejor *the best*
malo *bad*	peor *worse*	el peor *the worst*
grande *old*	mayor *older*	el mayor *the oldest*
grande *big*	más grande *bigger*	el más grande *the biggest*
pequeño *young*	menor *younger*	el menor *the youngest*
pequeño *small*	más pequeño *smaller*	el más pequeño *the smallest*

Note that the superlative is formed by adding a form of the definite article *(el, la, los, las)* in front of the comparative form.

EXERCISE

Rewrite each group of sentences as one sentence, comparing the differences. Choose an appropriate word to use in the comparison.

1. Hay tres productos, X, Y y Z, en este supermercado. X tiene unas cualidades deseables. X es un producto bueno. Y tiene más cualidades deseables.

   Y _____.

   Z tiene las cualidades de X y Y y otras también.

   Z _____.

2. Mi hermano es grande. Tiene veinte y cinco años. Pero papá tiene casi sesenta años.

   Papá _____.

   Mi abuelo tiene más de ochenta años.

   Mi abuelo _____ de nuestra familia.

3. Mi hermano es grande. Pesa doscientas libras y tiene seis pies y medio de altura. Papá pesa ciento setenta libras y tiene seis pies de altura. Yo peso ciento veinte y cinco y tengo cinco pies y medio de altura.

   Mi hermano _____ papá.

   Mi hermano _____ de los varones de la familia.

   Yo _____ de los varones de la familia.

4. Juana tiene siete años. Su hermana Ana tiene tres.

Ana _____. El bebé sólo tiene seis meses.

El bebé _____ de los tres.

Juana _____ Ana.

Juana _____ de los tres.

5. Es imposible andar rápido en esta carretera. Es una carretera mala. La otra es más moderna.

Esta _____ la otra. Pero hay en las montañas una poco usada que no es tan buena como ésta.

La de las montañas _____ de las tres.

6. Hay tres protegidos en nuestra casa: un perro, un gato y un pajarito.

El gato _____ perro.

El pajarito _____ de los tres.

<table>
<tr><td colspan="3" align="center">**G O A L   4**</td></tr>
<tr><td colspan="3">To use comparative and superlative patterns in referring to verbs.</td></tr>
</table>

Más and *menos* are used to compare differences with adverbs and verbs.

- Más (menos)

  Rosa habla **más rápido** que Ana.   *Rosa talks **more rapidly** than Ana.*

  Rosa habla **más que** Ana.   *Rosa talks **more than** Ana.*

  De todas las chicas Alicia habla **menos.**   *Of all the girls Alicia talks **(the) least.***

- There are two irregular usages in this pattern.

Positive	*Comparative*	*Superlative*
bien *well*	mejor *better*	(lo) mejor *(the) best*
mal *poorly*	peor *worse* (lo)	peor *(the) worst*

Lo, the neuter article, is used with an adverb, but the superlative uses an article only if there is an expressed comparison in the comparative phrase.

Habla **lo más rápido que** puede.   *She speaks **as rapidly as** she can.*

Hacen **lo mejor** posible.   *They do **the best** possible.*

EXERCISE   Rewrite each group of sentences as one sentence, making a comparison. Choose an appropriate word from the following list to use in the comparison:

lejos   rápido   bien
despacio   cerca   mal

1. Carlos cena en media hora. Su hermana cena en cuarenta minutos.

   Carlos cena _____ su hermana.

   Manuela cena en quince minutos. Ella _____ de los tres.

2. El presidente vive a diez cuadras de la universidad. El profesor de español vive a veinte cuadras de la universidad. El profesor _____. El profesor de historia vive en un pueblo a diez millas de la universidad. El _____.

3. Cristina sacó una "D" en el examen. Manuel sacó una "D+". Los dos salieron mal pero Cristina salió _____. Pedro sacó una "D–". El _____.

4. Rosita y Rafael viven a quince cuadras del centro. Rosita llega al centro en treinta minutos. Rafael llega al centro en una hora. Rafael camina _____. La mujer que vive al lado de ellos llega al centro en dos horas. La mujer camina _____.

5. Marta, recién llegada a este país, habla sin muchos errores. Roberto, que lleva seis años aquí, habla casi sin acento. Roberto _____. Guillermo, que ha pasado casi toda su vida en este país, habla como nativo. Guillermo _____.

6. Pedro se sienta en la segunda fila de la puerta. Mariana se sienta en la tercera fila de la puerta. Pedro _____. Ramón se sienta en la primera fila de la puerta. Ramón _____.

Communication Pattern Exercises

I. Use each cue to form a sentence using a comparative or a superlative according to the meaning given in parentheses.

1. Juan/ser/sentimental/María (El es sentimental. Ella no es tan sentimental.)

   Juan es más sentimental que María.

2. señor/hablar/despacio/mujer (El habla despacio. Ella habla rápidamente.)

_____

3. Anita/ser/bueno/estudiante/clase (No hay otro que aprenda tanto.)

_____

4. Mario/ser/hablador/familia (El habla más que los otros.)

_____

5. Bogotá/ser/bello/ciudad (No hay otra ciudad tan bella.)

_____

6. profesor/tener/dinero/el señor Rockefeller (El señor Rockefeller es más rico.)

_____

7. este/motores/ser/poderoso (No hay otros que sean tan poderosos.)

_____

8. Pepito/ser/pequeño/sobrinos (Todos los otros tienen más años.)

_____

9. este/clase/ser/bueno/otro (Me gusta más la clase en que estoy.)

_____

II. Work with a partner. Take turns asking and answering the questions.

1. ¿Es usted más alto(a) o más bajo(a) que su mejor amigo(a)?
2. ¿Es usted el más delgado(a) de su familia?
   (serio/cortés/independiente/quieto/cariñoso/intelectual)
3. ¿Quién es el(la) más gordo(a)?
4. ¿Aprendes con menos dificultad que los otros estudiantes?
5. ¿Aprendes más fácilmente que tus amigos?
6. ¿Eres el más inteligente de tu familia?
7. ¿Quién es el más inteligente?
8. ¿Quién sabe más?
9. ¿Manejan rápido los miembros de su familia?
10. ¿Quién maneja más rápido?
11. ¿Quién maneja menos rápido?
12. ¿Estudian ustedes más este año que el año pasado?

Actividades de comunicación

I. Con "más", escribe una descripción de cinco oraciones comparando lo siguiente:

Tú y tu mejor amigo(a)

Tú y un(a) hermano(a)

Tu papá y tu mamá

II. Con "el más", escribe una descripción de cinco oraciones de las varias personas en los siguientes grupos:

Tu familia

Tu clase

Tu escuela o universidad

III. Habla de estas comparaciones a un(a) compañero(a) de clase.

Refránes

Más vale ser cabeza de ratón que cola de león.
Más moscas se cazan con miel que con hiel.
Explica el sentido. Da ejemplos de la vida.

---

2 Comparisons of Equality

GOAL 1

To compare equal qualities or characteristics of two different people or things using adjectives and adverbs.

With a descriptive word the phrase *tan . . . como* is used in comparisons of equality.

Pattern: Spanish—*tan* + adjective or adverb + *como*
English—"as" + adjective or adverb + "as"

María es **tan inteligente como** Ana.   *María is **as intelligent as** Ana.*

Corre **tan rápido como** yo.   *He runs **as rapidly as** I.*

EXERCISE   Combine each pair of sentences into one using *tan . . . como* to express the comparison of equality. Choose an appropriate word from the list to use in the comparison:

generoso   despacio   amable   bien
grande   diligente largo   mal

1. José regala la mitad de su dinero. Pepe regala la mitad de su dinero también.

   Pepe es tan generoso como José.

2. Rosa habla español como nativo. Ramón habla español como nativo también.

3. El hombre trabaja todo el tiempo en el jardín. La mujer trabaja todo el tiempo también.

4. Todos quieren a la señora Rodríguez. Todos quieren a la señora Gómez también.

5. Los enamorados andan lentamente. Los turistas andan lentamente también.

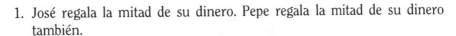

GOAL 2

To compare equals using nouns.

With a noun, the phrase *tanto, -a, -os, -as . . . como* is used in comparisons of equality. *Tanto* means "as much" or "as many."

Pattern: Spanish—*tanto, -a, -os, -as* + noun + *como*
English—"as much" ("many") + noun + "as"

Raúl bebe **tanta leche como** yo.	*Raúl drinks **as much milk as** I.*
Josefina lee **tantos libros como** el profesor.	*Josefina reads **as many books as** the teacher.*

EXERCISE

Combine each pair of sentences into one using *tanto . . . como* to express the comparison of equality.

1. Manuel tiene cuarenta discos. Anita tiene cuarenta discos también.

   Anita tiene tantos discos como Manuel.

2. Susana tiene muchas fotos. Isabel tiene muchas fotos también.

3. Había mucha nieve en enero. Había mucha nieve en febrero también.

4. En los Estados Unidos se come una libra de carne cada día por persona. En la Argentina se come una libra de carne cada día por persona también.

_____

5. Van a pasar una semana en la Ciudad de México. Van a pasar una semana en Acapulco también. (tiempo)

_____

6. Pedro estudia tres idiomas: el inglés, el español y el alemán. Roberto estudia tres también.

_____

GOAL 3

To compare equals with verbs.

With a verb, the phrase _tanto como_ is used in comparisons of equality.

Pattern: Spanish—verb + _tanto como_
          English—verb + "as much as"

Berta **habla tanto como** yo.   _Berta **talks as much as** I._

EXERCISE

Combine each pair of sentences into one using _tanto como_ to express the comparison of equality.

1. El profesor lee tres libros cada semana. Elena lee tres libros cada semana también.

   Elena lee tanto como el profesor.
   _____

2. Rodrigo hace natación una hora cada noche. Mariana hace natación una hora también.

   _____

3. Mi papá corre una milla todos los días. Yo corro una milla todos los días también.

   _____

4. Este abrigo cuesta cincuenta dólares. El otro cuesta cincuenta también.

   _____

5. Estos chicos juegan todo el tiempo. Estas chicas juegan todo el tiempo también.

   _____

6. José y Rosa se llaman cada fin de semana. Pedro y Susana se llaman cada fin de semana también.

_____

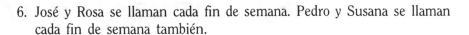

GOAL 4

To distinguish between the uses of *tan . . . como, tanto, -a, -os, -as . . . como,* and *tanto como.*

EXERCISE

Combine each pair of sentences into one sentence using *tan . . . como, tanto, -a, -os, -as . . . como,* or *tanto como,* as the situation indicates, to express a comparison of equality.

1. Rosita tiene diez y siete años. Catalina tiene diez y siete años también. *(joven)*

   Catalina es tan joven como Rosita. _____

2. Esteban es un dormilón. Duerme diez horas cada noche. Catalina duerme diez horas cada noche también.

   _____

3. Nuestro vecino anciano sólo anda treinta millas por hora en la carretera. Nuestra madre sólo anda treinta millas por hora en la carretera también. *(despacio)*

   _____

4. Los Rodríguez tienen tres televisores de colores. Los Fernández tienen tres televisores de colores también.

   _____

5. Usted aprende lo más posible. Yo aprendo lo más posible también.

   _____

6. Hace mucho viento en marzo. Hace mucho viento en abril también.

   _____

7. La madre es muy simpática. La hija es muy simpática también.

   _____

8. El ve tres flores. Nosotros vemos tres también.

   _____

GOAL 5

To combine two sentences into one containing either a comparison of equality or a comparison of inequality.

Más (menos) and *el más (menos)* are used in Spanish to make comparisons of difference. *Tan . . . como, tanto, -a, -os, -as . . . como,* and *tanto como* are used in Spanish to make comparisons of equality.

EXERCISE   Combine each pair of sentences into one sentence to express a comparison of inequality or a comparison of equality.

1. Un avión 707 lleva más de cien pasajeros. Un avión 747 lleva más de doscientos pasajeros. *(grande)*

   Un avión 747 es más grande que un avión 707.

2. Pablo ahorra dinero todos los días. Carlos ahorra dinero también.

   _____

3. Pablo toma el sol por quince minutos. Carlos toma el sol por quince minutos también.

   _____

4. Lola canta bien, pero Dorotea canta como un ángel. Su voz es magnífica. *(bien)*

   _____

5. Andrés lleva cinco paquetes. Yo lleva cinco también.

   _____

6. Mi hermana rompió un vaso. Mamá rompió tres. Papá rompió siete.

   _____

7. Hay tres perros. Fido pesa cincuenta libras. Capitán pesa ochenta libras. Y Lobo pesa veinte libras. *(pequeño)*

   _____

8. Mi papá tiene seis pies de altura. Yo tengo sólo cinco pies y medio de altura. *(alto)*

   _____

9. Hay tres hijos en mi familia. Manuel tiene diez y ocho años. Yo tengo quince años. Susana tiene doce años. *(pequeño)*

   _____

10. Después de un día largo de ir de compras, a Leticia no le queda ninguna energía. Y a su madre lo mismo. *(cansado)*

G O A L   6

To change a superlative to an absolute superlative.

The superlative indicates the extreme in any given group. For example, "Mary is the smartest girl in the class." It is also possible to say that someone is "very smart" without making any comparison.

María es **muy bonita.**	*María is **very pretty.***
María es **bonitísima.**	*María is **(very) extremely pretty.***

This type of word is formed by adding -*ísimo, -a, -os, -as* to the adjective minus the final vowel, if there is one.

grande	grandísimo
fácil	facilísimo
feliz	felicísimo
bonita	bonitísima

This same pattern is followed in changing adverbs to the absolute superlative.

elocuente	elocuentísimo	elocuentísimamente
rápido	rapidísimo	rapidísimamente

Note that with adjectives ending in *co, go,* or *z,* the spelling must be changed to *qu, gu,* or *c* before the *i* of -*ísimo.* Too, it is appropriate to note here that *muy* cannot be used with *mucho.*

E X E R C I S E

Change each sentence from a superlative to an absolute superlative using the -*ísimo* form.

1. Aquel edificio es el más alto de la ciudad.

   Aquel edificio es altísimo.

2. La familia que vive en aquella casa es la más rica de este distrito.

   _____

3. Raquel y Juana son las chicas más felices de la vecindad.

   _____

4. Esta profesora es la más exigente de todas.

   _____

5. El que ganó el premio gordo lo hizo muy fácilmente.

   _____

6. Elena hablo muy animadamente de los problemas.

   _____

7. Arturo recibió más becas. (mucho)

_____

8. Los vencedores salieron muy contentos.

_____

Communication Pattern Exercise

Work with a partner. Take turns asking and answering the questions.

1. ¿Eres tan alto(a) como tu padre?
2. ¿Eres tan inteligente como tu tía?
3. ¿Eres tan tímido(a) como tu mejor amigo(a)?
4. ¿Hablas tanto como tu mejor amigo(a)?
5. ¿Estudias tanto como tu amigo(a) íntimo(a)?
6. ¿Tienes tanta ropa como él (ella)?
7. ¿Gastas tanto dinero como él (ella)?
8. ¿Lees tantos libros como él (ella)?
9. ¿Escribes tantas cartas como él (ella)?
10. ¿Lees tan rápido como él (ella)?
11. ¿Sales con tu novio(a) tan frecuentemente como él (ella)?
12. ¿Tienes muchísimas tareas que hacer por la noche?
13. ¿Hay muchísimas revistas en tu casa?
14. ¿Es guapísimo(a) tu novio(a)?
15. ¿Es simpatiquísimo(a)?

Actividades de comunicación

Con "tan . . . como", "tanto, -a, -os, -as . . . como" y "tanto como", escribe una descripción de media página como mínimo comparando lo siguiente:

1. Tú y tu mejor amigo(a)
2. Tus hermanos(as) con los(as) de tu mejor amigo(a)
3. Tu madre con la de tu mejor amigo(a)
4. Tus profesores de este año con los del año pasado
5. La universidad con la escuela secundaria

Habla de estas comparaciones a un(a) compañero(a) de clase.

Refrán

Más hace el que quiere que el que puede.
Explica el sentido. Da ejemplos de la vida.

3 Relator Words

GOAL 1

To combine two sentences or ideas into one using *que*.

The word most commonly used in Spanish to relate a clause to a noun is *que*.

- Without a preposition, *que* may refer to either persons or things.

La señora **que** acaba de salir es
mi profesora de español.

*The lady **who** just left is my
Spanish teacher.*

Las clases **que** tengo ahora son
interesantísimas.

*The classes **that** I have now are
most interesting.*

In English the relator "that" may be omitted. It is never omitted in Spanish.

- With a preposition, *que* refers only to things.

El avión **en que** viajé era muy
viejo.

*The plane **in which** I traveled
was very old.*

Note that in Spanish the preposition always precedes *que*. Which preposition to use is determined by the verb and the meaning of the sentence.

EXERCISE

Incorporate the second sentence of each pair into the first using *que*.

1. Escogí un libro. El libro es fácil de leer.

   Escogí un libro que es fácil de leer.

2. El señor es un vendedor de seguros. El señor me llamó.

3. Berta tiene una máquina de escribir. Berta escribe sus lecciones en la máquina de escribir.

4. El profesor es muy exigente. El profesor me dió mala nota el semestre pasado.

5. La computadora es útil. La uso en las clases de matemáticas.

6. La bibliotecaria es mi tía. Trabaja los jueves por la noche.

G O A L   2

To combine two sentences or ideas into one using *quien*.

Another word commonly used to relate a clause to a noun is *quien*. In certain contexts *quien* is used instead of *que* to refer to persons. It is never used to refer to things. *Quien* has both a singular and a plural form.

- A clause containing *quien* may be used as the subject of a sentence.

Quien espera está perdido.	***He who*** *hesitates is lost.*
Quienes salen no pueden ganar.	***They who*** *leave cannot win.*

- *Quien* may be used in clauses that are set off by commas.

Los Cibrián, **quienes** son muy ricos, me dieron el dinero.	*The Cibriáns, **who** are very rich gave me the money.*

Que is also used in this type of sentence. When there are two possible antecedents, *que* or *quien* refers to the nearest one.

La hermana de Paco, **que** está en mi clase de psicología, se llama Ana.	*Paco, **who** is in my psychology class, has a sister named Ana.*
Dolores y su novio, **que** se llama Paco, vienen a la fiesta esta noche.	*Dolores and her fiancé, **whose** name is Paco, are coming to the party tonight.*

- *Quien* is also used after a preposition to refer to persons.

La señorita es mi hermana.

Hablaba **con** la señorita.

La señorita **con quien** hablaba es mi hermana.	*The girl **with whom** I was talking is my sister.*

Note that in Spanish the preposition used is governed by the verb in the clause. The preposition must always precede *quien*.

EXERCISE

Combine each pair of sentences into one using *quien* or *quienes*.

1. El señor Alborg es buen profesor. El señor Alborg me ayudó durante mi primer año.

   El señor Alborg, quien me ayudó durante mi primer año, es buen profesor.

   _____

2. El chico tenía el pelo rojo. Le di mensaje al chico.

   _____

3. Las recién llegadas son de la Argentina. Hablábamos de las recién llegadas.

   _____

4. Algunos van a ganar el partido. Son los que tienen más deseo.

_____

5. Juan González nos llevará en su coche. Juan se sienta cerca de mí en la clase de historia.

_____

GOAL 3

To combine two sentences or ideas into one using a form of *el cual.*

When the noun to which the relator word refers is not clear, *el cual, la cual, los cuales,* and *las cuales* are often used for clarity.

- When there are two nouns, a form of *el cual* refers to the more distant.

  La hermana de Paco, **la cual** acaba de recibir una beca de Harvard, quiere especializarse en las matemáticas.

  *Paco's sister, **(the one) who** just received a scholarship to Harvard, wants to major in mathematics.*

- A form of *el cual* is used after a compound preposition of more than three syllables to refer to things.

  Llegamos a las tiendas **delante de las cuales** ocurrió el accidente.

  *We arrived at the stores **in front of which** the accident occured.*

A form of *el cual* is also used in those cases in which the use of *que* might cause some confusion such as *por que* vs. *por el cual* or *sin que* vs. *sin el cual.*

  Se le perdió el mapa **sin el cual** era imposible encontrar el tesoro.

  *He lost the map **without which** it was impossible to find the treasure.*

- *Lo cual* refers to an indefinite idea or generality rather than a definite noun to which gender may be ascribed.

  La niña come poco, **lo cual** me preocupa.

  *The girl eats little, **which** worries me.*

EXERCISE

Combine each pair of sentences into one using a form of *el cual.*

1. Los parientes de mi amigo llegan mañana. Los parientes viven en Puerto Rico.

   Los parientes de mi amigo, los cuales viven en Puerto Rico, llegan mañana.

   _____

2. Por fin vimos un fuego. Alrededor del fuego había un grupo de jóvenes.

   _____

3. Algunos no tratan de mantener limpia la universidad. Esto me molesta.

_____

4. En el sótano había un baúl. Dentro del baúl los niños encontraron mucho ropa vieja con que jugar.

_____

5. La amiga de Andrés se sienta cerca de ti en esta clase. La amiga de Andrés tiene un portafolio.

_____

GOAL 4

To combine two sentences or ideas into one using *el que.*

A form of *el que* may be used, with a few exceptions, more or less like the forms of *el cual.* In fact, in the spoken language, forms of *el que* are more common.

- A form of *el que* may be used instead of *quien* at the beginning of a sentence.

  El que estudia aprende.   *He who studies learns.*

- *Lo que* is used like *lo cual.* However, *lo que* is also used to mean "that which" in English. The problem is that many times we say "what" instead of expressing the complete meaning.

  Lo que digo es verdad.   *What (that which) I say is true.*

  No entiendo **lo que** dice.   *I do not understand what (that which) he is saying.*

EXERCISE

Combine each pair of sentences into one using a form of *el que.*

1. El hermano de Rosa sacó buenas notas en la universidad. El hermano de Rosa es jugador de fútbol.

   El hermano de Rosa, el que es jugador de fútbol, sacó buenas notas en la universidad.

2. Unos son perezosos. Estos me extrañan.

_____

3. La hija del señor Gómez es abogada. La hija del señor Gómez vive en

   San Antonio.

_____

4. Te daré algo. Te daré cualquier cosa que tenga.

_____

5. Entrando en la sala vimos un escritorio. Encima del escritorio encontramos una nota.

_____

6. No tiene muchos amigos. Cualquier persona que siempre piensa en sí misma es así.

_____

G O A L   5

To combine two sentences or ideas into one using a form of *cuyo*.

Cuyo, -a, -os, -as expresses possession. It refers both to persons and to things. The form always agrees with the person or thing possessed.

Esta es la escuela **cuyo** equipo ganó el campeonato del estado.	*This is the school **whose** team won the state championship.*

Do not confuse *cuyo* with the interrogative word, *¿de quién?*, which also means "whose."

¿De quién es el sombrero?	***Whose** hat is it?*

EXERCISE

Combine each pair of sentences into one using a form of *cuyo*.

1. Esta es la casa de los Cid. Fue su perro que me atacó.

   Esta es la casa de los Cid, cuyo perro me atacó.

2. Voy con José y Manuela. Su padre es el jefe de su compañía.

   _____

3. Estudio bajo el señor García. Sus estudiantes son los mejores del distrito.

   _____

4. Manuel va a pasar el verano allí. Sus tías viven en España.

   _____

5. Pepe acaba de comprar un bote nuevo. Sus padres son riquísimos.

   _____

6. Mi amiga me invitó a pasar las vacaciones con ella. Su familia tiene un condominio en la Costa del Sol.

   _____

GOAL 6

To choose between *que, quien, el cual, el que,* and *cuyo,* depending upon context.

EXERCISE

Complete each of the following sentences with the appropriate form of *que, quien, el cual, el que,* or *cuyo,* depending on the context.

1. María no podía contestar porque no sabía _____ quería el profesor.

2. _____ tiene más suerte recibe el premio gordo.

3. Fue mi novio _____ me dio esta pulsera.

4. En el escritorio había un montón de papeles debajo de _____ encontré la foto perdida.

5. El niño lloraba continuamente, _____ irritaba a la madre.

6. ¿Es ésta la chica para _____ compraste el anillo?

7. Mi amiga, _____ padre es dentista, no tiene ni una carie.

8. El abrigo de pieles _____ quiero cuesta mucho dinero.

9. La hermana de José, _____ trabaja en la oficina, es administradora.

10. Los juguetes con _____ juegan los niños son de plástico.

11. El señor Fernández, _____ nació en Buenos Aires, hace un viaje a la Argentina el mes que viene.

Communication Pattern Exercise

Write an original sentence using the same pattern as that of the given sentence.

1. (person + *que* clause) Es la chica que te llamó anoche.

   _____

2. (thing + *que* clause) Busca el libro que perdió.

   _____

3. (thing + preposition + *que* clause) El cuarto en que duerme está en el primer piso.

   _____

4. (person + *quien* clause) Jaime, quien es muy amable, me ayudó mucho.

   _____

5. (person + preposition + *quien* clause) Busco un amigo con quien divertirme.

   _____

6. (two persons + *el cual* clause) Se casó con una amiga de José, la cual trabaja en Arizona.

_____

7. (thing + preposition + *el cual* clause) Vi a una señorita hermosísima alrededor de la cual habiá un grupo de admiradores.

_____

8. (whole idea + *lo cual* clause) Siempre hace mucho ruido, lo cual me irrita.

_____

9. *(quien* or a form of *el que* clause + verb) Quien aprende, gana.

_____

10. (verb + *lo que* clause) El pobre no entiende lo que pasa.

_____

11. (possessor + *cuyo* clause [including person possessed]) Pura, cuyo padre es médico, nunca se enferma.

_____

12. (possessor + *cuyo* clause [including thing possessed]) Pedro, cuya casa es muy grande, da muchas fiestas.

_____

Actividades de comunicación

Completa las siguientes oraciones.

1. Un tonto no sabe lo que _____.

2. El libro que me gusta más _____.

3. La persona con quien hablo más _____.

4. El profesor cuya clase me interesó más _____.

5. Quien trabaja _____.

6. El que tiene fe _____.

7. La actividad en que paso más tiempo _____.

Refránes

Dime con quien andas y te diré quien eres.
El que madruga, Dios le ayuda.
El que siembra recoge.
Explica el sentido. Da ejemplos de la vida.

4 The Subjunctive in Cause plus Desired Result Relationships

The subjunctive mood in Spanish is much more important than the subjunctive in English. In most cases it is used in structures that do not require the subjunctive in English. There is usually no separate subjunctive form in English to cue the use of the subjunctive in Spanish and to make its meaning absolutely clear.

GOAL 1

To learn the basic concepts of mood.

In Spanish and in English there are three moods that a verb may express: the indicative, the imperative, and the subjunctive.

Indicative:	He **goes.**
Imperative:	**Go!**
Subjunctive:	Mom insists that he **go.**

These three moods are used in different cases to express different ideas. The *indicative* mood may be used as a main verb in a sentence or as the verb in a clause. This mood describes facts, experienced reality, or certainty.

He went.	I found out that he **went.**
He goes.	I know he **goes.**
He will go.	I believe that he **will go.**

The *imperative* is used as the main verb in a sentence or as the main verb in a direct quotation. It is used to give a command or to make a request.

Come here.

Please **close** the window.

Dad said, "**Do** your homework."

The *subjunctive* is normally used only as the verb in a dependent clause. This mood describes an action that is not a fact, that is not experienced from the point of view of the main verb.

If **I were** you, I would go.	(I am not you.)
It is necessary that he **leave.**	(He has not left yet.)
Long **live** the king.	(His life is not over.)

The subjunctive is used much more in Spanish than in English. It is used to contrast with the indicative as a dependent verb. The indicative describes an action that is a fact. The subjunctive describes an action that is not a fact or that is a fact but toward which there is some emotional or personal opinion on the part of the speaker. Contrast the following examples:

Indicative

Sabe que **soy** estudiante.   *He knows (that)* **I am** *a student.*

Sabe que **estás** aquí.   *He knows (that)* **you are** *here.*

Subjunctive

Si **fuera** presidente yo. . .   *If* **I were** *president, I would. . .*

¡Cuánto me alegro de que **estés**   *How happy I am (that)* **you're**
  aquí!   *here!*

_E X E R C I S E_   The examples and questions in each item are based on the preceding discussion
                         of mood in English. Answer them in your own words.

  1. *Leave* your books in your locker.

      a. "Leave" is in what mood? _____

      b. Is it the main verb or a dependent verb? _____

      c. What idea does it express? _____

      d. Give another example of a command.

      _____

  2. John *knows* the answer.

      a. "Knows" is in what mood? _____

      b. Is it the main verb or a dependent verb? _____

      c. What idea does it express? _____

      d. Give another example of the indicative used as a main verb.

      _____

  3. We realize that Jane *has* a boyfriend.

      a. "Has" is in what mood? _____

      b. Is it the main verb or a dependent verb? _____

      c. What idea does it express? _____

      d. Give another example of the indicative used as a dependent verb.

      _____

  4. She insists that her son *study* his lessons.

      a. "Study" is in what mood? _____

      b. Is it the main verb or a dependent verb? _____

      c. What is the correct verb form in English if the part of the sentence
         after "that" stands alone? _____

      d. Give another example of the subjunctive used as a dependent verb.

      _____

5. Logically, there is a close relationship between the imperative mood and the subjunctive mood. For each of the following sentences, indicate *I* for those sentences in which the italicized verb is imperative and *S* for those in which the italicized verb is subjunctive. In neither case has the action taken place.

_____ a. She suggested, "*leave* early or you won't make it on time."

_____ b. She suggested that he *leave* early.

_____ c. *Leave* early.

_____ d. It is necessary that he *leave* early in order to arrive on time.

6. In order to use the subjunctive correctly you must be able to distinguish between the indicative mood and the subjunctive mood. For each of the following sentences, indicate *I* for those in which the italicized verb is indicative and *S* for those sentences in which the italicized verb is subjunctive.

_____ a. She requested that he *open* his eyes.

_____ b. He *opens* the door for his mother.

_____ c. They noticed that the store *opens* tomorrow.

_____ d. He is demanding that she *give* the ring back.

_____ e. That mother *gives* her son too much to eat.

_____ f. They know that she *gives* him extra money.

7. At times either an indicative or a subjunctive verb may be used in the dependent clause, but the meaning is different for each. What is the difference in meaning between these two sentences?

_____ a. The mother insists that he *study* his lessons.

_____ b. The mother insists that he *studies* his lessons.

GOAL 2

To use the correct class vowel to indicate commands.

Most commands are given by using the present subjunctive form of the verb. To form the present subjunctive, use the opposite class vowel. In *A* verbs the *a* changes to *e,* and for *E* and *I* verbs the *e* or *i* becomes *a.*

EXERCISE

Complete each command form by adding the appropriate class vowel.

1. Juanita, no le habl_____s así a tu hermanito.

2. Señor Gómez, trat_____ usted de patinar con nosotros esta noche.

3. Sub_____n ustedes a nuestro cuarto.

4. Que demuestr_____n el otro ahora.

5. Que confies_____ ella sus delitos.

6. Despert_____mos a sus padres.

7. Durm_____mos aquí.

8. Volv_____mos temprano.

9. Veng_____n ustedes pronto.

10. Pepito, no huy_____s de él.

11. Que pagu_____ todo este cliente.

12. Que no pesqu_____n en ese río contaminado.

13. Recoj_____mos los soldados miniaturas esta tarde.

14. No vay_____is sin paraguas.

15. No se_____n ustedes antipáticos.

16. Que est_____ satisfecho con éstos.

GOAL 3

To convert direct commands to indirect commands.

A. A sentence containing a formal command in a direct quote can be converted into a sentence containing a subjunctive in the dependent clause by removing the quotation marks plus the subject pronoun and adding *que*.

El dependiente demanda, "Salga usted."
El dependiente demanda que salga.

EXERCISE

Change each sentence from a direct to an indirect command.

1. El científico demanda, "No ensucien ustedes este planeta."

   _____

2. Los padres les suplican a sus hijos, "No gasten ustedes tanto dinero."

   _____

3. La señora insiste (en), "Suba la calefacción."

_____

4. El médico le dice, "Extienda usted la pierna derecha."

_____

5. Les pide, "Traigan ustedes una ensalada."

_____

6. El viejo le aconseja, "Duerma usted más."

_____

B. This same pattern may also be extended to all the other command forms. However, there are two principal differences between direct commands and indirect commands that must be kept in mind. First, the affirmative command forms _tú_ and _vosotros_, which do not use the subjunctive verb forms, must be converted to the subjunctive. Second, in dependent clauses, the object pronouns always precede the verb.

El viejo demanda, "Sal tú."
El viejo demanda que salgas.
El viejo demanda, "Salid."
El viejo demanda que salgáis.
El viejo demanda, "Cómetelo ahora."
El viejo demanda que te lo comas ahora.

EXERCISE   Change each sentence from a direct command to a sentence containing a clause with a subjunctive verb. Keep the same subject with the verb.

1. Mamá insiste (en), "No comas con los codos en la mesa."
   Mamá insiste en que no comas con los codos in la mesa.

2. Juan advierte, "No le pidas un divorcio."

_____

3. Papá te dice, "Levántate pronto."

_____

4. La madre suplica, "No os quejéis tanto."

_____

5. Rafael ruega, "Creed en la libertad individual."

_____

6. Juan nos dice, "Votemos ahora."

_____

GOAL 4

To combine two sentences into one containing a clause plus a desired result relationship.

The indirect commands studied in Goal 3 all express cause plus desired result relationships. The main verb, which is in the indicative, is the cause; the dependent verb, which is in the subjunctive, is the desired result. The main verb is a fact. The dependent verb has not occurred at the time the statement is made although it may or may not come to pass later.

Pattern: main verb (indicative) + relator + desired result (subjunctive)

| El viejo demanda | que | salgas. |
| *The old man demands* | *(that)* | *you leave.* |

This cause plus desired result may be expressed in English in two different ways. Note that in English the word "that" is often omitted.

- main verb + relator + desired result

| They demand | (that) | we help them. |
| I insist | (that) | she go. |

- main verb + infinitive phrase

| They tell | us to help them. |
| I write | her to go. |

- With some English verbs either pattern may be used.

	They ask	that	we help them.
or	They ask	us to help them.
	I advise	that	she go.
or	I advise	her to go.

Which type of expression follows the main verb is governed by the main verb itself. With minor exceptions only the pattern main verb + relator word + clause is used in Spanish.

EXERCISE

Combine each pair of ideas into one that contains a cause plus a desired result relationship.

1. la madre ruega/su hijo maneja con más cuidado

   La madre ruega que su hijo maneje con más cuidado.

2. el policía recomienda/los ladrones se ponen las manos en la cabeza

3. mis padres quieren/te quedarás con nosotros

4. le pido al mesero/nos traerá el menú

5. sugieren/no me preocupo tanto

_____

6. ¿quieres?/vamos juntos a la fiesta

_____

7. el guía no permite/nadie saca fotografías

_____

8. el juez demanda/guardamos silencio

_____

GOAL 5

To distinguish between the use of the indicative and the subjunctive in the desired result clause.

If the sentence implies a cause plus a desired result, the second verb is in the subjunctive. If not, the indicative is used.

- Cause plus desired result (subjunctive)

  Demanda que le **diga** la verdad.   *He demands that **I tell** him the truth.*

  Quiere que le **diga** la verdad.   *He wants me **to tell** him the truth. (I have not told him the truth yet.)*

- Statement of fact (indicative)

  Sabe que le **digo** la verdad.   *He knows that **I tell** him the truth. (I have told him the truth. To the speaker this is experienced.)*

EXERCISES

I. Combine each pair of ideas into one sentence containing *que* plus a clause. Use either the indicative or the subjunctive for the second verb, depending upon the meaning of the sentence.

1. los empleados saben/no hay trabajo mañana

_____

2. los estudiantes quieren/no hay un examen después de las vacaciones

_____

3. Mariana entiende/a su comprometido no le gusta bailar

_____

4. Juana insiste/su novio baila con ella

_____

5. ¿quieres?/vuelvo antes de la medianoche

_____

6. contesta/vuelvo inmediatamente después del partido

_____

II. Change each of the following sentences from a direct quote to an indirect statement using either the indicative or the subjunctive for the second verb, as the context implies. Give the English meaning of each.

1. La madre grita, "Espere usted."

_____

_____

2. La madre grita, "¡Vuelve Rosa!"

_____

_____

3. Les dice, "Cierren ustedes los libros."

_____

_____

4. Les dice, "Todos cierran los ojos al dormirse."

_____

_____

5. Mamá insiste (en), "Vengan ustedes mañana."

_____

_____

6. Mamá insiste (en), "Ustedes siempre hacen demasiado ruido."

_____

_____

7. Me escribe, "Juan va a vender su motocicleta."

_____

_____

8. Me escribe, "Vende la tuya también."

_____

_____

GOAL 6
To combine two sentences into one using either an infinitive or a clause.

A cause plus a desired result is only possible when one subject attempts to influence the actions of another. Otherwise, the Spanish and English patterns are identical and an infinitive clause is used.

Quiero que Juan **abra** la ventana.   *I want Juan **to open** the window.*

Quiero **abrir** la ventana.   *I want **to open** the window.*

In the case of *dejar, hacer, mandar, prohibir,* and *permitir,* either a clause or an infinitive may be used with one subject attempting to influence the actions of another.

Le permiten **salir.**   *They permit him **to leave.***
Permiten **que salga.**

EXERCISE

Combine each pair of ideas into one sentence containing either a dependent clause or an infinitive, depending upon the situation. Give the English meaning of each.

1. María prefiere/María almuerza en casa

_____

_____

2. María prefiere/su madre almuerza en casa

_____

_____

3. los jóvenes quieren/los jóvenes oyen canciones populares

_____

_____

4. los niños quieren/su papá los besa

_____

_____

5. papá me deja/conduzco su coche

_____

_____

6. mamá nos hace/somos corteses

_____

_____

Communication Pattern Exercises

I. Work with a partner. Read each statement, then take turns answering the questions.

1. Juan no presta atención en la clase y el profesor lo ve.

   ¿Qué no quiere hacer Juan? ¿Qué ve el profesor? ¿Qué le recomienda a Juan?

2. Los niños no beben la leche y papá lo nota.

   ¿Qué no quieren hacer los niños? ¿Qué nota papá? ¿Qué les dice papá?

3. El niño escribe en la pared y mamá lo nota.

   ¿Qué hace el niño? ¿Qué nota mama? ¿Qué grita mamá?

4. No me gusta levantarme temprano. Mis padres saben esto pero insisten.

   ¿Qué no me gusta? ¿Qué saben mis padres? ¿En qué insisten?

5. José no se siente bien. Mientras le habla al médico confiesa, "Sólo duermo cuatro horas cada noche."

   ¿A qué está acostumbrado José? ¿Qué le confiesa José al médico? ¿Qué le advierte el médico?

6. Rosa siempre llega tarde a clase y el profesor siempre la mira cuando entra en la clase.

   ¿A qué está acostumbrada Rosa? ¿Qué sabe el profesor? ¿Qué le sugiere?

II. Take turns asking and answering the questions with your partner.

1. Al salir de casa por la noche, ¿qué te dicen tus padres?
2. En la clase de inglés, ¿en qué insiste el profesor?
3. Con respecto a los estudios de usted, ¿qué quieren tus padres?
4. Hablando de tus actividades, ¿qué prefieren tus amigos?
5. Con respecto a su carrera, ¿qué te aconseja el consejero?
6. Hablando de la ayuda que les das a tus hermanos, ¿qué te piden?

III. Give the Spanish equivalent of each of the English sentences. Remember the following:

• The wording is often quite different between the two languages.
• *Que* is never omitted in Spanish.
• The meaning of the main verb determines whether or not the subjunctive is used in the second verb.

1. We demand that they call.

_____

2. She wants us to read ten pages.

_____

3. Do you prefer to eat here?

_____

4. They know she lives upstairs.

_____

5. Her parents permit her to go.

_____

6. The teacher tells us that you do not study.

_____

7. We tell you to study.

_____

8. You tell us that you study.

_____

9. She insists that he play the piano every day.

_____

10. She insists that he plays the piano every day.

_____

Actividades de comunicación

Con cualquier verbo de la siguiente lista de verbos, o cualquier otro verbo, prepara un resumen de cinco oraciones como mínimo.

lo que tus padres esperan de ti

lo que esperas tú de ti mismo(a)

lo que el (la) profesor(a) espera de los estudiantes

lo que los padres de tu mejor amigo(a) esperan de él (ella)

advertir	pedir	prohibir	dejar	escribir
insistir	decir	demandar	mandar	aconsejar
rogar	permitir	preferir		

Habla de tus resúmenes a un(a) compañero(a) de clase.

Refrán

No firmes carta que no leas, ni bebas agua que no veas.
Explica el sentido. Da ejemplos de la vida.

5 The Subjunctive in Other Noun Clauses

To combine two sentences into one containing an expression of doubt
and the subjunctive.

If the speaker doubts the reality of the action of the second verb, the subjunctive
will be used.

Dudamos que **diga** la verdad.   *We doubt (that) he **tells** the truth.*

Remember that *que* must be used to join the two clauses.

EXERCISE   Combine each pair of sentences into one sentence using the subjunctive.

1. Los estudiantes cuidan sus animales. El veterinario no cree eso.

   El veterinario no cree que los estudiantes cuiden sus animales.

2. Mi hermana duerme bastante. Mamá duda eso.

   _____

3. Existen seres extraterrestres. ¿Crees eso?

   _____

4. Pepe tiene éxito con ese trabajo. Dudo eso.

   _____

5. Se matriculan aquí. ¿Creéis eso?

   _____

6. Yo hago esas travesuras. Mis padres no creen eso.

   _____

To distinguish between the pattern doubt plus subjunctive and the
pattern certainty plus indicative.

If the main verb does not imply doubt as to the reality of the second verb, the
indicative is used.

No dudamos que **dice** la verdad.   *We **do not doubt** that he **is
telling** the truth.*

EXERCISE

Combine each pair of ideas into one sentence using either the subjunctive or the indicative, as the meaning requires.

1. mis amigos dudan/yo voy al partido esta semana

   Mis amigos dudan que yo vaya al partido esta semana

2. creo/piensan firmar un acuerdo de paz

   _____

3. no dudamos/Juan se siente mal

   _____

4. sabe/esta joven es cristiana

   _____

5. no creen/la chica lee tan rápido

   _____

6. ¿cree usted?/tenemos suficientes recursos minerales

   _____

7. el joven no niega/su hermana conoce a José

   _____

8. Marta niega/Raúl está enamorado de ella

   _____

GOAL 3

To combine two sentences into one containing an expression of strong feeling and the subjunctive.

Even though an event may be experienced, known, or believed, the subjunctive is normally used if the speaker expresses an emotional reaction to the second verb.

Juan **está** en la sala.	*Juan **is** in the living room.*
¡Qué lástima que **esté** aquí esta noche!	***What a pity** he **is** here tonight!*

Remember that *que* must be used to join the two clauses.

EXERCISE   Combine each pair of ideas into one sentence using the subjunctive.

1. tengo miedo de/los otros no entienden

   Tengo miedo de que los otros no entiendan.

2. se alegran de/tomo cursos por correspondencia

3. ¿sientes?/tu amiga recibe más dinero que tú

4. tememos/ustedes pierden todo

5. ¡qué lástima!/no te mejoras más rápido

6. ¡ojalá!/recuerda de cerrar la puerta

GOAL 4

To combine two ideas into one sentence containing an impersonal
expression and the subjunctive.

Impersonal expressions may express a cause, a doubt, or an emotion. With such
expressions the subjunctive is used.

Es necesario que **vaya.**	*It is necessary that he go.*
Es dudoso que **vaya.**	*It is doubtful that he goes.*
Es lástima que **vaya.**	*It is a pity that he goes.*

EXERCISE   Rewrite each sentence, inserting the expression in parentheses.

1. Dejo el coche en el garaje. *(es preferible)*

   Es preferible que deje el coche en el garaje

2. Tú crees en la brujería. *(es lamentable)*

3. Reciben el paquete para esta tarde. *(es improbable)*

4. Me divierto en esta fiesta. *(puede ser)*

_____

5. Se apaga el televisor a las diez. *(es mejor)*

_____

6. Importamos tanto petróleo. *(es increíble)*

_____

GOAL 5

To distinguish between the pattern impersonal expression plus subjunctive and the pattern impersonal expression plus indicative.

If the meaning of the impersonal expression implies certainty or fact, the indicative is used.

Es verdad que Juan **está** aquí.   *It is true that Juan is here.*

EXERCISE

Combine each pair of ideas into one sentence using either the subjunctive or the indicative for the second verb.

1. es dudoso/atacan antes del amanecer

   Es dudoso que ataquen antes del amanecer.
   _____

2. claro está/esta mujer se queja mucho

   _____

3. es importante/entienden lo peligroso que es el paracaídismo deportivo

   _____

4. es evidente/Rosa prefiere salir con Pepe

   _____

5. es verdad/soy patriótico

   _____

6. es posible/atropellamos a un peatón si no tenemos cuidado

   _____

GOAL 6

To distinguish between the use of a clause and an infinitive.

In addition to those types of sentences in which the subjunctive is used as the second verb, it is possible in many cases to use the infinitive.

- Same subject

Me alegro de **ir.**   *I am glad **I am going.***

Note that with verbs of doubting, a clause is used even if there is no change of subject.

Dudo que **vaya.**   *I doubt (that) **I am going.***

- No expressed subject

Es necesario **ir.**   *It is necessary **to go.***

EXERCISE

Rewrite each sentence, inserting the expression in parentheses. The second clause will contain either the subjunctive or an infinitive, depending upon the situation.

1. Sale sin jugar. *(es lástima)*

   Es lástima que salga sin jugar.

2. Los dos llegan tarde. *(es lástima)*

3. Vamos en el avión Concorde. *(dudamos)*

4. El médium tiene contacto con los muertos. *(dudamos)*

5. Pesco durante las vacaciones. *(espero)*

6. Cumples con tu promesa. *(espero)*

Communication Pattern Exercises

I. Work with a partner. Read each statement, then take turns asking and answering the questions using either the subjunctive, the indicative, or the infinitive, as the context requires.

1. Julio quiere ir al baile. Su madre entiende esto, pero también sabe que tiene un examen mañana.
   ¿Qué quiere Julio? ¿Qué entiende su madre? ¿Va Julio al baile? ¿Es probable o improbable?

2. Cuando los alumnos llegan a la clase ven este anuncio en la pizarra: <<NO HAY CLASE HOY>> ¡Qué contentos están!
Al llegar a la clase, ¿qué aprenden los alumnos? ¿De qué se alegran los alumnos?

3. Raúl estudia mucho o por lo menos dice que sí. Sin embargo, sus amigos lo dudan porque recibe malas notas.
¿Qué dice Raúl? ¿Qué saben sus amigos? ¿Qué dudan sus amigos?

4. Rosita no come el desayuno porque no quiere engordar. Al mismo tiempo no tiene mucha energía. Su padre nota esto y le molesta.
Rosita no come mucho ¿verdad? ¿Qué nota su padre? ¿Qué le molesta a su padre?

5. Estos jóvenes tienen mucho talento. Eso es evidente. Pero no participan en ninguna actividad. Eso es una lástima.
¿Qué es evidente? ¿Qué es una lástima?

6. Pepe sale hoy para matricularse en la universidad. Sus padres están tristes porque van a echar de menos a su hijo, pero están contentos porque él quiere continuar sus estudios.
Pepe sale hoy. ¿No es cierto?
Los padres están tristes y contentos al mismo tiempo, ¿verdad?
¿Qué sienten los padres? ¿De qué se alegran?

II. Express the idea of each English sentence in Spanish.

1. I doubt that he will close the door.

_____

2. She does not doubt (believes) he is coming.

_____

3. We are sorry that you do not understand.

_____

4. Are you happy that I will be there?

_____

5. They are afraid he is working too much.

_____

6. It is a pity they break everything.

_____

7. It is evident that they write poorly.

_____

8. It is better for you to return early.

_____

Actividades de comunicación

Pensando en tu familia, habla con un compañero de clase de los siguientes temas.

1. Me alegro de que mi familia . . . , mi padre . . . , mi madre . . . , mis hermanos . . .
2. En mi familia es importante que . . .
3. Todos sabemos que . . .
4. Mis padres quieren que . . .
5. Es verdad que . . .

Refrán   No temas mancha que sale con agua.
                  Explica el sentido. Da ejemplos de la vida.

---

6 Other Tenses and Sequence of Tenses

GOAL 1

To change a verb from the present perfect to the present perfect subjunctive.

The present perfect subjunctive is formed by adding the regular perfective particple to the present subjunctive of *haber*.

Indicative	Subjunctive	
he llamado	hay a	llamado
has llamado	hay a s	llamado
ha llamado	hay a	llamado
hemos llamado	hay a mos	llamado
habéis llamado	hay á is	llamado
han llamado	hay a n	llamado

EXERCISE   Combine each pair of sentences into one sentence containing the present perfect subjunctive form of the second verb.

1. Sandra ha encontrado sus aretes. Me alegro de eso.

   Me alegro de que Sandra haya encontrado sus aretes.

2. ¿Han aprobado el curso? Eso es dudoso.

_____

3. Hemos visto ejemplos del poder psíquico. ¿No lo crees?

_____

4. ¿Te has acostumbrado a la vida estudiantil? Espero que sí.

_____

5. Habéis esperado tanto. Eso es lástima.

_____

6. ¿He recordado bien la fecha? Esperan que sí.

_____

G O A L   2

To change a verb from the imperfect or preterite to the imperfect subjunctive.

A conjugated verb form has three parts: the stem, the class vowel and tense-aspect suffix, and the person-number suffix. The stem and the class vowel for the imperfect subjunctive are the same as the stem and the class vowel for the third person plural of the preterite. The tense-aspect marker is *ra* or *se*. The person-number suffixes are the same as in all other tenses.

hablar (hablaron)	**ser** (fueron)	**volver** (volvieron)
habl ara	fu era	volv iese
habl ara s	fu era s	volv iese s
habl ara	fu era	volv iese
habl ára mos	fu éra mos	volv iése mos
habl ara is	fu era is	volv iese is
habl ara n	fu era n	volv iese n

Note the accent mark over the class vowel in the *nosotros* form. The *se* suffix is rarely used in Latin America; the *ra* form is used in this book.

EXERCISES

I. Change each verb from the preterite or the imperfect form to the imperfect subjunctive.

1. ayudaron   *ayudaran*

2. volvieron	_____	12. buscaba	_____
3. sirvieron	_____	13. vendían	_____
4. leíste	_____	14. estábamos	_____
5. trajeron	_____	15. ponía	_____
6. estuve	_____	16. entendíais	_____
7. cayó	_____	17. se divertían	_____
8. dijimos	_____	18. pagabas	_____
9. saliste	_____	19. era	_____
10. canté	_____	20. íbamos	_____
11. escribisteis	_____		

II. Combine each pair of ideas into a new sentence containing the imperfect subjunctive form of the first verb. Note that there is no distinction made in the subjunctive between perfective and imperfective actions.

1. No se enfadaron y me alegraba de eso.

   Me alegraba de que no se enfadaran

2. Dije la verdad pero era necesario.

   _____

3. Bajamos el volumen del estéreo porque nos pidió.

   _____

4. No nos gustaba el cuarto y ella temía eso.

   _____

5. Perdían mucho tiempo y era una lástima.

   _____

6. Ibamos en autobús y era mejor.

   _____

GOAL 3

To change a verb from the past perfect indicative to the past perfect subjunctive.

The past perfect subjunctive is formed by adding the regular perfective participle to the imperfect subjunctive of *haber*.

Indicative	Subjunctive	
había jugado	hub iera	jugado
habías jugado	hub iera s	jugado
había jugado	hub iera	jugado
habíamos jugado	hub iéra mos	jugado
habíais jugado	hub iera is	jugado
habían jugado	hub iera n	jugado

EXERCISE

Combine each pair of ideas into one sentence containing the past perfect subjunctive form of the second verb.

1. dudábamos/había obtenido un trabajo

   Dudábamos que hubiera obtenido un trabajo

2. era improbable/habían pensado en eso

   _____

3. esperaría/habías hecho lo mejor posible

   _____

4. habríamos sentido/habíais paseado solos

   _____

5. no habían creído/nos habíamos vestido así

   _____

6. temía/me había equivocado

   _____

GOAL 4

To use the various tenses in proper order and relationships.

The present subjunctive or present perfect subjunctive normally follows non-past verbs: commands, present, and future. There is no future subjunctive form.

Alégrese de que venga (haya venido).

Be glad he is coming (has come).

Nos alegramos de que venga (haya venido).

We are happy he comes (has come).

Me alegraré de que venga (haya venido).

I will be happy he is coming (has come.)

The imperfect subjunctive or past perfect subjunctive follows past set verbs: imperfect, preterite, conditional, past perfect, and conditional perfect.

Sentía que llamara (hubiera llamado).

She regretted that I called (had called.)

Sintió que llamara (hubiera llamado) en ese momento.

She was sorry that I called (had called) at that moment.

Sentiría que llamara (hubiera llamado).

She would be sorry that I called (had called).

Había sentido que llamara (hubiera llamado).

She had been sorry that I called (had called).

Habría sentido que llamara (hubiera llamado).

She would have been sorry that I called (had called).

Of course, it is quite possible to be happy, sad, etc., now about something that happened in the past.

Siento que **estuviera (hubiera estado)** enferma.

*I am sorry that you **were (had been** sick.*

EXERCISE

Combine each pair of ideas into one sentence containing the subjunctive in the appropriate tense.

1. es imposible/han bebido tanto

   Es imposible que hayan bebido tanto _____

2. es imposible/lees con este ruido

   _____

3. fue imposible/jugó tan bien

   _____

4. habría sido mejor/no habíamos ganado la lotería

   _____

5. no habían creído/encontré uno tan barato

_____

6. temo/se ha perdido

_____

7. ¿quieres?/te llamo

_____

8. ¿querías?/te llamé

_____

9. es lástima/ya se han perdido su amistad

_____

10. era lástima/no estuvieron aquí

_____
_____

GOAL 5

To use the proper subjunctive or indicative tense in sequence.

Of course, if the subjunctive is not required, the regular indicative forms are used. The sequence of tenses is the same as for subjunctive; non-past is normally used with non-past and past is normally used with past.

EXERCISE

Combine each pair of ideas into one sentence containing either the subjunctive or the indicative in the appropriate tense.

1. mi amigo sabía/yo iba al baile con Rosa

   Mi amigo sabía que iba al baile con Rosa.

2. pero él no quería/(yo) iba con ella

   _____

3. me pidió/(yo) iba con María

   _____
   _____

4. es verdad/todos tenemos miedo a veces

   _____

5. es lástima/tenemos un examen después del fin da semana

   _____

6. Juan me dijo/Ana estaba enferma la semana pasada

_____

7. Ana, siento/estabas enferma la semana pasada

_____

8. su mamá cree/su hijo ha realizado sus planes

_____

9. nosotros dudamos/su hijo ha realizado sus planes

_____

10. pero es posible/su hijo los había realizado antes

_____

11. se alegraba de/yo la visité

_____

12. también se alegraba de/yo había visitado a sus parientes

_____

Communication Pattern Exercise

Work with a partner. Read each statement, then take turns asking and answering the questions that follow.

1. Papá le pide. "Lava el coche," y lo lava.
   ¿Qué quiere papá? ¿Qué le pide papá? Y lava el coche, ¿verdad?

2. Ayer le dijo, "Vende tu motocicleta," pero no la vendió. La necesita para ir a clase.
   ¿Qué le dijo papá? No la vendió, ¿verdad?

3. El mes pasado la mejor amiga de mi hermana vino a visitarla. Desde ese día no vuelve a visitarla. Está enfadada. Es evidente, pero mi hermana no sabe por qué. Ella está triste.
   ¿Qué es evidente? ¿Qué siente su hermana?

4. Escriban ustedes todos los ejercicios con tinta azul para mañana. ¿Qué les ha dicho el profesor a los alumnos? ¿Es probable que los escriban?

5. Mamá le dice a su hijito, "Tienes algo en la boca. Ábrela."
   ¿Qué sabe mamá? ¿Qué le dice a su hijito?

Actividades de comunicación

A. Completa cada frase, pensando en cuando eras niño(a).

1. ¿De qué te alegrabas? Me alegraba de que _____.

2. ¿Qué te gustaba? Me gustaba que _____.

3. ¿Qué les pedías a tus padres? Les pedía que _____.

4. ¿Qué te pedían tus padres? Me pedían que _____.

5. ¿En qué insistían tus padres? Insistían que yo _____.

6. ¿Qué entendían tus padres? Entendían que yo _____.

B. Compara tus respuestas con las de un(a) compañero(a) de clase.

Refránes

El que no se aventura no cruza el mar.
Explica el sentido. Da ejemplos de la vida.

---

7 The Subjunctive in Adjectival Clauses

GOAL 1

To use the subjunctive in a clause describing an indefinite noun.

If a noun to which a clause refers is an indefinite or uncertain person, place, or thing, you must use the subjunctive form of the verb in that clause.

Quiero leer un libro que **sea** interesante.	*I want to read a book that **is** interesting.*
Buscamos un apartamento que **tenga** una máquina de lavar.	*We are looking for an apartment that **has** a washing machine.*

It is obvious that the speaker does not have a certain book or apartment in mind. He or she wants to read any book as long as it is interesting or find any apartment as long as it has a washing machine.

EXERCISE

Combine each pair of ideas into one sentence containing the subjunctive. Remember to make the sequence of tenses agree.

1. quiere un cuarto/está cerca del centro

    Quiere un cuarto que esté cerca del centro

2. buscamos una joven/ha visitado el país

3. ¿habia algunos?/no vieron el programa ayer

_____

4. dondequiera/va María/todos están contentos

_____

5. queremos un equipo/gana todos los partidos

_____

6. ¿hay alguien?/no entiende esto

_____

_____

G O A L   2

To use the subjunctive in a clause referring to a nonexistent noun.

If the noun to which the clause refers is nonexistent, the subjunctive form of the verb must be used in that clause.

No hay nadie que **pueda** hacerlo.   *There is no one who **can** do it.*

It is obvious that the speaker believes it is impossible to do whatever is being talked about. Therefore, the verb in the adjectival clause cannot be an accomplished fact or reality, and the subjunctive must be used.

EXERCISE

Combine each pair of ideas into one sentence containing the subjunctive in the adjectival clause.

1. no hay nadie/comprende completamente los reglamentos de los impuestos

   No hay nadie que comprenda completamente los reglamentos de los impuestos.

2. no había ningún cliente/me dio las gracias

   _____

3. no existe ningún profesor/enseña sólo por el dinero

   _____

4. no conozco a ningún policía/tiene un Cadillac

   _____

5. no me trajo ninguna máquina de escribir/funcionaba

   _____

6. no vi a ninguna mujer/estaba vestida de domingo

   _____

GOAL 3

To use the indicative in a clause referring to a definite noun.

If the noun to which a clause refers is definite, you must use the indicative form of the verb in the clause.

Conozco a un señor que vive en   *I know a man who lives in*
    México.   *Mexico.*

EXERCISE

Rewrite each of the following sentences using the words indicated to make the noun definite. Make the necessary change in the verb form in the adjectival clause.

1. Quiere un cuarto que esté cerca del centro.

    Tiene _____ *un cuarto que está cerca del centro* _____.

2. Buscamos una joven que haya visitado el país.

    Conocemos a _____.

3. Buscaba una librería en que se vendiera esa novela.

    Encontró _____.

4. Queremos un equipo que gane todos los partidos.

    Tenemos _____.

5. Buscaban una casa que tuviera dos cuartos de baño.

    Compraron _____.

6. No hay nadie que comprenda todos los reglamentos de los impuestos.

    Hay alguien _____.

7. No me trajo ninguna máquina de escribir que funcionara.

    Me trajo una _____.

8. No vi a ninguna mujer que estuviera vestida de domingo.

    Vi a una _____.

GOAL 4

To distinguish between the use of the indicative and the subjunctive in adjectival clauses.

Remember that the verb in a clause used with an indefinite or nonexistent noun must be in the subjunctive and that the verb in a clause used with a definite noun must be in the indicative.

EXERCISE

Complete each sentence using either the subjunctive or the indicative in the adjectival clause.

1. *(portarse)* ¿Hay algún joven que _____ bien?

2. *(portarse)* Conozco a un joven que _____ bien.

3. *(creer)* No había nadie que _____ la noticia.

4. *(vender)* Señor González, hay un señor aquí que _____ máquinas de oficina.

5. *(mudarse)* Tenemos unos amigos que _____ a Costa Rica.

6. *(preparar)* Buscaba una mujer que _____ comidas deliciosas.

7. *(hablar)* Vimos a un chico que _____ inglés.

8. *(manejar)* No vi a ningún chófer que _____ con cortesía.

Communication Pattern Exercises

I. Work with a partner. Take turns asking and answering the questions.

1. ¿Conoces a alguien que haya viajado por Sudamérica?
2. ¿Tienes un perro que sepa dar la mano?
3. ¿Quieres un pájaro que hable?
4. ¿Buscas una clase que sea difícil?
5. ¿Hay padres que no quieran a sus hijos?
6. ¿Hay alguien a quien no le gusten las vacaciones?
7. ¿Encontraste un libro que tuviera fotos de la corrida de toros?
8. ¿Recibiste una carta que estuviera escrita en español?

II. Complete each sentence.

1. Tengo un amigo que _____.

2. ¿Hay un (una) estudiante que _____?

3. Hay unos profesores que _____.

4. No conozco a nadie que _____.

5. Quiero un amigo que _____.

6. No hay nadie que _____.

Actividades de comunicación

I. Sueña con personas o casas ideales.

1. Los padres quieren hijos que _____.

2. A los profesores les gustan los estudiantes que _____

_____.

3. Los estudiantes prefieren un(a) profesor(a) que _____

_____.

4. Quiero un(a) amigo(a) que _____.

5. Prefiero una casa que _____.

6. Busco un(a) esposo(a) que _____.

Habla de tus respuestas a un(a) compañero(a) de clase.

II. Escriben ustedes en la pizarra varias oraciones que describan las características de un hijo, padres y amigos ideales.

Refránes

No hay mal que por bien no venga.
No hay olla tan fea que no encuentre su cobertera.
El bien que puedas hacer hoy, no lo dejes para mañana.
Explica el sentido. Da ejemplos de la vida.

---

8 The Subjunctive in Adverbial Clauses

GOAL 1

To combine two sentences into one using the subjunctive in the adverbial clause.

With some relator words connecting a clause to a verb, the meaning is such that the action in the adverbial (or dependent) clause is always "still to happen." In such cases the subjunctive is always used.

The most common relator words of this type are as follows:

a menos que	*unless*	con tal que	*provided that*
a fin (de) que	*in order that*	para que	*in order that*
antes (de) que	*before*	sin que	*without*

Saldré **antes que lleguen** mis padres.

*I will leave **before** my parents **arrive**.*

Salgo **antes que lleguen** mis padres.

*I leave **before** my parents **arrive**.*

Salí **antes que llegaran** mis padres.

*I left **before** my parents **arrived**.*

In each example above, from the point of view of the main verb, the second verb was "still to happen"; the parents still had not arrived at the time of the speaker's departure. In other words, if A (the main verb) occurs before B (the clause verb), then the subjunctive is used.

EXERCISE

Combine each pair of sentences into one using the subjunctive in the adverbial clause.

1. Vamos a burlarnos de él a menos de eso. Nos dice que sí.

   Vas a burlarnos de él a menos que nos diga que sí.

2. Iban a su apartamento a menos de eso. Les decía que no.

   _____

3. Pago antes de eso. Me envían la cuenta.

   _____

4. Nos acompañará con tal de eso. Nos damos prisa.

   _____

5. Los padres trabajan para eso. Sus hijos pueden asistir a la universidad.

   _____

6. Siempre poníamos el radio así sin eso. Los vecinos se quejaban del ruido.

   _____

7. ¿Saliste antes de eso? Sonó el timbre.

   _____

8. Los estudiantes estudiaron mucho para eso. El profesor no les dará una tarea para el fin de semana.

   _____

To combine two sentences into one using the subjunctive in the
adverbial clause if future time is implied.

In the case of other relator words, the meaning is such that the clause verb is
"still to happen" only when the main verb is in the future, or if future time is
implied.

The most common relator words of this type are as follows:

cuando	*when*
después (de) que	*after*
en cuanto	*as soon as*
hasta que	*until*
luego que	*as soon as*
tan pronto como	*as soon as*

Le hablaré **cuando llegue.**	*I will talk to him **when he arrives.***

EXERCISE　　Combine the cues into one sentence using the present subjunctive in the adverbial
clause.

1. me dará el mensaje/cuando/lo veré

   Me dará el mensaje cuando lo vea.

2. almorzaremos/en cuanto/servirán la comida

   _____

3. cerraré la puerta/después de que/todos entrarán

   _____

4. ¿esperaras?/hasta que/el programa comenzará

   _____

5. nos llamaréis/en cuanto/querrán hablar los rebeldes

   _____

6. les escribirán/luego que/Susana sabrá los planes

   _____

To combine two sentences into one using the indicative in the
adverbial clause.

With the relator words listed in Goal 2, the indicative is called for if the main verb is in the present or past.

Le hablo **cuando llega.**	*I talk to him **when he arrives.***
Le hablaba **cuando llegaba.**	*I always talked to him **when he arrived.***
Le hablé ayer **cuando llegó.**	*I talked to him yesterday **when he arrived.***

In each case the indicative is used because it describes "something that happened."

EXERCISE

Combine the cues into one sentence using the indicative in the adverbial clause.

1. me da el libro/cuando/se lo pido

   Me da el libro cuando se lo pido.

2. me dio el libro/cuando/se lo pedí

3. almorzamos/en cuanto/sirven la comida

4. cerré la puerta/después que/todos entraron

5. ¿esperabas?/hasta que/el programa empezaba

6. les escribió/luego que/María supo los planes

7. ¿nos llamáis?/en cuanto/quieren hablar los rebeldes

GOAL 4

To combine two ideas into one in adverbial clauses in which either the subjunctive or the indicative may be used.

In the case of a few relator words either the subjunctive or the indicative may be used in the adverbial clause, depending upon the meaning the speaker wishes to express. As in other uses of subjunctive, "still to happen" actions are expressed with the subjunctive.

The most common relator words of this type are as follows:

aunque *although*	de modo que *so that*
adonde *where*	de manera que *so that*

Indicative

Voy adonde vas.	*I go where you go.*
Todos entienden de manera que salen bien en los exámenes.	*Everyone understands so they do well on the exams.*

Subjunctive

Voy adonde vayas.	*I am going wherever you go.*
Explica de manera que entiendan todos.	*He explains so that everyone understands.*

EXERCISE

Form sentences using either the subjunctive or the indicative, as the meaning indicates.

1. no me dará socorro/aunque/me hace falta

   _____

2. no me dará socorro/aunque/me hará falta

   _____

3. viajaremos/adonde/el jefe nos dice

   _____

4. viajaremos/adonde/el jefe nos dirá

   _____

5. papá me da el dinero/de manera que/iré al cine esta noche

   _____

GOAL 5

To distinguish between the use of the indicative and the subjunctive in adverbial clauses.

EXERCISE

Form sentences using either the subjunctive or the indicative in the adverbial clause, as the meaning indicates.

1. Pedimos permiso antes de eso. Mis padres salen de casa.

   Pedimos permiso antes de que mis padres salgan de casa.

2. Tendremos suficiente comida para todos a menos de eso. Habrá un aumento de la población.

_____

3. Mamá compró "Cabeza y Hombros" para eso. La familia no tendrá caspa.

_____

4. lo llamé/después que/Marta me dio el mensaje

_____

5. ¿irás al hotel?/en cuanto/el avión aterrizará

_____

6. ¿jugáis?/hasta que/el entrenador se pone fatigado

_____

7. mis amigos fueron a la reunión/aunque/no querían ir

_____

8. todos lo leen/aunque/no lo entienden

_____

9. todos lo leen/aunque/no lo entenderán

_____

10. la calle ya está reparada/de modo que/podemos ir por aquí

_____

GOAL 6

To combine two ideas into one using the infinitive form of the second verb.

Normally, if both verbs have the same subject the infinitive is used with the following relator words:

a fin de *in order to*	después de *after*
a menos de *unless*	hasta *until*
antes de *before*	para *in order*
con tal de *provided*	sin *without*

Note that usually a clause is or may be used in English.

Estudio para aprender. *I study **in order to learn.** (I study in order that I learn.)*

Estudiamos hasta terminar. *We study **until we finish.***

EXERCISE   Form sentences using an infinitive after the relator word. Give the English meaning of each.

1. guardo mi dinero/a fin de/me jubilaré temprano

   _____

   _____

2. nos graduamos/antes de/ganaremos un salario adecuado

   _____

   _____

3. mira la televisión/hasta/se acostará

   _____

   _____

4. tendrán un picnic/con tal de/terminarán los quehaceres

   _____

   _____

5. viajaba por España/para/aprendería más de la lengua y de la cultura española

   _____

   _____

6. me acosté/después de/yo había visto "Slime Theater"

   _____

   _____

GOAL 7

To distinguish between uses of the infinitive, the subjunctive, and the indicative.

A clause is used in Spanish with the relator words listed in Goal 6 when each verb has a different subject.

Vengo cuando me llama.	_I come when he calls me._
Juan vino para hablarme.	_Juan came to talk to me._
Juan vino para que habláramos.	_Juan came so we might talk._

EXERCISE

Complete each sentence using either an infinite or a clause as the sentence requires. Remember that the verb in the clause may be either subjunctive or indicative.

1. El señor García le hablará cuando *(terminar)* _____*termine*_____ con esta entrevista.

2. Cada mes la señora González va a la biblioteca para *(hacer)* _____ investigación.

3. Todos los martes por la noche mi padre se queda en la casa para que me madre *(asistir)* _____ la reunión de un club.

4. Sí, te busqué hasta que *(empezar)* _____ el partido.

5. Sí, espero en la acera hasta *(ver)* _____ el autobús.

6. Sí, te auydaré hasta que *(sonar)* _____ el timbre.

Communication Pattern Exercises

I. Work with a partner. Read each statement, then take turns asking and answering the questions.

1. Fui a la tienda. Compré leche. ¿Para que fuiste a la tienda?
2. Ayudé a mi amigo. Entonces él podía ir al cine. ¿Para qué ayudaste a tu amigo?
3. Pagaremos la cuenta. Nos la enviarán. ¿Cuándo pagarán ustedes la cuenta?
4. Leen. Es la hora de dormirse. ¿Leen hasta qué?
5. Comes. Más tarde llegarán los invitados. ¿Como antes de qué?
6. Comes. Más tarde mirarás la televisión. ¿Como antes de qué?
7. Viviré aquí. Ya sé que no me gusta. ¿Vivirás aquí? *(Answer with aunque.)*
8. Viviré aquí. No sé si me gusta o no. ¿Vivirás aquí? *(Answer with aunque.)*
9. Contesta. Pero su amigo le dijo la respuesta. ¿Contesto después de qué?
10. Nos acompañaréis si salimos temprano. ¿Os acompañeremos con tal de qué?
11. Usted volvió a casa. Los vecinos no lo vieron. ¿Volví sin qué?
12. Voy solo sí no me lleva José. ¿No vas a menos de qué?

II. Express the idea of each of the following sentences in Spanish.

1. We talk until the bell rings.

2. We will talk until the bell rings.

_____

3. We talked until the bell rang.

_____

4. We are studying although we do not understand.

_____

5. We are studying although we may not understand.

_____

6. We study in order to understand.

_____

7. We play (a game) before the class begins.

_____

8. We played before the class began.

_____

9. We will play before the class begins.

_____

Actividades de comunicación

Completa las siguientes oraciones.

1. Iremos al cine el sábado por la noche con tal que _____.
2. Hacen el viaje en el verano a menos que _____.
3. Habrá paz en el mundo cuando _____.
4. Nos robó el dinero sin que _____.
5. Lo llamaré tan pronto que _____.
6. Estaré satisfecho cuando _____.
7. Mis padres me permiten usar el coche con tal que _____.
8. Iré al partido aunque mis amigos _____.

Refránes

Antes de que te cases mira lo que haces.
Nadie sabe lo que puede, hasta que prueba.
Explica el sentido. Da ejemplos de la vida.

9 The Subjunctive in "If" Sentences

The subjunctive is used in an "if" sentence when something is not true. (The basic reason for using subjunctive in these sentences is the same as the reasons for using the subjunctive in other types of sentences.)

GOAL 1

To combine two sentences into one using "if" to express an intention.

"If" sentences with the main verb in the future express something intended or expected. The pattern of tenses is fixed and unchangeable.

Pattern: *Si* (present tense), (future tense)

or

(future tense) *si* (present tense)

Si **llueve,** no **iré.**   *If it **rains,** I **will** not **go** (am not **going**).*

Te **daré** el dinero si lo **tengo.**   *I **will give** you the money if I **have** it.*

Note that the pattern of tenses is the same as in English.

EXERCISE

Combine the two ideas in each item into one using *si* with the first to express an intention or expectation in the future.

1. Julia posiblemente nos acompañará. Con tal de eso iré a la boda.

   Si Julia nos acompaña, iré a la boda.

2. Posiblemente tendremos el dinero. Con tal de eso compraremos un helado.

   _____

3. Posiblemente lo verás. ¿Con tal de eso me lo saludas?

   _____

4. Posiblemente tendré la oportunidad de jugar. Con tal de eso, jugaré lo mejor que pueda.

   _____

5. Posiblemente tendrá éxito el ejército voluntario. Con tal de eso evitará la conscripción militar.

   _____

6. Posiblemente excederán la velocidad máxima. Con tal de eso tendrán que pagar una multa.

   _____

GOAL 2

To combine two ideas into one sentence using "if" to express the opposite in the present.

An "if" sentence may be used in the present to express the opposite of what is stated. Students are often surprised to realize that a positive "if" sentence really implies a negative (and vice versa) and that a past tense verb is often used to describe a present situation. The sentence, "If I *had* the time, I *would go*." really means "I *do not have* the time, and therefore I *am not going*."

Since the "if" verb in the sentence means the opposite of what it seems to say, the subjunctive is used both in Spanish and in English. The pattern of tenses is fixed and unchangeable in both languages.

Pattern: *Si* (imperfect subjunctive), (conditional)
                                    or
            (conditional) *si* (imperfect subjunctive)

No iría si **lloviera.**   *I would not go if it were raining.*

Si **tuviera** el dinero,   *If I had the money, I would give*
    te lo **daría.**   *it to you.*

EXERCISE

Combine each pair of ideas into one sentence using "if" with the first verb to describe the present situation.

1. Ellos no viven cerca de aquí y por eso no los visito.

   Si vivieran cerca de aquí, los visitaría

2. No existe un sistema de transporte público y por eso no voy a mi trabajo en autobús.

   _____

3. No hacen ejercicios y por eso no tienen un cuerpo sano.

   _____

4. Tengo otro y por eso vendo éste.

   _____

5. Hoy llueve y por eso tenemos que trabajar adentro.

   _____

6. Se preocupan mucho y por eso siempre están tristes.

   _____

7. Jugamos al ping-pong y por eso no comemos.

   _____

8. No se lo comen y por eso tienen mucha hambre.

   _____

G O A L   3

To distinguish between an "if" sentence expressing a truth in the present and one expressing something contrary to fact.

An "if" sentence may also be used to describe a situation that is customarily true. If this is the case, the indicative tense is used.

Pattern: *Si* (present indicative),(present indicative)

or

(present indicative) *si* (present indicative)

Si llureve, no **voy.**   *If it **rains, I do** not **go.***

EXERCISE

Give the English meaning of each sentence.

1. a. Si María come mucho, engorda.

    _____

    b. Si María comiera mucho, engordaría.

    _____

2. a. Si Juan necesitara dinero, trabajaría.

    _____

    b. Si Juan necesita el dinero, trabaja.

    _____

3. a. No te pondrías tan irritado si durmieras más.

    _____

    b. No te pones tan irritado si duermes más.

    _____

4. a. Corremos por la noche si tenemos tiempo.

    _____

    b. Correríamos si tuviéramos tiempo.

    _____

G O A L   4

To combine two ideas into one sentence using "if" to express the opposite in the past.

An "if" sentence may be used in the past to express the opposite of what is stated. The sentence, "If I *had had* the time, I *would have gone.*" really means "I *did not have* the time, and therefore I *did not go.*"

Since the "if" verb in the sentence means the opposite of what it seems to say, the subjunctive is used both in Spanish and in English. The pattern of tenses is fixed and unchangeable in both languages.

Pattern: *Si* (past perfect subjunctive), (conditional perfect)

or

(Conditional perfect) *si* (past perfect subjunctive)

No **habría ido** si **hubiera llovido.**   *I would **not have gone** if it **had rained.***

EXERCISE

Combine each pair of ideas into one sentence using "if" with the second verb to describe the past situation.

1. No los visitaba porque no vivían cerca de aquí.

   Los habría visitado si hubieran vivido cerca de aquí.

2. No iba a mi trabajo en autobús porque no existía un sistema de transporte público.

   _____

3. No tenían un cuerpo sano porque no hacían ejercicios.

   _____

4. Vendí éste porque tenía otro.

   _____

5. Tuvimos que trabajar adentro porque llovía.

   _____

6. Se cansaban tanto porque se sentaban todo el día.

   _____

7. No comimos porque jugábamos al ping-pong.

   _____

8. Perdían tanto tiempo porque no organizaban la agenda.

   _____

GOAL 5

To distinguish between an "if" sentence expressing a truth in the past and one expressing something contrary to fact.

An "if" sentence may also be used to describe a situation that was customarily true. If this is the case, the indicative tense is used.

Pattern: *Si* (imperfect indicative), (imperfect indicative)

or

(imperfect indicative) *si* (imperfect indicative)

Si **llovía,** no **iba.**   *If it **was raining, I did** not **go.***

EXERCISE   Give the English meaning of each sentence.

1. a. Si María comía mucho, engordaba.

    _____

    b. Si María hubiera comido mucho, habría engordado.

    _____

2. a. Si Juan hubiera necesitado dinero, habría trabajado.

    _____

    b. Si Juan necesitaba dinero, trabajaba.

    _____

3. a. Si hubieras dormido más, no te habría puesto tan irritado.

    _____

    b. Si dormías más, no te ponías tan irritado.

    _____

4. a. Corríamos por la noche si teníamos tiempo.

    _____

    b. Habríamos corrido si hubiéramos tenido tiempo.

    _____

Communication Pattern Exercise

Work with a partner. Take turns asking and answering the questions.

1. ¿Irás al cine este fin de semana si tienes el dinero?
2. ¿Habrá un partido de fútbol si llueve?
3. ¿Tendremos un exámen si el profesor está enfermo?
4. ¿Estarán Uds. aquí mañana si no hay clase?
5. ¿Si estudias, aprendes?
6. ¿Si estudiaras más, aprenderías más?
7. ¿Qué estudiarías si tuvieras la oportunidad?
8. ¿Si hay tiempo en clase, hablan ustedes español con sus compañeros?
9. ¿Si hubiera más tiempo en clase, hablarían ustedes más en español con sus compañeros?
10. ¿En qué país estudiarías si tuvieras la oportunidad?

(11–16)Antes, cuando eran mas joven . . .

11. ¿Comprabas un disco si tenías el dinero?

12. ¿Habrías comprado más si hubieras tenido el dinero?

13. ¿Qué habrías comprado si hubieras tenido más dinero?

14. ¿Viajaba la familia cuando su padre tenía vacaciones?

15. ¿Habrían viajado ustedes a México si hubieran tenido más tiempo durante las vacaciones?

16. ¿Adónde habrían viajado ustedes si hubieran tenido más tiempo?

Actividades de comunicación

I. Vamos a suponer la falta completa de restricciones—¿Qué harías hoy si todo fuera posible? Di diez cosas en diez oraciones distintas.

II. Describe en media página lo que habrías hecho el verano pasado si hubieras podido hacer cualquier cosa.

III. Habla de esta pregunta—¿Cómo sería diferente tu vida si fueras Superhombre?

IV. Prepara una lista de los personajes (reales o ficticios)

1. que te gustaría ser

2. que no te gustaría ser

3. que te parecen más admirables

Habla de tu lista a un(a) compañero(a) de clase. ¿Cuáles son las características que desean ustedes?

Refrán

Si a Roma fueres, haz como vieres.
Explica el sentido. Da ejemplos de la vida.

Glossary of Grammatical Terms

A

Actions   Verbs name actions, events, or conditions. These may be of different types: continuing or repeated, imperfected or perfected, durative, or singular.

Continuing vs. *repeated*   Depending upon the meaning the speaker wishes to convey, he or she may choose to stress that an event is going on (continuing) or that it happens several times (repeated). Both continuing and repeated actions are usually expressed by imperfective verb endings.

Continuing—Call me back later. **We are eating** now.

Repeated—Don't call at six We **always eat** around six.

Imperfective vs. *perfective*   Events may also be not completed (imperfective) or completed (perfective).

Imperfective—**Were** they **leaving** when we called?

Perfective—They **left** at 7:00.

Durative vs. *singular*   Some verbs name actions, events, or conditions that, by their very nature, last over a period of time. Others occur at one point in time.

Durative—She **loved** her children.

Singular—He **kissed** the baby and **closed** the door.

Adjective   An adjective tells something about a person, place, thing or idea.

Adjectives that point out—
   The picture over my desk
   has a special meaning.
   That man is **the** one.
Possessives—**Your** brother
   has **my** diary.
Limiting adjectives—Do you
   want **one** copy? I think we
   will need **several** copies.

Descriptive adjectives—Are
   you buying one of his horses?
   Yes, I am buying the **chestnut**
   colt.

Adverb An adverb tells us something about a verb, an adjective, or another adverb. It usually indicates how, when, where, or to what degree.

How—He drives **fast.**
When—She arrives **early.**
Where—Don't shout. I'm right **here.**

To what degree—Their uniforms are **bright** red.
They walk **very** slowly.

Agreement In Spanish, all adjectives, pronouns, possessives, and verbs must agree with the nouns with which they are used. Pronouns must agree with their antecedent(s). Possessives must agree with both the possessor and the thing possessed.

Adjectives Adjective endings change to correspond to the gender, number, and/or ending of the noun.

Articles—**El** rubio y **la** morena son **los** novios más popular**es.**

Adjectives—Mis mejor**es** amig**as** son muy creativ**as.**

Demonstratives—Est**a** camisa y est**os** calzoncil**los** son de José.

Perfective participles—Los padres estaban preocupad**os.**

Possessives—**Su** familia y **la** nuestra van a tener un picnic.

Pronouns The pronoun must agree in gender and number with the noun to which it refers.

¿Tienes las llav**es**? No, **las** dejé en mi chaqueta.
¿Me diste el horari**o**? Sí, **te lo** di esta mañana.
¿Conoces a Roberto? Sí, **me** siento cerca de **él.**
Nosotros vamos a la piscina.

Possessive pronouns have to agree with two nouns: the possessor and the thing possessed.

Sí, **los suyos** son razonabl**es.**

Verbs The ending of a Spanish verb agrees in person and number with the subject. Agreement is indicated by person-number endings added to the end of the verb or by a class vowel different from that used with other subjects. In other cases, there is no separate ending to indicate the exact subject, and a subject pronoun must be used to tell who the subject is.

Los jóvenes se diviert**en** los fines de semana.
Mir**o** televisión, pero él escuch**a** discos.

Antecedent An antecedent is the word to which another word refers.

Mary used **her** credit card.

Article An article precedes a noun or a word used as a noun. Articles are often classified as noun determiners. In Spanish the ending of the article must agree with the gender, number, or ending of the noun.

Definite article   In English we use "the." In Spanish four forms are used: **el** and l + **-a, -os,** and **-as.**

Mamá trae **el** pan, **las** verduras y **la** fruta.

Indefinite article   In English we use "a" or "an." In Spanish four forms are used: **un** and **un** + **-a, -os,** and **-as.**

En la familia hay **un** hijo, **una** hija y **unos** gatos.

Aspect   When considering an event, one may focus on different aspects of the action: the beginning, the middle, or the end.

Beginning—The game **started** at eight.
Middle—They **were playing** at nine.
End—They **finished** the contest at ten.

C

Clause   A clause is a combination of words containing a subject, either expressed or understood, and a verb.

Dependent clause   Some clauses are dependent because they make sense only when used in combination with another clause.

He stayed in the shower **until there was no more hot water.**

Independent clause   An independent clause expresses a complete, comprehensible thought and may be used alone.

He stayed in the shower.
There was no more hot water.

With rare exceptions, verbs in independent clauses are used in the indicative mood. Verbs in dependent clauses are either in the indicative or the subjunctive mood.

Noun clause   A dependent clause that takes the place of a noun in a sentence is called a noun clause. In Spanish the verb may be in the indicative or the subjunctive mood, depending upon the meaning.

Indicative—Sé **que tú eres**   Subjunctive—Espero **que**
    mi amigo leal.   **no estés enojado.**

If clause   If the verb in the "if" clause describes an event that is contrary to fact, the subjunctive is used. If the verb in the "if" clause describes a fact, the indicative is used.

Indicative—**Si mi invita,**   Subjunctive—**Si me invitara,**
    iré.   iría.

Adjectival clause   A clause that develops or limits a noun serves as an adjective in the sentence. If the noun with which the clause is used is nonexistent in the sense that it is negative or indefinite, the verb in the dependent clause is in the subjunctive. Otherwise, the verb is in the indicative.

Indicative—Tengo un ami-
go **que corre todos los
días.**

Subjunctive—¿Tienes un
amigo **que corra todos
los días?**

Adverbial clause   A clause that develops or limits the verb serves as an adverb in the sentence. If the action of the dependent verb has not happened yet from the point of view of the verb in the independent clause, the verb in the dependent clause is in the subjunctive. If it has occurred, the verb is in the indicative.

Indicative—Lloraron **cuando salimos.**

Subjunctive—Se reían
antes que saliéramos.

Comparative   A comparative is a word, form, or pattern used with an adjective or adverb to compare some quality of two entities or events.

Noun—Yo soy **más** astuto
que mis hermanos.

Verb—Me divierto **menos**
aquí **que** en casa.

Complex sentence transformation   A complex sentence transformation involves the transformation of two complete thoughts into one sentence.

Comparisons of equality
—María juega bien. Rosa
juega bien también. Rosa
juega tan bien como María.
Comparisons of inequality
—Pepe toma mucho Pepsi.
Juan toma poco. Juan toma
menos Pepsi que Pepe.

Complex sentence—Mi mamá
se alegra de algo. Yo soy
cortés. Mi mamá se alegra
de que yo sea cortés.

Consonant   A consonant is a language sound produced by making some change in the air stream as it flows out of the lungs.

D

Demonstrative   A demonstrative is used to point out or replace a noun.

Adjective   If a demonstrative is used with a noun, it functions as an adjective.

Es imposible fomentar el
progreso con **estos** hábitos improductivos.

It is impossible to encour-
age progress with **these**
unproductive customs.

Pronoun   If the noun is omitted and the demonstrative stands alone, it functions as a pronoun and an accent mark is added.

Esta escritura y **ésa** son
similiares.

This handwriting and **that**
(handwriting) are
similar.

E

Entity Entity is a general term that encompasses the names of persons, places, things, emotions, or ideas. The grammatical synonym is noun.

juez, Acapulco, juguete, amor, democracia

Event Event is a general term that encompasses the names of actions and conditions. The grammatical synonym is verb.

esquiar, ser

F

Finite verb A finite verb denotes an action that is limited to a given subject at a given time.

Martha **played** on Friday. Bill **plays** today. Ryan **will play** at ten tomorrow.

G

Gender Grammatically, all Spanish nouns have traditionally been labeled either masculine or feminine. Four-ending adjectives and pronouns have separate masculine and feminine forms. Two-ending adjectives and pronouns use the same form with both masculine and feminine.

El señor es alt**o**, pero su esposa es baj**a**.

The gentleman is tall, but his wife is short.

Tus ojos profund**os** tienen **un** poder mágic**o**.

Your deep eyes have a magic power.

¿Le dio **la** joven **el** mensaje de **la** llamada?

Did the young woman give you the message about the call?

I

Imperfective participle An imperfective participle describes an action in progress. In Spanish the imperfective participle is used either as part of the progressive form of the verb or as an adverb.

Se está **peinando** ahora.

He is combing his hair now.

Gana la vida **engañando** a la gente.

He makes his living by tricking people.

Impersonal expression An impersonal expression is characterized in English by the subject "it" before the verb.

It is important to have a perspective on current affairs.

Infinitive   In Spanish the infinitive is the verb form ending in *r*. The *r* is always preceded by the class vowel *a, e,* or *i.*

ensuciar, suspender, conducir

Intonation   Intonation refers to the rise and fall of the voice while one is speaking.

M

Modifier   A modifier changes or develops the meaning of a noun or verb in the sentence. A modifier may be an adjective, an adverb, or a phrase or clause functioning as an adjective or adverb.

Adjective—One hears about **our permissive** society.

Adverb—We live **here now.**

Adjectival phrase and clause—The boy **with the broken arm** is the one **who fell off the horse.**

Adverbial phrase and clause—She went slowly **into the house after they told her the tragic news.**

Mood   Verbs are classified into three different categories of mood.

Indicative   Indicative is the factual mood. In Spanish the indicative may be used in either a dependent or an independent clause.

I **have** a toothache.

I just **called** the dentist to tell him that my tooth **hurts.**

Imperative   An imperative verb form makes a request or gives a command. In Spanish subjunctive verb forms, with the exception of the familiar affirmative commands, are used for the imperative mood. The imperative is always the main verb in the sentence or in a direct quote.

Help! Leave me alone! Don't ever say that again!

Subjunctive   A subjunctive verb form describes an action or condition that is not a fact at the time of the action of the main verb or an action toward which the speaker has a subjective, emotional reaction. With only a few exceptions the subjunctive is used in a dependent clause.

It is important that you **be** here this evening.

I wish I **were** more sure of myself.

May he **treat** you with love and respect.

If I **knew** the answer, I would tell you.

N

Neuter   Neuter is neither feminine nor masculine. The neuter forms in Spanish **(ello, esto, eso,** and **aquello)** refer to specific nouns. (**Lo** may be used as a neuter.) In Spanish, neuters are used to refer to something unknown or to a general situation or idea.

¿Qué es **esto**?	*What is **this**?*
No me gusta **eso** de entregarle al gobierno tanta información.	*I don't like handing over so much information to the government.*

Non-finite verb   A non-finite verb describes an action but does not limit it to a certain subject or time. Infinitives, imperfective participles, and perfective participles are non-finite verbs.

Ver es **creer.**	**Seeing** is **believing.**
Estudian **escuchando** discos.	They are studying **while listening** to records.
Encontraron los cheques **perdidos.**	They found the **lost** checks.

Noun   A noun is a naming word. It is used to designate entities as such: people, places, things, and ideas.

citizens, the United States, frisbee, liberty

Noun phrase   A noun phrase is made up of a noun plus its modifiers.

The **big** book **with the yellow cover that is lying on the end table** is due at the library.

Number   The grammatical concept of number refers to whether or not the speaker is talking about one or more than one. In Spanish all nouns, adjectives, verbs, and pronouns have number.

Nouns—El **joven** siguió los malos **ejemplos** de sus **amigos.**	Verbs—El joven **siguió** los malos hábitos que **tienen** sus amigos.
Adjectives—**El** joven siguió **los malos** ejemplos de **sus** amigos.	Pronouns—**El** siguió los malos ejemplos de **ellos.**

O

Orthographic change   At times a Spanish sound may be represented by more than one spelling, depending upon the context in which it occurs. This change in spelling is an orthographic change.

P

Past set verbs   There are five groups of Spanish verbs in the past set.

Conditional   A conditional verb describes an action that is to occur in the future from some point in the past. It is often called the past future tense. The helper verb in English is "would." There is no helper verb in Spanish. The sound *ría* signals the conditional in Spanish.

Me dijo que **llamaría.**	*She told me she **would call.***

Conditional perfect   A conditional perfect verb describes an action, viewed from the past, that is to be completed prior to some point in the future. The signal for conditional perfect is "would have" in English and a conditional form of *haber* in Spanish.

Vamos. **Habrían llegado** para las seis.	*Let's go. They **would have arrived** by six.*

Imperfect   An imperfect verb describes an action uncompleted and in progress. It represents an action that is continuing or repeated. It is one of two ways of looking at actions, and in the past it contrasts with the preterite.

Repeated—Se **dormía** en clase a veces.	*He sometimes **fell asleep** in class.*
Continuing—Se **dormía** cuando el profesor lo vio.	*He **was falling asleep** when the professor saw him.*

Past perfect   The past perfect describes an action completed by some point in the past. The helper verb is "had" in English and an imperfect form of *haber* in Spanish.

Insistieron en que **habían visto** una nave espacial.	*They insisted that they **had seen** a space ship.*

Preterite   A preterite verb describes a singular past action or the beginning or end of a continuing or repeated action. It contrasts with the imperfect in the past.

¿Por qué no nos **llamaste** anoche?	*Why didn't **you call** us last night?*
Se **enamoraron** la primera vez que se vieron.	***They fell in love** the first time they saw each other.*
Hace quince años que **vivimos** allí.	***We lived** there fifteen years.*

Perfective participle   A perfective participle describes a completed action. A perfective participle is used in passive voice and compound tenses and may also be used as an adjective.

Los jóvenes **fueron castigados** por sus padres.	*The young people **were punished** by their parents.*

Los padres han **castigado a** los jóvenes.	*The parents **have punished** the young people.*
Los jóvenes **castigados** no pueden salir de casa.	*The **punished** young people are not able to leave the house.*

Person   There are three persons in Spanish: person(s) speaking, person(s) spoken to, and person(s) spoken about.

Estoy bien, gracias. ¿Y **tú?**
Así, así. ¿Cómo está **tu novio** hoy?

Possessives   Possessives show ownership or possession. In Spanish the possessive must agree with the possessor, and the possessive ending must agree with the ending of the thing possessed.

Adjectives   Possessive adjectives may come before the noun, after the noun, or after the verb *ser.*

Tu idea de un paraíso es muy extraño.	*Your idea of paradise is very strange.*
Es que no te gusta cualquier idea **mía.**	*It's that you don't like any of **my** ideas.*
No es **mía** esta opinión. Todos están de acuerdo.	*It's not **my** opinion. Everyone is in agreement.*

Pronouns   Possessive pronouns are used without the noun and are preceded by an article.

La nuestra está en casa.	***Ours** is in the house.*
¿Dónde esta **la suya?**	*Where is **yours?***

Preposition   A preposition shows a relationship in space or time. In contrast to a clause, the prepositional phrase has no verb. Like an adjectival or adverbial clause it functions to modify a noun or verb.

Sure, I can introduce you to the guy **in the blue suit.**
He lives **near me.**
Tell me the answer **without looking.**

Present set verbs   There are four groups of verbs in the present set.

Future   A future verb describes an action to occur some time after the present. The helper verb in English is "will" or "shall." In Spanish there is no helper verb. The sound that signals future is "r" plus a vowel and the person-number ending.

Se comportar**án** mejor la próxima vez.	*They **will behave** better next time.*

Future perfect   A future perfect verb describes an action viewed from the present that is to be completed prior to some point in the future. The signal for future perfect is "will have" or "shall have" in English and a future form of *haber* in Spanish.

Me dice que **habrá considerado** todas las alternativas para mañana.	*She tells me that she **will have considered** all the alternatives by tomorrow.*

Present   A present verb describes an imperfect action going on or being repeated in the present or an action that is to occur in the near future. In English we may use three different patterns: I read, I do read, and I am reading. Normally, in Spanish one verb *(leo)* is used for each of the three English patterns.

Cada verano **pasan** sus vacaciones cerca de un lago.	*Each summer **they spend** their vacation near a lake.*
Pasan esta semana en Madrid.	***They are spending** this week in Madrid.*
Vuelven a casa el sábado por la noche.	***They are returning** home Saturday evening.*

Present perfect   A present perfect verb describes an action completed in any recent indefinite time up to the present. The helper verb in English is "have" or "has." In Spanish the present tense of *haber* is used.

¿Has llamado a Jorge? No, no lo **he llamado** todavia.	***Have you called** Jorge? No, **I haven't called** him yet.*

Pronoun   A pronoun is a word that is used instead of the noun to which it refers.

Direct object pronoun   A direct object pronoun substitutes for a noun object of the verb.

Do you know Bob? Yes, I know **him.**
And Karen? No, I do not know **her.**

Indirect object pronoun   An indirect object pronoun substitutes for a noun indirect object of the verb.

Did you give the message to your parents?
Yes, I gave it **to them,** but they did not send anything **to you.**

Object of preposition   An object of preposition pronoun substitutes for a noun used after a preposition.

They camped near **us.**

Reflexive   A reflexive pronoun refers to "self."

Did you do all that **yourself?** Yes, I did everything **myself.**

Subject   Subject pronouns tell who is performing the action of the verb. In Spanish they are normally used to clarify or to emphasize. Otherwise, the verb ending itself indicates the subject.

¿Crees lo mismo? Sí, **creo** los mismo, pero ¿qué **creen él y ella?**	***Do you believe** the same? Yes, **I believe** the same, but what do **he and she** believe?*

R

Relator word   Words in this category show relationships between parts of a sentence. Relator words introduce clauses and show the relationship between a dependent clause and the noun or verb with which it is used.

Object of verb—¿Sabe **dónde tienen los cohetes?**

Adjectival clauses—Es el coche **que vendí el año pasado.**

Adverbial clause—El juez lo condenó a la muerte **des pués de que confesó.**

If sentences—**Si la saludamos,** no nos va a contestar.

S

Simple sentence transformations   A simple transformation involves the change of a basic sentence to a somewhat more complex simple sentence.

¿Han llegado ya los otros? ¿No han llegado ya los otros?

Stem   The stems of the verb in Spanish is that part of the verb that precedes the class vowel of the infinitive. The stem carries the name of the action being described.

bailar, **quer**er, **re**ír

Suffix   A suffix is an ending attached to a word.

sociedad   sociedad**es**
sociedad permisi**va**   sociedades permisi**vas**
La sociedad result**a** permisiva. Las sociedades result**an** permisivas.
Ell**a** es más responsable que ell**os.**

T

Tense   Verb tense refers to the time associated with the verb. There are two times in both English and Spanish: past and present.

Past and related to past—**I went** last week.
They **told** me they **would go** tomorrow.

Present and related to the present—**I do** not **know** now, but **I will know** before **I leave. I have not given** up.

V

Verb   A verb designates an event, action, or condition. In Spanish the stem of the verb names the event, action, or condition and the suffixes give the necessary additional information about the verb to comprehend the speaker's message.

¿**Vas** a nadar? No, **voy** a tomar el sol solamente.
¿Lo **han visto** ustedes? No, no **estuvo** en su oficina. **Estaba jugando** al golf.

Verb class   There are three verb classes in Spanish: *A, E,* and *I* verbs. This information is extremely important because the speaker must know to which class a verb belongs in order to use the correct suffix and to express the exact meaning.

Verb phrase   A verb phrase is made up of a verb plus its modifier(s). The modifier functions as an adverb and it may be a word, a phrase, or a clause.

They worked **hard on the first** day after the supervisor **criticized their progress.**

Vowel   A vowel sound is a language sound produced without restricting or making changes in the flow of air from the lungs. The vowels are *a, e, i, o,* and *u.*

Vocabulario

This vocabulary includes all Spanish words found in the text except exact cognates, adverbs ending in -*mente* when the adjectives from which they are derived are listed, proper names, numbers, superlatives, and diminutives. The following abbreviations are used:

adj. adjective
adv. adverb
art. article
conj. conjunction
f. feminine

inf. infinitive
m. masculine
pl. plural
prep. preposition
pron. pronoun

A

a *prep.* to, at
  al (a + el) to the
abajo *adv.* below; down; downstairs
abeja *f.* bee
abierto,-a open, opened
abogado,-a *m.,f.* lawyer
abril *m.* April
abrigo *m.* coat
abrir to open
abuelo,-a *m.,f.* grandfather, grandmother
aburrido,-a boring, bored
acá *adv.* here
acabar to finish, to conclude
acabar de to have just
a causa de because of
accidente *m.* accident
acción *f.* action
  acciones stocks
aceite *m.* oil
acento *m.* accent
acentuar to accent
aceptar to accept
acera *f.* sidewalk

acerca de *prep.* about, regarding
acercarse to approach
acertar to guess
acompañar to accompany
aconsejar to advise
acordar to agree
acostar to put to bed;
acostarse to go to bed
acostumbrar to accustom;
  acostumbrarse to get accustomed
actitud *f.* attitude
actividad *f.* activity
actriz *f.* actress
actualmente *adv.* at present
actuar to act, to perform
acuático,-a aquatic
  esquiar acuático to waterski
acuerdo *m.* agreement
  de acuerdo in agreement
adecuado,-a adequate
adelante *adv.* farther on; later on
adentro *adv.* inside
adivinanza *f.* riddle, guess
adivinar to guess

administrador,-a *m.,f.* administrator
admirar to admire
adonde *conj.* where
adorar to adore
adorno *m.* ornament
aduana *f.* customs
adverbio *m.* adverb
adversidad *f.* adversity
advertir to notify, to warn
aeropirata *m.,f* skyjacker
afeitadora *f.* shaver
aficionado,-a *m.,f.* fan
afortunado,-a fortunate
afuera *adv.* outside
agencia *f.* agency
agente *m. & f.* agent
  agente de bienes raíces real estate agent
  agente de seguros insurance agent
agitado,-a agitated
agradable *adj.* agreeable, pleasant
agradecer to appreciate; to thank
agresivo,-a aggressive
agricultor,-a *m.,f.* farmer

agua *f.* water
águila *f.* eagle
ahí *adv.* there
ahogar to choke
ahora *adv.* now
   ahora mismo right now
ahorrar to save
aire *m.* air
aire libre open air
aislado,-a isolated
ajedrez *m.* chess
al + *inf.* on, upon
alabado *m.* hymn
alabar to praise
alcanzar to reach, to acquire
alcoba *f.* bedroom, alcove
alcohólico,-a *m.,f.* alcoholic
alegrarse de to be happy about
alegre *adj.* happy
alemán,ana *adj. & m.,f.* German
alfombra *f.* rug
algo *pron.* something
algodón *m.* cotton
alguien *pron.* someone
algun,-o,-a some
aliento *m.* breath, gasp
alimento *m.* food
aliviar to alleviate
almacén *m.* department store
almorzar to eat lunch
almuerzo *m.* lunch
alquilar to rent
alquiler *m.* rental, rent
alrededor *adv.* around
   alrededor de *prep.* around
alternativo,-a alternative
alto,-a tall, high
   ¡alto! stop! halt!
altura f. height
alumbrar to give light
alumno,-a *m.,f.* student
allá *adv.* there, over there
allí *adv.* there
amable *adj.* kind, amiable
amanecer *m.* dawn
amante *m. & f.* lover
amar to love
amarillo,-a yellow
ambiente *m.* atmosphere,
   ambience
ambos *pron.* both
amenaza *f.* threat
americano,-a *adj. & m.,f.* American
amigo,-a *m.,f.* friend
amistad *f.* friendship
amistoso,-a friendly

amor *m.* love
amoroso,-a loving, affectionate
amplificador *m.* amplifier
amplificar to amplify
ancho,-a wide
anciano,-a *adj.* old;
   m.,f. old person
andar to walk
anillo *m.* ring
animado,-a animated
   película animada cartoon
animal doméstico *m.* pet
año *m.* year
anoche *adv.* last night
anteayer *adv.* day before yesterday
anteojos *m.pl.* glasses, spectacles
anterior *adj.* front; previous
antes *adv.* before
antes de *prep.* before
antes de que *conj.* before
anticipación *f.* anticipation
   con anticipación eagerly
antigüedad *f.* antique
antiguo,-a old; former
antipático,-a unfriendly
anti-transpirante *m.* antiperspirant
anunciador,-a *m.,f.* announcer
anunciar to announce
anuncio *m.* advertisement,
   announcement
apagar to put out, to turn off
aparato *m.* apparatus, appliance
aparecer to appear
apenas *adv.* scarcely
aplicar to apply
aprender to learn
apretar to squeeze
aprisa *adv.* fast, quickly
aprobar to pass (an examination)
apropiado,-a appropriate
aquel, aquello, aquella, aquellos,
   aquellas *adj.* that, those
aquél, aquéllo, aquélla, aquéllos,
   aquéllas *pron.* that one, he, she,
   the former, that, those
aquello *neuter* that
aquí *adv.* here
   por aquí this way
árbol *m.* tree
arena *f.* sand
arete *m.* earring
armario *m.* closet
arquitecto,-a *m.,f.* architect
arreglado,-a arranged
arreglar to arrange
arrepentirse to repent

arriba *adv.* up; above; upstairs
arrimarse to lean; to get near
artículo *m.* article
artístico,-a artistic
asado *m.* roast
ascensor *m.* elevator
asesinar to kill, to assassinate
asesino,-a *m.,f.* assassin
así *adv.* thus, that way
asiento *m.* seat
asignatura *f.* subject
asistir a to attend
aspiradora *f.* sweeper, vacuum
   cleaner
asunto *m.* matter
asustar to frighten; **asustarse** to
   be frightened
atacar to attack
atajo *m.* shortcut
ataque *m.* attack
   ataque de corazón heart attack
atención *f.* attention
   prestar atención to pay
   attention
atender to take care of
aterrizar to land
atmósfera *f.* atmosphere
atractivo,a attractive
atrapar to catch
   atrapar un catarro to catch
   cold
atrás *adv.* behind, back
atravesar to cross
atreverse a to dare to
atropellar to knock down, to run
   over
auditorio *m.* auditorium
aula *f.* classroom, lecture hall
aullar to howl
aumento *m.* increase, growth
aunque *adv.* although
autobiografía *f.* autobiography
autobús *m.* bus
automático,-a automatic
automovilista *m. & f.* driver,
   motorist
autopsia *f.* autopsy
autor,-a *m.,f.* author
auxilio *m.* aid
aventurar to venture;
   aventurarse to risk
avergonzado,-a ashamed
averiguar to verify, find out
avión *m.* plane
   avión de reacción jet plane
ayer *adv.* yesterday

ayuda *f.* help
ayudar to help
azafata *f.* stewardess
azteca *adj. & m., f.* Aztec
azúcar *m.* sugar
azul *adj.* blue

B

bachillerato *m.* bachelor's degree
bahía *f.* bay
bailador,-a *m., f.* dancer
bailar to dance
baile *m.* dance
bajar to go down, to descend
bajo,-a low, short;
  prep. underneath
balcón *m.* balcony
baloncesto *m.* basketball
bañar to bathe; **bañarse** to take a bath
banco *m.* bank; bench
banda *f.* band
bandera *f.* flag
bandido,-a *m., f* bandit
banquero *m. & f.* banker
banquete *m.* banquet
barato,-a inexpensive
barba *f.* beard
barbero *m.* barber
barco *m.* boat
barrio *m.* district, neighborhood
basado,-a based
básquetbol *m.* basketball
bastante *adv.* rather, enough
basura *f.* garbage
basurero *m.* garbage collector
bata *f.* robe
batido *m.* milk shake
baúl *m.* trunk, clothes chest
bebé *m. & f.* baby
beber to drink
bebida *f.* beverage
beca *f.* scholarship
belleza *f.* beauty
bello,-a handsome, beautiful
besar to kiss
beso *m.* kiss
biblioteca *f.* library
bibliotecario,-a *m., f.* librarian
bien *m.* good
bien *adv.* well
billete *m.* bill, ticket
  billete de lotería lottery ticket
biografía *f.* biography
biología *f.* biology

bistec *m.* steak
blanco,-a white
blando,-a soft
blusa *f.* blouse
boca *f.* mouth
boda *f.* wedding
boleto *m.* ticket
bolígrafo *m.* ball-point pen
bolsa *f.* purse, bag
bolsillo *m.* pocket
bombero,-a *m., f.* fire fighter
bombilla *f.* light bulb
bonito,-a pretty
bosque *m.* forest
bote *m.* boat
botella *f.* bottle
boxeo *m.* boxing
Brasil *m.* Brazil
brillante *adj.* brilliant
brillar to shine
broche *m.* clasp; brooch
broma *f.* joke
brujería *f.* witchcraft
bueno,-a good
  buenos días good day
  buenas noches good night
  buenas tardes good afternoon
bufanda *f.* scarf; blanket
burlar to mock;
burlarse de to make fun of
burocracia *f.* bureaucracy
buscar to look for
buzón *m.* mail box

C

caballo *m.* horse
  montar a caballo to ride horseback
caber to fit, to be capable
cabeza *f.* head
cada *adj.* each, every
caer to fall
  dejar caer to drop
café *m.* coffee; small restaurant
caja *f.* box
caja fuerte strong box, safe
calcetín *m.* sock
calculadora *f.* calculator
calefacción *f.* heating system
calendario *m.* calendar
caliente *adj.* hot, warm
callar to be quiet
calle *f.* street
calmado,-a calm
calmante *m.* sedative

calor *m.* heat
  tener calor to be hot
caloría *f.* calorie
cama *f.* bed
camarero,-a *m., f.* waiter, waitress
cambiar to change; to exchange
cambio *m.* change
caminar to walk
camino *m.* road
camisa *f.* shirt
campana *f.* bell
campaña *f.* campaign
campeón *m.* champion
campeonato *m.* championship
campesino,-a *m., f.* country person, farmer
campo *m.* country
canal *m.* channel
canasta *f.* basket
cancha *f.* court, ball park
canción *f.* song
candidato,-a *m., f.* candidate
canoa *f.* canoe
cansado,-a tired
cansar to tire; **cansarse** to get tired
cantante *m. úf.* singer
cantar to sing
capítulo *m.* chapter
cara *f.* face
característica *f.* characteristic
caramelo *m.* caramel
carbón *m.* coal
caridad *f.* charity
carie *f.* cavity
cariño *m.* affection, love
cariñoso,-a affectionate
carne *f.* meat
caro,-a expensive
carrera *f.* career; race
carretera *f.* highway, road
carta *f.* letter
cartel *m.* poster
cartera *f.* bag; wallet; briefcase
casa *f.* house
  en casa at home
casado,-a married
casarse to get married
casi *adv.* nearly, almost
caspa *f.* dandruff
castigar to punish
castigo *m.* punishment
castillo *m.* castle
catarro *m.* cold
catedral *f.* cathedral
católico,-a *adj. & m., f* Catholic

cazar to hunt
celebración *f.* celebration
celebrar to celebrate
celoso,-a jealous
cena *f.* dinner
cenar to eat dinner
cenicero *m.* ashtray
centro *m.* downtown, center
cepillo *m.* brush
cerámica *f.* ceramics, pottery
cerca *adv.* nearby
  cerca de *prep.* near
cercano,-a neighboring
cero *m.* zero
cerrado,-a closed
cerrar to close
cerrar con llave to lock
cesta *f.* basket
ciclista *m. & f.* cyclist
ciego,-a *m.,f.* blind person
cielo *m.* heaven, sky
ciencia *f.* science
  ciencia ficción science fiction
científico,-a *m.,f.* scientist
ciento,-a hundred;
cien shortened form of **ciento**
cierto,-a true, certain
cine *m.* movie theater
cinematográfico, -a cinematographic
cinta *f.* tape
cinturón *m.* belt
circunstancia *f.* circumstance
cirujano,-a *m.,f.* surgeon
cita *f.* date, appointment
ciudad *f.* city
cuidad universitaria campus
ciudadano,-a *m.,f.* citizen
civilización *f.* civilization
clarinete *m.* clarinet
claro of course
claro,-a clear, light
clase media middle class
clásico,-a classical
cliente *m. & f.* client
clima *m.* climate
cobertera *f.* cover; lid
cobija *f.* cover; shawl
coche *m.* car
cocina *f.* kitchen
cocinar to cook
cocinero,-a *m.,f.* cook
cocodrilo *m.* crocodile
codicia *f.* greed
codo *m.* elbow

coger to pick; to take hold; to catch
cohete *m.* rocket
cola *f.* tail; waiting line
colcha *f.* bedspread
colección *f.* collection
colega *m. & f.* colleague
colegio *m.* high school
colgar to hang
colina *f.* hill
colocar to place
colono *m. & f.* colonist
colombiano,-a *adj. & m.,f.* Colombian
columnista *m. & f.* columnist
collar *m.* necklace
comedor *m.* dining room
comentar to comment on
comenzar to begin, to commence
comer to eat
comerciante *m. & f.* merchant
cometer to commit
cómico,-a comic
comida *f.* meal, food
como *prep. conj.* as, like
  ¿cómo? how?, what?
cómodo,-a comfortable
compañero,-a *m.,f.* companion
compañía *f.* company
comparación *f.* comparison
comparar to compare
compasión *f.* sympathy
compartir to share; to divide equally
competencia *f.* competition
complejo,-a *adj. & m.* complex
completar to complete
complicado,-a complicated
composición *f.* composition
comprar to buy
compra *f.* purchase
  ir de compras to go shopping
comprometido,-a fiancé; fiancée
comprender to understand
comprensivo,-a comprehensive
computadora *f.* computer
comunidad *f.* community
con *prep.* with
  con anticipación eagerly
  con tal de *prep.* provided
  con tal que *conj.* provided that
concierto *m.* concert
concurso *m.* contest; assembly
condenar to condem
conducir to drive, to lead
conferencia *f.* lecture; meeting

conferenciante *m. & f.* lecturer
conferencista *m. & f.* participant in a conference; lecturer
confesar to confess
confianza *f.* confidence
confiar en to count on, to trust in, to rely on
conformarse a to conform to
conformista *m. & f.* conformist
congelado,-a frozen
congelar to freeze
conjunto *m.* group
conmigo with me
conocer to know; to meet
conocido,-a well-known
conocimiento *m.* knowledge
conquistar to conquer
conscripción *f.* conscription, draft
conseguir to get, to obtain
consejero,-a *m.,f.* advisor
consejo *m.* advice
conservador,-a *adj. & m.,f.* conservative
construcción *f.* construction
construir to construct
contacto *m.* contact
contaminación *f.* pollution
contaminado,-a contaminated
contaminar to contaminate
contar to tell; to count
contemporáneo,-a contemporary
contener to contain
contento,-a happy
contestar to answer
contigo with you
continuar to continue
contra *adv.* against
contrastar to contrast
contrato *m.* contract
conversación *f.* conversation
conversar to converse
convertir to convert
corazón *m.* heart
corbata *f.* necktie
correcto,-a correct
corregir to correct
correr to run
  corrida de toros *f.* bullfight
correspondencia *f.* correspondence
corriente *adj.* current
  cuenta corriente *f.* checking account
cortar to cut
corte *m.* court
cortés *adj.* courteous

cortesía *f.* courtesy
corto,-a short
cosa *f.* thing
coser to sew
costa *f.* coast
costar to cost
costarle a uno to be difficult for
costumbre *f.* custom
creación *f.* creation
crecer to grow; to create
creencia *f.* belief
creer to believe
crema *f.* cream
criado,-a *m.,f.* servant
cristiano,-a *adj. & m.,f.* Christian
cronista (de televisión) *m. & f.* anchorperson
cruzar to cross
cuaderno *m.* notebook
cuadra *f.* block
cuadro *m.* painting
cual,-es *pron.* which
    ¿cuál? which?, which one?
cualidad *f.* quality
cualquier,-a *adj. & pron.* anyone, whichever
cuando *conj.* when
    ¿cuándo? when?
cuanto,-a,-os,-as *adj. & pron.* how much, how many
    ¿cuánto,-a? how much?, how many?
    cuantos few
    en cuanto *conj.* as soon as
    unos cuantos a few
cuarto *m.* room
cubano,-a *adj. & m.,f.* Cuban
cubrir to cover
cuchillo *m.* knife
cuenta *f.* bill
    cuenta corriente checking account
    darse cuenta to realize
cuento *m.* story
cuerpo *m.* body
cueva *f.* cave
cuidado *m.* care
cuidadoso,-a careful
cuidar to take care
culpa *f.* blame
cultivar to cultivate
cumpleaños *m.* birthday
cumplir to complete, to fulfill
cuñado,-a *m.,f.* brother-in-law, sister-in-law
cura *f.* cure; *m.* priest

curar to cure
curioso,-a curious
curso *m.* course
cuyo,-a,-os,-as *adj.* whose, of whom

Ch

chaqueta *f.* jacket
charada *f.* charade
charlar to chat
cheque *m.* check
chico,-a *adj.* small; *m.,f.* boy, girl
chisme *m.* gossip
chiste *m.* joke
chistoso,-a funny
chofer *m. & f.* chauffeur
chuleta *f.* chop, cutlet
    hacer chuletas to cheat (Mexico)

D

dañar to harm
dar to give
    dar las gracias to thank
    dar la mano to shake hands
    dar un paseo to take a walk
    darse cuenta de to realize
    darse prisa to hurry
de *prep.* of; from
    del (de + el) of the, from the
debajo *adv.* underneath
deber *m.* duty, debt
deber to have to; to owe
decidir to decide
decir to say, to tell
declarar to declare
decoración *f.* decoration
dedo *m.* finger; toe
defender to defend
dejar to give up; to leave
    dejar caer to drop
    dejar de to omit
delantal *m.* apron
delante *adv.* in front, before
delante de *prep.* in front of
delgado,-a slender, delicate
delicioso,-a delicious
delito *m.* crime
demandar to demand
demás *adj. & pron.* rest, others
    lo demás the rest
demasiado,-a *adj.* too much, excessive; *adv.* excessively
democracia *f.* democracy
demócrata *m. & f.* Democrat

democrático,-a democratic
demostración *f.* demonstration
demostrar to demonstrate
dentista *m. & f.* dentist
dentro *adv.* inside
    dentro de inside of, within
dependiente *m. & f.* store clerk
deporte *m.* sport
deportista *m. & f.* sportsman, sportswoman
depresión *f.* depression
deprimido,-a depressed
deprimir to depress
derecha *f.* right (side)
derecho *m.* (civil) right
deseable *adj.* desirable
desagradable *adj.* disagreeable
desanimado,-a listless, discouraged
desafío *m.* challenge; contest
desaparecer to disappear
desarreglado,-a disarranged
desastre *m.* disaster
desayuno *m.* breakfast
descansar to rest
descomponer to break
descompuesto,-a broken
desconcertado,-a disconcerted
desconocido,-a *adj.* unknown; *m.,f.* foreigner
descontento,-a discontented
descortés *adj.* discourteous
describir to describe
descripción *f.* description
desde *prep.* since, from
desde hace since
desear to desire
deseo *m.* wish
desesperado,-a desperate
desgraciado,-a unfortunate
desierto,-a deserted; *m.* desert
desinflado,-a deflated
desmayarse to faint
desocupado,-a empty
desodorante *m.* deodorant
despacho *m.* office
despacio *adv.* slowly
despedir to emit; to fire
    despedirse de to say goodbye to
despertar to awaken;
    despertarse to wake up
despierto,-a awake
despoblado,-a uninhabited
después *adv.* afterwards
    después de *prep.* after

después que *conj.* after
destino *m.* destination
destruir to destroy
detalle *m.* detail
detener to stop
detenidamente *adv.* cautiously
determinación *f.* determination
detrás *adv.* behind
  detrás de *prep.* behind
devolver to return
devoto,-a devout
día *m.* day
  día de fiesta holiday
  día de las bromas April Fool's Day
diablo *m.* devil
dialecto *m.* dialect
diario,-a daily
dibujar to draw
dibujo *m.* drawing
diente *m.* tooth
dieta *f.* diet
dietético,-a dietetic
diferencia *f.* difference
diferente *adj.* different, various
difícil *adj.* difficult
dificultad *f.* difficulty
diligente *adj.* diligent
dinero *m.* money
dios,-a *m.,f.* god, goddess
  Dios *m.* God
dirección *f.* address, direction
directamente *adv.* directly
dirigir to direct
disco *m.* record
discoteca *f.* discotheque
discriminación *f.* discrimination
discurso *m.* speech, discussion
discusión *f.* discussion
discutir to discuss
disertación *f.* dissertation
disfrazar to disguise;
  disfrazarse to masquerade
disminuir to diminish
disobediencia *f.* disobedience
disponer to dispose
distancia *f.* distance
distinguido,-a distinguished
distinguir to distinguish
distinto,-a different
distrito *m.* district
divertido,-a fun, entertaining
divertir to amuse; **divertirse** to have a good time
dividir to divide
divorcio *m.* divorce

dócil *adj.* docile
dólar *m.* dollar
doler to hurt
dolor *m.* ache, pain
doméstico,-a domestic
domingo *m.* Sunday
don,ña *m.,f.* sir; madam
donde *adv.* where
¿dónde? where?
dondequiera *adv.* wherever
dormilón *m. & f.* dull person, one who sleeps a lot
dormir to sleep;
dormirse to go to sleep
dormitorio *m.* bedroom, dormitory
droga *f.* drug
drogadicto,-a *m.,f.* drug addict
duda *f.* doubt
dudar to doubt
dudoso,-a doubtful
dueño,-a *m.,f.* owner
dulce *adj.* sweet;
  m. candy
durante *prep.* during
durar to last
duro,-a hard

E

echar to throw; to mail
  echar de menos to miss
económico,-a economical
ecuatoriano,-a *adj. & m.,f.* Ecuadorian
edad *f.* age
edificio *m.* building
editor,-a *m.,f.* editor; publisher
educación *f.* education
eficiente *adj.* efficient
ejemplo *m.* example
ejercer to exercise; to practice
ejercicio *m.* exercise
ejército *m.* army
el *art.* the
él *pron.* he, him
eléctrico,-a electric, electrical
electrónica *f.* electronics
elegir to choose, to elect
eliminar to eliminate
elocuente *adj.* eloquent
ella *pron.* she, her
ello,-s *pron.* it, they, them
embajada *f.* embassy
embajador,-a *m.,f.* ambassador
emocional *adj.* emotional
emocionante *adj.* exciting

empanada *f.* pie, meat pie
empeñarse en to insist on
empezar to start, to begin
empiezo *m.* beginning
empleado,-a *m.,f.* employee
emplear to employ
empleo *m.* job
en *prep.* in; on; upon
enajenación *f.* absence of mind, alienation
enamorado,-a *adj.* in love; *m.,f.* lover
encantar to delight
encender to light; to set fire
encima *adv.* above
  encima de on top of
encontrar to find; to meet
enemigo,-a *m.,f.* enemy
energía *f.* energy
enfadar to anger;
enfadarse to get angry
énfasis *m.* emphasis
enfermedad *f.* sickness
enfermarse to get sick
enfermero,-a *m.,f.* nurse
enfermo,-a sick
enfrentarse to face
enfrente de *adv.* in front of
engañar to deceive
engordar to get fat
enojado,-a angry
enojar to anger;
enojarse to get angry
enojo *m.* anger
enorme *adj.* enormous
ensalada *f.* salad
ensayo *m.* practice, essay
enseñar to teach; to show
ensuciar to dirty
entender to understand
entero,-a entire
entonces *adv.* then
entrada *f.* entrance; admission
entrar to enter
entre *prep.* between
entregar to deliver
entrenador,-a *m.,f.* coach, trainer
entrenamiento *m.* training
entrevista *f.* interview
entrevistar to interview
entristecerse to become sad
entusiasmado,-a enthusiastic
envejecer to make old; to age
enviar to send
equipo *m.* team
equivocado,-a wrong

equivocarse to make a mistake
escalera *f.* stairs
escaparate *m.* show window, showcase
escaparse to escape
escena *f.* stage; sketch
escoger to choose
esconder to hide
escribir to write
   escribir a máquina to type
escrito,-a written
escritor,-a *m.,f.* writer
escritorio *m.* desk
escuchar to listen
escuela *f.* school
ese, esa, esos, esas *adj.* that, those
   a eso de about
ése, ésa, ésos, ésas *pron.* that one, those things
eso *neuter* that
   a eso de approximately
espacial *adj.* spatial, space
   nave espacial spaceship
espacio *m.* space
España *f.* Spain
español,-a *adj.* Spanish; *m.,f.* Spaniard
especial *adj.* special
especializarse to specialize in, to major in
espectáculo *m.* spectacle
espejo *m.* mirror
esperanza *f.* hope
esperar to wait; to hope
espía *m.,f.* spy
espina *f.* thorn
esposo,-a *m.,f.* husband; wife
esquí *m.* ski
esquiar to ski
   esquiar acuático to waterski
esquina *f.* corner
esquizofrenia *f.* schizophrenia
establecido,-a established
establecer to establish
estación *f.* station; season
estacionar to park
estadio *m.* stadium
Estados Unidos *m.pl.* United States
estar to be
   estar bien to be OK
   estar de acuerdo to agree
   estar listo to be ready
este east

este, esta, estos, estas *adj.* this, these
éste, ésta, éstos, éstas *pron.* this one, the latter, these
estéreo *m.* stereo
estereofónico,-a stereophonic
estilo *m.* style
estimar to esteem
esto *neuter* this
estómago *m.* stomach
estrella *f.* star
estudiante *m. & f.* student
estudiantil *adj.* student
estudiar to study
estudio *m.* study
estufa *f.* stove
europeo,-a *adj. & m.,f.* European
eutanasia *f.* euthanasia
evidente *adj.* evident
evitar to avoid, to shun
exactamente *adv.* exactly
examen *m.* exam, test
examinar to examine
exceder to exceed
exclamar to exclaim
excusa *f.* excuse
exigente *adj.* demanding
éxito *m.* success
experiencia *f.* experience
experimento *m.* experiment
explicación *f.* explanation
explicar to explain
expresión *f.* expression
extender to extend
extrañar to seem strange; to miss (a person)
extranjero,-a *m.,f.* stranger; foreigner
extrasensorial *adj.* extrasensory
extravagante *adj.* extravagant
extravertido,-a *m.,f.* extrovert

F

fábrica *f.* factory
fácil *adj.* easy
falda *f.* skirt
falta *f.* lack; absence
   hacer falta to lack; to need
faltar to be absent, to need
farmacia *f.* drugstore
fascinar to fascinate
fatigado,-a fatigued
fatigar to tire
favor *m.* help, aid
   por favor please

favorito,-a favorite
fe *f.* faith
febrero *m.* February
fecha *f.* date
felicidad *f.* happiness
feliz *adj.* happy
feo,-a *adj.* ugly
feria *f.* fair
ferrocarril *m.* train
ficción *f.* fiction
   ciencia ficción science fiction
fiel *adj.* faithful
fiesta *f.* party
figura *f.* figure
fila *f.* row
filosofía *f.* philosophy
fin *m.* end
   a fin de *prep.* in order to
   a fin de (que) *conj.* in order to
   fin de semana *m.* weekend
   por fin finally
finca *f.* farm
firmar to sign
físico,-a physical
fisiología *f.* physiology
flor *m.* flower
folklórico,-a folk
fomentar to foster, to promote
fondo *m.* bottom
   fondos *m.pl.* funds
fortuna *f.* fortune
fotografía *f.* photograph
fraile *m.* monk, friar
francés,-cesa *adj.* French; *m.,f.* French person
Francia *f.* France
frazada *f.* blanket
frecuente *adv.* frequently
fregar to wash (dishes)
freno *m.* brake
frente *m.* front
   en frente de in front of
fresa *f.* strawberry
fresco,-a cool, fresh
friega *f.* friction, rubbing
frío,-a cold
   tener frío to be cold
frito,-a fried
   papa frita french fry
fuego *m.* fire
fuera *adv.* outside
fueres go
fuerte *adj.* strong
fumar to smoke
funcionar to work; to function
fútbol *m.* soccer

G

gafas *f.pl.* glasses
  gafas oscuras sunglasses
galleta *f.* cookie
gallina *f.* hen
ganancia *f.* earnings
ganar to earn; to win
ganga *f.* bargain
garantizado,-a guaranteed
gastar to spend
gasto *m.* expense
gato,-a *m.,f.* cat
generación *f.* generation
generoso,-a generous
genética *f.* genetics
gente *f.* people
gerente *m. & f.* manager
gimnasio *m.* gymnasium
gobierno *m.* government
goma *f.* eraser
gordo,-a fat
gozar to enjoy
gracias *f.* thanks, thank you
  dar las gracias to give thanks
  tener gracia to be funny
graduarse to graduate
grande *adj.* great; big
granja *f.* farm
grano *m.* grain
gratis *adv.* free
gritar to shout
grupo *m.* group
guantes *m.pl.* gloves
guapo,-a good-looking
guardar to save; to keep
  guardar silencio to keep quiet
guardarropa *m.* clothes closet
guerra *f.* war
  Segunda Guerra Mundial World
  War II
guía *f.* guidebook, directory;
m.úf. guide
guiar to guide
guitarra *f.* guitar
guitarrista *m. & f.* guitarist
gustar to like
gusto *m.* taste

H

haber to have
  haber de to be to
había there was, were
habilidad *f.* ability
habitación *f.* room
habitante *m. & f.* inhabitant

hablador,-a *adj.* talkative;
m.,f. talker, gossip
hablar to talk, to speak
habla española Spanish speaking
habrá there will be
hacer to make; to do
  hacer autostop to hitchhike
  hacer camping to go camping
  hacer calor to be hot
  hacer chuletas to cheat
  (Mexico)
  hacer ejercicios to do exercises
  hacer falta to lack, to need
  hacer fresco to be cool
  hacer investigación to do
  research
  hacer buen tiempo to be good
  weather
  hacer mal tiempo to be bad
  weather
  hacer preguntas to ask
  questions
  hacer una excursión to take a
  tour, trip
hambre *f.* hunger
  tener hambre to be hungry
hasta *prep.* until
  hasta que *conj.* until
hay there is, there are
  hay que it's necessary
hecho,-a *adj.* made; *m.* fact
  hecho a mano handmade
  mal hecho badly done
helado *m.* ice cream
helicóptero *m.* helicopter
hemisferio *m.* hemisphere
hermano,-a *m.,f.* brother; sister
hermoso,-a beautiful
hielo *m.* ice
hierba *f.* grass
hijo,-a *m.,f.* son; daughter
himno *m.* hymn
hipnotizador,-a *m.,f.* hypnotist
hispano,-a *adj. & m.,f.* Hispanic
historia *f.* history, story
  historietas cómicas comics
hoja *f.* leaf; sheet (of paper)
hombre *m.* man
hombro *m.* shoulder
hondo,-a deep
honradez *f.* honesty, integrity
hora *f.* hour; time
horario *m.* schedule
horóscopo *m.* horoscope
hotelero,-a *m.,f.* hotel keeper
hoy *adv.* today

huelga *f.* strike
hueso *m.* bone
huésped *m. & f.* guest
huevo *m.* egg
huir to flee
huracán *m.* hurricane

I

ida y vuelta *f.* round trip
identidad *f.* identity
idioma *m.* language
iglesia *f.* church
igualmente *adv.* equally
imaginar to imagine
imaginario,-a imaginary
imitar to imitate
imperativo,-a *adj. & m.* imperative
impedir to prevent
impermeable *m.* raincoat
importación *f.* importation
importante *adj.* important
importar to matter
imposible *adj.* impossible
improbable *adj.* improbable
impuesto *m.* tax
inagotable *adj.* inexhaustible
incapaz incapable
incitar to incite
incluir to include
increíble *adj.* incredible
independiente *adj.* independent
indicar to indicate
industrializado,-a industrialized
inferioridad *f.* inferiority
inflación *f.* inflation
influir to influence
información *f.* information
informar to inform
informe *m.* report
ingeniero,-a *m.,f.* engineer
inglés,-esa *adj.* English;
m.,f. English person
iniciar to initiate
injusto,-a injust
insistencia *f.* persistence
insistir to insist
instrucción *f.* instruction
inteligencia *f.* intelligence
inteligente *adj.* intelligent
intérprete *m. & f.* interpreter
interés *m.* interest
interesante *adj.* interesting
interesar to interest
interior *adj.* interior
interrogar to interrogate

interrogativo,-a *adj. &*
 m. interrogative
íntimo,-a intimate, secret
introvertido,-a introverted
invención *f.* invention
inventariar to take inventory
investigación *f.* investigation
 hacer investigación to do research
investigar to investigate
invierno *m.* winter
invitado,-a *m.,f.* guest
inyección *f.* injection
ir to go
 ir a + *inf.* to be going to
 ir de compras to go shopping
 ir de paseo to go for a walk
irritar to irritate
italiano,-a *adj. & m.,f.* Italian
izquierda *f.* left (side)

J

jabón *m.* soap
jamás *adv.* never, ever
jamón *m.* ham
Japón *m.* Japan
japonés,-esa *adj.* Japanese;
 m.,f. Japanese person
jardín *m.* garden
jaula *f.* cage
jefe,-a *m.,f.* boss
jinete *m. & f.* horseman,
 horsewoman
joven *adj.* young;
 m. & f. young person
joya *f.* gem, piece of jewelry
jubilarse to retire (from a job)
juego *m.* game
juego de acertar guessing game
 Juegos Olímpicos Olympic
 Games
jueves *m.* Thursday
juez *m. & f.* judge
jugador,-a *m.,f.* player
jugar to play
jugo *m.* juice
juguete *m.* toy, game
julio *m.* July
junio *m.* June
junto,-a next to, together
juntos together
justo,-a just, fair
juzgar to judge

L

la, las *f. pron.* you; her; them;
 art. the

laboratorio *m.* laboratory
laca *f.* hair spray
lado *m.* side
ladrón,-ona *m.,f.* thief
lago *m.* lake
lágrima *f.* tear
lámpara *f.* lamp
lana *f.* wool
lanzamiento *m.* launch
lápiz *m.* pencil
largo,-a long
lástima *f.* lament, pity
lavadora *f.* clothes washer
lavaplatos *m.* dishwasher
lavar to wash
le, les *pron.* to you, him, her,
 them; for you, him, her, them
lección *f.* lesson
leche *f.* milk
lechería *f.* dairy
lectura *f.* reading
leer to read
legumbre *f.* vegetable
lejos *adj.* far away
 a lo lejos in the distance
lengua *f.* language; tongue
lentes *m.pl.* eye glasses
 lentes de contacto contact
 lenses
lentitud *f.* slowness
lento,-a slow
león *m.* lion
letra *f.* letter
letrero *m.* sign
levantar to raise; **levantarse** to
 get up
ley *f.* law
libertad *f.* freedom
libra *f.* pound
libre *adj.* free
 aire libre open air
librería *f.* bookstore
libro *m.* book
licencia *f.* license
 licencia para conducir driver's
 license
lider *m. & f.* leader
limitar to limit
limón *m.* lemon
limpiar to clean
limpio,-a clean
línea *f.* line
liquidación *f.* sale
listo,-a ready
 estar listo,-a to be ready
 ser listo,-a to be bright

lo, los *pron.* you, him, it, them
 lo que what, the thing
lo *neuter* it
lobo *m.* wolf
locación *f.* location
loción *f.* lotion
loco,-a *adj.* crazy;
 m.,f. crazy person
lógico,-a logical
lotería *f.* lottery
 billete de lotería lottery ticket
luchar to fight
luego *adv.* then
luego que *conj.* as soon as
lugar *m.* place
lujoso,-a luxurious
luna *f.* moon
lunes *m.* Monday
luz *f.* light

LL

llamar to call, to knock;
 llamarle la atención to attract
 attention
 llamarse to be named
llanta *f.* tire
llave *f.* key
llegar to arrive
 llegar a ser to become
 llegar con anticipación to
 arrive early
llenar to fill
llevar to wear; to take
llevarse bien to get along with
llorar to cry
llover to rain
lluvia *f.* rain

M

madera *f.* wood
madre *f.* mother
madrugar to get up at dawn
maestro,-a *m.,f.* teacher
magnífico,-a magnificent
mal *adv.* poorly, incorrectly
mal *m.* evil, bad
malo,-a bad
 mal hecho poorly done
maleta *f.* suitcase
mamá *f.* mama
mañana *adv.* tomorrow
mañana *f.* morning
mancha *f.* spot
mandar to send
manejar to drive

manera *f.* way, method
  de manera que *conj.* so that
manifestación *f.* demonstration
mano *f.* hand
  a mano by hand
  dar la mano to shake hands
mantener to maintain
mantequilla *f.* butter
mantilla *f.* mantilla (Spanish scarf)
manuscrito *m.* manuscript
manzana *f.* apple; block of houses
mapa *f.* map
máquina *f.* machine
  escribir a máquina to type
mar *f.* sea
maravilloso,-a marvelous
marca *f.* make, brand
marido *m.* husband
marinero,-a *m.,f.* sailor
mariposa *f.* butterfly
martes *m.* Tuesday
marzo *m.* March
más *adj.* more
más que more than
matar to kill
materia *f.* subject
matricular to matriculate, to enroll
máximo,-a maximum
mayor *adj.* older, oldest;
  m. adult
me *pron.* me, to me, for me, myself
mecánico,-a mechanical;
  m.,f. mechanic
mecanizado,-a mechanized
medianoche *f.* midnight
medicina *f.* medicine
medico,-a *m.,f.* doctor
medio,-a *adj. & m.* half; average
mediocre *adj.* mediocre
mediodía *m.* noon
meditación *f.* meditation
médium *m. & f.* spiritual medium
mejor *adj.* better, best
mejorar to improve
menor *adj.* younger, youngest;
  m.,f. young person
menos *adv.* less, least
  a menos de *prep.* unless
  a menos de que *conj.* unless
  echar de menos to miss
  por lo menos at least
mensaje *m.* message
mensajero,-a *m.,f.* messenger
mentir to lie

mentiroso,-a untruthful
menudo,-a small
  a menudo often
mercado *m.* market
mercancía *f.* merchandise
merecer to deserve
merienda *f.* lunch, snack
mes *m.* month
mesa *f.* table
mesero,-a *m.,f.* waiter; waitress
meta *f.* goal
meter to put in
metro *m.* subway; meter
mexicano,-a *adj. & m.,f.* Mexican
mi, mis *adj.* my
miedo *m.* fear
miel *f.* honey
miembro *m. & f.* member
mientras (que) *conj.* while
miércoles *m.* Wednesday
mil *adj. & m.* thousand
militar *adj.* military
milla *f.* mile
miniatura *f.* miniature
minifalda *f.* miniskirt
minuto *m.* minute
mío, mía, míos, mías *adj.* mine
mirar to look at
mismo,-a same, self
  lo mismo the same thing
  sí mismo,-a himself, herself
mitad *f.* half
moda *f.* fashion
modelo *m. & f.* model
moderno,-a modern
modesto,-a modest
modo *m.* mode, manner
  de modo que so that
  de modos que at any rate
molestar to bother
momento *m.* moment
moneda *f.* coin
montaña *f.* mountain
montar to mount; to ride
  montar a caballo to ride horseback
monte *m.* small mountain
montón *m.* pile, heap, mass
moreno,-a brunette, brown
morir to die
mosca *f.* fly
muchacho,-a *m.,f.* boy; girl
muchedumbre *f.* crowd
mucho,-a much, many
mudar to change;
mudarse to change residence

muebles *f.pl.* furniture
muerte *f.* death
muerto,-a *adj.* dead;
  m.,f. corpse
mujer *f.* woman
multa *f.* fine
mundial *adj.* worldwide
mundo world
muñeca *f.* doll
municipalidad *f.* municipality
museo *m.* museum
música *f.* music
músico,-a *m.,f.* musician
muy *adj.* very

N

nacer to be born
nación *f.* nation
nacionalidad *f.* nationality
nada *pron.* nothing, anything
nadar to swim
nadie *pron.* no one
naranja *f.* orange
nariz *f.* nose
narrador,-a *m.,f.* narrator
natación *f.* swimming
nativo,-a *adj. & m.,f.* native
nave espacial *f.* spaceship
Navidad *f.* Christmas
necesario,-a necessary
necesidad *f.* necessity
necio,-a ignorant, stupid
negar to deny
negocio *m.* business
negro,-a black
neón *m.* neon
nervioso,-a nervous
nevar to snow
ni *adv.* not even
  ni . . . ni neither . . . nor
nieve *f.* snow
nilón *m.* nylon
ningun,-o,-a none; no one
niñera *f.* baby-sitter
niño,-a *m.,f.* child
noche *f.* night
  anoche last night
nombrar to name
nombre *m.* name; noun
norte *m.* north
norteamericano,-a *adj. & m.,f.* North American
nos *pron.* us, to us, for us, ourselves
nosotros,-as *pron.* we, us

nota *f.* note; grade
notar to note
noticia *f.* news
novelista *m. & f.* novelist
novienbre *m.* November
novio,-a *m.,f.* boyfriend; girlfriend; fiancé; fiancée
nube *m.* cloud
nuestro,-a,-os,-as our, ours, of ours
nuevo,-a new
  de nuevo again
número *m.* number
nunca *adv.* never
nutritivo,-a nutritious

O

o . . . o either . . . or
obedecer to obey
objetivo *m.* objective
obligar to oblige
obra *f.* work
obrero,-a *m.,f.* worker
obscenidad *f.* obscenity
obscuridad *f.* obscurity, darkness
observar to observe
obtener to obtain
ocasión *f.* occasion
occidental *adj.* western
aciosidad *f.* idleness
oculto,-a hidden
ocupado,-a busy
ocupar to occupy
occurrir to occur
oeste *m.* west
oficial *adj.* official; *m. & f.* officer
oficina *f.* office
oficioso,-a officious
ofrecer to offer
oír to hear
¡ojalá! I hope that!
ojo *m.* eye
ola *f.* wave
oliva *f.* olive
olivo *m.* olive tree
olvidar to forget
olla *f.* pot, kettle
operación *f.* operation
oportunidad *f.* opportunity
optimista *m. & f.* optimist
oración *f.* sentence
orador,-a *m.,f.* orator
oreja *f.* ear
organizar to organize
orgullo *m.* pride

orgulloso,-a proud
oro *m.* gold
oruga catepillar
os *pron.* you, to you, for you, yourselves
oscuro,-a dark
otoño *m.* autumn
otro,-a other, another
oveja *f.* sheep

P

paciencia *f.* patience
paciente *adj. & m.,f.* patient
padre *m.* father
padres *m.pl.* parents
pagar to pay
página page
país *m.* country
paisaje *m.* landscape, countryside
paja *f.* straw
pájaro *m.* bird
palabra *f.* word
palabrota *f.* big word; bad word
palacio *m.* palace
pan *m.* bread
panadería *f.* bakery
pantalones *m.* pants
pañuelo *m.* handkerchief
papa *f.* potato
  papa frita french fry
papá *m.* dad
papel *m.* paper; role, part
  hacer un papel to play a role
paquete *m.* package
par pair
para *prep.* for, in order to
  para eso for that purpose
  para que *conj.* in order that
  ¿para que? why, for what purpose
  para siempre forever
paracaidismo *m.* parachuting
parada *f.* stop
paraguas *m.* umbrella
pardo,-a brown
parecer to seem
parecerse to resemble
pared *f.* wall
pareja *f.* couple, pair
pariente *m.* relative
parque *m.* park
  parque de atracciones amusement park
párrafo *m.* paragraph
participar to participate
participio *m.* participle

partido *m.* athletic game
partir to leave; to divide
pasado,-a last; past
pasajero,-a *m.,f.* passenger
pasar to spend; to pass; to happen
pasatiempo *m.* pastime
pasear to walk
  ir de paseo to take a walk
pasillo *m.* hall
pasivo,-a passive
pasta *f.* paste
  pasta dentífrica toothpaste
pastel *m.* pastry, dessert
pata *f.* foot, leg (of animal or furniture)
patinar to skate
patria *f.* homeland
patriótico,-a patriotic
paz *f.* peace
peatón *m. & f.* pedestrian
pecado *m.* sin
pedir to ask, to ask for
pegar to hit
peine *m.* comb
pelear to fight
película *f.* film
  película animada cartoon
peligro *m.* danger
peligroso,-a dangerous
pelo *m.* hair
pelota *f.* ball
peluca *f.* wig, toupee
peluquería *f.* hairdresser's
peluquero,-a *m.,f.* hairdresser
pensar to think
  pensar + infinitive to intend to
  pensar en to think about
pensión *f.* boarding house
pentágono *m.* pentagon
peor *adj.* worse, worst
percepción *f.* perception
pequeño,-a small
perder to lose
perdido,-a lost
perdón *m.* pardon
perezoso,-a lazy
perfectamente *adv.* perfectly
periódico *m.* newspaper
periodista *m. & f.* journalist
permanecer to remain
permiso *m.* permission
permitir to permit
pero *conj.* but
perro,-a *m.,f.* dog
persona *f.* person
personaje *m.* character, personality

personalidad *f.*   personality
pertenecer   to belong
peruano,-a *adj. & m.,f.*   Peruvian
pesadilla *f.*   nightmare
pesado,-a   boring, tiresome
pesar   to weigh
pescar   to fish
peseta *f.*   unit of Spanish currency
pesimista *m. & f.*   pessimist
petróleo *m.*   petroleum
pez *m.*   fish
picante *adj.*   hot, spicy
pico *m.*   peak
pie *m.*   foot
  a pie   on foot
  de pie   standing
piedra *f.*   rock, stone
piel *f.*   skin; fur
pierna *f.*   leg
pieza *f.*   piece
piloto,-a *m.,f.*   pilot
píldora *f.*   pill
pintar   to paint
pintor,-a *m.,f.*   painter
pintoresco,-a   picturesque
pintura *f.*   painting
pirámide *f.*   pyramid
piscina *f.*   pool
piso *m.*   floor
pizarra *f.*   chalkboard
placer *m.*   pleasure
placer   to please; **placerse a**   to
take pleasure in
plátano *m.*   banana
plato *m.*   dish; plate
playa *f.*   beach
plaza *f.*   square
pluma *f.*   pen; feather
población *f.*   population
pobre *adj.*   poor, pitiable;
  m.,f.   poor person
pobreza *f.*   poverty
poco,-a   little; few
poder *m.*   power
poder   to be able
poderoso,-a   powerful
política *f.*   politics
político,-a *adj.*   political;
  m.,f.   politician
póliza *f.*   policy
pollito *m.*   chick
polvo *m.*   dust

poner   to put, to turn on;
  ponerse   to put on
por *prep.*   for, through, by
  por ejemplo   for example
  por eso   therefore
  por favor   please
  por la noche   in the evening
  por la tarde   in the afternoon
  por lo general   in general
  por lo menos   at least
  ¿por que?   why?
  por seguro   for sure
pornográfico,-a   pornographic
porque *prep.*   because
portafolio *m.*   portfolio
portarse   to behave
portugués,-esa *adj. &*
  m.,f.   Portuguese
posibilidad *f.*   possibility
posición *f.*   position
positivo,-a   positive
posesión *f.*   possession
postal *f.*   postcard
postre *m.*   dessert
potro *m.*   colt
practicar   to practice
práctica *f.*   practice
preciar   to value
precio *m.*   price
precioso,-a   precious; nice
preciso,a *adj.*   necessary
predecir   to predict
  predecir la fortuna   to tell one's
  fortune
predicar   to preach
preferible *adj.*   preferable
preferir   to prefer
pregunta *f.*   question
hacer preguntas   to ask questions
preguntar   to ask
prejuicio *m.*   prejudice
premio *m.*   prize
premio gordo *m.*   first prize
prender   to seize, to grab, to turn
on
prendido,-a   on (to leave a light
on)
preocupación *f.*   worry
preocupado,-a   worried
preocuparse   to worry
preparar   to prepare
preposición *f.*   preposition
presentación *f.*   presentation
prestar   to lend
  prestar atención   to pay

attention
prestigioso,-a   prestigious
primavera *f.*   spring
primero,-a   first
  primeros auxilios   first aid
primo,-a *m.,f.*   cousin
principe *m.*   prince
principio *m.*   beginning
  al principio   at first
prisa *f.*   haste
  tener prisa   to be in a hurry
probar   to taste, to try, to test
problema *m.*   problem
procesión *f.*   procession
producción *f.*   production
producir   to produce
producto *m.*   product
profesor,-a *m.,f.*   professor, teacher
programa *m.*   program
progreso *m.*   progress
prohibido,-a   prohibited
promesa *f.*   promise
prometido,-a   engaged
pronombre *m.*   pronoun
pronto *adv.*   quickly
  de pronto   suddenly
propaganda *f.*   advertising,
propaganda
propina *f.*   tip
propio,-a   own
proponer   to propose
proteger   to protect
protegido *m.*   pet
protesta *f.*   protest
protestar   to protest
protestante *m. & f.*   Protestant;
protester
próximo,-a   next
proyecto *m.*   project
psicología *f.*   psychology
psicólogo *m. & f.*   psychologist
psiquiatra *m. & f.*   psychiatrist
psíquico,-a   psychic
publicar   to publish
público,-a   public
pueblo *m.*   town
puente *m.*   bridge
puerta *f.*   door
  puerta principal   main door
  puerta de atrás   back door
puerto *m.*   port
pues   well
puesto *m.*   position
pulga *f.*   flea
pulsera *f.*   bracelet
punto *m.*   point

Q

que *pron.* that, who, which
  que than
  lo que what, the thing, that which
  ¿que? what? which?
  ¡Que¡ How! What!
  ¿qué tal? how are things?
quedarse to stay
quehacer *m.* chore
quejarse to complain
quemar to burn
querer to want; to love
querido,-a *m.,f.* dear one
quien,-es *pron.* who, whom, the one who
  ¿quién? who?, one who
quieto,-a quiet
química *f.* chemistry
quinta *f.* villa, country house
quisiera I would like
quitar to remove;
quitarse to take off (clothing)

R

raíz *f.* root, origin
ranchero,-a ranch
rápido,-a fast
raqueta *f.* racket
raro,-a rare; strange
rascacielo *m.* skyscraper
rato *m.* a while
ratón,-ona *m.,f.* mouse
razón *f.* reason
reacción *f.* reaction
  avión de reacción jet plane
realidad *f.* reality
realista *m. & f.* realist
realizar to realize, to fulfill
realmente *adv.* really
rebelarse to rebel
rebelde *m. & f.* rebel
recibir to receive
recién *adv.* recently
recoger to collect, to gather
regalado,-a given
reconocer to recognize
recomendar to recommend
recordar to remember
recreación *f.* recreation
recreo *m.* recreation
recuerdo *m.* souvenir
recurso *m.* resource
reducir to reduce
referirse to refer
refrán *m.* proverb

refresco *m.* refreshment
regalar to give a gift
regalo *m.* gift
regatear to bargain
regla *f.* rule
reglamento *m.* rule, regulation
regresar to return
regularidad *f.* regularity
reina *f.* queen
religioso,-a religious
reloj *m.* clock; wristwatch
relucir to shine
relumbrar to glare, to glitter
renta *f.* rent
reparar to repair
repasar to review
repente *m.* sudden movement
  de repente suddenly
repetir to repeat
reportero,-a *m.,f.* reporter
representante *m. & f.* representative
representar to represent
republicano,-a *adj. & m.,f.* Republican
resfriado *m.* cold
resignar to resign, to submit
resolver to solve, to resolve
respetar to respect
respeto *m.* respect
responder to answer
responsabilidad *f.* responsibility
respuesta *f.* answer
restricción *f.* restriction
resumen *m.* summary
reunión *f.* meeting
reunirse to meet
revista *f.* magazine
revolución *f.* revolution
rey *m.* king
rico,-a *adj.* rich; *m.,f.* rich person
río *m.* river
risa *f.* laughter
robar to rob
rogar to beg
rojo,-a red
romántico,-a romantic
romper to break
roncar to snore
ropa *f.* clothing
rosa *f.* rose
roto,-a broken
rubí *m.* ruby
rubio,-a blond
ruido *m.* noise
ruta *f.* route

rutina *f.* routine
rutinario,-a routine

S

sábado *m.* Saturday
sábana *f.* sheet
saber to know
saber + *inf.* to know how
sabio,-a *m.,f.* wise person
sabroso,-a savory, tasty
sacapuntas *f.* pencil sharpener
sacar to get, to take out
saco *m.* sack, bag, coat
sal *f.* salt
sala *f.* living room
  sala de recreo game room, family room
salario *m.* salary
salida *f.* exit
salir to leave
  salir bien to do well
  salir con to go out with
  salir mal to do poorly
salud *f.* health
saludar to greet
salvavida *f.* life preserver
sandalia *f.* sandal
sangre *f.* blood
sano,-a healthy
santo,-a *m.,f.* saint
sarape *m.* blanket (Mexico)
satisfecho,-a satisfied
se *pron.* yourself, himself, herself, themselves, each other
secador *m.* dryer; *f.* hairdryer
secar to dry
sección *f.* section
secreto *m.* secret
secuestrador,-a *m.,f.* kidnapper
secundario,-a secondary
sed *f.* thirst
  tener sed to be thirsty
seguir to follow, to continue
  en seguida right away
  seguir derecho to go straight ahead
seguro,-a sure
seguro *m.* insurance
seleccionar to select
sello *m.* stamp
semana *f.* week
  fin de semana weekend
  por semana a week
sembrar to sow
semestre *m.* semester
semilla *f.* seed

señalar to point out
senador,-a *m.,f.* senator
sencillo,-a simple
sensualidad *f.* sensuality
sentado,-a seated, sitting
sentarse to sit
sentido *m.* meaning
sentimiento *m.* feeling
sentirse to feel, to regret
   lo siento I'm sorry
septiembre *m.* September
ser to be
   ser de to become of
   ser humano human being
serenidad *f.* serenity
serie *f.* series
serio,-a serious
servicio *m.* service
servilleta *f.* napkin
servir to serve; to work
sesión *f.* session
si if
sí yes
sicólogo,-a *m.,f.* psychologist
siempre *adv.* always
siesta *f.* rest, nap
significante *adj.* significant
siguiente *m.* next
sílaba *f.* syllable
silencio *m.* silence
guardar silencio to keep quiet
silla *f.* chair
símbolo *m.* symbol
simpático,-a nice
simplemente *adv.* simply
sin *prep.* without
   sin duda without a doubt
   sin embargo nevertheless
   sin que *conj.* without
sindicato *m.* union
sinfónico,-a symphonic
sino *conj.* but
sitio *m.* place, site
situado,-a situated
sobre *adv.* over
sobrepoblación *f.* overpopulation
sobrevivir to survive
sobrino,-a *m.,f.* nephew, niece
sociedad *f.* society
socio *m. & f.* member, partner
socorro *m.* help
sol *m.* sun
solar *m.* lot, plot of ground
soldado *m.* soldier
soledad *f.* solitude
soler to be in the habit
solicitar to apply for, to request

solo,-a alone, lonely
sólo *adv.* only
solución *f.* solution
sombra *f.* shade, shadow
sombrero *m.* hat
son *m.* sound
sonar to ring
soñar (con) to dream (about)
sonido *m.* sound
sopa *f.* soup
sótano *m.* basement
sorprender to surprise
su, sus *adj.* your, his, her, its,
   their
suave *adj.* soft
subir to climb; to get in; to raise
sujeto *m.* subject
suceder to happen
sucio,-a dirty
Sudamérica *f.* South America
sudamericano,-a *adj. &*
   m.,f. South American
suéter *m.* sweater
suelo *m.* floor
sueño *m.* dream; sleepiness
suerte *f.* luck
   tener suerte to be lucky
suficiente *adj.* sufficient
sufrir to suffer
sugerir to suggest
Suiza *f.* Switzerland
sumamente *adv.* chiefly
superastro *m.* superstar
Superhombre *m.* Superman
supermercado *m.* supermarket
suplicar to supplicate, to implore
suponer to suppose
sur *m.* south
suyo,-a,-os,-as *adj.* his, of his, her,
   of hers, your, of yours, their, of
   theirs

T

tabla *f.* board
   tabla de surf surfboard
tal *adj.* such
   con tal de que provided that
   ¿qué tal? how are things?
talento *m.* talent
taller *m.* shop
también *adv.* also, too
tampoco *adv.* neither, either
tan *adv.* so
   tan ... como as ... as
   tan pronto como *conj.* as soon
   as

tanto,-a so much
   tanto,-a ... como *conj.* as
   much ... as, as many ... as
   por lo tanto therefore
tardanza *f.* delay, tardiness
tardar to delay, to be late
tarde *adv.* late;
   f. afternoon
tarea *f.* homework
tarjeta *f.* card
   tarjeta de crédito credit card
   tarjeta postal postcard
taza *f.* cup
te *pron.* you, to you, for you,
   yourself
té *m.* tea
   té helado iced tea
techo *m.* roof; ceiling
telenovela *f.* serial
   telenovela de amor soap opera
televisor *m.* television set
tema *m.* theme, topic
temer to fear
tempestad *f.* storm
temprano,-a early
tener to have
   tener ... años to be ... years
   old
   tener buena cara to be good
   looking
   tener calor to be hot
   tener cuidado to be careful
   tener en cuenta to take into
   consideration
   tener éxito to be successful
   tener frío to be cold
   tener ganas de to feel like
   tener gracia to be funny
   tener hambre to be hungry
   tener la culpa to be guilty
   tener miedo to be afraid
   tener prisa to be in a hurry
   tener que to have to
   tener razón to be right
   tener sed to be thirsty
   tener sueño to be sleepy
   tener suerte to be lucky
   tener vergüenza to be ashamed
   of
tenista *m. & f.* tennis player
teoría *f.* theory
terminar to finish
tesis *f.* thesis
testigo *m. & f.* witness
testimonio *m.* testimony

tiempo *m.* time; weather
  a tiempo on time
  al mismo tiempo at the same time
tienda *f.* store
tierra *f.* land, earth
timbre *m.* bell; stamp
tímido,-a timid
tinta *f.* ink
tío,-a *m.,f.* aunt; uncle
tío político uncle by marriage
tía política aunt by marriage
típico,-a typical
tipo *m.* type
toalla *f.* towel
tocadiscos *m.* record player
tocar to play (an instrument)
tocino *m.* bacon
todavía *adv.* still, yet
todo,-a all, entire
todos,-as everyone
tolerante *adv.* tolerant
tomar to take; to drink
  tomar el sol to sunbathe
  tomarle el pelo to kid, to tease
tonto,-a *m.,f.* fool
torero,-a *m.,f.* bullfighter
tormenta *f.* storm
torneo *m.* tournament
toro *m.* bull
torta *f.* cake
tortura *f.* torture
tostada *f.* toast; toasted tortilla
trabajador,-a *m.,f.* worker
trabajar to work
trabajo *m.* work
traer to bring
traje *m.* suit, outfit
  traje de baño bathing suit
trampolín *m.* diving board
tranquilizante *m.* tranquilizer
tranquilo,-a tranquil
transporte *m.* transport
tratar to treat; to deal (with)
tratar de to try to
travesura *f.* prank
tremendo,-a tremendous
tren *m.* train
tribu *m.* tribe
trigo *m.* wheat
triste *adj.* sad
tristeza *f.* sadness
trono *m.* throne
tropa *f.* troop
tu, tus *adj.* your

tú *pron.* you
tuerto,-a *m.,f.* one-eyed person
turbado,-a disturbed, troubled
turismo *m.* tourism
turista *m. & f.* tourist
tutear to address in the familiar
tuyo,-a,-os,-as *adj.* yours, of yours

U

último,-a last
uno,-a *art.* a, an
  unos,-as some, a few
único,-a only; unique
universidad *f.* university
universitario,-a university
usted *pron.* you
usado,-a used
usar to use
útil *adj.* useful
uva *f.* grape

V

vaca *f.* cow
vacación *f.* vacation
valer to be worth
  valer la pena to be worth the trouble
valiente *adj.* brave, courageous
valle *f.* valley
valor *m.* value
vamos a + *inf.* let's
vándalo,-a *m.,f.* vandal
vaquero *m.* cowboy
varios,-as several
varón *m.* male, man
vaso *m.* glass
vecindad *f.* neighborhood
vecindario *m.* neighborhood
vecino,-a *m.,f.* neighbor
vela *f.* candle
velocidad *f.* speed
  velocidad máxima speed limit
vencedor,-a *m.,f* winner
vendedor,-a *m.,f.* vendor
vender to sell
venir to come
ventana *f.* window
ventilador *m.* ventilator
ver to see
  a ver let's see
verano *m.* summer
verdad *f.* truth
  de verdad really
  ¿verdad? right?

verdadero,-a real
verde *adj.* green
verdura *f.* vegetable
vergüenza *f.* shame
vestido *m.* outfit, dress
vestir to dress;
vestirse to get dressed
veterinario,-a *m.,f.* veterinarian
vez time
  a la vez at the same time
  a veces at times
  muchas veces often
viajar to travel
viaje *m.* trip
viajero,-a *m.,f.* traveler
vicio *m.* vice, bad habit
víctima *f.* victim
vida *f.* life
viejo,-a *adj.* old; *m.,f.* old person
viento *m.* wind
vieres see
viernes *m.* Friday
viga *f.* beam
vinagre *m.* vinegar
vino *m.* wine
visita *f.* visit
visitante *m. & f.* visitor
visitar to visit
vivir to live
vivo,-a alive; bright
vocabulario *m.* vocabulary
volar to fly
volumen *m.* volume
volver to return
vosotros,-as *pron.* you
votar to vote
voto *m.* vote
voz *f.* voice
  voz alta loud voice
  voz baja low voice
vuelo *m.* flight
vuestro,-a,-os,-as *adj.* yours, of yours

Y

y *conj.* and
ya *adv.* already; now
yo *pron.* I

Z

zapato *m.* shoe
zorro,-a *m.,f.* fox
zumbido *m.* buzz, hum

Index